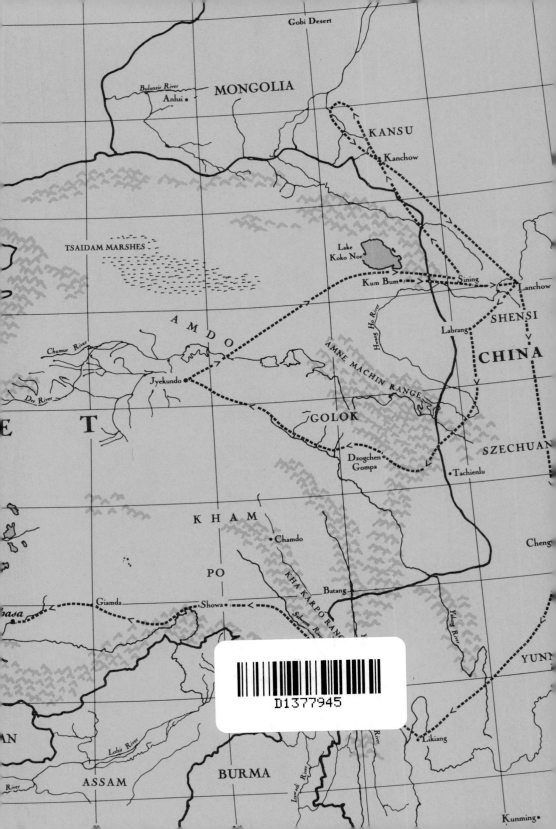

The Secret Lives of Alexandra David-Neel

The Secret Lives
of
Alexandra
David-Neel

A Biography of the Explorer of Tibet
and Its Forbidden Practices

BARBARA FOSTER AND MICHAEL FOSTER

THE OVERLOOK PRESS
WOODSTOCK & NEW YORK

First published in the United States in 1998 by
The Overlook Press, Peter Mayer Publishers, Inc.
Lewis Hollow Road
Woodstock, New York 12498

Library of Congress Cataloging-in-Publications Data

Foster, Barbara M.
The Secret Lives of Alexandra David-Neel /
Barbara & Michael Foster—Rev. ed.
p. cm.
Includes bibliographical references and index.
1. David-Neel, Alexandra, 1868—1969. I. Foster, Michael. II. Title.
BQ950.A937F67   1998   294.3'092—dc21 [B]   96-50127

BOOK DESIGN AND FORMATTING BY BERNARD SCHLEIFER
Original Maps by Letha Hadady

Manufactured in the United States of America
ISBN 087951-774-3

First Edition
1 3 5 7 9 8 6 4 2

Contents

Book Two: The Pilgrim

Book Three: The Savant

The Voyages of
Alexandra David-Neel

1891-1893	India
1911-1912	Ceylon, India
1912-1916	Sikkim, Nepal, southern Tibet (expelled)
1916-1918	India, Burma, French Indochina, Japan, Korea, China
1918-1921	Eastern Tibet (Kum Bum)
1921-1924	Journey to Lhasa through eastern Tibet, Mongolia, western China, and southern Tibet
1925	Return to France
1937-1945	Soviet Union, China, Sino-Tibetan border, India
1946	Final return to France

Chronology

October 24, 1868	Louise Eugénie Alexandrine Marie David is born in Paris.
1871	The Commune lives and dies.
1873	The Davids move to Belgium.
1888-1890	Alexandra investigates the Society of the Supreme Gnosis, London. She discovers the Theosophical Society in Paris and Buddhism and other oriental philosophies.
1891	Departs for India.
1895	Sings with l'Opéra-Comique in Indochina
1898	Publishes *Pour la vie*, a libertarian essay
1904	Marries Philip Neel; her father dies
1911	Undertakes second Asian sojourn
1912	Meets Prince Sidkeong of Sikkim, glimpses Tibet and has two interviews with the Dalai Lama.

1914-1916	Lives as a hermit in the Himalayas
1917	Tours Japan and Korea
1918-1920	Lives among the monks at Kum Bum monastery
October 1923	Sets out on a four-month journey afoot to Lhasa
February 1924	Reaches Lhasa, remains for two months
1925	Returns to France
1927	*My Journey to Lhasa* is published in New York, London, and Paris.
1928-1936	Alexandra buys and inhabits Samten Dzong in Digne, France. Completes *Magic and Mystery; Buddhism; Initiations*
1937-1945	She lives in China during the Sino-Japanese war.
1941	Philip Neel dies.
1946	Alexandra returns to France to settle estate.
1955	Yongden, her adopted son, dies.
1959	Marie-Madeleine Peyronnet comes to Samten Dzong.
1968	Alexandra's 100th birthday is celebrated at Digne.
September 8, 1969	Alexandra, much honored, dies at Digne. Several projects are left incomplete.

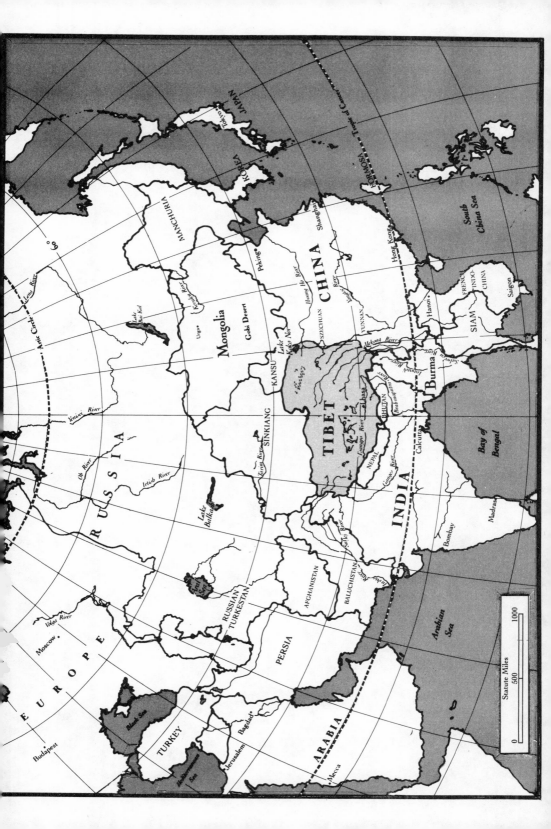

Preface to the Revised Edition

At the start of the winter we were in North Beach. It was a nostalgia run that brought back memories of hippie San Francisco rather than today's techno-town at the head of Silicon Valley. While we didn't wear flowers in our hair, we did head for the City Lights Bookstore. In front of the shop there was a photo shoot of Lawrence Ferlinghetti in the grey-bearded flesh, wearing a dark sweater and a dented bowler hat. We had mutual acquaintances—Allen Ginsberg for one—but with photographers shouting instructions and flashes popping, this was no time to bother the man. But we did want to talk to him about Buddhism and his publication, in 1967, of *The Secret Oral Teachings in Tibetan Buddhist Sects*, by Alexandra David-Neel and her Tibetan son Lama Yongden.

Alan Watts called this the "I-told-you-so-book," because it validated his crystal-clear approach to meditation and enlightenment. When the crowd had cleared and Ferlinghetti had gone back inside, we approached the show window. There, where it has stood for the last thirty years, was *The Secret Oral Teachings* with the same picture of bespectacled Lama Yongden seated, prayer beads in hand and what appears to be a wizard's cap on his head. The format was larger than our original copy, but we were pleased to discover not a word had been changed. When we finally spoke to Ferlinghetti he told us this late work by David-Neel was selling better than ever.

Alexandra David-Neel, French by birth, English by education and American in temperament, lived—really lived—for nearly one hundred and one years, a span that stretched from the mid-nineteenth to the mid-twentieth centuries. In that time she led a youthful life as a student radical, had a career as an opera singer admired by Massenet, became a feminist journalist who flirted with Mussolini, tried conventional marriage at which she failed, journeyed to India, Tibet, and, China where she studied, traveled, and wrote despite famine, plague, and civil war, and where she was effortlessly at home.

The woman shed her past lives like a serpent does its old skin. In each life she buried the previous one, concealing its traces. In her very last incarnation, as the Eastern savant, she effaced her whole previous history. Why? Because she had done or said things she wished to deny, or at least hide. She was making for herself a stainless myth of the intrepid explorer, the philosopher above and beyond passion.

Alexandra's act has been good enough to fool her previous biographers. However, in their attempts at the telling of her life, they turn her into a stick figure—either a sexless saint or a liar who never went to Tibet. They attribute her deliberate actions, in which they cannot find motive or reason, to a divine destiny. At their most banal, writers on this relentless seeker of clarity of mind gush about her heroism or her devotion to Buddhism. She had both, but they do not explain the woman.

In *Forbidden Journey* (1987), our initial attempt to chart Alexandra David-Neel's mysterious course, we employed—for the first time among her biographers—third-party sources, original maps, and copious footnotes citing secret archives and personal letters. We proved that, at age 55, she had indeed trekked to Lhasa, Tibet against an incredible array of obstacles. This entirely revised edition follows a somewhat different path. Since we have been living with David-Neel's life for nearly two decades, we trust more to our own observations and opinions. We try to answer the question why, as well as the questions where and when. We believe that a biography, especially of such a large character, is a no-holds-barred effort, or it must fail.

For the global edition, we have fleshed out the comments about David-Neel made by distinguished persons who knew her, such as Christmas Humphreys, Lawrence Durrell, and John Blofeld—from the latter we received an extraordinary deathbed commentary. We have again consulted our mainstay Hugh Richardson, Britain's last man in Tibet. We have dug deeper into the Secret Files of the India Office to unearth startling evidence that confirms the relentless, underground character of our protagonist. Unfortunately, the disoriented state of the David-Neel Foundation in Digne, France prohibits our lushly reproducing Alexandra's own voice. But the reader will find that her presence permeates the tale of a karmic journey at once both hugely successful and tragic.

Alexandra David-Neel's influence lives on in surprising ways. If we are just beginning to appreciate the role of Beat writers such as Kerouac and Ginsberg in transmitting Buddhism to America, much of what they learned of Tibetan Buddhism stems from her. Alexandra and the Beats shared a love of the big, blue sky over an expanse of land undesecrated by man. There is, as Carole Tonkinson expresses it, "an American brand of mountain mysticism based on Buddhist sources," but in terms of the mountains as well as the mysticism. The western peak in *The Dharma Bums* that Jack Kerouac, no matter how spaced, can't manage to fall from, might as well be in the Himalayas.

David-Neel's work influenced James Hilton's *Lost Horizon* and led to the notion that hidden in Tibet was Shangri-La, an ageless Eden. Her more esoteric writings have been studied by occultists throughout the world. Not least, they helped to shape the ideas of L. Ron Hubbard, who took them in the very different direction that has become the Church of Scientology. Yet, WHAT IS TRUE FOR YOU IS TRUE was not only Hubbard's but also her credo.

This Frenchwoman of obscure antecedents, with not a great deal of formal education, produced thirty fascinating books that have been translated into as many languages. Women still find in her a hero, and men an example. But we suspect that most of her fans wish only to escape for a time into a rousing adventure story set in that exotic East, especially Tibet, which is fast vanishing. At any rate, David-Neel's works are her legacy to all, and it was through one in particular that we made the acquaintance of this remarkable woman.

Introduction:
Our Journey to Alexandra

The setting was perfect: a spacious whitewashed room with slowly turning ceiling fan, decorated with tropical flowers and opening onto a lush garden that mitigated the heat of south India. Pondicherry, a former French colony, retained its Mediterranean air, and at dusk with the chirps of crickets and hums of insects wafting through the opened doors, we felt immeasurably far from the roar of New York. Time: the late seventies; place: the library of the ashram founded by Sri Aurobindo Ghose, the patriot and philosopher who on the Subcontinent rivals Gandhi in the esteem accorded to his memory. A portrait of Aurobindo, the rational mystic, hung on the wall, flanked by a luminescent photo of the Frenchwoman known as the Mother, who had become the master's consort and successor. Partly it was this lack of sexual prejudice, found too often among the allegedly enlightened, that had drawn us to this idyllic spot.

As well, we had heard of the small, private gatherings of seekers under the guidance of the learned librarian Mehtananda held to discuss subjects that were of pressing interest to David-Neel herself: psychic phenomena and occult forces. Around us this evening sat a dozen others, ranging from fair-haired Swedes to a British couple (burned red as lobsters from lingering too long on the beach) to several Asians. Imagine our surprise when the tall, graying, dignified Indian announced that his topic was tantric sexual rites. In soft, well-bred English he spoke of the higher purpose of sexual initiation, how arduous practices were undergone to achieve an evolved consciousness rather than erotic gratification, which after all could be come by in the usual ways.

The speaker told of male initiates trained to reserve their seminal fluid, even to retract after expending it. These adepts chose not to sacrifice the seed of life but to reabsorb it along with a complement of female energy. Their consorts, whom they worshiped, gained powers to rival the *dakinis* (or *kandomas*, literally sky-dancers). These in Tibetan lore were considered as mother goddesses who taught mystic doctrines and magical sciences. Some adepts deep in practice sought intercourse directly with the goddess, bypassing her human surrogate. Alexandra, when she traveled in Tibet, was taken by the common folk to be a dakini, and she didn't entirely disagree.

A member of our group was a Tibetan, Burmese in features rather than Mongol. He verified the speaker's assertions, pointing to the example of the Sixth Dalai Lama, Tsanyang Gyatso, whose name means "Ocean of Pure Melody." The rebel potentate, to the despair of his advisors, became the scandal of eighteenth-century Tibet. Recognized as the incarnation of the revered Great Fifth, this Dalai Lama had an eye for loose women. Come nightfall, he made the rounds of taverns and brothels in his capital, Lhasa. He wrote songs about his exploits until, at the instigation of the Chinese emperor, he was deposed and murdered. Some scholars, despite describing him as "the only erotic poet of the country," claim he was not a playboy but an initiate of secret knowledge, which is borne out by a couplet of his verse:

> Never have I slept without a sweetheart/
> Nor have I spent a single drop of sperm.

While were were playing the skeptical roles natural to an occidental education, our leader abruptly switched to the apparently morbid: rites practiced with the aid of the dead. We were invited to close our eyes and mentally transport ourselves over the Himalayan range to a rockstrewn plateau sixteen thousand feet high in Tibet, the roof of the world. *Rolang*—"the corpse who jumps up"—was one of the secret practices of the pre-Buddhist shamans of Tibet. Even today a body is not dismembered and fed to the vultures until a Buddhist lama has extracted what we would call its "soul" in the required fashion. The lama chants the service, which contains directions for the "soul" to find its way to the paradise of Maitreya, the

Buddha-to-come. Otherwise, the spirit will turn into a hungry ghost that wanders about causing harm.

In rolang, the shaman, after obtaining a corpse, lies on it mouth to mouth; holding it in his arms he continually repeats a magic formula. The corpse begins to move, then stands up and tries to break loose. The shaman clings to it though the corpse leaps and bounds to extraordinary heights, dragging with it the man, who keeps his lips on the mouth of the cadaver and continues to mentally repeat the magic words.

Then comes the vital moment when the tongue of the corpse protrudes. The adept has to seize it in his teeth and bite it off, at which time the corpse collapses. If any part of the operation should backfire, the cadaver may escape to kill indiscriminately. The tongue, properly dried, will become a magic weapon dreaded by all but the most enlightened Tibetans.

By narrative's end, the room in sweltering Pondicherry felt chilly to us. Without discussing our doubts, we asked how such closely held secrets had become known. In reply, Mehtananda produced a copy of *Magic and Mystery in Tibet,* which he informed us was the most widely read book of Alexandra David-Neel. We remarked that we had not heard of the author, and shortly after the group, no doubt appalled by our ignorance, broke up. In the midst of a squall, palms clashing as the rain fell in sheets, the borrowed volume tucked in to stay dry, we hurried to our hotel.

We were struck most forcefully by the author's source for her tale of rolang: A *ngagspa* (wizard) whom she met on the Tibetan steppe claimed he had performed the rite himself. He even described his dread when the corpse's tongue touched his lips and he would have to bite it off or succumb to the cadaver's deadly force. The ngagspa showed Alexandra the dessicated tongue in a jar, which he claimed was a powerful magic tool. She in turn wondered if the wizard hadn't succumbed to a form of self-hypnosis, imagining the whole affair in a trance.

Skeptic, rational mystic, indefatigable traveler, and explorer— here was a woman who had gone to India and Tibet, lived there for fourteen years among a wide variety of types from maharajas to bandits to *naljorpas* (adepts), and returned to write intriguing but dispassionate accounts of what she had observed. Here was the lost world of Tibet before the Chinese occupation, indeed before the wheeled vehicle. If there were masters of secret knowledge beyond the Himalayas, practictioners of the sort of psychic phenomona the *New York Times* had dubbed "astral bodies and tantric sex," David-Neel must have gotten to know them. And so might we, though the physicality of the world they inhabited had been blown to bits, through an acquaintance with her life and work. We commenced the search that would consume our next decade.

We left Pondicherry for Adyar, near Madras, and the ample library at the headquarters of the Theosophical Society. Here at the turn of the century, a youthful Alexandra had sat under the spreading banyan tree to discuss arcane lore. "There is no religion higher than truth" is the theosophical motto, and appropriately we discovered David-Neel's *My Journey to Lhasa,* her breakthrough work in every respect. Published almost simultaneously in 1927 in New York, London, and Paris, *Journey*, more wonderful than any work of fiction, tells of the explorer's trek across the trans-Himalayas in dead of winter disguised as a beggar and accompanied only by her adopted Sikkimese son Yongden.

To gain an understanding of how this lone woman in her mid-fifties could gain the Tibetan capital—a quest that had defeated the most accomplished and acclaimed male explorers—we browsed among the twenty-five additional books she had published during her long life, as well as her more important articles. We located several short pieces about her, but these were confused and repetitious, a sign of the biographer's original sin: regurgitating the errors of others. Then we came upon *A. David-Neel au Tibet* by Jeanne Denys.

This slim volume, published shortly after Alexandra's death in 1968, had caused a minor sensation by claiming she had never gone to Tibet. Denys called her subject an actress and alleged that she was an imposter who invented the stories of her travels and studies. The motives of this ill-tempered, anti-Semitic tract were made obvious by the author's insistence that Alexandra's parents had been modest shopkeepers and that they were Jewish and spoke Yiddish at home. Still, it deepened our suspicion that the truth about David-Neel would not come easily. Denys, a dedicated enemy, had spent years digging for dirt, and she claimed to have found some. We booked a flight for Paris.

The French intellectual René Grousset once quipped, "There exist two Madames David-Neel: the one who writes and the one who knows." The seeker began her quest for enlightenment at the Musée Guimet, where in her youth the murals adorning the grand staircase presented scenes from the great Eastern religions, including the life of Siddhartha, the Nepalese prince who became Gautama the Buddha two-and-a-half millenia ago. But the murals have faded and traces of Alexandra are few in the City of Light that first tantalized, then defeated and, perhaps too late, rewarded her. We crossed the English Channel to London.

Alexandra spent her days on foot, horse, and yak crossing the trails of an Asia dominated by three empires—the British, Russian (afterward Soviet), and the fading Chinese. The contest for political supremacy among these behemoths had been dubbed by Rudyard Kipling, "The Great Game." But on the ground, among the caravan traders, bandits, soldiers, and pilgrims with whom Alexandra rubbed shoulders, authority was exercised by the local warlord or the party with the greatest firepower. The Parisian dakini got by on her guerilla instincts and charm and a handy knowledge of English, the *lingua franca* of this Asian stew.

It was in the British Library, then housed at the British Musuem, that we made the acquaintance of Sir Charles Bell through his unpublished papers, resident political officer in the Himalayas and a leading hawk eager to place Tibet wholly within the ambit of the British Empire; his aim was to fill the vacuum of power in Central Asia by extending north the influence of British India. Bell, who was at first David-Neel's patron, soon became her rival and nemesis. As fluent in Tibetan as she, equally fearless and certain of his mission, Bell had the backing of the empire and its secret service as well as that of the Thirteenth Dalai Lama and his servants.

It was at the same historic library, under whose magnificent dome Karl Marx had scribbled notes toward *Das Kapital*, that we found traces of Alexandra's love affair with the handsome Tibetan, Prince Sidkeong Tulku of Sikkim. The progress and sudden end of this relationship irrevocably set her course toward Lhasa and fame. Her life story, we decided, had everything—love, adventure, betrayal, and victory. But what about it was true?

Over lunch in a small restaurant tucked among the rare book

shops of London, we queried Peter Hopkirk, author of several
books on Central Asia: was he convinced that Alexandra had made
that forbidden journey to Lhasa? "David Macdonald would have
been hard to fool," he replied. Then he suggested we consult
the Secret Files of the India Office for additional clues. Macdonald?
Secret Files? We were in for more than one surprise.

Housed across the Thames in a nondescript South Bank neighborhood, these splendid if musty archives of the India Office offered
up rare nuggets from the intrigue and duplicity typical of the Great
Game, a web in which David-Neel was unknowingly caught. The
secret service had watched her, giving her the code name French
Nun. By tracking her, they verified beyond doubt her travels across
the vast Tibetan plateau—where they had tried to keep her from
going. Eventually, we were able to obtain the other side of this story
from Bell's eventual successor Hugh Richardson, the Westerner who
best knows Tibet, and who in himself sums up all that is excellent in
Britain's vanished empire.

Possessing hard facts made us wonder more about the "whys"
of Alexandra's adventures. Again we crossed the Channel, headed
this time for the spa town of Digne in the Basses Alpes of southern
France, where at sixty she had finally bought a home. Settled in
with her extensive collection of Tibetan manuscripts and curios, she
called the place Samten Dzong, or "Fortress of Meditation." Here we
met Mademoiselle Marie-Madeleine Peyronnet, who had acted as
Alexandra's cook, housekeeper, and secretary for the last decade of
her centenarian life. Under her custody (nominally supervised by
the mayor of Digne) were crates of Alexandra's papers and photos—
she was an early camera buff—including some three thousand type-
script pages of the wanderer's letters to her stay-at-home husband,
Philip Neel.

But what husband? None of her books published in David-Neel's
lifetime mention such a person. Alexandra had carefully guarded her
private life in order to cultivate a rarified public image. On separate
occasions she ordered both her husband and secretary to destroy
portions of her letters. Philip, who usually acquiesced to his wife's
demands, once refused, but Marie Madeleine, feeling she had no
choice, consigned to the flames a substantial packet of documents.

The remaining letters, only one-third of which have been published, reveal that behind the pose of an enlightened being beat the heart of a real woman, alternately troubled or elated, happy or desperate. At times Alexandra's intimate letters are at odds with her published accounts. Yet the correspondence has its own slant, since the turn-of-the-century wife, traveling far from home, had no intention of telling all to her bourgeois husband, who grudgingly paid her bills. As we browsed among the letters, the debris of Alexandra's explosion of living, the image of rolang came to mind: writing the biography of this woman was like bringing her corpse back to life. At any moment it could jump up, shatter our preconceptions, and make off on its own.

"She was born an explorer," remarked Marie-Madeleine, as we took tea in the garden, a habit Alexandra borrowed from the English. But why had she chosen the mountain fastness of Tibet? "It was bigger than life, just as was her character. It exhilarated her."

But again, *why* had she made that suicidal trek to Lhasa in dead of winter? Marie-Madeleine thought for a moment: "She was turned back twice in the south—literally, 'put out the door'—and twice in the north. It hurt her monumental pride."

So here was one answer, and Alexandra herself had given several others to the same question. Suppose her story was made into a screenplay: the central action—her quest and the chase that followed—lacks a credible motive. Mademoiselle Peyronnet thinks of her former employer as a journalist, a reporter on the oddities of a bygone Asia. The National Geographic Society to promote their coffee-table book *Into the Unknown* termed David-Neel a "gentlewoman explorer," while headlining: "She defied East and West in her quest to explore a forbidden land." And the authorized French biography (by Jean Chalon) persistently refers to this Buddhist agnostic as "Our Lady of Tibet," one who followed a divine destiny.

What a varied life she led! Alexandra was progressively a debutante, a radical student and bohemian in Belle Epoque Paris, a failed opera singer, and the frustrated wife of a colonial bureaucrat in Tunis. However, once she turned East she found her course. So it was that, following on a similar path, we returned to India. At holy Benares on the Ganges, Alexandra had strained to accept the impersonality of life and death. In Nepal she pilgrimaged to the fragrant gardens of Lumbini, birthplace of Siddhārtha, the historical Buddha.

It was at the border of Tibet that she paused on the edge of a mystery. Alexandra's destiny was not written in the stars; she made it happen in the face of the mightiest empire on earth.

This is being written on March 10, 1997, the thirty-eighth anniversary of the uprising of the Tibetan people against the occupation of their land by the Chinese Red Army and its destruction of their culture and institutions. Most immediately for us, the 1959 popular resistance and the Red Army's bloody reprisals—some ninety thousand Tibetans lost their lives—caused the Fourteenth Dalai Lama and members of his government to flee across the border into India. His continuing exile has resulted in the formation of a substantial, thriving Tibetan diaspora that rings the Himalayas from Dharamsala, India in the west to Bhutan in the east. Here we meandered in search of a vanished time, country, and person.

In the Himalayas Alexandra had camped and stalked wolves and snow leopards to photograph. The paintings of another lover of these monstrous mountains, the Russian Nicholas Roerich, only slightly prepared us for the fire-opalescent sunrise—"the flowering of the snows"—over five-peaked Kanchenjunga, viewed as Alexandra had seen it from Gangtok, Sikkim on a clear dawn. At last in tiny Kalimpong, terminus of the mule trains from across the mountains in what in her day was British Bhutan, we began to delineate our own portrait of Alexandra David-Neel. A woman of mature years, Victoria Williams, daughter of the British official David Macdonald, told us about the encounter between Alexandra and her father.

At the Himalayan Hotel, a Macdonald family operation, we began to write the story of "the most astonishing woman of our time," as Lawrence Durrell called her. But first we asked Mrs. Williams, who succored the haggard but cheerful traveler when Alexandra came out of Tibet, why she supposed Alexandra had made that nearly suicidal journey to Lhasa.

"Why?" she repeated. "To show that a woman could do it!"

BOOK ONE
The Seeker

He who would harm another
is no seeker after truth.

—*from* DHAMMAPADA

Chapter 1
The Eye of Empire

David Macdonald was napping after tea in May 1924. Spring afternoons were pleasant in southern Tibet, and since he was not expecting visitors, the British Trade Agent had retired to a bedroom in his house that was located within the mud brick fort overlooking Gyantse and the surrounding fields still bare of grain. The town, Tibet's third largest, was strategically located at the confluence of the Route of Wool from the southeast, the Route of Wood from the Bhutanese border, and trade routes from Nepal through the Himalayan passes. But the most important route of all was that of Religion from India, along which Buddhism had entered Tibet beginning in the seventh century.

When an Indian servant awakened Macdonald, he was surprised to hear that a woman in a white native dress, wearing a hat with pointed flaps, and a young man in tattered lama's robes were demanding to see him. Despite his unassuming title, the half-Scottish, half-Asian official represented the British Empire in these parts, and his supporting detachment of Indian troops, officered by a few Britons, was the sole military force. It was this far—two hundred and forty miles north of the Sikkimese border—that British might had penetrated into Tibet on a permanent basis.

The servant described the pair as looking like tramps, yet the woman spoke English tersely in the European manner. Macdonald had an ugly thought: the two might be another set of miscreants who had sneaked across the border, found the natives hostile, and were pleading for help. A few years ago an American daredevil, Schary, a strange little man, had crossed over from Ladakh. His pony died and a servant ran off with his money; he had to beg and became an object of ridicule. By the time he crawled on hands and knees to the fort, he was covered with festering sores and was half-mad. He said he wanted to find the *Mahatmas*—the legendary wise men—-and write a book about his adventures.

Coming fully awake, Macdonald realized he did indeed have a woman for a caller. Annie Taylor, the missionary lady who used to live at Yatung on the Sikkimese border where his own family stayed at this season, was in the habit of donning a disguise and slipping into Tibet in an attempt to convert the lamas to Christianity. But she had long since departed for England and, he guessed, heaven. No, it was probably his daughter Victoria and some friend. She was often up to tricks to fool him. She must have come by buggy—the sole wheeled vehicle in Tibet—to bring her dad preserved fruits and vegetables, for they grew there in the milder Chumbi Valley. Well, he would have the laugh on her.

Macdonald instructed his servant to show in the lady. He pretended to be asleep. He heard steps, a voice, "Mr. Mac-do-nald?" Oh, Victoria was putting on a French accent.

"Go away! I've no time for a silly girl!"

"I am Alexandra David-Neel," replied the mature woman.

Macdonald popped up. Along with other border officials, he had been alerted to watch for this mysterious Frenchwoman, who was suspected of spying, though no one was certain for which country. Aside from feeling like an ass, he knew she had no business being in Tibet.

However, the agent was a kindly man who, from his mustache down to his riding boots, resembled an oriental Teddy Roosevelt. He apologized and led his visitor into the sitting room. He noticed her eyes, filled with the light of the mountains, and that she was short, pale, and, save for an odd bulge round her waist, much slimmer than he'd expected. He wouldn't have dreamed that in the belt strapped beneath her clothes she carried exquisite gold jewelry—the gift of a maharaja—which she kept on her person. That she had stashed an automatic pistol might have surprised him even more.

Madam David-Neel sipped tea, disappointed it was English style rather than the salty, buttered Tibetan tea that was almost a broth. She did not wait long to state her errand: she was bound from Peking to Calcutta through the heart of Central Asia, a journey that so far had taken several years. She and her adopted son Lama Yongden had traveled the last several months on foot from Yunnan, China, crossing through the unexplored Po country to Lhasa, Tibet's forbidden capital. She had circumvented Chinese, Tibetan, and British authorities by walking through rugged terrain, often by night, and by disguising herself as a beggar.

Macdonald, who had achieved his position, unusual for a Eurasian, by exercising both diligence and wit, asked his visitor in Tibetan how she had found her way. She replied with the ease of a native, but she said nothing about the maps lining her yak-hide boots. They had been given to her by a former British officer, a man whom Macdonald greatly respected. Instead, Alexandra emphasized that as a Buddhist she was able to assume the role of a beggar-pilgrim without qualm. She and Yongden had slept outdoors or in the huts of the natives, poor but generous, eating what scraps they were fed. They had spent two months in Lhasa undetected. Now she wished permission to lodge in the guest bungalow for a few days before crossing the Himalayas into India.

Macdonald was amazed. Assuming madam was telling the truth, she had performed a wonderful feat for a woman of her fifty-odd years and slight physique. He knew Tibet and took a keen interest in its people and customs. David-Neel would have had to travel through jungles and over snow-covered mountain ranges, cross wide chasms on flimsy rope bridges, and stumble down miles of crumbly rocks to find roads no wider than tracks in the mud. She must have fended off wolves and bears and the giant mastiffs that defended every village and mauled strangers on sight. Most incredibly, she had slogged through that wild, inaccessible country in the dead of winter! Macdonald pressed her for further details.

Alexandra at first refused, because she intended to write a book in which he and everyone who liked could read about her journey. She was thinking of going to America where she was certain to lecture before packed houses. The official reminded his visitor that the government of India had denied her permission to travel in Tibet, indeed had expelled her from Sikkim and India. She shot back that it was none of their affair because Tibet was an independent nation. Besides, she happened to be a French citizen.

Macdonald kept his counsel. He could recall that not many years past a high lama had been flogged and then drowned for unwittingly aiding an Indian spy in reaching Lhasa. Others who were implicated had their arms and legs chopped off and eyes gouged out. Although Tibetans were by nature kindhearted and eager to gain merit through good deeds, no word in the language aroused more distrust than *philing* (foreigner).

Alexandra removed her cap to reveal a wave of grey-tinged brunette hair and reluctantly offered proof of her exploits. She spoke of nights on the snowy wastes, of villagers who had opened their doors to them, hoping that if Yongden blessed their yaks they would proliferate like stars in the Central Asian sky. Thoughtful householders had invited the mendicants to share a stuffed sheep's belly. Because they were on pilgrimage, the peasants filled their begging bowls with *tsampa* (barley gruel) to assure a propitious rebirth in future lives.

Once at Lhasa, the interlopers had mingled with the thousands of pilgrims flocking in from the countryside, and twenty thousand monks from the three great monasteries ringing the capital, to joyously celebrate the Tibetan New Year. They had witnessed the dances of the masked lamas, the horse races and archery contests among big fur-hatted nomads who resembled Genghis Khan's Golden Horde, as well as the ritual hounding out of town of the poor fellow chosen as scapegoat, who took on the community's sins. Packed in the motley crowd, they watched colorful pageants of giant figures made from butter—in no danger of melting at twelve thousand feet.

Alexandra and Yongden had toured the Dalai Lama's awesome Potala Palace with its riches of gold, silver, and bejeweled statues of deities, its countless rooms filled with priceless porcelains and jades donated by pious Chinese emperors. From its roof topped with gilt pagodas, they took in a view over the plains and distant mountains that repaid all their efforts.

Macdonald, one of the handful of outsiders who had visited Lhasa, doubted his guests no longer. But when the woman, who was beginning to seem much taller than her diminutive five feet, two inches, requested a signed statement to verify their journey, the Trade Agent hesitated.

"Madam," he said, "you have undergone incredible hardships. Your courage and vitality have succeeded where others failed. Unfortunately, by reason of the disguise you adopted, you saw Tibet only from the viewpoint of a poor pilgrim."

He had almost said "an outlaw." The political air of Tibet was ominous due to a power struggle between the Panchen Lama (domiciled in Tashilhunpo monastery near Shigatse) and the Thirteenth Dalai Lama, and each was being courted by the rival great powers. Macdonald needed to weigh his goodhearted instincts against official policy. On the next day, May 7, he would notify his immediate superiors in Sikkim and India about his visitors.

While Alexandra might smile—she had won sweet revenge for earlier humiliations—she couldn't afford to let on how sick and weary she and Yongden felt. She had shown what the will of a woman could do; it was now time to tell the world. Neither she nor the astute Scot could gauge the extent of her victory: the fame and honors due her in a life that would span more than a century. Yet, this woman of power would know much disappointment and sorrow in her heart.

Alexandra, prodded by Yongden, noticed a nearby haversack and what appeared to be an eye resting on it. Macdonald, seeing her surprise, explained that the Telegraph Master had come up from India to inspect the newly installed line to Lhasa, which via Gyantse was now connected to the entire world. "He has a glass eye," continued Macdonald, "and he places it on his property to guard it from pilfering. The natives, being superstitious, give his things a wide berth."

Alexandra at once inquired if she could telegraph the news of her triumph to Paris. But Yongden, regarding the small blue object of glass said, "That is the eye of empire."

And the telegraph was the ear of empire. Lhasa was no longer closed to the world and its doings. From the day telegraphic service began until the Chinese invasion of 1950 there were always British or British-trained operators in Lhasa. The pristine Tibet, unknown and unmapped, portrayed in the books of the first foreign woman to reach Lhasa was already becoming a memory. But in 1924 it was unforseen that not Britain but the Red Army of China would perform the drastic surgery of severing the Tibetan nation from its ancient religious and cultural roots. To Alexandra, the British

Government of India was the antagonist she feared.

Ironically, David Macdonald, Trade Agent at Gyantse, furthered David-Neel's ambitions by sending her on to his family at Yatung in the Chumbi Valley. Their loving treatment may have saved her life and Yongden's, so weakened had they become through fatigue and illness. Victoria, then only twenty, gave her respectable clothes to wear down into India. She thought Alexandra the handsomest woman she had ever seen.

Chapter 2
Prisoner of a Dream

On a baking mid-August evening in 1911, thirteen years before David-Neel's encounter with Macdonald, the steamer *City of Naples* sounded its horn and pushed off from the quay at Bizerte, Tunisia. The Arab women hanging on the rail sent up a cacaphony of shrill howls to match. Third class was above rather than below decks, and the poorer travelers, headed for the Suez Canal and beyond, kept their belongings bundled on top. Down in the hold stirred a tribe of rats, intent on good meals to come. The passenger Madame Alexandra David-Neel, wearing a preposterous feather hat, was pressed among the natives, while her husband Philip stood on the dock in the fullness of his starched-collar dignity. In the tumult about her, she watched in silence as his silhouette grew smaller, dimmer, erased by the night.

Why, she wondered, did thoughts of Philip arouse a physical disgust in her? Instead, she ought to feel grateful. The chief engineering officer of the French Railroads in North Africa was not the inspiring life companion she had dreamed of, but she had chosen to marry him. So the obscene pictures of him that flashed to mind caused her to feel guilty and to flee ever farther from the poor man. Yet he seemed preferable to the husbands of women that she met in her constant travels.

To all appearances, Alexandra, who had married Philip Neel in Tunis in 1904, was both successful and content. A feminist and orientalist of some repute, she kept on the move. During the years subsequent to marriage, she made a circuit of Paris, Brussels, London, and Rome, taking out time to visit Philip in Tunis. She attended various conferences, took tea along the boulevard, Saint-Germain, where this meant champagne, and in London where she and her cultured friends drank actual tea. An increasingly successful journalist, she stalked editors in their dens, particularly M. Rachilde at the influential review *Mercure de France*. She was rewarded by his publishing her "Contemporary Buddhist Thinkers" in December 1909.

In 1910 Alexandra lectured to attentive crowds at the Theosophical Societies of both Paris and London. She was delighted to address a group of Indian medical students at Edinburgh. She wrote and published in Paris in 1911 *Modern Buddhism and the Buddhism of Buddha*, a title that reads no less awkwardly in French. She was on the right path, the author assured her husband. Keeping busy allowed her to feel better than she had in years.

Yet Alexandra felt something essential to be missing. She wrote to Philip from London that she was fed up with poseurs who took a facile interest in the East. She'd met one eccentric who insisted on writing a life of Buddha in Miltonic blank verse. Most enthusiasts passed off secondhand opinions and could only quote the critics. At the Paris salon of Professor Sylvain Levi, the Sorbonne's most distinguished Orientalist, when Alexandra had spoken animatedly of a living Eastern philosophy that was not limited by the past, she found that the guests deserted the professor to gather around her. Still, she felt like a poseur herself. Her work was based on book learning rather than the hard-won knowledge gained from experience.

To her surprise, Philip responded by proposing that she visit India to perfect her oriental languages, particularly Sanskrit. He would pay for a sojourn of about one year. This woman approaching her mid-forties, despite suspecting that her husband had found a mistress, jumped at the chance, and by August she was aboard a steamer bound east of Suez. While the odor of rancid food wafted to her, she could hardly believe that she was truly en route.

Alexandra introduced *My Journey to Lhasa* by recalling that even as a little child in a Parisian suburb she longed to escape from the garden of her home, to investigate far away places. Alexandra's enemy, Jeanne Denys, admits that "from the age of five on, she manifested her taste for travel and liberty by escaping from the arms of her nurse to explore the Bois de Vincennes." But Denys failed to see that Alexandra was not only running *away*, but also *toward* something: here was a duality of captivity and flight that, once established, would become habitual. In this case the precocious little girl, or so she tells us as an adult, was fleeing from her family's plans to move from Paris to Brussels.

Alexandra once compared her parents to two statues who faced each other over a lifetime with nothing to say, closed and cold. Her father, Louis Pierre David, was born in Tours on July 6, 1815, into an old Huguenot family. He was distantly related to Napoleon's favorite painter Jacques Louis David, and the name has Jewish antecedants. Alexandra hinted that the family once had been Albigensian (a heretical sect during the Middle Ages) and suffered religious persecution. Her mother, Alexandrine Borghmans, came of mixed Dutch, Norwegian, and Siberian ancestry, and because of the latter the explorer of Tibet would claim to have Mongol blood.

It was the only positive thing she ever said about her mother. From photos, Alexandrine's ample presence appears intimidating in the way of those who are securely anchored and care little for speculation. In Flemish lace and pleated blouses, she ordered about her family and the servants, and in the marketplace she tried the patience of merchants with her demands. At home everything had to be kept spotless, but the damask napkins and the fine porcelain dishes were never used.

As a girl Alexandra fought against her mother's restrictions, and as a woman she never entirely forgave her. In contrast Alexandra adored and bonded with her indulgent father. Louis David came to manhood under the reign of Louis-Philippe, the bourgeois monarch brought to power by the Revolution of 1830, who could be seen strolling the promenades of Paris in everyday clothes. It was a period of economic liberalism, material improvements, and spiritual malaise that perversely spawned the heroic poetry of young Victor Hugo and the titanic canvases of Delacroix. At first, Louis chose his father's occupation, the prosaic one of provincial schoolmaster.

Louis, slim, earnest, with eyes alight and handsome features finely hewn, considered himself a political activist. And the French genius for controversy was merely slumbering. In the 1840s, with the relaxation of censorship, Louis founded a Republican journal, *Courier d'Indre et Loire*. This was a local weekly that combined official notices, advertisements for land sales, humorous remarks, and veiled editorial comment. David became a prominent citizen of Tours.

The 1851 coup d'etat of Louis Bonaparte, who would declare himself Napoleon III, sent Louis into exile in Louvain, Belgium. The mature bachelor, who prided himself on his appearance, tried to keep his head high and his graying beard trimmed—the badge of a Republican. Nearly penniless, he gave French lessons to the young daughters of the Flemish mayor of this thriving industrial town. Protestant, Mayor Borghmans may have been a fellow Mason. There also lived at his house his adopted daughter Alexandrine. She was now twenty-two and becoming old maidish. Thus the mayor made no objection when, in 1854, Louis asked for Alexandrine's hand. The couple was married with a minimum of ceremony.

According to Alexandra, who is our only authority, her parents were unhappy from the start. The new Madame David was a practical soul who cared little for politics or ideas. Not formally religious, she had a mystical streak and had converted to Catholicism. A stocky woman who looked older than her years, she liked to wear her thick hair in a bun atop a round, complacent face. Why had the intense Louis taken this *terre a terre* woman as his wife?

An exile, he faced bleak economic prospects, while in contrast Alexandrine, though an orphan, had been left a boutique that sold fabrics as well as a tidy sum by her natural father. The money, loaned to merchants in the textile trade, brought in a secure income. During Alexandra's youth, her family did not lack for possessions, servants, and social standing. Until Louis suffered severe losses on the Bourse in the Panic of 1893, he was able to indulge his only daughter in governesses, music and English lessons, and in pocket money.

It is curious how the Davids, after fifteen years of a steadily souring marriage, finally conceived a child. Alexandra told Philip that during her mother's pregnancy the dour woman read the novels of James Fenimore Cooper. In her mind she traversed grasslands and forests, lived harrowing adventures, while carrying Alexandra in her womb.

An immediate effect of Alexandrine's pregnancy was that Louis demanded his offspring be born on French soil, so the child would be a citizen. In 1868 the couple moved to Paris. Their daughter was born on October 24th at St. Mandé, a comfortable suburb of Paris wedged between the Bois de Vincennes and the defensive wall surrounding the city. Three days later at the parish church the infant was baptized Louis Eugénie Alexandrine Marie David, but to the despair of her mother and pleasure of her father she preferred to be called Alexandra.

Louis David, the earnest Republican of 1848, found a drastically altered, imperial capital. Baron Haussmann had rammed through wide boulevards, destroying the tortuous alleys of the medieval burgh. Everywhere rose gleaming new buildings with cafes spread out under rows of trees. Fashion and laughter ruled the day and more the night. At all hours Paris amused itself under the glow of gaslights. Jacques Offenbach wrote the gay tunes to which dancers kicked and showed their red satin-clad derrieres.

As soon as she was old enough, Alexandra tagged along with her father and his hunting dogs on walks around their placid, leafy neighborhood. Undeterred by brisk winter days, they chatted together like grownups. Often their longer excursions ended at the Gare de Vincennes or the Gare de Lyons to watch the trains come and go. A great network of tracks had been built out from Paris to every corner of the country, and the Impressionists were soon to discover the lure of painting outdoors in the provinces. However, the dreams of this precocious child—fussily dressed with tiny drop earrings and necklace to match—did not stop at the French border. On the station platforms she yearned for vast, snowbound places like Russia. Infinite space lured her.

Alexandra's first escape was triggered by a situation more complex than she later admitted. She never cared to acknowledge that from her maternal line she inherited stamina, longevity, and good looks. For Alexandrine was solidly handsome, a complement to Louis' slender sensitivity. Their union was maintained by an attraction of opposites. Yet Alexandra claimed that when on January 26, 1873, after nineteen years of marriage, Alexandrine gave birth to a boy, Louis was more embarrassed than delighted. Certainly his five-year-old daughter was less than pleased. While watching her baby brother in the bath, she is said to have commented about his tiny penis, "Well, that I do not have."

Even if this story, related by more than one biographer, is apocryphal, the demanding little girl felt jealous about the shift of attention to her sibling. When Louis Jules died at the age of six months, Alexandra acted openly content, but the episode may have planted within her a certain guilt. This, at least, is classic Freudian theory. Nonetheless the woman when grown could and did enjoy sex. Initially, her attitude toward men was typical of the milieu in which she was raised.

After the baby's death the David household was in uproar. The distraught Alexandrine demanded to return to live near her adoptive mother. Louis, living in a Third Republic constantly under the threat of a Bourbon restoration, without significant friends or hopes, could not resist for long. It was then, on the eve of the family's departure for Brussels, that the girl gave an inattentive nurse the slip in the Bois de Vincennes. The horrified domestic alerted a gendarme, and after a widespread search Alexandra was captured and brought to the station. For his trouble, she scratched the policeman. When her chagrined father came to collect her, she showed no remorse, lending some credence to her adult boast that she was born a savage.

It was in March 1874 that Louis was ready to surrender to Alexandrine's demand to return to Belgium. But first, he did something that remained a secret between father and daughter. Louis had Alexandra baptized again, this time as a Protestant. She never revealed her feelings about when, standing in a strange, bare church, the minister in black touched her forehead and left a chill spot. In later years Alexandra spoke well of the Huguenots and she identified with their independent spirit and social conscience. But in time of need she couldn't find comfort in their austere services.

Catholic and Protestant, dreamer and activist, loving at once the sensual and the severe, Alexandra's nature was built on dualities. Living in the suburbs of Brussels in a tense bourgeois household, the young girl fled into the imaginary realm of books. Her favorites were the fantasies of Jules Verne and she swore to herself to surpass the exploits of his heroes, whether in the air or under the sea. Dolls and dresses bored her, and for her birthdays she demanded books about faraway places, or better yet the whole world—a globe! She dreamed not of growing up to be a coquette, of fancy dress balls, but of wild country and glacier-tipped peaks. At least, her parents might take her traveling on school holidays.

They failed to, and so Alexandra tried vainly to escape. In Belgium at that time primary schools were all taught by the clergy.

When Alexandra's governess became a nun, and the ten-year-old turned sickly, her mother packed her off to Bois Fleuri, a convent school where rows of rosy-cheeked little Flamandes were stuffed like geese, fed half-a-dozen times a day. Here, among girls her age, she fattened. Yet this hardly satisfied her soul. Instead, she was struck by reading a tale about Buddha—an earlier incarnation than Gautama—who, on meeting a tiger in the jungle, gave his own flesh to feed her starving cubs. The sacrificial quality of the story thrilled Alexandra's imagination.

Already she had begun to read authors intellectual enough to intimidate an adult: Augustine, Proudhon, Kierkegaard. Imitating the ancient Stoics, she subjected her body to rigorous trials, which included using boards for a bed. That habit stuck, and even in old age she permitted herself only the luxury of dozing in an armchair. She would joke that the soul of a medieval theologian had been reincarnated in the body of a schoolgirl. And this pessimism, too, stayed with her, even when it yielded first to social radicalism, then Bohemianism. Finally Buddhism—concerned with putting an end to suffering—became the solace of a desperate young woman who felt betrayed by the crassness of the world.

At fifteen, when Alexandra had already begun to study music and voice privately, an odd thing happened to break her routine. She got hold of an English journal put out by the Society of the Supreme Gnosis. It had been sent to her, at her request, by a certain Mrs. Elisabeth Morgan who, although she remains a shadowy figure, was to become Alexandra's first patron. She was a mature woman, an occultist, who befriended French students visiting England. Alexandra, as she sat alone in the garden, stared at the pale blue cover with its enigmatic oriental symbols. The contents were still more perplexing: unfamiliar language, twists of thought, snatches of Sanskrit. At first she supposed it was all craziness, but she soon determined to find out in person.

That summer while her family vacationed at Ostend, Alexandra walked into Holland and crossed the channel to England. Here she found Mrs. Morgan, who then persuaded her to return home. When we observe a photo of Alexandara taken at the age of sixteen, her desire to flee from a stiffling milieu becomes obvious. She was tightly corseted into a bustled, ruffly gown that is buttoned up to her chin, holding a fan in her white-gloved hand. Alexandra puts on a proper face, though she looks swallowed up in her gown. Still, her brown hair piled high, dark, luminous eyes, a regular nose and almost sensuous mouth, as well as a note of melancholy, produce the contrasting impressions of elegance and vulnerability.

Alexandra the debutante is about to be presented to the emperor and empress of the Belgians, who also ruled with brutal terror over millions of black subjects in the Congo. How did the dashing Leopold II react, or his equally dissolute wife, Henrietta Maria? We can only guess. But already Alexandra can sense that men will want her, and not knowing how to respond makes her miserable.

In 1885, in her seventeenth year, Alexandra again absconded, hiking alone over the Saint-Gotthard Pass through the Alps to the Italian lake country. She was furnished with little more than an umbrella and the *Maxims* of Epictetus, the Stoic philosopher. However, she permitted her mother to recover her at Milan. This excursion backfired when Madame David, weary of her daughter's eccentricities, put her to work in a family shop selling fabrics for women's clothing. Louis David was not in accord, but as usual his wishes counted for little.

Alexandra tried to assume the obliging air of a merchant but failed. From outside the shop came an air played on a North African hand organ. It set her to dreaming in total oblivion of the customers. She soon parted company with the world of commerce, never to reunite. At eighteen a romantic streak lay beneath Alexandra's reserved exterior. This was to find an initial outlet in the continued study of music, begun at boarding school. In preparation for the entrance exam of the Royal Conservatory of Brussels, Alexandra practiced piano and reviewed music theory. She entered the conservatory in April 1886, but it was for her soprano voice that she won first prize three years later. Louis David, who had faith in his daughter's talents, vigorously promoted her singing. To her mother it seemed the lesser of evils and might enhance her daughter's marriage prospects.

In 1888 Alexandra was offered another opportunity to escape, at least temporarily, when Mrs. Morgan sent for her. She could study in London and board cheaply at the Supreme Gnosis. She was under respectable sponsorship, and in her heart she had already chosen the career of medical missionary in the East. Her mother objected that women, other than nuns, did not become missionaries, but Alexandra persisted and won out. She knew she would need to perfect English, the common language of educated Asians.

Traveling toward London, Alexandra set out for the Dutch port of Flushing. Here the passenger was guaranteed more hours aboard ship than at Calais. To the very end of her hundred years, she would love the momentum of travel for its own sake. That evening Alexandra strolled along the quay at dusk. Fog crept in, making passers-by into apparitions. A strange peace took hold of the rebel. She was alone and entirely unknown here. Waves of happiness swept over her. All mental and physical agitation disappeared, and she felt—no, tasted—life pure and simple.

The young philosopher, on the threshold of her first serious challenge, had experienced an insight, a breakthrough of the quality termed by Zen Buddhists *satori*. According to Christmas Humphreys' *Dictionary of Buddhism*, "It is the beginning and not the end" of the direct experience of reality. Next must follow "a period of maturing."

Chapter 3
The Ego and Its Own

Jeanne Denys was a medical doctor who in 1958 helped the ninety-year-old Alexandra David-Neel to arrange her library at her home in the south of France. Yongden had passed away three years earlier. Denys, who'd hoped to find an enlightened sage, instead had to deal with a crotchety woman who complained of her aches and pains and, instead of discoursing on Buddhism, avidly followed the stock market. Denys finally told David-Neel to her face that she was a fraud: "Madame, you never went to Lhasa or received a mystical initiation." The canny one smiled, and replied, "Prove it!" She understood that there is no such thing as bad publicity.

Denys spent the next decade investigating David-Neel's life and tracking her winding course throughout Asia. In *Alexandra David-Neel au Tibet*, Denys outlines Alexandra's travels beginning in 1911 at Adyar, India, traversing Benares, Sikkim, Nepal, Shigatse, Tibet, India again, China, Burma, Korea, Japan, Manchuria, Peking, Eastern Tibet, finally to Lhasa. She ends by stating: "With that, this female traveler would have crossed a good part of the immense Asian continent, some 30,000 kilometers on horse, yak, rickshaw, sedan chair, train, boat and even on foot, and all this during only fourteen years. You have to admit it is a fantasy." No, David-Neel's adventures are fantastic—incredible, amazing—but she really lived them.

Biographical research requires an open mind, and it can't be accomplished from a Paris café, employing a derisive logic as one's chief tool. Nonetheless we agree with Denys' comments about "the extreme reserve of the author [David-Neel] concerning the first forty years of her life." Alexandra made a deliberate attempt to picture herself as a superwoman, without emotion, or in a phrase she often used: a "rational mystic." She obscured and destroyed evidence of any less elevated or darker side. A trunkful of costumes that Marie-Madeleine stumbled over after her employer had died was her first clue that Alexandra had made a career as an opera singer. Alexandra was reluctant to deal with wounds received or given, though deeply felt. Her inner probing was done in a specifically Tibetan Buddhist context.

For the first time on March 18, 1913, Alexandra informed her husband from Benares, India that, while watching dead bodies heaped on the cremation ghats, the odor of charred flesh had forced to the surface her earliest conscious memory, one that gnawed at her throughout life. Because this trauma formed the basis of David-Neel's view of humanity, we reconstruct it in detail:

Paris—divided and burning, 1871. Under a sky leaking rain, a well-dressed man with a neat gray beard totes a young girl in his arms along the deserted boulevard Voltaire. The girl in her pretty starched dress, hair braided and beribboned as though going to a party, slightly resembles *monsieur*. Ragged gunfire can be heard ahead. The man has difficulty peering through the haze compounded of a gray day and smoke from the remains of the palaces on the Right Bank. Out of view, the romantic revolutionaries known as the Paris Commune are making a last stand behind a barricade of cobblestones at the corner of rue de Faubourg du Temple and rue de la Fontaine, 11th arrondissement. Army cannons overwhelm their scattered musket shots.

Fearful, Louis David pushes on, keeping clear of the fighting. He has a reputation as a liberal journalist, a dedicated Republican. He is close to Victor Hugo, France's foremost man of letters and the scourge of the now dethroned emperor, Napoleon III. The connection is enough to hang a man during this week of reactionary terror that follows the French defeat at the hands of the Prussians. Under orders from the new government at Versailles, the army has uprooted the rebels of Paris and is systematically executing thousands, perhaps twenty-five thousand in all. Men, women and children.

The pair eventually reach the destroyed gate of Pere Lachaise cemetery. No one stops them from entering. The muddy ground is littered with toppled tombstones, and fresh corpses still clutch their enemies, locked in timeless combat. Casualties from both sides have fallen round the bust of Honoré de Balzac. Louis David trudges on, cradling his only child.

Ahead stands a stone wall. A few minutes earlier neatly uniformed soldiers had formed into ranks, shouldered arms, and on command fired. Figures, hands tied behind them, fell like puppets with their strings cut. Those not quite dead moaned while another group was lined up against the wall. This well without bottom—defiant men, pregnant women, boys with fuzz on their cheeks weeping—would be plumbed to its depth by the *haute bourgeoise* regime determined to exorcise the devils of the Commune.

The soldiers have marched off, leaving the burnt smell of gunpowder and a heap of bodies that hangers-on are shoveling into the holes they themselves dug. Louis David has to brace himself to keep from trembling, but his little daughter's round face remains placid, her gaze elsewhere. She has just caught sight of her "invisible companion," who will guide her through a distraught youth. Still, for the fancily dressed Alexandra of two-and-a-half years, the pile of fresh corpses will coalesce into a phantom in the depths of her psyche. She will never forget that humanity is the most ferocious species.

If Alexandra's left-wing politics were a reflex inherited from her father, the streak of mysticism she rarely displayed to those in the West stemmed from her mother's side. She complained of being a pawn in her parents' endless chess match, yet her whole life long she oscillated between the attractions of reason and ritual. Alexandra's actions from the late 1880s until she married Philip Neel in 1904 are difficult to make sense of because she was going in two or more directions at once. In London at twenty she came under the influence of occultism, which proved merely diverting to her, and Theosophy, which she took more seriously.

One evening in 1888 the twenty-year-old mademoiselle descended on Victoria Station, unsure of herself. Confused by the swirl, she summoned nerve to ask directions in halting English. Fortunately, James Ward, a member of the Supreme Gnosis, picked the young woman out of the crowd and conducted her to the home of the society. Although Alexandra had eagerly awaited this moment, once deposited in her dimly lit room she burst into tears. Alone in a foreign capital, she felt homesick.

When Alexandra lay down to sleep, vibrations from French doors covered by a shade pulled down smoothly like a lacquered panel disturbed her. What was behind them? She had read of secret societies that subjected candidates for admission to gruesome and terrifying ordeals. Drifting off, she was startled awake by a ghostly procession marching through the doors and around in arcane circles.

Alexandra was determined to get hold of herself. Hadn't she always derided her mother for her baseless superstitious fears? She crept out of bed to examine the doors. When she managed to pry up a corner of the stiff canvas paneling to peek beyond, she saw only darkness. There was an electric lamp in the room, and Alexandra seized on this product of science. She kept the unaccustomed object lit by her bed, ready if the phantoms invaded to point it at them and scare them away.

At seven the next morning a maid bearing tea and biscuits awoke the soundly sleeping young woman. She pressed a tiny latch and parted the doors to disclose a pleasant garden, common enough behind London townhouses. Alexandra hurried through her toilette to arrive at breakfast, but here she found only a few emaciated-looking tablemates. When she complained about the sparse diet, they reprimanded her with a story about their president: he subsisted on a dozen almonds a day and an occasional orange.

Alexandra grew used to life among the gnostics, older than she, urbane, and discreet. They enforced no rules or dogma. Normally, they congregated in the large, comfortable library, rich in works on alchemy, metaphysics, and astrology, and they read whatever treatise struck their fancy. Smoldering incense sticks lent an oriental aroma to the book-lined room. Some puffed incessantly on Turkish cigarettes, while others in trailing white robes glided soundlessly through the thick blue smoke.

Even at twenty, Alexandra's critical faculty kept her aloof from true believers or a mushy mysticism. In old age she wrote a reminiscence of her youthful search, which she then declined to publish. Since she was always eager for the attention and money a book would bring in, this was unusual. However, this veiled memoir might prove embarrassing if someone could read between its lines. Issued posthumously, *Le sortilege du mystere (The Spell of Mystery)* chronicles the seeker's occasional adventures in the fin-de-siècle world of metaphysics and kooky cults.

Long afterward Alexandra termed the gnostics extravagant, but where else in Victorian London could a young lady be housed so cheaply and safely? The gnostics left her free to study English and to delve into the wealth of knowledge stored at the British Museum. Her carrel at that famous library began to be piled high with commentaries on Hindu philosophy, Buddhism, and Chinese Taoism. Down the sidestreets were bookshops specializing in such matters, into which would stroll real turbaned Indians and pigtailed Chinese!

Elisabeth Morgan exercised some supervision over the still naive, attractive young woman. Alexandra referred to this shadowy figure as her "godmother," although *marraine* may also mean "sponsor." London at this time presented a smorgasbord of occult societies and personalities. The Kabbala and the Rosy Cross had their devotees, as did cenacles of Egyptian magical rites. Spiritualism was a craze among high and low alike. Victor Hugo had adopted it while living on Guernsey, and he spent days on end tipping tables to contact the spirit of his drowned daughter. Distinguished intellectuals such as Sir Arthur Conan Doyle investigated the phenomena. The popular field belonged to the great performing mediums, such as Douglas Home, who could levitate individuals; Florence Cook, who materialized beings; and the master of the trance, William Stainton Moses.

Alexandra, in spite of her excellent recall, never mentioned seeing any of these famous mediums. However, we know that she attended seances because she would later give a reasoned explanation of the process. The spirits that people perceived at seances were "elementals"—disembodied spirits that, lacking a material envelope, strive to incarnate, to become involved with living beings. Failing in this, they may temporarily possess a willing medium, who uses them to produce spiritual "phenomena"—sounds or sensations— or an unwilling medium, whom they may lead to destruction. These elementals were never human but fall into the class termed "demons" by the Tibetans. They inhabit a shadowy nether world and have been through the ages the servants of magicians, shamans, and wizards.

Alexandra, then, believed in another, nonmaterial world, the so-called astral or etheric planes where the boundaries of material reality are transcended. This places her more directly in the line of that preeminent figure of nineteenth century metaphysics—Madame Helena P. Blavatsky. The founder of the Theosophical Society in 1888 resided in a little villa on Lansdowne Road, South London. On Saturdays, starting in the afternoon and often lasting till the wee hours, Madame Blavatsky would hold forth on the principles of the Secret Doctrine, imparted telepathically to her by the spiritual masters of Tibet. These *mahatmas*, wiser than mere gurus, formed a Secret Brotherhood in a Shangri-La beyond the Himalayas, and their wishes were made known only via selected disciples.

Madame orated in a stentorian voice—audible for blocks in that quiet neighborhood—to rapt audiences of her followers, her soon-to-be-enemies from the Society for Psychical Research, and those who wished to seem fashionable. Alexandra, in an undated entry in her diary, recalled that Elisabeth Morgan had introduced her to Madame Blavatsky's salon and this had opened a new dimension of her life. Blavatsky's thought contained strong feminist and anticolonial elements, and her influence on David-Neel was far greater than she later cared to admit. According to Blavatsky's biographer Maurice Leonard, "It's obvious that there were certain things in her past which Madame was terrified would be resurrected." The same can be said for David-Neel.

David Macdonald wrote that "for some time [David-Neel] was associated with the organization inaugurated by Madame Blavatsky." Partly the reason was convenience. Leonard noted that "in 1883 forty-three new branches of the Theosophical Society opened in India and Ceylon, in addition to branches in London, New York, Paris, and the rest of Europe. Madame Blavatsky was by now an international figure whose career was followed with interest by millions." There were advantages and a sense of identity in being a Theosophist.

Alexandra was especially attracted by the character of Annie Besant, who became Blavatsky's disciple in 1889 and the leading figure (and eventually president) of the Theosophical Society after the founder's death in 1891. Not coincidentally, Alexandra formally joined the society the next year, stayed with Besant in London, followed by a lengthy stay at the Theosophical compound near Adyar, India in 1893. After returning from her first trip to the East, she continued to ask advice of Besant. This strong-willed woman had been a feminist and outspoken advocate of what was then termed Free Love, that is, free sexual choice.

The young woman boarding at the Gnossis was more concerned with her covertly romantic relationship with Jacques Villemain, *artiste parisien*. She was attracted to the slim, elegant esthete, with his delicate features and pale complexion, as she would be to others of this monkish type who also held some knowledge she wanted. He also gave the impression of being a gentleman, which reassured Alexandra. She remarked with satisfaction that she couldn't imagine him dressed up in a costume at the Beaux Arts Ball.

Villemain painted in a metaphysical style: landscapes alive with menacing anthropomorphic forms, as though each rock or tree held a secret inner self peering at the viewer. In the artist's room, where she visited him, Alexandra regarded one such landscape of a snow-capped peak dominating a deserted salt lake, the whole vast and empty yet peopled with indistinct figures. Thoroughly absorbed, as she moved to touch the painting, the artist whisked it away. He warned her that she was going to enter into the landscape.

Alexandra begged Villemain to explain himself, but he put her off with tea and toast. Shortly after, he went into seclusion. Miss Holmwood, another eccentric member of the Gnosis, confided that he was a probationer who desired admittance to the secret, inner circle of the society. After a while the young man turned up gaunt and withdrawn, health damaged by a routine of privation. To cheer him, as well as to corner him into answering her questions, Alexandra suggested that they visit the Crystal Palace remaining from the Great Exposition of 1851. Incidentally, the structure had been moved to the same neighborhood in which Madame Blavatsky held her Saturdays.

The pair boarded a train in the midst of a London fog. Villemain was silent, sunk in thought, and Alexandra promptly fell asleep. She awoke at a siding and, calling out, discovered they had boarded an express to Scotland. They would have to wait until evening when a local came through to return to London. It began to drizzle, and they sat under a little shelter. Alexandra, seizing her chance, demanded to know what Villemain had meant by "entering into a painting."

The youthful occultist launched into a strange tale of how our fate is determined by our astral double in the other world. The hours sped by, and although the notions elaborated by Villemain to his fascinated friend harked back to the neo-Platonists, they also corresponded to the beliefs of Tibetan Buddhism. Alexandra was especially struck by one story that, taken symbolically, was filled with portent.

> An artist had painted a picture of an oasis in Africa. A woman initiate went to view it. She became lightheaded, as though she was falling down among the palms. She walked about in the desert and, feeling warm, she wiped her face with a handkerchief. A sudden convulsion attacked her, and the woman, after dropping the kerchief, found herself back in the artist's atelier, in an armchair where evidently she had fainted. Searching for her kerchief, she saw it painted into the landscape at the foot of a palm! The artist swore he hadn't committed such an incongruity, and others affirmed they had seen the painting without the offending kerchief. Had the woman dropped it while she was strolling in the landscape?

Villemain might believe in astral doubles who inhabited a nonmaterial reality, but Alexandra sought a more tangible explanation. Perhaps all concerned had been victims of a communicable delusion? On their return to town, she demanded they eat a good Italian dinner. Too soon the young man returned to his austerities, and James Ward, her first friend in London, succumbed to a drug habit. Alexandra, still financially dependent on her parents, decided to leave London. Yet she couldn't rid her mind of the painting of an eerie snowcapped peak set in barren terrain shown her by Villemain. Decades afterward, the traveler finally found herself crossing from the hostile terrain of massive, guardian ice-mountains onto the vast Tibetan plain, the sun setting over a lake, from the shore of which a gold-crowned bird cawed its displeasure at the passing caravan. She recalled Villemain and the prescient tale of entering into a painting.

Alexandra returned to Brussels in 1889 to resume the study of music and voice. She was included in a circle of young intellectuals revolving around the old radical and friend of her father, Elisée Reclus. One of two brothers who fought on the barricades for the Paris Commune, his mother had been the rebels' Commissioner for Girls' Education. Either practical or intellectual schooling for girls was then a radical idea. Hadn't the great Balzac written: "The destiny of woman and her sole glory are to make beat the hearts of men. . . . She is a chattel . . . only a subsidiary to man." The Reclus family passed on the cause of women's education to Alexandra, who would personally suffer from the rabid antifeminism found in French universities.

While Alexandra's parents quarreled over her future, she took it in her own hands. Elisabeth Morgan arranged for her to board cheaply with a branch of the Theosophical Society in the Latin Quarter of Paris. It was a dimly lit, shabby flat fronting on the boulevard Saint-Michel, and its proprietors, one of several antagonistic factions of the society, claimed to be descended from moon beings. Dinner consisted of hunks of rock-like potatoes and a bloated piece of bread swimming in boiled dishwater. A few spoonfuls of this soup and the dejected young woman retreated to her room to gaze out the window. The pedestrian traffic below caught her eye.

Alexandra stood at the center of that gaudy merry-go-round dubbed *La Belle Epoque*. The habitues of the Latin Quarter streamed along the boulevard, gay, lively, or rude, flaunting their costumes or wares. These comings and goings were a river she could not fathom. She was disturbed by the gestures of a fancy harlot to hoped-for customers seated at a café, themselves too drowned in absinthe to notice. Had humans descended from the moon to arrive at this?

Alexandra enrolled at the College de France, studying Sanskrit under the venerable Professor Philippe-Edward Foucaux. Her teacher had translated Sanskrit works into Tibetan and written a grammar of that lanugage. Typical of scholars of his time, he had never visited the Land of Snows—forbidden to Western eyes—and he never dreamed of doing so, let alone that his pupil would reach its mysterious capital.

Alexandra repeated the pattern set in London, replacing the British Museum with the Musée Guimet. Here she read on Eastern themes, not only religion but also history, geography, and folklore, regarded the paintings and statuary, and met people of like mind. Settling into Paris, she sampled from the broad menu of esoteric societies. The most intriguing was the salon held by Marie Duchess de Pomar (Lady Caithness) at Holyrood, her mansion on rue de l'Université.

Alexandra eagerly climbed a flight of rose marble stairs to Pomar's ornate bedroom where the Duchess, wearing crimson velvet and a long chain of huge diamonds around her neck, received visitors. The ceiling was painted with angels circling a gold star. The

Duchess, a Spanish beauty, had married first an aged nobleman who obligingly died, then the Scottish Lord Caithness. Since she considered herself to be the reincarnation of Mary, Queen of Scots, a chapel in her boudoir contained a portrait of that unfortunate. Pomar had steeped herself in the lore of the dead queen and surrounded herself with "Mary relics." Habitually, twelve votaries led by a female medium sat around a table, fingertips touching. They silently awaited a presence, while the sensitive mumbled and drifted into a trance. Flashing lights, gray smoke, and a delicious rose perfume heralded the arrival of Mary's ghost—head intact—who when she kissed someone was supposed to leave a visible mark.

Pomar was not the light society quack that Alexandra pictured her. Rather, the Duchess authored some weighty tomes, notably *Serious Letters to Serious Friends*. Due to their heretical views, her books had shocked the clergy of Europe. Pomar was an associate of Madame Blavatsky and Annie Besant and became cofounder of the Paris Lodge of the Theosophists. This ambitious woman was a radical thinker who advocated the "reign of the feminine brain." Her models harked back to neolithic days when female divinities possessed the traits that once again would be valued in future society. Woman—fecund, sensual, intuitive, and nonviolent—should lead the way to a new race and an era of peace. The old warlike male rulers, such as those lords who had usurped the power of Mary of Scotland, would become obsolete and vanish.

In *fin-de-siecle* Paris decadence constituted both a style and an atmosphere. But Alexandra claimed not to be tempted by the cells of pagan worship of which she was aware. Yet she listened to her cleaning woman's talk of midnight gatherings in the woods outside of town, which also featured the so-called cult of the woman. Her problem with these meetings was that they were attended by the wrong sort of people—bank clerks and the like. The satanic mass was inevitably followed by a sexual free-for-all, for which our Victorian young woman was not prepared.

In her early twenties, Alexandra was pursuing her studies at the Sorbonne, but as a woman she could not be a full-time student. Still, this was typical of the older European system: T. E. Lawrence, who earned a bachelor's degree from Oxford, spent most of his time wandering about England or reading medieval literature. Alexandra had to return often to Brussels to continue her musical studies. The stern judge within her refused to let her rest. She could prepare for no definite career because those open to women were too limited.

However, the unhappy and frustrated young woman did not convert smoothly to Buddhism. Later in life she liked to give that impression, but in reality she painfully oscillated from pole to pole. Born a Catholic then rebaptized Protestant, she had been attracted to the ideas of Plato and the cadences of the Koran. When she felt the need to pray, she knelt in front of a devotional lamp, chanting prayers from the Hindu Vedas. Her travels to date, though mainly mental, ranged far and wide.

In 1889 the government of the Third Republic determined to hold another universal exposition, or world's fair, to commemorate the centenary of the French Revolution. President Sadi Carnot inaugurated the proceedings, which were intended to display France's worldly and artistic wealth and to attract a horde of tourists to Paris. This city of two-and-a-half million had outstripped every rival as the capital of pleasure. Thanks to the appearance of what Parisians termed "the electric fairy," it was becoming a true city of light.

The exhibitions ranged from an enormous gallery of machines to the reconstruction of a street in Cairo complete with belly dancers. Scientific discoveries such as Edison's phonograph and the Curies' radium were of the greatest interest to the throngs of visitors. In the center of the grounds stood that summation of French genius in the form of soaring iron and glass: the Eiffel Tower. Most Parisians hated it at first, certain it would tumble down on their heads. Gustave Eiffel had to guarantee indemnity in case of an accident. A committee of artists dashed off a manifesto denouncing the edifice "dominating Paris like a black, gigantic factory chimney." On the other hand, Alexandra looked kindly on this great symbol of scientific progress, in which she then believed, and of masculine power—which she sorely lacked.

1889 also marks the first of Alexandra's so-called neurasthenic crises. "Neurasthenia" is a term currently replaced by "depression," which is almost as vague. Alexandra internalized her dependent situation and attempted to emancipate herself from what she deemed unworthy passions and habits. She claimed to have seen the banality of most human pleasures. She knew of higher things but lacked the strength to pull herself out of despair. Young, pretty, petite, she was tormented by desires and fears. To her diary (fragments have surfaced and been published in *La Lampe de Sagesse*, 1986) she confided that she could not believe in romantic love, which would only lead to infidelity, betrayal, and a broken heart.

Death preyed on Alexandra's mind. Under the appearance of beauty or wealth she saw a rotting corpse, and she predicted, wrongly, that she would die young. But she nearly made the prophecy self-fulfilling by attempting suicide. Without warning, a demonic voice would whisper in her ear that she could put a quick end to her troubles. She knew she mustn't let it triumph.

"I belong to a new breed," she would reply. "We are few in number but we will accomplish our mission. I am doing what I must."

In our own time of suicidal cults, the above suggests that Alexandra was involved with an extremist political or messianic group. If so, she destroyed the evidence. However, in her diary the former debutante mentions that she kept a pistol and ammunition in her Paris room. Alexandra was trying to accept her instincts, demanding admiration from her comrades yet fearful of giving them anything deep. One evening during the winter of 1890–1891, she loaded her handgun, held it to her head and commanded: "Pull the trigger!" Then she began to reason with herself: a bullet could only disperse the atoms which made up her body, not kill her spirit. She already believed that she would be reincarnated to suffer the consequences.

More telling at the time, suicide meant desertion. True, Alexandra did not trust her comrades and she habitually lied to them. She had her hands on large sums of money—perhaps as a courier—which made her uncomfortable. Alexandra also had access to drugs. These are strong hints that she was leading an underground life as a political radical. She scribbled in her diary about how her blood boiled at injustice and the need for revolt—a stance that has been chic on the Left Bank for a long time.

Alexandra knew how to use a pistol. Her father had hunted and took along his daughter and taught her to shoot. She had sufficient familiarity with the sport to hate it, terming it the mere murder of animals. Jeanne Denys insisted that Alexandra "must have had a run-in with the law." The Belgian authorities informed Denys,

"There exists [on Alexandra] dossier number 508-533 at the Foreign Police of the Ministry of Justice." Denys requested the folder but was denied. The authors have determined that such files are open only for governmental purpose or to relatives.

From the viewpoint of the Belgian police, Alexandra was involved in shady doings. Over two decades later, the British Government of India, concerned about her activities there, investigated her past. They concluded that, at the least, she had radical associates in Paris and Brussels. The answer to the puzzle lies in the influence of the old Communard Elisée Reclus. After years of wandering he had settled at Ixelles, a suburb of Brussels, and embarked on the composition of his grand *Geographie universelle*, one of the first genuinely scientific works in the field. But Reclus was always at the service of his comrades. One of these was Louis David, his neighbor at Ixelles.

Reclus was an uncompromising radical. He continued to edit the far-left review *La Rive Gauche* and to write such provocative manifestos as *Worker Take the Machine! Farmer Take the Land!* Dispensing with priest or magistrate, he officiated at the marriages of his two daughters to like-minded young men. Most important, he threw open his pleasant home with its lush garden to young people whom he encouraged to gather and air controversial notions. It was under his roof that Alexandra met political exiles, bearded freethinkers, emaciated poets, and other merchants of dreams.

Here men and women, genteel or working class, were welcomed equally. These hopeful ones would sit around a table on which perched a couple of bottles of cheap wine and argue philosophy or politics late into the night, each ecstatic face lit by an interior flame. Alexandra, the mature author, wondered what had become of those early comrades. Older, wiser, she knew that some while searching for justice had died as martyrs, or worse, died young after becoming disillusioned with humanity. These rebels would be reincarnated on the streets of the Left Bank during the 1968 student uprising that toppled the government, and to which Alexandra gave her blessing in her hundredth year.

But to understand the extreme bent of Alexandra's thought, we must glance at Max Stirner, the German anarchist whose work dominated her outlook as a young rebel—and as an old one! Stirner, an opponent of his more successful countryman Hegel, led an unremarkable mid-nineteenth century life. He taught at a respectable girl's school in Berlin and was known for his translations of Adam Smith. But his magnum opus, *The Ego and Its Own*, converted Alexandra from a libertarian in spirit to one in doctrine and practice.

Stirner, scorning the common person as "a dog dragging his chain," celebrated the egotist brave enough to heed his natural instincts, which he assumed were in accord with "the laws of the universe." In the German romantic tradition, he glorified the self above society. "Every moment," he wrote, "the fetters of reality cut the sharpest welts in my flesh. But my own I remain." Indeed, Stirner denied any truth beyond the individual's free will.

Stirner anticipated Nietzsche and even Freud. He reflected Alexandra's inner turmoil by picturing the self as divided between its wants and needs on the one hand, and on the other a police force determined to restrain it from satisfying itself. Give the ego free reign, he implored; deny so-called honesty by having "the courage to lie." Commit crimes to weaken the "cement" (respect for law) that holds the state together. At his most bellicose, Stirner announced, "I prefer one free *grisette* [whore] over a thousand virgins grown gray in virtue." All this has the ring of *La Bohème* mingled with the nasty romanticism that in time would provide the underpinning for a fascist aesthetic. But Alexandra, who couldn't stand to obey orders, echoed the frustrated German, who declared: "Every moment a man submits to an outside will is an instant taken away from his life."

Elisée Reclus was a kinder man who provided a figure counter to her own weak-willed father. He became her mentor—the next in a line that was mostly male. A photo of Alexandra from circa 1890, taken in Reclus' garden, shows her dressed soberly in a high-collared blouse, a man's tie folding into a skirt that falls to her boots. She appears to be a perfect bluestocking. Her hair is curly, short, and unadorned; not a frill relieves the austerity of the ensemble. Clearly, she doesn't frequent the Paris *maisons* of Worth or Doucet, where socialites flock to spend lavishly on the latest fashions. This young woman stands at attention, right foot forward as though ready to be off to some distant land.

That summer in Paris was a lark to young Havelock Ellis. In *From Rousseau to Proust* he recalled that he was welcomed along with the budding esthetes who frequented the poet Mallarme's Tuesday evenings. He observed Paul Verlaine (whose love for young Arthur Rimbaud had wrecked his marriage) drinking himself to death at a café on the boulevard des Italiens. It exhilarated the aspiring bohemian—explorer of the forbidden realm of sex—to stroll along the wide, chestnut tree-lined boulevards. His admiring glances were returned by expensively garbed, if suspect, ladies who were accustomed to midnight suppers at Maxim's. They expected their entrance on a man's arm to make heads turn.

Whether in the silly farces of the period, the superb posters, or the absurd dreams of men far and wide, the Parisienne had become the universal sex symbol. Meanwhile the artistic milieu was as insurrectionist as the French working class, among the worst paid in Europe. Paul Gauguin and his followers began to make a change in academic perceptions with their *Salon des independants*. At war with the taste of the bourgeosie, Gauguin, despairing of Europe, left for Tahiti to rediscover the splendor of barbarism. In effect, he declared the chasm between individual creativity and the constraints of Western society to be unbridgeable. He helped to launch the vogue of Orientalism, which was to find its way into the parlors of the middle class and into the heart of our susceptible young Frenchwoman.

By 1891 Alexandra was in her early twenties, and her alternatives were narrowing. She might teach or, as her parents hoped, marry. If she were more of a coquette she could find a wealthy old protector and scheme to get included in his will. The properly brought up mademoiselle hesitated at a singing career with its inevitable demands of the flesh.

Then Elisabeth Morgan died and Alexandra inherited a small but tidy sum. Madame David insisted that she invest it in a nice tobacconist shop. Louis, semiretired, living off stocks and rents, weakly seconded his wife's practical plan. He wished his only child to remain close to him. In Paris Alexandra, to resolve her dilemma, resorted to the cult led by Sri Ananda Saraswati. The followers of this popular guru used drugs, particularly North African hashish (concentrated pollen of the marijuana plant, often laced with opium) for the purpose of obtaining visions in astral travel. Alexandra disguised herself as a young man, joined them, and smoked a hash cigarette. She was hoping for a revelation.

A few drags on the butt induced a dreamlike reverie. The "young man" saw his astral double in the parlor of his parent's home, enveloped in a gloomy light. He became frightened, weak, doubled-up in pain. He was afraid that he would be made a prisoner and never allowed to leave. Moaning, he was jarred awake at the salon. Alexandra writes that the "young man" left that same evening for Marseilles and a ship bound for India.

In fact, Alexandra did not break her ties so quickly. She resorted again to her temple of learning, the Musée Guimet. Ascending the grand staircase past frescos of a Brahmin tending a ritual fire, Buddhist monks in saffron togas carrying begging bowls, a Japanese temple amid cherry blossoms with icy mountains in the background, she felt like a pilgrim proceeding toward the unraveling of the supreme mystery.

In the library, presiding over books and readers alike, sat a large gilt Buddha, a smile hinting up his moon-shaped face. Alexandra had made a practice of saluting the statue. Now she brought her problems to the Buddha—and he answered her with a blessing. The statue spoke to the young scholar, although not in French or English. An object of prayer for ages, the statue had stored some of the energy, the devotion, poured into it, much as the earth holds the heat of the sun. As the sand of the desert can in the middle of the night give off warmth, so the stone Buddha returned the radiance of his vanished devotees. But this is Alexandra's rationalization, not her experience, which she at first resisted.

Another instance of such communication comes from the noted author and Buddhist John Blofeld. He writes of hearing an image of Kuan Yin, the Chinese goddess of compassion and granter of favors, reply to his doubts with the following words: "Look not for my reality in the realm of appearances. . . . Seek it in your own mind." Blofeld kept this experience secret from Westerners for decades out of fear of ridicule. Finally, he accepted the belief that the being Kuan Yin did communicate with him.

Whether Alexandra's feeling of oneness with the Buddha stemmed from a subjective or an objective basis—a tenuous distinction in the East—in front of this statue, while paying homage in the traditional manner with palms pressed together in front of the heart, head bowed, she received an instance of what her Huguenot forebears called "God's grace." Between her and the Buddha image passed an intimation of things to come. She was off to "somewhere east of Suez."

Chapter 4
The Saddest Story

In 1951, following Indian independence, Alexandra David-Neel, then eighty-three, published in Paris a memoir (*India Yesterday, Today and Tomorrow*) of her several voyages to the Subcontinent. She is unabashed about the sights she witnessed—gorgeous and gruesome—but, as usual, indifferent to the integrity of genre. David-Neel, who loathed chronology, would let nothing stand in the way of telling a good story. Impressions from her first and later sojourns are mingled if they suit the theme. But why did she wait so long to reminisce about the first Asian country to seize her imagination?

Beginning in 1891, at age twenty-three, Alexandra traveled for over a year through Ceylon and India to the foot of Mount Kanchenjunga on the Nepali-Sikkimese border, its five snowy crowns visible on a clear morning from Darjeeling, beckoning the seeker on to the mysterious beyond. Here she stopped, although not in imagination. In an article published in 1904, "The Religious Power of Tibet," Alexandra wrote of the lamas as "superhuman beings" who lived so high and distantly they had reversed the Greek myth of the gods descending from Olympus to mingle with humans. It would have amazed her to think that she would one day study with these masters.

On the outward passage to India through the Red Sea, the heat grew unbearable and everyone dozed all day. Alexandra, probably still a virgin, was struck by the lean, blonde beauty of one of the passengers, stretched out on a deck chair by the first-class cabins. Although she had the air of a goddess, Alexandra suspected she was a high-class practitioner of the oldest profession. She noticed that one of two monks who had come aboard at Suez—Christian but of an Eastern order, wearing coarse robes—felt compelled to stare at the woman. When this tall, thin, young monk realized that Alexandra was aware of this, he blushed, raised his cowl and went below. But not before he and the woman had exchanged a glance of unmistakable meaning.

The beautiful courtesan and the handsome monk continued their dance of passion in the dimness of the voluptuous, Eastern night. As the ship approached Ceylon, with the sea a sheet of silver lamé, Alexandra watched one evening while the woman, seductively draped in a sheer dress, lounged against the rail and the monk hesitantly approached her. They spoke a few words that Alexandra could not get close enough to hear; then the monk, trembling, embraced the woman. He follwed her to her cabin. When the young traveler disembarked at Colombo, neither of the pair was on deck and she supposed she'd seen the last of them.

Alexandra, on her first sojourn in India, brought with her certain European preconceptions of the hygienic sort that kept her at a distance from the land and its people. She studied Sanskrit with the Theosophists at Adyar near Madras, and after an interview with Annie Besant, she formally joined the society there. In Benares, holy city on the banks of the Ganges, Alexandra studied yoga with a naked eminence, Bashkarananda, who lived year round in a rose garden. She felt that the swami had a deep understanding of Indian thought, and she was preparing to be initiated as a *sanyassin* (renunciate) in her twenty-fifth year. Before this could happen, she ran out of money and had to return to Brussels.

She was once again dependent on her parents. However, encouraged by Elisée Reclus, she set to work on an anarchist "hymn to life," the lengthy essay *Pour La Vie*. "This is a proud book," Reclus would state in its preface, "written by a woman prouder still." He could speak with authority, since eventually he was going to bear the risk of publishing this immoderate tract that blasted all laws that interfered with individual liberty.

The most intriguing aspects of *Pour La Vie* are those that stem from Alexandra's heartfelt experience. She damned the artificial faith of her mother and a cruel god who demands pain and tears in life as payment for going to heaven after death. She viewed the society of her day as her mother's morality writ large, the enforcer of constraint and death. She condemned the singleminded pursuit of wealth, particularly by inheritance. Ironically, the Panic of 1893 gripped the stock markets of the world, and, compounded by the collapse of French efforts to build a Panama Canal, it was especially acute on the Paris Bourse. Louis David's investments turned into worthless pieces of paper. He could no longer afford to underwrite his daughter's fancies, and her inheritance was much diminished.

While Alexandra faced the prospect of earning a living, anarchist cells such as "The Terribles" counterfeited, robbed, and assassinated in the name of the people. Never very many, these terrorists—who made bombs out of cast-iron soup pots with the lids fastened over sticks of dynamite and iron scraps—succeeded in thoroughly frightening the government. In 1893 a bomb was thrown from the gallery into the Chamber of Deputies, wounding several lawmakers. In 1894 the execution by guillotine of Emile Henry, aged twenty-two, drew a large, enthusiastic crowd. He had hurled a bomb into the cafe of a railway station filled with people sipping aperitifs. When asked whether he intended to wound innocent people, he replied, "There are no innocent *bourgeoises*."

The wave of terror crested with the assassination of the popular president of the Republic, Sadi Carnot, on June 24. An Italian stabbed him to death. France had been pushed too far, and the police raided leftist dens and homes. Thirty allegedly anarchist writers and journalists were put on trial, but their witty replies turned the proceedings into a fiasco. Nonetheless radicals fled into exile and others went underground. Elisée Reclus accepted the safe position of professor of geography at the New University of Brussels. Anarchy, as a political movement, was finished.

Although Alexandra David hadn't published her subversive "hymn"—and wouldn't until five years had passed—she was well-known to the police in Brussels and Paris. They retained dossiers on her, which nearly twenty years later they would pass on to British officials in India. For the present, Alexandra was obliged to fall back on her feminine assets: brunette good looks and a fine soprano voice. In pursuing a new career, she found it prudent to forget most of her old comrades and to assume an alias.

From 1894 to the end of the decade, Alexandra David lived and worked as an aspiring chanteuse, performing under the name of Alexandra Myrial (a character in the writings of Hugo). She had a coloratura voice, delicate enough to attempt the ornamentation of Leo Delibes's "Bell Song." She sang roles composed by Bizet, Gounod, Puccini, and especially Jules Massenet. Whatever her other preoccupations, Alexandra had clung to the love of music. In her mid-twenties, she studied with a feverish diligence at the Brussels Conservatory and then moved on to Paris. She composed music and her goal was to win the coveted Prix de Rome. In this she did not succeed.

Living as an aspiring actress/singer in Paris was difficult. Alexandra later reminisced about her so-called herring days when a grocery store would give her potatoes and a dozen herring on credit. Boiled together, this was all she had to eat as she practiced scales. Still, the glamorous world of the opera promised a way out. She devoured musical scores, impassioned by them as though they were romantic novels. But Alexandra commented grimly on how she watched backstage mothers turn their daughters into whores. She, however, had a backstage father: Louis David was always full of helpful advice or nostrums. He was delighted when, solely on her talent, his daughter was selected in autumn 1895 to tour Indochina with the road company of L'Opéra-Comique. She was to be billed as their *premiere chanteuse* in Hanoi and Haiphong.

Alexandra once quipped that she had nostalgia for Asia before ever going there. On board the steamer bound for the Gulf of Tonkin, the singer's cabinmate criticized her for bathing daily, claiming it would ruin her skin. Alexandra didn't care for the libertine society in which she found herself. Nor did she have any compliments for France's devilish colony, where the young men and women of the company gave themselves up to sexual intrigues. Rich plantation owners were surprised that they could not buy her favors.

Her first triumph was as Violetta in *La Traviata*. She immediately sent a clipping from the local paper to Louis David with instructions to bring it to the notice of the Belgian papers. This was a pattern she was going to repeat in different circumstances with the man we may term her backstage husband. The premiere chanteuse was creating a certain image. She studied her roles with care and oversaw the making of her costumes. She sang the role of Thaïs in a coat of silk covered with pearls and gold that she had copied from a description given by a courtesan of ancient Alexandria. She portrayed Delibes's Lakmé—a role of great delicacy—with success, fed herself well, and obeyed her father's injunction to take quinine regularly and avoid the early morning mists.

Then Alexandra made a mistake. The director of the opera house at Hanoi, impressed by her ability to fill the house, offered her two hundred francs per night to sing Carmen several nights running. Recalling her herring days, the singer, in her prime at twenty-eight, accepted. Carmen is a part for a mezzo-soprano, a huskier voice than Alexandra's, and though she might manage it occasionally, at Hanoi she began the process of using up her voice.

The would-be prima donna returned to Paris for the season of 1897. She had already initiated a correspondence with Jules Massenet, cleverly asking his advice concerning the character of Manon. He had taken unusual pains with the psychology of his opera. Alexandra perfectly understood that lost but striving woman, unwilling to accept a mediocre lot; France's leading composer in a letter of that spring praised her voice and acting ability. Although a projected rendezvous failed to take place, Massenet, an obliging man, recommended her to Leon Carvalho, director of L'Opéra-Comique, before he fled the Paris winter for the south.

Carvalho, despite being the composer of sentimental operas, was a hardheaded businessman. He recognized the singer's potential but offered her a bit part at three hundred francs per month. This was little more than she had earned each night at Hanoi. Alexandra could starve in Paris or sing for better pay in the provinces. In the spring of 1897 she departed for a fateful tour of the Midi.

Here Alexandra experienced her first sexual encounter. Previous biographical opinion has claimed that she had an aversion to men, indeed a horror of the opposite sex. The idea is patently absurd; this was a woman who loved her father, had a long marriage, adopted a son, and who dreamed of her own sort of romance. In reality David-Neel, like Blavatsky, got on much better with men than women, if only because it was more profitable. She had a great need for, and responded to, fatherly affection. Victor Hugo, a bear of a man, was the first to bounce the little girl on his knee. Physical authority was an essential quality that Alexandra would look for in a man.

Eventually she was able to transmute the father role into that of mentor (even guru), and these men too would be physical types. Finally they became her equals, fellow explorers.

Alexandra was attracted to another sort of man, the younger brother or companion. Possibly this made up for the early loss of her own brother. A certain sexual aura, although muted, pervaded these relationships. Eventually this need was filled by her adopted son Yongden. Alexandra's ideal man would have to play both roles simultaneously, to be at once authoritative and sensitive. He must be worthy to arouse in her a great love. If Alexandra hadn't understood the passion for which her characters in *Manon* or *Thaïs* were willing to die, she could not have sung the roles so meaningfully. And she would not have found the real life story of the courtesan and the monk—the duality of sensuality versus austerity—so terribly moving. Because once again, this time in Paris, she glimpsed the "goddess from Olympus." She learned from the proprietor of a beauty salon, with whom she loved to gossip, that the goddess was Clare de Langy, a fabulously expensive prostitute.

For now, the woman of nearly thirty had tired of her chastity. Alexandra was slipping from the status of maiden to that of old maid. Conventional marriage appalled her, since it would deprive her of most legal rights. What she needed in order to live in Paris was a roommate rather than a husband.

Alexandra found the right young man: Jean Haustont, composer and fellow orientalist. A photo shows a tall, slender, earnest fellow without much force of character. He is attractive, appropriately bearded, and fair-haired. Jean had been born in Brussels in 1867, and he was introduced to Alexandra by a painter at a meeting of the Theosophical Society. They shared similar interests but hardly a grand passion.

Toward the end of this period of her development, Alexandra wrote a long, soppy, more or less autobiographical novel that she tried but failed to have published. "High Art" (subtitled "Memoirs of an Actress") reveals the author's extreme sensitivity, conflicting desires and dual identity. It handles sexuality in a manner typical for its day: rough, masculine sex is counterpoised against feminine sentimentality. For one reason or another, the author never destroyed this work of fiction.

Jean is depicted as the opera company's pianist, Pierre: blue-eyed and melancholy. He falls in love with Cecile (Alexandra), the glamorous soprano, while she feels a tender pity for the grown man she will come to term her "child." While they flirt innocently at rehearsals—the touring opera company is at Bayonne—a Greek stagehand is eyeing Cecile. He has a more vivid idea of what she will look like with her clothes off than does Pierre.

In the novel the stagehand brutally rapes Cecile, who swoons and falls into a brain fever that lasts for weeks. Her life hangs by a thread as loyal Pierre nurses her, soiled woman that she is. This sort of melodrama was popular in its day, but in reality Alexandra was never so passive. The stagehand probably was her first lover, but only because she had wearied of her virginity and decided to make use of him. Jean Haustont, whom she desired, was not the type to initiate an affair, still less to deflower a virgin. Alexandra, we should note, had a limited admiration for the brute, and when decades later she began to write original, indeed captivating, fiction, one of her best realized heros was just such a fellow.

Alexandra was at her pitch of beauty at this time. A photo of her dressed in an elaborate opera costume shows a fully rounded but still petite figure, a symmetrical face whose most striking feature is a pair of brooding almond eyes set in high cheekbones. The nose is her father's, straight but delicate, and her mouth is set in a sensual pout, lower lip turned out. The ensemble is capped by a frizzed coiffure from which trails a fake braid. Later, although her looks turned matronly, she still carried herself with the air of a beauty.

Alexandra and Jean moved in together in a flat in suburban Passy, and here they lived and worked for most of the next three years. Significantly, they went under the name of Monsieur and Madame Myrial, which Alexandra would adopt as a *nom de plume*. Together they wrote a lyrical drama in one act—"Lidia"—Jean the music and she the words. No one could be found to stage it. Quiet bohemians, they visited Elisée Reclus, who gave them his blessing, as did Louis David. The elderly gentleman liked Jean and wrote to him from time to time. He envied what he supposed was the couple's true love.

The singer's career was going nowhere, and as novelist and essayist she was rejected and unnoticed. But she hadn't yet tired of *la vie de boheme*. She looked for salvation in art and wrote approvingly of its sensual satisfactions. When, in the autumn of 1899, the opportunity arose to perform with the Opera of Athens, a second-rate house, she didn't hesitate to go. However, her voice was no longer reliable. Louis David sent a remedy for her bad throat: a decoction of dried figs and raisins with honey added. To herself the singer admitted that her career in high art was a failure.

In the summer of 1900—while Paris indulged in another universal exposition—Alexandra sent her parents a curt note from Marseilles stating that she had accepted an engagement with the municipal opera in Tunis. Her career was on a predictable downward spiral: from the second company to the provinces to the colonies. For a time Louis David received no more news from her, and he wrote anxiously to Jean. The earnest young musician knew no more than did her father. Alexandra had dropped him for another man.

Alexandra had mothered Jean and she felt for him a sweet, calm affection. But their relationship was ultimately neither practical nor passionate. Haustont, an introspective man, invented a novel musical notation scheme based on vibrations. He eventually went to China where he taught music and lived out his days. Alexandra, who for a time visited and corresponded with him, made no effort to find her former lover in the Orient.

Once she had met the stranger she was going to marry, she never accorded Jean much weight. Philip Neel, a bachelor at the age of thirty-nine, was a man who appeared to have everything except a wife. Born at Ales in the south of France, his family was of ancient Norman stock and came from Jersey, and his father had been a Methodist missionary. His mother was the daughter of a Protestant minister. Philip, in contrast to Alexandra, was one of ten children; however, his parents saw to it that he got the best education—in engineering—then available. Philip was instrumental in constructing the railroad line from Bône, Algeria, to Guelma, Tunisia, of which he was made the chief engineering officer.

With his air of an English gentleman, Philip favored frock coats, high collars with cravat and stickpin, or while on duty a cutaway jacket worn with contrasting knickers and high socks, as well as a jaunty cap. His features were finely cut, eyes cold blue, mustache alert. Alexandra found him to be elegant and a perfect gentleman.

But he was no Don Juan and she never fell madly in love with him. Philip was more of a country Casanova, crude in his advances and riddled with guilt. Meanwhile, the Parisienne who called herself Alexandra Myrial, thirty-two and worldly wise, must have caused a stir among the lonely Frenchmen at Tunis.

Alexandra met Philip at the casino. This was the center of social life for colonial society, at least for the men, and here they gathered to gamble, gossip, and listen to a chanteuse from Paris sing café ballads. Thus the military officers and bureaucrats forgot, for the moment, they were far from home in an Arab land. By September of 1900 the entertainer at the piano was Alexandra Myrial, formerly of L'Opéra-Comique. She sang light arias for her polite, if not deeply attentive, audience, one of whom was the chief engineer. Philip had a yacht of sorts, the *Swallow*, to which he invited the glamorous Parisienne. Not only did she accept on September 15, but, according to her diary, she went to bed with him then and there. For a change, Philip Neel found himself involved with a woman he had to take seriously.

The yacht was the usual scene of Philip's trysts, but these had involved whores from Marseilles who serviced the colonial class. When one of the girls asked for more than the going price, Philip sent her away rather than pay up. This missionary's son liked to sin, but on the cheap. He had a postcard made up with a photo of the *Swallow* on one side, and he mailed it with identical gallantries to all the girls. Naturally, at first, he assured Alexandra she was the only woman in his life. If there had been others, he couldn't recall their names.

In 1902 Alexandra accepted the more attractive post of artistic director of the casino, possibly obtained through Philip's influence. In contrast, she temporarily joined an expedition of German botanists into the southern desert, where she indulged her interest in ethnology and studied the Bedouins. She continued to write occasionally for radical reviews. In "The Origin of Myths and Their Influence on Social Justice" (*Free Thought* [Brussels, 1901]) she attacked the Judeo-Christian tradition and its priests as the descendants of witch doctors. Buddhism, on the other hand, she declared to be rational and liberal. She hoped for a revolution of thought and sentiment not for the masses but to free the individual.

Alexandra traveled sometimes to Paris where she stayed with Jean Haustont at their old flat in Passy. He came to visit her in Tunis during the summer of 1902. Perhaps she aimed to make Philip jealous, playing on an attraction that, for both, was winning out over their caution and mutual prudence. The budding author needed to maintain a link with her Paris editors, and that same year she published two articles in the influential *Mercure de France*, including one on "The Tibetan Clergy and Its Doctrines." It was as though she could glimpse her own future.

By the winter of 1904, Alexandra, Philip's avowed mistress, had moved into his lovely native-style home, La Goulette (Waterwheel). On account of his curly hair, she chose the pet name "alouche," which she supposed meant "sheep" in Arabic. The nickname "Mouchy" stuck to him. For a while, though, it appeared that Alexandra and her sheep were going to part bitter enemies. Philip had a kinky side: he took and kept intimate photos of his paid-for conquests, posed *Penthouse*-style. Ever the bureaucrat, he carefully filed the photos with the girls' letters. Either by accident or design, Philip left the incriminating evidence where his mistress might discover the whole lot. She did, and far worse, she found her own letters mixed in with the rest.

Philip's reaction to Alexandra's barely suppressed rage was nonchalance. Forgetting how he'd lied to her, he amiably exhibited his gallery of whores. None of these overweight, lower-class women was pretty, and Philip and Alexandra laughed like comrades over their crudeness. To herself Alexandra tried to rationalize away her anger. So what if the man was a skirt chaser? And now he strutted around proud as a peacock! But he had led her on, telling her she was his all-in-all. Worse, all the girls had his picture and could exhibit it to future clients.

Once she cooled down, Alexandra realized she was dealing with a coxcomb. Mouchy had delivered to her his past as hostage. Alexandra divined the Methodist guilt that lurked beneath his pose as man of the world. Philip at forty, patron of prostitutes, had to redeem himself through marriage. She, thirty-six, had trouble keeping her weight in check and owned nothing but some books and inexpensive jewelry. Her feminist principles were strong, her Buddhist yearnings real, but the prospect of a poor, lonely middle age was bleak.

On August 4, 1904, Alexandra David married Philip Neel at the

French consulate in Tunis. Her choice of husband proved brilliantly correct and her timing downright lucky. Philip formally wrote to the astonished Louis David to request his consent. The elderly gentleman, approaching ninety, agreed—after he had checked with the president of the railroad, who praised the engineer's salary, character and pension. For their honeymoon, the newlyweds sailed to France, then went by train to the spa town of Plombiers, where they took the waters. After a week they parted. Philip returned to Tunis, Alexandra went on to Paris to make the rounds of publishers. There she received word that Louis David was dying, and she hurried to Brussels. Her mother, who was practically senile, fell ill. In her time of trouble and grief, while watching over her father's last days, Alexandra could depend on steady Philip.

Over the next several years La Goulette, the Neels' villa by the Mediterranean Sea, would provide a healing refuge for Alexandra's frequently bruised ego. It was a lovely Moorish home with whitewashed walls, arcades, and arches, a cool patio, and playing fountains. In August 1905, while redecorating her home, she learned that her mentor Elisée Reclus had died. She could afford to cry like a little girl, resting her head on Philip's shoulder. For the time being she had found a substitute father. But lurking in the background was an older, more profound paternity: the shadow of Genghis Khan.

Try as she might, Alexandra couldn't tolerate indefinitely the role of bureaucrat's wife or amateur woman of letters. A photo snapped in the patio of the Neels' home sometime before 1910 shows her reclining on a chaise lounge, a prosperous, slightly overweight matron in an oriental dressing gown. The lady is about to summon a servant to refill her cup of tea. Her hair is tidy, upswept, and parted in the middle. Around the patio are plants that give an illusion of the tropics, but nothing is wild except the eyes of the caged wife.

Alexandra would advance to meet her desinty on the wind-swept plateau of Tibet, the Roof of the World. She would penetrate a mysterious realm known to few European men and no European women. But on returning from her travels and staying briefly in Paris to taste the acclaim due her, she once again encountered Clare de Langy, who was still beautiful and a viscountess and terribly sad. Clare, an admirer of Alexandra's writing, invited her to her home and poured out her story.

Clare de Langy had seduced the young monk aboard the ship on a whim. She was excited by the thought of overcoming his asceticism, his vows to God. Lightning flashed as she felt the coarse cloth of his robe against her soft white skin. By morning she was hopelessly in love with the Viscount de Trévaux, who had joined a monastic order and planned to give them his fortune. They went ashore at Colombo together, the viscount wearing a fashionable tropical suit and black turban. Only then did Clare realize how handsome her lover was—like a Greek god. But she knew she had sinned mortally.

The pair became ardent lovers but Trévaux insisted on marriage. Under his spell, Clare succumbed. The couple lived in luxury on the French Riviera. Clare sensed her husband's restlessness, and indeed one morning he left the house and didn't return. His lawyer informed Clare that she was wealthy and could keep the house but her husband, who had retreated to an unknown monastery, would never see her again. Clare hired detectives and searched everywhere for her husband, whom she deeply loved, but it was no use. At last the lawyer informed her that Trévaux had died and she had inherited his entire fortune.

Clare had this to ask of Alexandra: is there a life after death? She couldn't bear the thought of never again seeing her loved one. The beautiful viscountess, in effect a nun, looked forward only to joining him in death. She was hopeful that Alexandra had learned the secret of contacting his spirit. David-Neel, the Buddhist, advised her to pray for the welfare of all sentient beings to benefit her departed husband. But she could see that the woman, despite her promiscuous past, thought only of this one man.

Alexandra, as she left, realized that Clare had lived the role of the penitent courtesan that she had acted on the operatic stage. Clare's story was, in a sense, her own story, which is why she was so moved by it. Except that while Clare had nowhere to run from her grief, she had taken refuge in travel and the study of Buddhism.

Chapter 5

India Absurd and Marvelous

In 1911 on her second voyage to India, Alexandra David-Neel, aged forty-three, although traveling first class, had a bad time of it. The Arabs eating with their hands from grimy baskets, the odors from poor sanitation and a scorching sun, the vermin that got into her cabin, made her feverish. She believed that odd microbes had infected her, and she thought wistfully of an early return. But the die was cast: Alexandra wouldn't see her "dear Mouchy" for fourteen years. By then she would have graduated from being a student of the East to a learned lama; from a seeker to a pilgrim to a savant.

Despite her discomfort, David-Neel thought lucidly about what she proposed to accomplish. She was known in feminist circles, and she had both attended and addressed various conferences, including the first Congress of Women in 1907 in Rome, which she found overly tame and dominated by women of the leisure class. She had a reputation as a journalist who wrote on a variety of subjects, from reform of marriage to Zionism, for small magazines. She was perhaps best known as the author of a book on the oldest form of Buddhism, that of the Theravada as practiced in Ceylon, Burma, and Thailand. This would go through many permutations and titles and remains still in print.

In reality the author had exhausted her stock of knowledge, and the woman, despite her apparently productive life, was miserable. Alexandra complained continually of headaches, fatigue, poor appetite. She felt she was growing old, coming to resemble her mother. She had lost touch with her guardian spirit. Yet her growing involvement in Buddhism gave her hope, and she determined to take her place in French Orientalism: not as a specialist but an advocate of the living philosophy of the East. She (rather rashly) hoped to reform and rationalize the teachings of Buddhism.

Meanwhile Alexandra the gourmet complained about the food on board ship, especially lentils boiled with onions for dinner. If she had guessed what slops she would one day beg for—and relish! Colombo, Ceylon, where she disembarked on August 30, pleased her no better than had the voyage. Under the swaying palms merchants swarmed like flies, buzzing about their silks and sapphires. She was infuriated by the sight of a canary yellow statue of Buddha into whose open hands a devotee had placed a pack of toothpicks, while another left a jar of peas. She lectured at the Theosophical Society and gave a conference at the Royal College before heading into the countryside.

At a hermitage founded by the German scholar Nyanatiloka (born Anton Gueth), Alexandra studied Pali. This ancient tongue is the scriptural language for Theravadins, and its revival was akin to the study of Hebrew by the early Protestants. Indeed, her understanding of Buddhism at this time was entirely rational: Buddha was an exceptionally wise man who had taught a means of collective action that involved the renunciation of worldly gain. Thus Buddhism was compatible with her other beliefs, such as in science and anticolonialism.

Nonetheless Alexandra enjoyed playing the *mem sahib*. Dressed in white, wearing a huge hat with a white veil, she was pulled about in a rickshaw. For two months she visited the holy sites, including the Bo tree grown from a cutting of the original one under which Gautama had received enlightenment. But it was all too sweet and simple, and modern Buddhists were scarcer than in Paris.

Alexandra was pleased to sail away across the Gulf of Mannar on a tub without electric lights. At Madurai she passed an enchanting evening under the stars, intoxicated by the perfume of India. She had arrived in the south, land of the fine-boned, dark-skinned, emotive Dravidians. These people, who had resisted the conquering armies of both Aryans (bearers of Sanskrit) and Moghuls (Muslims), were ardent worshipers of the Hindu trinity. This is composed of Brahma the creator (to whom there are no temples, no images); Vishnu the preserver (sometimes pictured as a boar but whose best-known incarnation is as Krishna the blue cowherd); and Shiva the great destroyer (whose many arms flail a whirlwind of blades) who represents the fire of purification and of generation in the shape of a giant stone *lingam*, a phallic symbol adored by matrons and maidens and over which they pour pots of melted butter or cover with garlands of flowers—sweet and suffocating.

Alexandra grew more at ease with customs of which she theoretically disapproved. She frequented the baroque, indeed seething with statuary, Meenakshi temple that still dominates this bustling center of pilgrimage. The enormous rectangular structure dating from 1560 has always been a beehive of commerce. Figures in bright silks flitted about or hovered over stalls in the outer courtyard. Beggars begged, peddlers hawked glass bracelets while folk gossiped and bargained for flowers and fruits with which to propitiate Shiva, the temple's reigning deity. At intervals gourds were sounded to summon the faithful to prayer amid billows of incense, marigold petals, and a rosewater mist. It all reminded Lanza del Vasto, the Sicilian nobleman who became a follower of Gandhi, of Biblical descriptions of the Temple at Jerusalem in the time of Jesus.

Alexandra liked best the processions on the feast days. First the enclosure rang with a racket of conchs and gongs, which the former singer described as commanding, almost violent. Then the Brahmin priests issued from the temple precincts with the enthusiasm of a charge, while the devotees dragged a huge wooden-wheeled chariot through the streets, atop which Krishna danced death and rebirth. This chariot was called Juggernaut, and, because it sometimes crushed those in its way, gave the term its meaning. Men naked save for their loincloths, smeared with ash or painted with symbols, held up torches like weapons. The devout crouched along the way of the cortege or flung themselves down to kiss the paving stones after the god had passed. The pandemonium sent chills to the marrow of the supposedly rational observer's bones.

Alexandra admitted that the scene appeared to be straight out of the Middle Ages, even Satanic. Yet it was far more inspiring than the insipid holiday parades held in what remained of Christian Europe. The pagan Greeks had known of a similar sacred terror. Within the temple, a grand sight was the hall of a thousand exquisitely carved stone pillars, each illustrating an aspect of Hindu mythology. The inner sanctum was closed to the public (it still is). Here priests with half-naked torsos performed elaborate ceremonies, and here took place the tantric rites, sexual practices of which most Westerners have heard but continue to misunderstand. Alexandra, hiding in a secluded spot, witnessed the rites one evening.

David-Neel claims in her memoir, written nearly half-a-century after the fact, that she sneaked into the inner sanctum. Perhaps she bought admission. At any rate, in the house of the fish-eyed goddess Meenakshi, Shiva's consort, there were beautifully shaped statues of her, with rounded hips and breasts, which Alexandra admired. Upon Meenakshi were modeled the *Devadasis*, the temple's sacred prostitutes. These dancers were slaves wedded to Shiva at birth. Occasionally, a woman's freedom was bought by a wealthy admirer who paid the temple treasury a large sum. He then took her away to become his own concubine. The dancers performed only for high caste Hindus, and sons of the best families attended the rites.

Alexandra watched forty women whirl in dim light to the accompaniment of flute and drums. The musicians followed the steps of the performers, to mimic in sound the lascivious sway of dark, willowy torsos. A steady rhythm built and was accentuated by gauzy revelations of bare bosoms, which entranced the male congregants. Although the dancers, trained from childhood, were skilled in the erotic arts, Alexandra found nothing refined or graceful in the display. She termed it an Asian burlesque. No Puritan, she had read the *Kama Sutra* and, with Mouchy, practiced its complicated sexual postures. But the women before her were soft from a lazy life and violated her standard of beauty.

The Madurai males went nearly wild. Stimulated by spiraling hips and breasts, their lust rose to a crescendo. One, eyes dilated, began to writhe and gulp in ecstatic parody of *samadhi*, the state of unthinking bliss. Suddenly, the dancers fled from the platform and the devotees tore after them toward an innermost chamber where dwelled Shiva, his consort and their offspring. Alexandra didn't follow to witness the supposedly divine fulfillment. Instead, flattened between the legs of a giant stone horse, keeping company with his outsized lingam, she let the wave of horny males pass by. Then she exited, feeling not a little superior.

Alexandra realized she had found merely a perversion of the

tantric rite. In his *Tantra: The Yoga of Sex*, Omar Garrison reports on his investigation of a "night school" in Brindaban where a guru was training several disciples in the Secret Ritual—the taking of five forbidden substances, including meat and liquor, which would climax in *maithuna*, the conjugal union between a disciple and his *shakti*, or ceremonial partner. The guru complained that, although he had carefully chosen his pupils and trained them for over a year, when he arranged a ritual circle with women for their final initiation, the disciples all failed the test. The guru continued:

> The nececessary thing in this practice is control of the senses, especially control of the seed or semen. Emission is not allowed for any reason.
>
> But one of the boys did not restrain himself as I have taught him. Instead, he is spending his seed . . . To the others of the circle, he is saying, 'This is very jolly. Let us indulge.'
>
> They were all discharging with shouts like players at a polo match. So the fruit of their long *sadhana* (practice) was lost. Now they must find some other path to liberation.

Tantric sex, despite its adoption by hip couples throughout the Western world, is originally a sacred practice. Its aim is to make the sexual life cosmic in scope and intensity. Significantly, Lord Shiva is the chosen deity of both tantric adepts (*shaktas*) and the most ascetic of yogis, who seek from him the destruction of desire. Shaktas worship Shiva through the several images of his consort, for it is not pleasure but the female power that they seek. Found among this cult are those we would call magicians, or as Lanza del Vasto wrote in his *Return to the Source*, "the distillers of love-potions, amulet-makers, spell-casters, healers and miracle-makers—their holy books are the Tantra."

Tantrism, though despised by proper Brahmins, may be older than Hinduism itself. The Tantra looks back to the practices of the Vedic Rishis before the invasion of the Aryans; the latter brought with them the northern matrix of beliefs termed shamanism, from which Tantrism also borrowed. Tantrism demands the oral transmission of secrets from master to disciple, and its aim is the acquisition of magical powers in order to immediately affect both the world within and without. Rather than denying the erotic, Tantrism seeks to harness its energy. It is the sixth sense that the sexual organs seem to have, that is a mysterious inclination of their own, that the shaman seeks to obtain. Until relatively recently, this occult tradition was practiced most purely in a few regions of India—and in Tibet, the land where time had stood still.

The importance of this previously obscure system to the life of Alexandra, the rational Buddhist, would be crucial. Although she grew learned in several branches of Eastern thought, she became famous due to what she knew and wrote of Tibetan Buddhist tantrism. Generally, this is not sexual but employs the root power for other means. Only the difficult techniques she had studied in a Himalayan cave—such as *tumo* breathing, generating a protective body heat—turned her perilous journey to Lhasa into a success. As we shall see, Alexandra was identified as a tantric adept even before she became one.

The seeker traveled northward by train through forests of teak and past clearings in which drowsed age-old villages, a kind of psychic hum emanating from the click-clack of the train's wheels. Along the southeast coast the beaches were dotted by palmyra palms, and Alexandra expressed her approval of a people whose domestic economy was based on the coconut rather than the cow. At the major stations comfortable bungalows awaited Europeans where the native chambermaid could skillfully massage weary legs. Her companions proved interesting, and the Brahmins respectful, to the lone woman traveler.

But Alexandra was wearied by the heavy monsoon rains. She found the sky too gray and the fields almost too verdant. Everywhere she looked there was mud. Forgetful of time, she dreamed of her first trip to India nearly two decades earlier. Then she was a young woman whose spirit was in tune with the brief pink dawns that presaged a golden hot day. It wasn't India that had changed, but she. The full story of the tortured decade during which Alexandra had acted as Philip Neel's mistress and wife can only be glimpsed through the mirror of her own meditations. Their intimate correspondence for those years she consigned to the flames.

Alexandra arrived at Pondicherry, all that was left of French India, and was cheered by meeting with Sri Aurobindo Ghose, who was just then undergoing a conversion from political activist to spiritual leader. A Bengali by birth in 1872, he was taken at the age of seven to study in England. In 1893, after two years at Cambridge studying classics, Aurobindo returned to India in the service of a native maharaja. While he taught English he began to learn Sanskrit and finally to educate himself in the culture of India. In 1905 the British scheme to partition Bengal between west and east (Hindus and Moslems) gave rise to violent protests. Aurobindo became a leading Bengali nationalist and an important figure in the so-called Extremist wing of the Congress party: those who called for prompt, total independence from Great Britian.

In 1907 Aurobindo founded a newspaper, *Bande Mataram*, which laid out a program of noncooperation with the British government and laws, the boycott of foreign manufactured goods, and, when necessary, civil disobedience, that when adopted later by Mahatma Gandhi would lead to independence. But the plan was premature (Gandhi didn't return to India until 1915), and the government arrested Aurobindo for sedition. All in all he was arrested three times and each time acquitted, but the government still imprisoned him for a year. When he was released in 1909 he found the Congress Party broken, its leaders in prison or exile, and in 1910 Aurobindo took refuge in French Pondicherry, just ahead of another arrest warrant.

The government could not know that while in prison the political radical had metamorphosed into a spiritual philosopher. Aurobindo started on a period of silent yoga, which he would end in 1914, after which he wrote his more important works and founded his ashram, and, via the efforts of his consort, the Parisienne Mirra Alfassa (known to her followers as the Mother), the new city of Auroville. That Aurobindo would break his silence to converse with Alexandra is surprising, but she was to benefit from exceptions of this sort on the part of other spiritually or temporally powerful men, among them the Thirteenth Dalai Lama.

When Alexandra met Aurobindo in November 1911, he was a handsome man approaching forty. The room in his home had only a table and two chairs, and Aurobindo was seated with his back to the wide-open window, the great sky of India as stage set to his glowing conversation. Four young men hovered nearby—the disciples who had followed him into exile. Outside in the street the Indian "secret police," typical of their kind, made their presence known.

The meeting of these two exemplars of reform Buddhism and the twentieth century revival of the ancient Indian knowledge was rife with possibilites. Perhaps the philosopher spoke to Alexandra about his concept of the Supermind, which is conscious of eternal truth but can be made to infuse matter and all of life. The state that Aurobindo sought was not very different from the enlightenment achieved by Gautama Buddha, and the philosopher and his interlocutor had much in common. But though Alexandra praised Aurobindo's lucidity, she later would term their conversation "gossip."

This innocent talk had profound consequences on David-Neel's quest, leading to a series of incidents that found her, a dozen years later, entering Lhasa in disguise. Although she realized that Aurobindo and his guests were being watched, she was surprised when at Madras her train was met by the Chief of Police. He politely grilled her on her purpose in visiting India. She replied by showing the chief her letters of introduction from London officials to the viceroy and the governors of provinces. According to Jacques Brosse, the best of her earlier biographers, the chief left her completely reassured that she was a political naïf.

This error has been compounded by later biographers, who like to stress Alexandra's respectability and prominence, as though she was a society matron on a charity outing. True, not long afterward she dined sumptuously at the right hand of the governor of Madras. They even chatted amiably about Aurobino. But this was the beginning of a deliberately two-faced policy toward her that was determined at the highest levels of the Government of India. A confidential report (discovered by the authors in the Secret Files) made two years later to Sir Arthur Hertzel of the India Office, London, stated:

> Mme. David-Neel's visit to . . . Pondicherry to visit the leading extremist there. You will see from [a previous] telegram of 19, Dec. 1911 that the governor in Madras was advised to inform the Viceroy at Calcutta of her proceedings. In the circumstances we may perhaps assume that the G of I knows all there is to be known about her?

This overly optimistic assumption was based on "secret enquiries in Paris" begun immediately after Alexandra's interview with Aurobindo, and which had turned up elements of her radical past.

The British were worried by her former associates and by her use of various names, and they suspected she might be an agent of the French or some other government. The governor had been alerted promptly in the following words: "It might be well therefore not to lose sight of her, and to inform the . . . criminal investigation department of Calcutta."

The Government of India performed its surveillance with diplomatic finesse; its agents kept a wary eye on the Frenchwoman's travels and contacts. Several officials who proved most helpful to her also reported her movements to the viceroy. When they supposed it necessary, they thwarted her efforts. This ambiguity on the part of British officialdom continued throughout David-Neel's stay in the East. For her part, it took painful experience to learn that the British government was a collective opponent worth outwitting. Fortunately, their spying has left us an objective record of the traveler's moves across the chessboard of Central Asia. Jeanne Denys was mistaken: a lone middle-aged woman did get through to Lhasa.

Alexandra had the amusing faculty of denouncing the colonial bureacracy while occasionally sounding like the most chauvinistic of them. She compared Madras to a heap of rags and denounced the entire Brahmanic system based on the Vedanta (the sacred Vedas, or scriptures) and caste. The Brahmins, by suppressing Buddhism in the land of its birth, had brought India to the state of slavery in which it found itself. Besides, the homes of the Brahmins, contaminated by the habits of their domestics, were too filthy for her to eat in. So she avoided invitations by moving to the comfortable headquarters of the Theosophical Society at nearby Adyar.

Here Alexandra voiced complaints of a different sort. She luxuriated in a vast room in a house that resembled the Trianon of Louis XIV. The grounds by the sea were extensive, and in the evenings a collection of what she termed lunatics wandered over them, lanterns in hand. There was a European count, a beautiful circus performer turned missionary, a contingent of mature ladies. A certain Herr Grunewald peered through gold-rimmed glasses at old texts in the library to ascertain how medieval rabbis had manufactured *golems*, robots that did their will. A Swedish girl who vowed to starve herself to death for the experience was only dissuaded by a last minute cable from Annie Besant.

The meditating Theosophists were equally indifferent to the venomous snakes on the grounds. Alexandra wrote her husband how one might encounter a king cobra, marked with the sign of Shiva. When he rose upon his coil, neck swelling, eyes like fire, the victim could only pray. The cobra's bite meant a quick but agonizing end. Alexandra, after scaring Philip, assured him that she was in no real danger. Agitating and then pacifying her husband was part of her program to manage him from a distance.

Nights enthralled David-Neel, who sat in the dark listening to nature's tropic symphony. Many of the disciples, determined to concentrate on some assigned mantra, couldn't bear the uncanny racket of birds and insects humming, buzzing, whistling, and flying joyously about in search of nourishment or their mates. Alexandra cleverly made this creative chaos the subject of her meditation. In the darkness human vanity shrank to its proper insignificance. The night sounds were the voice of truth.

Alexandra maintained that the practitioners of yoga—either in its physical or more spiritual branches—could tell one another by the light in their eyes. This way or some other, several Vishnuites found her at Adyar and begged her to come join them. Adorned with togas and smeared with ash, they were a throwback to the ancient India of unvarnished mysticism. They appeared to revere Alexandra, and they quizzed her on the Hindu scriptures, giving her answers the rapt attention accorded to the Cybele pronouncing on the outcome of the Persian War.

On further inquiry, Alexandra learned that the yogis' guru was an elderly woman who sat naked under an arbor in a public park. She had been meditating there for decades and was growing worn out. Her disciples were seeking a likely replacement. Alexandra was amused that the disciples took her for an *avatar*, or goddess incarnate, and she rightly felt that even the greatest of French Sanskrit scholars would not have been so honored. But she hadn't, as yet, the desire to live without furniture or servants. She dispatched her would-be disciples by reminding them she was a married woman whose husband would not approve of his wife's public nudity.

Alexandra was more interested in an invitation to represent France at the International Congress of Moral Education to be held at The Hague in August 1912. That she accepted shows her expectation of returning by the next summer. She assured Philip she was gathering valuable documents and hoped to write a book on the living Hindu philosophy, the material for which would be gained by her actual experience. Her works would be pleasant to gaze on in their old age together. In fact, as it turned out, she did not write about India until Philip Neel had passed on.

Alexandra's first Christmas far from her home depressed her. It rained, and as though to emphasize her loneliness, the Europeans merrily celebrated the birth of Jesus. Those who preached of Christ, she complained, were among the ones who would have stoned him. Crucifixion was the reward for those who tried to save humanity, she reminded her husband, who had no such intentions. She missed Mouchy and wished he were close so she could hug him. But she quickly added that India would bore him; he would only be interested in the excellent railroad bridges built by the British.

Looking ahead to the New Year, Alexandra prepared to journey to the north. Rail as she might against the Europeans, whether Theosophists, officials, or missionaries, she remained the *mem sahib* who dressed in spotless white and preemptorily ordered about her coolies. As Luree Miller, a travel-writer, has pointed out, "A liberating achievement many women of means as modest as David-Neel might envy was that she never learned to cook but always managed to be served."

Chapter 6
City of Joy

By the New Year, 1912, David-Neel had moved north to Calcutta. The city, aggressively Bengali but at that time the capital of all British India, sprawled helter-skelter along the Hooghly River. A commercial creation of the nineteenth century, it was home to the Hindu revival, fierce and conflicting nationalisms, and poets and intellectuals such as Rabindranath Tagore, the first Asian to win a Nobel Prize for literature. It was divided into a native and British quarter, the latter with its Anglican cathedral, park (the Maidan), and stately homes.

Although Alexandra was welcomed and feted by wealthy Bengalis, she couldn't stomach their food and soon moved to the English pension of a Mrs. Walter. She was ready to dismiss the city as tattered and unhealthy. Each year when the river receded a plague broke out. In a reforming mood, she refused to make obeisances to renowned swamis, instead shaking their hands. On occasions when asked to speak, she preached the Buddhist *dharma* (doctrine) in a militant style. But her carping attitude was as empty of conviction as the Brahmanic ritual and caste system that she damned as lacking charity and compassion.

More to David-Neel's liking, she was known in Calcutta from reprints in the *Indian Mirror* and the *Statesman* of articles she had published in Europe. She admitted that parts of town resembled London's St. James's or Kensington Park, and that the evening's gray mist on the river reminded her of the Thames. Prominent persons in the British community also welcomed her, and soon she found herself dressing for dinner among the ladies in low-cut gowns and jewels and the gentlemen in tails. She missed her escort, Philip, and supposed the pair of them would have cut an impressive figure. But this sort of thing soon grew stale.

Besides, King George VI was soon to arrive to be installed as Emperor of India and to announce the transfer of the capital to Delhi. The British hoped that by reuniting Bengal they would conciliate the Bengalis and in any case remove the capital from their frequent demonstrations for home rule. The Government of India only succeeded in angering the Moslems, who had favored the separation of east and west, and who now formed the Moslem League that was to be instrumental in the partition of India in 1946.

However, Alexandra found a type of official that did not resemble the bumbling sterotype we have seen in films set during the Raj, such as *Heat and Dust* or *Gandhi*. Sir John Woodruffe, Justice of the High Court, was the first senior official to befriend Alexandra, indeed to influence her work and life. A highly cultured man, he was then in his mid-forties and wouldn't begin to publish until 1918, under the pen name Arthur Avalon, his vitally important studies of the Tantra. In translating the ancient books and revealing the rituals, Sir John had to be circumspect; he was, in Omar Garrison's words, "writing for two Puritan audiences"—the British Victorians and the Indian Vedantists.

Sir John immediately took Alexandra into his confidence. He escorted her to the temple of Kali—Calcutta means the place where Kali debarked—a ferocious manifestation of the universal mother. Here humans had been sacrificed until the British stopped the practice in the mid-nineteenth century. In Alexandra's day, sheep, goats and water buffalo were slaughtered in such profusion that she had to lift up her skirts to wade through the blood. The charnel house didn't disconcert Sir John, a devotee of Kali, a model husband and kindly father of four.

Although Alexandra failed to understand what he meant when he spoke of realizing material benefits from his *sadhana* (practice), she was pleased to accompany him and his wife to Indian receptions and secret *kirtans*. These devotions included a concert and could grow as unruly as a revival meeting. To the rhythm of tambours and cymbals—a music then unknown to the West—partcipants would exclaim the name "Hari!" (Vishnu). Seized by a worshipful frenzy, they grew louder, danced with arms akimbo and even fell into convulsions, foaming at the mouth. The others, sunk into a kind of trance, ignored them.

David-Neel was outwardly critical of elaborate processions where, in spite of the grinding poverty of the masses, dozens of elephants were decked out in cloth of gold, emeralds, and rubies, and camels in a network of beaten silver and gold. In fact the spectacle thrilled her to the core. She did grow angry over the custom of infant brides. Often these girls were wed to older men, a marriage that couldn't be consummated until menstruation. If their intended groom died, they found themselves widowed at twelve or thirteen—still virgin. Barred from remarrying, they often became prostitutes, and they were and still are displayed in cagelike rooms in sections of the major cities. Alexandra felt it was praiseworthy that an American school was educating some of the unfortunates.

In her own case, curiosity sometimes outweighed the evidence of misery. While in a boat on the river, her rower pointed to an object washed up on the bank. It looked like a chubby leather doll but closer up proved to be a dead man. A ravenous dog was gnawing his face, leaving a gaping hole and exposed teeth. Alexandra watched as the dog eventually tired of its tough meal. Then she ordered the rower to pull nearer so she could get a proper photo. She hoped her shots would come out. She warned Philip not to show such pictures to anyone because Europeans were so fearful of death.

Little by little the spell of the East won over the activist. Her criticisms became muted or clever. When a Brahmin priest haughtily refused an offering of chocolate, she tossed him rupees, which he avidly scooped up. Alexandra was reminded of how the Roman Emperor Vespasian had replied to criticism of a tax he had placed on public urinals: "Money has no odor." Once, annoyed by the antics of the fakirs, she lay down on a vacant bed of nails. She explained to a passing British tourist that she needed a nap and was lucky to find a handy couch.

Although Alexandra continued to see herself as the author of a shelf of fat books, she couldn't decide in which tradition to write. She studied the thoughts and lives of the two great figures of the Hindu (Vedantic) revival—the saintly Ramakrishna and his disciple Vivekananda, from whose examples flow most of the yoga ashrams in the West today. She was impressed that the ascetic Vivekananda had willed himself to death at an early age while seated in a chair apparently meditating. But she was even more taken with the wife of the late Ramakrishna, whom she visited in her sixty-sixth year. Caroda Devi had no wrinkles and bright, shining eyes, and Alexandra tried to coax from her the secrets of perpetual youth.

Facilitated by Woodruffe, David-Neel turned toward the mystery of the Tantra. She partook of the ritual of the so-called "five forbidden substances": meat, fish, grain and wine—all but the grain religiously forbidden to Brahmins. The fifth is *maithuna* (sexual union), which follows the ceremonial tasting of the first four. In her books on India and Nepal, written in the 1950s, Alexandra admits to at least witnessing three diverse tantric ceremonies that included all five elements.

At the first, to which she was invited by a guru, ten upper-class Hindu men attended, each accompanied by his wife and a *shakti*, or adored female. In an opulent house the richly attired threesomes formed into a *chakra* (mystic circle) seated on cushions on the floor. Alexandra was herself a shakti and chanted in Sanskrit while incense burned, the lights of oil lamps flickered over smooth, chiseled faces, and bronze bells tinkled. Finally, her eager nostrils could scent the perfume of adventure—now she was alive.

In this instance, the fifth element—sex—was performed virtually as each man wrapped himself and his wife in the extra length of her sari. Within their multicolored cocoons the couples appeared to be immobile for a long time. Actually each man had "laced" or intertwined himself with his partner and both meditated on supreme union with the universal power. Presently both emerged to gaze on and adore their shakti. Alexandra does not make clear what else happened, but she claimed it made her feel humble.

Another instance of tantric sex took place in an isolated pavilion in a garden, while jackals howled outside. Alexandra had bribed the gardener, whose employers worshiped the goddess, or female power, on certain moonless nights. She was secretly installed on a stairway leading to a terrace, and from there she looked on undetected. She was disguised in a dark blue sari like those worn by women of a low caste. By craning her neck, she was able to see everything.

First a goat was slaughtered, then the attractive, well-off participants, seated in the chakra, drank a lot of wine from a communal jug. Then each of the ten men embraced his shakti. This was his consort or partner in the cult and could be any woman except his actual wife. The couples, without entirely disrobing, consummated with first one sexual pose and then another to resemble the tantric statues that decorate certain Indian temples. Alexandra enjoyed watching a scene that she found perfectly decorous. But it is likely, from what she admitted to a confidant late in life, that she was a participant as well as a voyeur.

A third instance of Alexandra's spying on tantric sexual intimacies went less smoothly. That one took place a year later in Nepal, and it involved the sort of native helper that colonial society termed a "boy," no matter his age. Alexandra had a penchant for young, handsome, clever boys, and in Nepal she was guided by a young man named Passang. When she asked him why a giant stone lingam should be considered a symbol of Shiva, he scornfully replied that only foreigners thought that way: "For us the lingam is Shiva himself."

Passang installed Alexandra, disguised as a Tibetan male, in a hay loft above the scene of a rural tantric rite. Five men and an equal number of women participated while the seeker peered through the widely separated floorboards. After prayers a goat was brought in and beheaded, and the tantrikas dipped their fingers in its blood and made signs on their faces. Food and drink—four of the elements—were indulged in without moderation. Suddenly the lamp went out and, amid the odor of blood, Alexandra heard "bestial groans." She silently crept out after Passang, her taste for voyeurism dampened.

In late January 1912 David-Neel complained to her husband that she was rushed, confused, and suffering from dizzy spells; she dwelt on everything that was tragic about India. Yet one month later, as she prepared to journey to the Himalayas, she was all enthusiasm. She wrote Philip that she had a vision of a good genie who walked in front of her, finding the path, making things easy. This need not be taken as a metaphor. Although Alexandra adapted the form of her spirit guide to conform with the environment, she had a reassuring faith in an outer force that watched over her. Only when she lost contact with this force did she fall into despair.

After a year of travel in Sikkim and Nepal, in March 1913 Alexandra returned to the Ganges Valley, to holy Benares (Varanasi).

Again she fell into a depression. During the year she had pried open a crack in the door to Tibet, but had it shut in her face. She was racked by a burning desire to be the first Westerner to truly understand that forbidden land. Now, at forty-four, she again compared herself to an old woman. She turned once more to the scholarly study of Sanskrit and Vedanta.

Benares, which means "resplendent with light," has been the religious capital of India since the dawn of history. When Gautama Buddha came there around 500 B.C., he saw ancient temples contemporary with Babylon, Nineveh, and Thebes. All devout Hindus yearn to worship at its holy places and to expire on the banks of its sacred Ganges. In this way they further their wish for no additional rebirths on earth but rather immersion in the Oversoul, Brahmin. Ultimate liberation from the wheel of life is assured to those who repeat, as does Shiva himself, "Rama!"—a name of God—directly before they die in Benares.

Alexandra explored the maze of small streets containing innumerable temples and shrines. She observed the *ghats*—stone steps stretching for miles to lead down from the steep bank to the river— and the crowds on them. She was out at dawn to watch devotees young and old execute yoga poses; zealots, eyes on the rising sun, stare into its blazing rays; a votary of Vishnu, hair matted and filthy, holds his shriveled up arm permanently high and immobile. Phantom forms emerged from the low-lying mist to bathe while cows ambled along the terraces. *Saddhus* (holy men) intoned mantras to the cosmic One. Mother Ganges made a grander stage than any Alexandra had sung upon. While maids and matrons with lightning speed changed wet saris for dry ones, the widows, segregated in houses along the banks, called plaintively for their own deaths.

Alexandra fell into sympathy with this atmosphere of charged piety. She took a step by adopting the saffron robe of the *sannyasin*, or renunciate. When Philip, who felt their marriage was threatened by this gesture, accused her of consulting only her own ego, she assured him she hadn't become a nun. The dawn-colored robe constituted a refuge that did away with the need for the stone walls and iron grilles of a convent. Although she didn't intend to meditate and fast all the time, she warned Philip that, if he pressed her to return at once, she would retire to a cave in the Himalayas.

Alexandra confessed to missing the shelter of their marriage, the beautiful house, the delicious dinners . . . but she had lived like a sleepwalker, not her true self. Now she needed to learn the illusory quality of this self. Like a saddhu, she wanted to own nothing. In almost the same breath, Alexandra assured Philip that he had married a person of note and could be proud of their name. The College of Sanskrit had called a conference to honor her with an honorary doctorate of philosophy. Imagine, here in the citadel of Hindu orthodoxy, a European, a woman, a Buddhist, to be so exalted! Brahmin priests attended, squatting on their haunches and listening raptly to her discourse on Vedantism. It was an event without parallel.

Alexandra had made rapid progress in Sanskrit, the notoriously difficult language of the Vedas, due to the tutoring of an elderly pundit who came to her in the morning and again in the evening. The Brahmin possessed amazing knowledge of the ancient texts but scant common sense. When a cholera epidemic broke out, he declared it to be the invention of evil foreigners. He scoffed at the European for having her room at the Theosophical Society scrubbed daily with disinfectant: it was useless to keep clean.

At night funeral processions went by, chanting the divine name: Ram! Ram! Their torches cast a gleam over the protective net under which Alexandra slept, cursing the mosquitos whose buzzing kept her awake. She stayed away from the worst infected zones, for the poor, dying like crushed ants, couldn't afford to burn their dead relatives' linen and by reusing it, unwittingly spread the disease. She tried to stick to her studies while the temperature soared to 104 degrees Fahrenheit.

Partly to gauge the epidemic's progress, more out of curiosity, David-Neel went down to the burning ghats. She squatted among the relatives and the yogis to watch dead bodies being incinerated on wooden beds, their ashes afterward fed to the Ganges. Day and night the spectacle continued, people carrying on their religion by setting others aflame, knowing that soon enough their turn to be consumed by fire would come. Alexandra was fascinated by the solid fellows who did the work, torsos naked, a brief garment draped over their muscled thighs. The operation reminded her of a ghastly sort of cooking. The workers, armed with long poles, flipped pieces of disjointed bodies into the heart of the fire, turning them like meat on a spit. The pelvic bones, seat of procreation, resisted longest.

Meanwhile the pundit was consumed with money worries. He spoke to Alexandra transparently of a friend who was losing all his disciples. They no longer believed in the Hindu gods and wished to emigrate to England. But if this friend could learn to work miracles, disciples would flock round him. Since Alexandra knew the Tantra, she must take him to magical ceremonies. He would do anything, the pundit whispered, eyes wide—even eat the brains of a dead person.

Alexandra realized it was no use to explain that she didn't believe in the sort of magic he wanted. Hadn't she been to the Himalayas? Every Indian knew that sorcerors lived there and even the English said so. Alexandra laughed when the pundit demanded to meet practitioners of the black arts. But she took seriously the illness that afflicted her in late summer. She felt feverish, dizzy, depressed—were these the first symptoms of the plague? Practically delirious, she saw visions of the mountains, of lakes that reflected snowy peaks. The delusion eerily resembled the painting showed to her long ago by Jacques Villemain, the young artist at the Gnosis, when he warned her about falling into the landscape.

Alexandra didn't have cholera, but rather an ailment of the soul. She longed for the chill of the Himalayas, the vistas and pure sparkling air of the high steppes. A brief glimpse of Tibet had captivated her, turned her plans topsy-turvy. At her last home in Digne, France, there exists an unfinished manuscript, begun at Benares, concerned with the Vedanta. She was going to abandon it to pursue her dream.

Suddenly word came that an apartment in the royal monastery of Sikkim awaited her. Instantly recovered, Alexandra packed her bags, tent, folding cot, and a galvanized tub she claimed to be portable. From her stays in Britain, the traveler had acquired two unlikely habits: she drank great quantities of tea, and wherever she might find herself—meditating in a cave in the Himalayas, slogging through the jungle, or under siege by bandits—she insisted on a hot bath daily.

Chapter 7
The Genie and the Demon

"Sikkim is the most mountainous country in the world. More so than Switzerland," said the prince. In his orange brocade robe, a diamond in his hat, Alexandra thought he must be a genie come down from these very mountains. Not only was he heir to the throne of Sikkim, he was an incarnated lama. With his dressed-up horse and a party of Oriental followers in colorful, silken clothes, the prince reminded Alexandra of a character from one of her operas.

He had just invited her to his capital, Gangtok. He would have to continue on before she was ready, but he would leave her one of his subjects, Kazi Dawasandup, as guide and interpreter. She must be dreaming, she decided, as the prince and his entourage rode off. But Dawasandup, a compact man in traditional dress who waited by her side, was real enough. David-Neel wrote of her adventures in the Land of the Thunderbolt over fifteen years after they had occurred and from the distance of southern France, yet her tone was underlaid by emotion. Perhaps this is why *Magic and Mystery in Tibet*, translated into every major language, has remained her most popular book.

The seeker had first ventured toward the Himalayas on a lark. In March 1912, while she was sweltering in Calcutta, David-Neel received an offer from the venerable Sanskrit college at Hardwar on the Ganges—room and vegetarian board, servants, a private tutor, and access to the faculty for explications. This would enable her to become a scholar the equal of any in the West. She told Philip it was what she wanted. She accepted and casually informed her husband that while waiting she would take a trip to Sikkim.

The monotonous clatter of the train across the verdant Bengal plain, broken by patches of scarlet—the "flame of the forest" tree—soothed her. Although the land was under cultivation, principally for rice, the vitality of Nature lurked in bamboo thickets and groves of palms—and its evils. In another month the temperature would rise to over 100 degrees fahrenheit, the rainstorms would begin and the mosquitos would breed, spreading malaria. At Siliguri, where the change was made to the narrow gauge Darjeeling-Himalayan railway, Alexandra noted people with yellow skins and slanted eyes wearing heavier, native dress.

The toy train puffed along at ten miles an hour through the timber. At times the grade was so steep that a man who rode at the front of the engine tossed sand on the tracks for traction. At the hill station of Darjeeling the scenery opened out to a tremendous amphitheater: on the farther side of the Rungeet River rose ranges of mountains in gigantic tiers—Sikkim—and in the far distance the lofty highlands of Tibet. The panorama culminated in the massive, five-peaked Kanchenjunga, twenty-eight thousand feet above the plain at its height.

Alexandra forgot the feverishness of the plains and her own discontents. She took a small mare and porters, traversing the high jungle, a dense curtain of foliage that hid its mysterious goings-on. While crossing tea plantations at over seven thousand feet, she encountered horsemen in Tibetan garb wearing huge curved cutlasses. Recalling her forebear Genghiz Khan, she exulted in Mongol Asia—though her behind ached something awful.

Alexandra took refuge in the *dak* bungalow at Kalimpong. Center of an area sometimes termed British Bhutan, it was the terminus of the mule trains carrying wool from across the Himalayas. The bungalows were built by the government to house its traveling officials, but these simple, comfortable, out-of-the-way accomodations were also frequented by European wayfarers. They were not always up to par, and the Frenchwoman complained about the poor service. The staff bustled about but were occupied by the person and entourage fo the Prince of Sikkim. She perked up when he sent over his card and immediately paid him a call.

Alexandra had met her prince charming: the Maharaj Kumar (Crown Prince) of Sikkim, Sidkeong Tulku. A *tulku* means roughly a "phantom body." In the popular mind this person is a living Buddha, or to be more precise, the successive incarnation of a great and holy spirit. The Dalai Lama is the best-known example of a tulku. Sidkeong had received this emanation—a concept more indefinite than the Western "soul"—from his granduncle, who died shortly before he was born.

The prince at thirty-three was the eldest son of the Maharaja of Sikkim and pro forma abbot of the royal monastery. Not much taller than Alexandra, with a penchant for satins and embossed leather belts, he was handsomer than Alexandra would reveal to Philip. Sidkeong had deeply thoughtful almond eyes, even features, a strong nose, and sensuous mouth, wore his hair caught up in a thick braid clasped in silver, and carried himself with a fitting air of command. Jacques Brosse shrewdly remarked that ordinarily David-Neel wrote with exactitude, but so correctly that it seemed cold, as if she feared to say too much, to reveal herself. She was wary, especially when she wrote to her husband."

Alexandra was at once struck by Sidkeong's warmth and intelligence despite his crowd of retainers, each carrying a dagger stuck in his belt. This model of an oriental despot had been given a European education, first by tutors, then at Oxford. Afterward he was sent on a grand tour of Asia to acquaint him with the reigning monarchs. His passions were agriculture, forestry and public education, to which he diligently attended. The prince had to make an impression on his people, but he himself preferred the tweeds and manner of a country gentleman.

Sidkeong's father, the ailing Maharaj Thutob, was a well-intentioned but superstitious man, traditional in all things. Disillusioned by politics, his great joy was to go gaming for bird or beast. He was certain that if he neglected to hunt successfully for more than a week, and thus offer a sacrifice to the native god he worshipped, he would be destroyed. This god, a fiery character who wore a crown made of five skulls and rode a snow lion, lived among the peaks of Kanchenjunga. The royal family was Tibetan, imposed in the sixteenth century along with Buddhism on the indigenous Lepcha, forest dwellers who had been animist and carefree. The British general Mainwaring, who studied the shy Lepchas, considered them "the original, unspoilt children of Adam and Eve." Indeed, Sikkim in Alexandra's day had the pristine quality of Eden—complete with a serpent.

Maharaj Thutob had lost his first wife, Sidkeong's mother, then married a noblewoman from Lhasa by whom he had a second son. This queen, Yeshe Drolma, although named for the Tibetan goddess of mercy, had an iron will that she attempted to impose on her lackadaisical husband. She wanted her son and not Sidkeong to inherit the throne. In ancient times the women of Tibet had ruled forts and whole provinces. In the late nineteetn century, W. W. Rockhill, the American ambassador to China, claimed that their legal and social position was superior not only to other Asian women but also to women in Europe. Yeshe Drolma, according to the prevailing custom of polyandry, was married to both Thutob and his younger brother. She wrote a history of Sikkim (under her husband's name), and she appears to have been "a practitioner of the Black Art." She kept the state seal, and to the extent she had leeway under the protection of the Government of India, she ruled.

British officials, taking their cue from the expansionist policy of the former viceroy, Lord Curzon, had definite plans for the tiny principality wedged between the larger, independent monarchies of Nepal, Tibet, and Bhutan. In the words of the Indian historian George Kotturan, Sikkim "is the only pass, in a big stretch of formidable natural barriers, connecting two of the most populous nations in the world"—China and India. The Government of India's resident political officer in Gangtok, Claude White, who had overseen the upbringing of Sidkeong, was acutely aware that Sikkim was the gateway across the Himalayas to Tibet.

Thus White took the lead in "regularizing" the administration and economy of Sikkim. "Chaos reigned everywhere," he wrote. "There was no revenue system. . . . No court of justice, no police, no public works, no education for the younger generation. . . . [E]verything was in my hands." White cut the maharaja's retainers from three hundred to fifty, and he encouraged commercial development of the land. Since the surrounding monarchies hadn't recognized Britain's protectorate over Sikkim, the Foreign Office chose to cement imperial ties by arranging a dynastic alliance between Prince Sidkeong and a Burmese princess he hardly knew. The British had defied the tradition of the maharani being Tibetan, and, by reinstating Sidkeong as heir apparent, gone against the wishes of Yeshe Drolma.

Alexandra, unaware of this plot of operatic complexity, instantly was attracted to Sidkeong by his charm and a pixyish quality. She soon discovered he was a rational Buddhist after her own heart. Although revered by his people, he treated folk beliefs lightly and was a reformer whose model was Milarepa, the great twelfth century Tibetan poet–sage. The prince, thrilled to find a Western woman who thought as he did, immediately invited Alexandra to his capital. Since he had to travel ahead, he provided Kazi Dawasandup as her escort.

For three days, the pair journeyed on horseback through a landscape of shifting fog that obscured the ranks of trees draped with moss and climbing vines. The trees seemed to gesture a warning to the travelers, as though they would speak of hidden influences. Alexandra, in her descriptions, will periodically resort to the metaphor of an impenetrable curtain to suggest occult forces. Dawasandup proved a companion to match the landscape. Born of hillmen forebears of the landlord class, he carried on their penchant for the mysterious. As a youth he'd studied with a Tantric guru, lived in a cave in the mountains of Bhutan, and courted secret intercourse with the *dakinis* (feminine deities) to gain magical powers. But the dapper little man was the slave of two passions: he drank and read to excess. His drunken bouts were only occasional, but he carried on his reading at any time or place and was known to fall into a long, ecstatic trance over a text that pleased him.

Dawasandup was currently headmaster of the Tibetan boarding school at Gangtok. According to Alexandra, he couldn't bear to spend time in the classroom and assigned his duties to a lower master who felt much the same. The pupils would run wild until one day without warning the headmaster appeared to quiz them as sternly as a judge of the dead. He ordered one boy at a time to answer questions, and if the lad failed, the next in line had to slap his face. When the students wouldn't hit hard enough, Dawasandup beat every one. Waving a heavy stick, he jumped around hollering "Han!" as he whacked the boys' arms. They howled a chorus of laments but never studied any harder.

Unfortunately, David-Neel had a habit of denigrating her competitors in a sneaky fashion. In fact, Dawasandup was an interpreter often relied on by the British. The Earl of Ronaldshay, Governor of Bengal, thought highly of him as "a man of learning with a good knowledge of English and a scholarly knowledge of Tibetan." W. Y. Evans-Wentz, the American-born Oxford scholar who compiled the *Bardo Thodol* (*Tibetan Book of the Dead*) adopted Dawasandup as his guru. The pair worked diligently at Rumtek monastery in Sikkim, Dawasandup translating and Evans-Wentz (then quite a young man) editing what has become the most famous Tibetan text—instrumental in making Buddhism a living tradition in the West.

Evans-Wentz also edited his mentor's life of Milarepa, which the latter had translated into English from traditional sources. He later remarked that Dawasandup began in June, 1902, "and, working on it periodically when he could spare time—he being the sole support of an aged father and mother and a wife and three children—completed it [in] January, 1917." The headmaster ended his days in 1923 as a respected professor at the University of Calcutta, dying of a fever before he could complete a Tibetan–English dictionary. But we shall see that it was Evans-Wentz the American, not his Asian mentor, that David-Neel was out to discredit.

Gangtok, the capital of Sikkim, is nestled among terraced rice fields at six thousand feet. In those days it was an important trade depot, "a kaleidoscope of races and costumes," as an observer put it, "where many tongues are spoken by the Tibetans, Sikkimese, Lepchas, Indians, Sherpas, and Bhutanese who load and unload their pack trains." The Tibetans, daggers stuck in their belts, swaggered as they walked the streets of what to them seemed a big town. A small European colony was made up mainly of missionaries, while the British Resident oversaw His Majesty's affairs in both Sikkim and southern Tibet. Once a year he trekked over the mountains to visit the trade agency at Gyantse, one hundred and thirty miles away, the furthest salient of British power in the Land of Snows.

As Alexandra and her escort approached Gangtok, they were greeted by a sudden, severe hailstorm that descended from a clear blue sky as though by magic. Dawasandup, frightened by the freakish storm, rushed off to consult a *mopa* (oracle), and Alexandra went on to be welcomed by the prince at his private villa. The first floor, containing the sitting room, was furnished according to European taste, but on the floor above she found snarling images, a Tibetan altar, and statues of Buddhas and saints. Scattered about were excellent works of art gathered by the prince in his travels. The modest villa, set in the lovely palace gardens, reflected both the sensitivity of the man and the split in his personality.

Wonderful conversations followed. First a Yellow Hat lama arrived from Tibet—this is the reformed branch, headed by the Dalai Lama and celibate—and shortly thereafter a Red Hat lama—the older, less numerous branch whose members may marry. Sidkeong, in a robe, modestly presided from a low couch. Alexandra sat opposite him in an armchair, while the lamas, draped in their garnet-colored robes, sat to either side of the prince. Dawasandup as interpreter squatted tailor fashion on the rug. A strange tea was served, flavored with salt and churned butter. Rich Tibetans, of whom it was said, "Their lips are always moist," drank endless bowls of this concoction. Although most Westerners refused it, Alexandra took to the brew, not least because she realized the importance of the tea ceremony to oriental etiquette.

Talk on the finer points of Buddhism continued for hours, and the seeker plied the lamas with questions on the mysteries of initiation, magical powers, death, and the beyond. A lama is not an ordinary monk (or *trapa*) but usually more venerable and better educated, and these two were the equivalents of doctors of philosophy. Alexandra delighted in bringing together two stalwarts of the sometimes feuding Red and Yellow Hat schools. But a much greater divide existed between the Theravadin and Mahayana schools, and for that matter between Tibetan Lamaism and the rest of the Buddhist world—which at the time numbered two-thirds of the human race.

Alexandra, perhaps out of mischief, recounted the story of the Greek King Menander's question about the existence of a human soul to the monk Nagasena (ca. 100 B.C.) who replied by taking to pieces and discarding one by one the component parts of the king's chariot, such as the pole, the axle, the wheels, to demonstrate that no such thing as a chariot, in and of itself, existed—let alone a soul. Dawasandup pointed to a *tanka* (painting) on the wall, which illustrated the *Bardo Thodol* by showing the transmigration of the soul from life through the *bardo* (purgatory) to life again through rebirth. "How can such a description be given if there is no human soul?" he demanded.

Since the *Bardo Thodol* was considered the work of Padmasam-bhava, the eighth century founder of Buddhism in Tibet, the lamas couldn't disagree with what amounted to sacred scripture. The prince seemed intently interested and agreed with Dawasandup's argument. But it failed to convince Alexandra, who would take no authority as final—not even the word of Buddha. However, Sidkeong was generally less concerned with metaphysics than the practical affairs of his kingdom and in reforming the small monastic establishments, all Red Hat. He was determined to put an end to their feudal privileges (such as compulsory labor from the peasants) and to make them contribute to social progress. Alexandra did not take long to accept the prince's offer to accompany him on an inspection tour to the outlying monasteries, although she was surrendering her chance at becoming a Sanskrit scholar.

The night before the pair set out for Podang monastery, of which the prince was nominally abbot, was the first of May, the anniversary of Gautama Buddha's enlightenment. A full moon blazed in the sky. By its light the man and woman spoke in subdued tones. Sidkeong told Alexandra about his father, who was under the thumb of Yeshe Drolma. To increase her own influence she had encouraged him to defy British rule. The Resident, Claude White, retaliated by placing him in solitary confinement on bread and water. Sidkeong complained that he was caught between his stepmother's faction of conservative clergy, and on the other hand, the British who had no regard for Sikkimese customs or the land. He couldn't bring his reforming ideas into practice. Indeed, he struck Alexandra as a bird of exotic plumage kept in too small a cage, and she decided to help free him.

She went to bed but barely slept. Outside a small orchestra played through the night, consisting of two *gyalings* (oboes), two *ragdongs* (very long trumpets), and a pair of kettledrums. The Tibetan-style concert sounded sinister enough to raise the dead. Now, since rock and classical composers have adopted the elements of Tibetan music, many more Westerners are familiar with it. But an earlier traveler, Captain Knight, called it "the most diabolical uproar . . . since the first invention of music." Alexandra found that the grave, slow, deep sounds thrilled her to the core.

The former diva arose next morning delighted but giddy from missed sleep. The prince's party was followed by an honor guard of musicians playing trumpets so long that small boys had to go ahead to hold them off the ground. Gradually, they wended their way upward, accompanied by a cortege of lamas who, in pointed bonnets, reminded Alexandra of medieval inquisitors. The monks' red hats and robes added extra splashes of color to a scene adorned with rainbow tinted waterfalls and hundreds of varieties of orchids.

Sidkeong, like Alexandra, was an amateur botanist, and he showed his guest a few of the four thousand plants and ferns that make Sikkim an exquisitely varied garden. Farther up, the tropical vegetation gave way to hardier Alpine species, spruce, firs, and birch. Here and there a gigantic lily poked its graceful neck through the shade of the forest. Gaudy butterflies struck the visitor's fancy, and she observed at least seventeen different varieties: one with a jet-black body and huge wings resembling a bird in flight. The explorer-to-be responded more naturally to the cooler heights than the hothouse closeness of the lowlands.

It rained, frustrating Alexandra's efforts at photography. She yearned to record the startling specimens of plants and people to send to Philip (with instructions to save for inclusion in future works). However, the prince diverted her with tales of his gaily dressed subjects, many of whom lined the road to pay homage, spinning prayer wheels that sighed in the wind. These implements offer up quotations from scripture, which are meant as salutations to spirits in other realms to ensure their favorable regard for those on earth. Sidkeong knew his people well—the commercially minded Nepalis, the creamy skinned Lepchas, and the sturdy Bhutanese herdsmen. But Alexandra's gaze kept roaming to the lordly Tibetans wearing ear ornaments of turquoise, jade, and coral, worked charm boxes around their necks; they led horses draped with saddlebags in bright, clashing colors.

Podang *gompa*, like other Sikkimese monasteries, was relatively small, housing no more than one hundred monks. It was a bastion of unreformed conservatism. On a terrace dominating the valley, prayer flags waving from every space, it appeared to be a Chinese landscape painting sprung to life. The monks welcomed their abbot reverentially despite his Western style of life. It annoyed Alexandra when a delegation of notables prostrated themselves on their stomachs three times. The prince, too, was embarrassed before his guest. Alexandra, to show respect to the holy place, folded her palms and gave the Hindu salutation. Let the lamas judge her rude, she refused to bow to men or images.

Certainly there existed a vast gulf between David-Neel's rationalist beliefs and those of the inhabitants of Sikkim's sixty-seven monasteries. These monks of several older sects peopled an infernal spirit world with ferocious deities dressed in diadems of human skulls and necklaces of bone. Still, the frightful aspects of the tantric universe weren't as alien to the orientalist as they had been to more naive, if intrepid, travelers. Even the great travel-writer Isabella Bird—the first woman admitted to membership in the Royal Geographical Society—called Buddhist sacred literature, which she couldn't read, "fairy tales and stories of doubtful morality."

To Alexandra, the paintings that she found on the monastery walls of male and female beings copulating—intertwined in difficult and explicit postures while trying to escape the many tiered Tibetan hell—struck home. Her sexual entanglements, whether casual encounters or the Kama Sutra practices done with Philip, had helped to trap her in *maya*, the world of illusions thought to be real. On the walls terrible looking men and women, teeth clenched, naked with many serpentine arms, were not enjoying lust but joined against it; the corpses beneath their feet were slain passions.

At least this was Alexandra's understanding of this horrifying yet erotic art. After what seemed endless prostrations by the monks, she and the prince adjourned to the oratory for the usual tea and conversation. She joked to Philip that her relish for the salty beverage was a sure sign of past lives in Tibet, and she promised to bring home the recipe so they could brew it in Tunis. She informed him that in the evening she had addressed the assembled monks. Taking a Theravadin approach, she emphasized the virtues of early Buddhism and the need to banish the fetishes that had distorted the great doctrine's message. The congregation heard the foreign woman respectfully, although they distrusted her influence on their abbot. For Buddhists, decadent or not, tolerance was a pillar of their creed.

The dance of Yama—lord of Death—concluded the festivities. Young boys danced with skeletons, rattling and clanging actual human bones. The actors wore masks featuring fanged mouths full of ulcers, and bloody, bulging eyes. Meanwhile Sidkeong told Rabelaisian jokes to his cronies. He seemed unaware of the dancers, who were pretending to eat the brains of the dead. Alexandra, stupefied by the show, was even more taken aback by the childish, irreverent attitude of the audience. She comforted herself with the thought that, in the Buddhist tradition, they regarded death as an incident in life, no sadder than other events.

The night had more to offer. Alexandra was allowed to sleep in the sanctuary, and the prince's divan was arranged on one side of the high altar, hers on the other. Although domestics hovered about to serve them, they couldn't impede the fleas that climbed up and down her legs. Mosquitoes, relentless as demons, also devoured her, and the patter of small feet indicated rats scurrying around to nibble at the food offerings. All these creatures, she understood, had as much right to live as she.

Annoyances couldn't dim the moment's hypnotic splendor. Soft moonlight intruded through the balcony and caressed the face of the pillars. A lamp cast dancing shadows on a golden statue of Buddha, while yellow zinnias emitted a subtle perfume. Alexandra recalled how in ancient Greece a novice who aspired to initiation had to sleep in the sanctuary at the foot of the altar. Would some strange magic befall her? As she drifted into a half-slumber, acutely aware of the prince's light, easy breathing a few feet away, she had a feeling that at last she was going to learn secrets never before revealed to a European.

Alexandra's euphoric mood deflated with her descent to Gangtok. Letters from Philip awaited her, wondering when she would return, complaining of her growing mysticism as once he had complained of her being too mental. She quickly replied and tried to reassure him that she was gathering material to write books while they grew old together. But she soon admitted that intellect had its limits, that she was opening another door onto experience. Alexandra's more immediate problem was the buzz of gossip going the rounds of the missionaries in the diminutive capital. Her outings and late night tete-a-tetes with the bachelor prince had caused tongues to wag. The Europeans were certain that all Asians were immoral, and since she was sleeping at the royal palace, near Sidkeong's villa, the good Christians suspected the pair of being lovers.

Ironically, the most serious accusation against Alexandra was that, by mixing with the prince and high lamas of the land, she was acting dangerously democratic. The inherent superiority of white skin was threatened! Amusingly, the former Bohemian in her turn damned the local British as mediocre *petite bourgeoisie*. The women talked endlessly of cooking, and their husbands played badly on some instruments.

The sort of evangelical personality abhorred by David-Neel was beautifully depicted by James Hilton in his classic *Lost Horizon*, the novel published in 1933 that was influenced by Alexandra's work, and whose theme bears a curious resemblance to her life. Hilton gives us a sympathetic if obtuse Miss Brinklow, who is courageous, narrowly sensible, and inquisitive up to a point. "Aren't you going to show us the lamas at work?" she demands at Shangri-La. This mature maiden lacks any genuine openness of mind but is eager to see "something picturesquely primitive that she could talk about when she got home. She had an extraordinary knack of never seeming very much surprised, yet of always seeming slightly indignant . . ." For Miss Brinklow the heathen existed to be converted, and so, stuck in Shangri-La, she dutifully learned Tibetan, in order to save the souls of those already in paradise.

The missionary Annie Taylor presents a real-life case. In 1892 this intrepid zealot entered Tibet from China, in what Luree Miller terms "a naive and ill-prepared . . . attempt to reach Lhasa." Yet this small, middle-aged woman, a semi-invalid in childhood, was turned back only one week's march from the forbidden capital. She had a propensity for handing out cards with biblical texts printed in Tibetan, and although most of the natives were illiterate, someone may have spotted these. Of the Buddhist lamas she remarked, "Poor things, they know no better; no one has ever told them of Jesus."

An Englishman of a different stamp resolved David-Neel's housing problem. The Resident Political Officer, Charles Alfred Bell, invited her to lodge with him. Although Bell, later Sir Charles, did a number of favors for Alexandra and initially forwarded her research, the two were natural rivals and antagonists. Bell was born at Calcutta in 1870, the son of a Barrister practicing before the High Court. Typically, he went home for schooling, first to Winchester on scholarship and then to Oxford. By 1891 he had joined the Indian civil service and was posted to Bengal.

The fair-haired, bright-eyed, strong-willed young official was not physically rugged, and the climate of the Indian plains nearly killed him. He struggled with malaria, and a transfer in 1900 to the hills of Darjeeling saved his life. Bell himself continues, "Here I spent three years, devoting in the main such little leisure as I had to the study of the Tibetan language, customs, and ideas." In 1905 he published a *Manual of Colloquial Tibetan*, an excellent guide to the spoken language.

In 1908 Bell was appointed to succeed Claude White in Sikkim. During the ten years he served as Political Officer, he came to dominate the relations of the British government with this principality and to influence its policy toward Bhutan and Tibet. When in 1910 the Thirteenth Dalai Lama fled an invading Chinese army, crossed the Himalayas, and went into exile at Darjeeling, His Holiness found in Bell a firm ally of Tibet. The two continued a remarkable lifelong friendship, and the Great Thirteenth was pleased to say of the Ideal Civil Servant, "We are men of like mind."

Bell was representative of an extraordinary group of scholar-diplomats whom Britain sent to her empire in Asia. He was observant, free of racial prejudice, and able to mingle freely with Tibetan lay and Buddhist officials. Alexandra recognized at once that the Resident was the actual power in the principality, and she insisted in her letters to Philip that Bell had designs on Tibet. Certainly he was Britain's point man in the Himalayas as the Great Game of Central Asian rivalry played out. "From very early on his career," writes historian C. J. Christie, "Bell had become one of the foremost advocates of the need for a British forward policy in the [Himalayan] area." But he was handicapped by the appeasement policies of the Foreign Office and of the Government of India.

In 1906 Britian concluded a treaty with China that conceded China's right to negotiate on behalf of Tibet. The next year Britain and Russia formally agreed not to interfere in Tibet's domestic affairs and not to send diplomatic representatives to Lhasa. Each empire would police its side of the border with Tibet, closing the country to any trespass whatever. Bell, to his disgust, was not allowed farther north than Gyantse. But he worked quietly to reverse this policy of retreat, and the flight of the Dalai Lama presented him with an opportunity to befriend a ruler as astute as himself. In the spring of

1912 he wrote in his private notebook, "Tibet would be delighted to be under a British protectorate, controlling their external affairs, and leaving their internal independence on the lines of the Bhutan Treaty of 1910." Bell had brokered that treaty, and it was his model for the benevolent overlordship that Britain—and he—might exercise over Tibet.

After his retirement, Charles Bell wrote several authoritative books on Tibet, its people and its culture. No European man knew the country better, and if David-Neel, with her sharp eye, had accurately taken his political measure, she may have also detected a literary rival. Meanwhile Bell had to be concerned with this attractive Frenchwoman's growing influence of over Prince Sidkeong. In diplomatic fashion the future Sir Charles ushered Madame Neel into the flower-gardened residency where, free of scandal, she would be comfortably lodged—and he could watch her.

Chapter 8

The Living Buddha

If the small European community of Gangtok liked to gossip about Alexandra's relationship with Sidkeong, the dust from their liaison hasn't settled yet. The official line emanating from the David-Neel estate is that, in the words of biographer Ruth Middleton, Alexandra became Sidkeong's "confidante, his traveling companion, his spiritual sister." Middleton cites as evidence Alexandra's letters to Philip—as if she would admit an affair to the husband who paid all her bills!—as well as letters from Sidkeong to Alexandra—those that she, and Marie-Madeleine Peyronnet after her, chose not to destroy. Middleton accepts a provincial, biased spin on what really went on.

Yet elsewhere the tiptoeing biographer indicates that she knew better: "Within the subconscious of almost every woman, however independent and emancipated, however indifferent to the lure of romance, lies buried a sleeping beauty who waits to be awakened. . . . How appropriate that when [Alexandra's] prince finally arrived on stage, he should be fitted out in gold brocade!" Alexandra, although no sleeping beauty, was a Romantic at heart. She once wrote to her husband that all her life she had been searching for a grand passion—and he did not fill the bill.

David-Neel was also a hard-driving, mature woman who generally got what she wanted. She was not "dedicated to a religious vocation, and therefore celibate," as Middleton claims, on no evidence. Alexandra's mentors, her "masters," who were dedicated to the pursuit of Enlightenment, were not celibate. As for Sidkeong, in the family tradition he was something of a lady's man. After all, he had received his mantle of *tulku*—the reincarnation of a great spirit—from his uncle, the second (simultaneous) husband of his stepmother.

Sidkeong's youth was marred by the death of his natural mother and his father's losing battle against Claude White, the first Resident Political Officer. The Indian historian Lal Basnet writes that Maharaj Thutob was "sorely tried by an unabating succession of unkind events," and that he led "an existence reduced to penury." White had Thutob kept under arrest for two years at a stretch. He claimed that Yeshe Drolma, whom he described as a "born intriguer and diplomat," was behind all the trouble. While the British backed Sidkeong as an alternative to his father, Drolma favored her own son. Sidkeong, then, was emotionally orphaned but still accustomed to a decisive surrogate mother figure—now provided by Alexandra.

The prince treated her in a manner almost worshipful. He collected her remarks in a scrapbook that he kept by his bedside. At other times Sidkeong acted more like a playmate to the plump woman a dozen years his senior. He took to loading her with presents, and on one occasion, when she was at her desk writing, he cradled a baby yak (the hairy Tibetan buffalo) in his arms before her window, offering it to her. Alexandra, a Parisian who knew how to flirt, responded to the erotic undertone.

It is harder to understand why she deliberately informed Philip how enchanting she found the thirty-three-year-old prince, and how he made everyone around him happy. Nonetheless, he was a hard worker who took his administrative duties seriously. Although he did not wish to marry the Burmese princess that the British had chosen for him, Alexandra concluded, he would make the right woman a fine husband. It seems she was still fighting the marital war with Philip, pointing out his failure to become the husband she'd hoped for.

Still more indiscreetly, Alexandra described her jaunts with the prince into the mountains. Sidkeong, short but sturdy, was a first-rate mountaineer who, no matter how high or slippery the climb, never showed fatigue or ill humor. After one particularly steep ascent that caused Alexandra's head to swim, she glanced up to see her partner scurrying fearlessly ahead. All this outdoor activity made the matron appear younger, slimmer. Looking in the mirror, she saw that care and disappointment had vanished from her features. Her eyes were radiant with an inner light.

In late May, following a day's trek on the route to Tibet, night in an isolated bungalow was cozy. Outside, the demons might prowl and witches gather, but within there were no closed doors between the two soul mates. First they dined together by candlelight; then, with incense perfuming the air, they spoke and dreamed of a better world. Until late, the pair indulged in what Alexandra called their private cult. Then, she assured her husband, the prince discreetly retired.

Philip, who knew Alexandra only too well, didn't believe her. He was having erotic dreams about his lost wife. Not overly suspicious, he sensed something more going on than a platonic affair. There was no denying a strong romantic current between the mature woman—charming and attractive when she chose to be—and the dashing young prince. That their feelings for one another were based on a shared view of the world only fanned the growing flames. Alexandra had never before found this quality of understanding, of spiritual dedication, in a man who physically pleased her. Sidkeong combined ease of companionship with the intensity of a believer. He was everything that the mundane, hypochondriacal Mouchy could never be, and Alexandra didn't mind so informing her husband.

Philip felt betrayed. He had undertaken to support a scholar, not an oriental potentate's mistress. Worse, he realized that he had failed to come close to the one person who mattered to him. According to his next letter, he went for a long melancholy Sunday walk along the margin of the sea, lonely and miserable. Was his desperation such that he contemplated suicide? The letter in which he detailed his feelings was discarded by Alexandra—just as she discarded his others, although she did respond to this one with unusual urgency.

She offered to return immediately if the pain caused by her absence was truly severe. She called Philip pet names and reassured him of her fidelity and that she would one day return to Tunis. Begging for patience, Alexandra switched the subject, reminding Philip that Buddha had been an active man of affairs just like himself. Alexandra was going through a gradual process of abandoning the *sexual* for the *sensual*. She devoured her exotic surroundings, including the tawny beauty of both men and women, through its sights and sounds, through her eyes, ears, through every one of her five sense organs. This is not Puritanism but a quickening of perception that is a step on the tantric path to power. However, her development was far from complete, and we are left with the question of whether she did or did not have a love affair with the Prince of Sikkim. Philip supposed so, likewise the missionaries. Charles Bell, who would have made it his business to find out, is silent on the matter, even in his unpublished notebooks.

Sidkeong gave Alexandra some remarkable gifts. At Digne we have seen some of these precious bracelets, earrings, and objets, and as is the custom in the East, they are often solid gold. The explorer, no matter how desperate her plight, how poor, hungry, and cold she grew, refused to sell even one piece. She carried the jewelry on her person during her marathon journey through unmapped Tibet, when if anyone had caught sight of the treasure, it could have cost her and her adopted son their lives.

Alexandra's training as a singer stood her in good stead in her climbing excursions. Born with strong lungs, she had studied breath control. Yet she was nervous before her first solo camping expedition in early June. She admitted that her daring was a triumph of will over unwilling flesh. She never quite lost the fear of hurting herself. The prince obtained for her mounts, yaks, tents, and bearers and waved her off on a trek up fifteen thousand feet—just below the line where the abominable snowman is rumored to prowl.

Thrilled at being her own woman, Alexandra sped along in front of the party, climbing higher, headed past Lachen and Tangu, the last outposts before Tibet. In the snow-clad mountains, home of anchorites and sages, Alexandra sensed the imminent presence that lurked behind the burnished peaks, the nonmaterial being more shadowy than the deepest ravines. She had to wait three hours in stinging snow for her servants to come up and boil tea. Her tent was leaky, and by next morning it was an inconspicuous dot on the heights. Alexandra, too ill to budge, felt her chest bound by pain. She had to do something quickly or the snow would be her shroud. If she had pneumonia or heart trouble, the odds were against her.

Then she grew calm. How noble to perish among these majestic mountains, alone with the gods! Her last wish was to get a picture of her death site—for Philip, she told him, but more likely for the press. Bulky camera in hand, Alexandra crawled from the tent, pointed, and snapped. She felt better and groaned for her retainers. Hot tea and a steaming footbath revitalized her blood, and she realized she had nothing worse than a chest cold. Soon, in the saddle, she was heading for the next ridge.

This trek proved to Alexandra the joys of solitude, of sleeping in a tent in the high Himalayas, and of eating rations cooked over a yak dung fire, but always provided a servant did the cooking. The Tibetan plateau lay before her: small, icy lakes dominated by glowing peaks that penetrated the intense blue sky. This surreal landscape resembled the mystical painting shown to her years before at the London Gnosis. Should she descend to it? She knew such a step was strictly forbidden by both British and Tibetan authorities. The question was settled for her by the Sikkimese porters, who were freezing and demanded to turn back. They took to fighting one another for a place at the fire, and Alexandra had to separate them with a whip.

She wasn't faring much better. The glare burned her eyes, the cold blistered her skin and spread her nose across half her face. She cured a huge white blister on her lip by slitting the skin with a sharp knife. Yet after her return to Gangtok, Alexandra had an irrepressible desire to make another expedition, to get stronger bearers—Tibetans—and climb back, this time to cross the forbidden line. All the Europeans in the tiny capital felt the same strange fascination, although none dared act. When Dawasandup revealed to her that the hailstorm had been a warning and the oracle had predicted she would face terrible difficulties if she attempted to live in Tibet—the Land of the Religion—the rational Buddhist didn't bother to reply.

Outwardly, David-Neel—who to some seemed a dilettante, to others worse—quietly continued with her studies. She said nothing of her evolving scheme to Sidkeong or Charles Bell or the missionaries. But, veiled as the Cybele, she confided to Philip that she was on the edge of solving the mystery that had long bewitched her.

"Forbidden Tibet! Westerners have called it that for centuries!" wrote Lowell Thomas, Jr. Naturally the least accessible land on earth, it has always lured explorers, missionaries, and searchers after both spiritual truth and the secrets of perpetual life. Shangri-La may be a fictional place, yet its equivalent has been sought for both above and below ground in this kingdom protected by the ramparts of the Himalayas. Despite its location on the roof of the world, with valleys at fourteen thousand feet, and until recently its official policy of remaining closed to outsiders, Tibet has drawn an array of adventurers who dared to penetrate the sacred, if haphazardly guarded, realm. For the rest, even now when Tibetan refugees live among us, we hold many misconceptions of their country.

Ethnographic Tibet is large—equal to one-third of the continental United States—and the influence of its culture has been decisive over an area of Central Asia far greater than its own size. Even its neighbors have been difficult to reach or politically unstable: to the west, Ladakh and Kashmir; to the south, the mountainous states of Nepal, Sikkim (now incorporated into India), Bhutan, and little-known portions of Assam and Burma; to the east, the Chinese marches, formerly inhabited by brigands and Tibetan-speaking nomads, or inhospitable portions of Szechuan and Kansu provinces; and to the north, the vast desert spaces of China's Sinkiang province. Mongolia lies beyond, and more to the west, Afghanistan. Population statistics are murky and politically entangled; there are some six million ethnic Tibetans, two-thirds of whom live in what is presently western China, and the remaining one-third in the so-called Tibetan Autonomous Region of China, the old heartland, which includes Lhasa. Since 1959, when Red Army troops crushed a popular uprising, a considerable emigré community has taken root in India, concentrated in the north, and more recently in Europe and America.

Historically, because of its altitude and the sparseness of the land, Tibet was seldom invaded. Even the hordes of Genghiz Khan or the later Mogul conquerors of India went around the great mountain fastness. But the nominal ruler of the land, Fourteenth in the line of Dalai Lamas, and perhaps the last, today lives in exile in India. So did his predeccessor, the Great Thirteenth, from 1910 to 1912 after he, too, fled from a Chinese invasion. Indeed, what was at stake then remains at stake today: the status of Tibet vis-à-vis China. This makes it particularly important that Alexandra met and interviewed the Thirteenth Dalai Lama. Although initially he was skeptical, the lord of Mahayana Buddhism came to accept the foreign woman as an insider—a member of the faith. The Thirteenth went out of his way to further her mission, encouraging her studies and answering many abstruse questions.

Yet Alexandra did not speak glowingly of the Thirteenth Dalai Lama. She admitted his profound knowledge of Buddhism, yet privately she claimed that he was cold, affected, and lacking in compassion. This was unusual criticism. Charles Bell, who knew the Thirteenth intimately over a period of years, was certain that he fit the generic description of the Dalai Lama: "He was regarded as a god, being an incarnation of Chen-re-zi, the Lord of Mercy, himself an emanation of Buddha. As Chen-re-zi is held to be the founder of the Tibetan race, and is worshipped as its partron diety, this gave the Dalai Lama an overpowering position in Tibet." That remains true today, much to the annoyance of the occupying Chinese officials, who have made the possession of photographs of the Fourteenth Dalai Lama a criminal offence.

Tibetans, at the end of an evening of light diversion, will sit cross-legged, and someone will say, "Let's talk about religion!" In order to understand the unique phenomenon that is the Dalai Lama, as well as Alexandra's reaction to the Thirteenth, it is necessary to take a quick glance back at the origin of Buddhism and how it came to reach Tibet.

The historical Buddha, Siddhartha Gautama Sakyamun—his given, family, and clan name—was born in the sixth century B.C. in what is now southern Nepal. According to Alexandra in her *Buddhism: Its Doctrines and its Methods*, he was of the Kshatriya (warrior) caste, and his immediate family was noble and wealthy. Bell remarks that "Buddha may well have been Mongoloid (perhaps Tibetan) rather than Indian, by race." The young nobleman received the best education of his day and grew up unfettered by worldly cares. He married, had a son, and appeared content. Then at twenty-nine Siddhartha had his head shaved, donned the plain yellow robe of a *sannyasin*, or renunciate, and rejected the goods of this world. Although the tradition of religious mendicants was well established, the young man's family was horrified. There is a certain parallel to Alexandra's own situation, and she once remarked that one first has to be comfortable to become a Buddha; otherwise, the allure of material things will be too engrossing, too persuasive.

Siddhartha sought Enlightenment by studying with the famous teachers of his day and then by fasting and ascetic practices, but to no avail. It came to him while sitting under a great canopy of a tree, from within his own mind. Siddhartha had become the Buddha, the Awakened One. He preached his first sermon at the Deer Park outside Benares. Though differing in content and emphasis, as a statement of belief it has made an impact on people's minds no less than Jesus' Sermon on the Mount. Here in the citadel of the Brahmins—much as Jesus dared the high priests—Buddha denied the value of self-mortification and denigrated the uses of ritual and sacrifice. He declared that all things spring from a cause, and the cause of human suffering is the craving for life. The search for pleasurable sensation leads inevitably to pain. But following the Eightfold Path puts an end to *karma*, successive rebirths, and leads to *nirvana*, cessation, the blissful void.

Buddhism, destined to nearly die out in its native India, spread to other lands. The term *Mahayana* is used to differentiate the Buddhism of northern Asia from the original Theravadin. According to Sir Charles Eliot, diplomat and scholar, the newer faith proved "warmer in charity, more personal in devotion, more ornate in art, literature, and ritual." Especially in Tibet, the Mahayana stressed the supernatural spirit of the Buddha, of which innumerable Buddhas past, present, and future are but emanations. Along with this concept, as mystical as the Christian theology that the young Alexandra rebelled against, came the worship of *bodhisattvas*—beings who reject nirvana until all of humankind can join them. Cults are dedicated to these heroes, who must continually reincarnate to fulfill their beneficent purpose.

"Warriors, warriors we call ourselves," began a favorite text of David-Neel's. "We fight for splendid virtue, for high endeavor, for sublime wisdom." It was the warrior king Strongtsan Gampo who, in the seventh century, bent to the will of his two wives, one Chinese the other Nepali, and sent scholars into India to study and translate Buddhist texts. They had to fashion an alphabet, since Tibet had none, and physically carry the books on their backs over the sky-high barrier of the Himalayas. This tradition became central to Tibetan Buddhism, and Alexandra would become rightfully proud of her translations *from* Tibetan and the collection of texts she hauled back over the mountains *to* India and the West. No other woman has performed such an astonishing task, and nearly at the cost of her life.

Not until the mid-eighth century did the tropical plant of Buddhism take root in the frigid soil of the Tibetan plateau. Tibet had become an important military power that had overrun areas of Turkestan, India, and China. The king sent for Padmasambhava, a

renowned yogi-sage, skilled in magic and mysticism. He was a harsh
but clever man able to adapt his teachings to the demonology already
in place. The preexistent shamanist religion, known as Bon, emphasized protection against a horde of malicious spirits. Considering
their environment of biting winds, glaciers, sudden storms, forbid-
ding mountains, chasms through which rush icy torrents, and a light
that presents distant objects as near and near ones as receding, the
Tibetans' bone-deep belief in sorcery is scarcely surprising.

Padmasambhava presented himself as the great exorcist empow-
ered to subdue the most ferocious demons. This is the sort of fellow
a barbarian king, or a well-to-do merchant or herdsman, is pleased
to hire, and Guru Rinpoche, as he is referred to by Tibetans, was able
to build the country's first monastery, Samye, and to become
the fountainhead of the several Red Hat sects. Apparently he drank,
consorted with women, and practiced tantric sexual rites.

At first, David-Neel regarded the Buddhism descended from
Padmasambhava as decadent and superstitious. She leaned toward
the reforms of Tsong Khapa, born in 1357 near Lake Koko Nor in
Amdo. This founder of the Yellow Hat discipline, the established
church of most Tibetans and Mongols, became a monk at seven and
absorbed instruction from a variety of teachers, including Roman
Catholic missionaries. In early manhood he went to Lhasa and,
under the secular rulers, began to implement his reforms. He insti-
tuted a true monastic discipline complete with hierarchy, celibacy,
and communal prayer, while discouraging magical practices. Tsong
Khapa was behind the founding of the three great monasteries of
Ganden (Joyous Mountain), Sera (Rose Fence), and Drepung (Rice
Heap), thereby surrounding the capital with yellow-hatted monks
and insuring a clerical veto over the acts of government. He also
established Tashilhunpo at Shigatse, which became the seat of the
Panchen Lama, who would rival the Dalai Lama in prestige—and
eventually in bestowing favors on David-Neel.

The author of *Buddhism* remarked that of all the Dalai Lamas
who preceded the Thirteenth, only two others achieved a measure
of fame: the Great Fifth and his successor, the infamous Sixth. The
Fifth, with the aid of Mongol troops, seized secular power in the seventeenth century. Indeed, *Dalai* is Mongol for the sea, vast and profound. The Fifth built Lhasa's enormously impressive Potala Palace,

and he determined the powers of the Dalai Lamaship as definitively as had Innocent III determined those of the Roman papacy. When the Manchus succeeded to the Celestial Throne of China in 1644, the Fifth journeyed to Peking where the emperor bestowed upon him the title "Universal Ruler of the Buddhist Faith."

The death of the Great Fifth was concealed for over a decade while his chief adviser, said to be his natural son, continued to preside in his name. But there can be no dynasty of Dalai Lamas; the successor is not his son but his reincarnation in a newborn male child. Thus Tibet's ruler has often been an infant of rude peasant parentage raised in the halls of state. However, due to the conniving at court, the Sixth Dalai Lama was not announced until 1697 when he was in his teens. He had been discovered but left to live normally with his parents.

Alas, the remarkably winning lad was a merry one: he drank, wore jewelry, and chased women all night long. Melodious Purity— so he was named—wrote beautiful love songs that are still sung by Tibetans, for the people adored him. Indeed, Alexandra insisted that she had found in Lhasa a half-secret cult that venerated his memory. She translated some of the Sixth's poetry, which often contains sharp social satire, mocking the monks who are not true to their vows, but more often is lyrical in praise of his sweethearts. She wrote that he led a life of "what appears to us [as] debauchery, and would indeed be so in the case of any other than an 'initiate' into that singular training"—of tantricism. The Indian scholar Agehananda Bharati adds: "The famous, or infamous, Sixth Dalai Lama had his problems vis-à-vis the orthodox reformed clergy, but I feel reasonably sure that they did not recognize the tantric disciplinary element in his case."

Certainly the Manchu emperor failed to be amused. He invited Melodious Purity to Peking under guard, in a mockery of the usual honorifics. On the way he had him poisoned. The Tibetan people were outraged, but this initiated the unfortunate habit of murdering young Dalai Lamas when they approached manhood. The Ninth, Tenth, Eleventh, and Twelfth conveniently shed their earthly guise at about the same age. The Tibetan noblemen acting as regents preferred it, and so did the two Chinese *Ambans* (ambassadors) residing in Lhasa. However, the Thirteenth proved more canny than had his predecessors, outwitting his enemy the Emperor of China. Indeed, he lived to grant an audience to a determined Frenchwoman, aged forty-four, who claimed to be a Buddhist and who barraged him with such exacting questions about the faith that he had to consider his answers carefully.

Kalimpong, India—twenty miles from Darjeeling—April 15, 1912. The inhabitants of this bustling trade mart, whether Nepali mule drivers, broad-faced Bhutanese, mustachioed Tibetans, or swarthy Hindus, or even the handful of British functionaries, were in a state of excitement bordering on the feverish. Flags flew, banners waved, and a bust of the late Queen Victoria presided benignly over this outpost of empire. In a chalet belonging to the Maharaja of Bhutan on the outskirts of town, Tibetan servants bustled about preparing tor the day. Despite a drizzle, some were planting bamboo poles to form an avenue in front of the modest building. Others hovered near their master, the living Buddha, who was seated cross-legged on an elevated bench draped in yellow in a corner of the topmost room. None of the retainers was too busy to chatter and gossip.

From the marketplace with its crowds lining shuttered shops, came a chorus of approval: a European woman was being carried past in a dandy, her four bearers doing their best not to jiggle her. The crowd caught only a glimpse of her, swathed in a raincoat, face covered by a light salmon veil. If the populace had been told, "She is Alexandra David-Neel," they wouldn't have cared. By sticking out their tongues (a sign of respect) and pointing to the bust of Victoria, they showed they regarded the lady as an emanation of the empress, who in turn really was Palden Lhamo, patron goddess of Tibet. In the East, truth can be as manifold as a "thousand-layered" Burmese pancake!

Within the dandy, Alexandra's mind was wandering back to the past. The weather reminded her of Belgium, of walks under rainy skies with her father. He had been her first mentor, and how proud he would be of her now. Sadly, Alexandra wished her dead father would appear magically on the road so she could stop everything to hug and kiss him. But she knew that Louis David would be embarrassed. Finally, he hadn't loved her any better than her mother.

Once inside the chalet, Alexandra had to pass the royal chamberlain, whom she felt was brusque. Although the protocol for her visit had been decided in advance, lapses occurred. Ushered into the presence of the Dalai Lama, she found that he had abandoned his throne to sit in a simple chair by the window. This was extraordinary, since he always sat higher than anyone else. Had he divined her dislike of pomp?

Alexandra recognized him from his portrait: a slightly stooped figure with wide open, riveting eyes, slightly evasive, a waxed mustache, and enormous ears (a sign of wisdom), wearing a peaked yellow cap and maroon robes. She pressed her palms together before the heart in salutation. Someone slipped a white silk scarf into her hands and she presented it but forgot the proper words. He wasn't very tall and, a trifle unwillingly, the rebel bowed her head, whereupon the Dalai Lama reached out to bless her.

As the two conversed, the Thirteenth wondered aloud how the Frenchwoman, alone in her faith in a foreign land, could have become a practicing Buddhist without a master. To himself he must have questioned whether she was a Buddhist at all. The Christian missionaries, fond of disguises, would go to any lengths to convert his people. But David-Neel's knowledge ran deep, and she soon satisfied him on that score, even made him smile. She tried to ignore the officious chamberlain who continued to interrupt. However, she had to admit that those Europeans interested in Buddhism were generally of the older, Theravadin school.

"The religious doctrines of Tibet are not understood in Europe," Alexandra informed His Holiness. "I am hoping you will enlighten me."

This pleased the Dalai Lama, and Alexandra went on to interrogate her host about the path of salvation, of gaining wisdom. She wasn't being impolite but merely employing the traditional method of discourse. Lamas must commit hundreds of sacred texts to memory, and when they are called on, repeat the appropriate answer to a question. The eager visitor fired off so many queries that she and the Dalai Lama agreed she should submit them in writing. He promised to answer them fully, and she would have unique documents, of great value to the world.

The interview over, the visitor received another silk scarf and backed out. Luckily there was no furniture to bump into, and besides she had practiced this maneuver at the court of Belgium. The crowd outside was awestruck when she emerged, since the Compassionate

One had allowed this European woman—the first ever—an hour of his precious time. Alexandra was thinking that the episode would make a splash in a French magazine. The silk scarf smelled so musty she couldn't wait to get rid of it.

The crowd stirred with anticipation. His Holiness appeared, and with legs bowed from meditating for hours each day since childhood, he mounted a makeshift throne. The pilgrims began to pass before him: rich or poor, traders and cowherds, Buddhists, Hindus, and animists. On the highest born he placed both hands, on landowners one hand, on merchants just a finger or two. Even the lowliest beggar could expect to be touched with a tassel to complement the blessing from the incarnation of Chenresi—bound to bestow good fortune.

After all, hadn't this god on earth through the power of his spells overthrown the Emperor of China? Was he not about to return triumphant to Lhasa, the universal ruler of the Buddhist faith?

Chapter 9
An Invisible Barrier

Events leading up to 1912, when David-Neel first ventured into culturally Tibetan territory, markedly anticipated the Red Chinese invasion and occupation of Tibet that began in 1949 and continues as of the date of this writing. The issues of law and power that Charles Bell and his colonial contemporaries struggled to resolve are with us today. Indeed, Bell's diplomatic maneuvers have shaped current Western policy toward Tibet. Remarkably, the eye of the hurricane remains the Dalai Lama—the Thirteenth then, the Fourteenth now. But there has been only one Dalai Lama in fourteen different human bodies; the task has been to find the emanation after each death and rebirth as an infant.

In the past, the method of locating him was fixed. Within a year or two of the previous sovereign's passing away, a council of lamas would consult the state oracle for general directions. Then a high lama was sent to a particular lake under the waters of which resided the Dalai Lama's imperishable soul. While staring into the icy blue water, the lama would have a vision, and perhaps that night a helpful dream. He should picture the looks and the whereabouts of the child-sovereign too clearly to be mistaken.

Once located, the candidate was put to the test. According to Charles Bell, the tiny Thirteenth, born in a peasant's hut in 1876, had several of the appropriate bodily marks, such as "large ears" and "an imprint like a conch-shell on one of the palms of his hand." An unearthly light issued from his countenance, and he was able to recognize the everyday religious articles used in his past life: the sacred thunderbolt (*dorje*), a bell, and a much-fingered rosary. He had to choose from among lookalikes with unfailing accuracy. Later, memories of previous incarnations would come to him, and he would feel instantly at home with unknown places and people. But now that the old order is overthrown and the Chinese occupy Tibet, will there even be a next Dalai Lama?

Traditionally, the Manchu emperor had the right to confirm the choice of a new Dalai Lama. This was done in a manner subject to manipulation: the names of several likely candidates were dropped into a golden urn, and the Chinese Amban picked out one with the aid of chopsticks. We suspect he had tucked the successful slip up his enormously long sleeve. In the case of the Thirteenth, the indications were clear and the suspicious Tibetans refused to employ the urn. The emperor grudgingly acquiesced, and so before he was aware of it, the Thirteenth had begun to defy China.

Taken from his mother and father at the age of two, enthroned at three before a horde of grave lamas prostrating themselves, he was then educated by learned professors in Buddhist ritual and metaphysics. Surrounded by serious-minded adults, he studied day and night, was denied playmates, and hardly ever saw a female. He learned little of the workaday world either personally or from books, and not much about lands outside Tibet. But his fate was to be different from those preceeding him.

Traditionally, when he reached eighteen, the Dalai Lama was expected to assume his temporal authority. First he had to make a journey to "The Heaven Lake of the Goddess" 150 miles southeast of Lhasa to commune with Palden Lhamo, guardian of the Tibetan state. Her chapel was "furnished with stuffed carcasses of wild animals and other fearsome objects . . . She is powerful and easily angered." On the way back to Lhasa, the living Buddha was given a holy pill, "to renew his vitality and make his countenance shine." Face aglow he passed into his next incarnation. A lavish funeral would be held where it was announced that the Compassionate One had departed the world due to despair at the wickedness of his people. The Thirteenth, who had a natural aptitude for politics, was clever enough to avoid swallowing the poison pill. According to Bell, a Chinese official remarked that "affairs had been managed very badly." Neither Peking nor the Government of India was accustomed to dealing with an adult sovereign of Tibet.

In the early years of the twentieth century the British in India, creeping northward, became worried by Russian expansion eastward into Buddhist Central Asia. A Russian Mongol, Dorjieff, had studied with the lamas and became a close adviser to the young Thirteenth. Lord Curzon, the viceroy, fearing that Dorjieff was an agent of the Czar, sent several letters to Lhasa to open discussions on trade. Always he received the same reply: "We have no dealings with foreigners."

In 1904 Colonel Francis Younghusband, backed by a small army of *sepoys* (Indian troops), was dispatched to pay a diplomatic call on the Dalai Lama. Younghusband was one of the most intrepid and knowledgeable officers on the Indian frontier. Interestingly, he would evolve into a mystic and an admirer of Alexandra David-Neel. Other officers on the expedition were Captain L. A. Waddell, who would write the comprehensive but biased *Tibetan Buddhism*, and young David Macdonald, just beginning his stint of twenty years in Tibet.

To the surprise of the British, the Tibetans fought bravely and held up their advance in the Chumbi Valley. Here Macdonald met Annie Taylor, who had penetrated farther into the country than any other missionary, male or female. Once the army had dragged its cannon over the mountains, the defenders, who had antique muzzle-loading rifles and no sense of modern warfare, could offer no serious resistance. Unfortunately, the Tibetan troops supposed that the blessing of the lamas would protect them from bullets. At every stage, Younghusband tried fruitlessly to negotiate, while the general in actual charge of the sepoys had to overcome the reluctance of his men to machine-gun the foolhardy Tibetans. The British pushed on, complaining of roads so poor they had never felt the weight of any wheeled vehicle. Soon everyone became entranced by the wild, magnificent scenery. As the army approached Lhasa and caught sight of the golden roofs of the Potala Palace, a race developed to be, in Macdonald's words, "the first living European to set eyes on the Forbidden City of the Lamas." On August 4 the British entered, "tearing aside the veil of centuries."

Because the Dalai Lama had fled north to Mongolia, Younghusband opened negotiations with the regent, the abbot of Ganden monastery. While the Dalai Lama camped in the remote grasslands of the steppes and his devout Mongol subjects flocked to pay him homage, an Anglo-Tibetan Convention was agreed upon and ratified by the Tibetan Assembly. The document laid the basis for Tibet's foreign policy in the twentieth century and strongly supports its claim to independence from China. Neither the Manchu emperor nor his Ambans were consulted. The convention forbade foreign occupation of any portion of Tibet or intervention in its affairs. Of most importance to Alexandra David-Neel, the convention stated: "No representatives or agents of any foreign power shall be admitted to Tibet." It did permit the British to open "trade marts" at Yatung (Chumbi Valley) and Gyantse. Alexandra realized that, in fact, the British empire had leaped the Himalayas to include part of southern Tibet. This arm-twisting diplomacy occurred the same year that she married Philip, and it was to have an impact on her doings that was nearly as important as her marriage.

Mongolia could not long support the Thirteenth and his entourage and although he made overtures to Russia, the Buddhist spiritual sovereign was forced to travel to Peking to bend his knee at the Celestial Throne. The Empress Dowager Yehonala and her nephew the emperor received him, after which at Yehonala's instigation his title was amended to include the phrase "Sincerely Obedient." The dowager, who claimed to be a good Buddhist, was above all an unscrupulous politician, and the 1908 subordination of the Dalai Lama to the last Manchus is an argument advanced by the People's Republic of China in asserting sovereignty over Tibet today. By fleeing the British, the Dalai Lama had leaped from the frying pan into the fire.

However, the Chinese emperor, addicted to drugs, was fading fast, and most likely a final dose of poison finished him. Yehonala selected an infant for the throne, and in her seventy-third year, she boasted she would surpass the years of Queen Victoria. She outlasted her nephew by only two days and died cursing the rule of women and eunuchs. The Dalai Lama conducted a joint funeral service, and after inspecting the monasteries of eastern Tibet he made his way toward Lhasa. Before he arrived Chinese armies under the capable general Chao Erh-feng had invaded his country, looted and set fire to monasteries, melted sacred images for bullets, murdered hundreds of monks, and ripped up ancient books to sole the boots of their soldiers. They were planning a military road from Batang in Kham province (later a key destination for Alexandra) to Lhasa. It was a preview of the pillage of Tibet in 1959 and afterward.

The Tibetans resisted as best they were able, but once a detachment of several thousand Chinese troops, including cavalry, reached Lhasa, the prematurely aged Dalai Lama fled over the Himalayan passes in dead of winter into the arms of his former enemy, the Government of India. In exile in Darjeeling he met Charles Bell, who became a lifelong friend and ally. Unfortunately, the Foreign Office found it convenient to consider itself bound by Britiain's treaties with Russia and China, though the latter was in obvious violation. Bell had to deny the Dalai Lama's request that Tibet become a protectorate under the British empire. Later the United States government would succumb to a similar ambivalence about the fate of Tibet.

Yet the prayers of the lamas proved effective: the senile Manchu dynasty collapsed under the weight of its depravity. Sun Yat-sen's Young China, taking time to establish itself, forgot about the Chinese garrisons in distant Tibet. The troops pillaged, then mutinied. The Dalai Lama sent word to his people to rise and kill the invaders. For this he was criticized by Prince Sidkeong, who began to take David-Neel's dubious tone toward the Thirteenth. Sidkeong told Bell, "It is a sin for a Buddhist to take a share in destroying life, a great sin for a lama, and a terribly great sin for the highest of all the lamas." But the Thirteenth emanation of the Bodhisattva Avalokiteśvara (Lord of Mercy), thrust rudely onto the stage of world politics, had learned his lines. This was the All Knowing One who had granted Alexandra an audience in 1912, and whom she would interview a second and final time in Ari, a tiny village just short of the Sikkim-Tibet border.

When writing to her husband, especially if she were asking for funds, Alexandra liked to stress the high-minded aspect of her journey. "When are you coming home?" Philip would inquire. He was writing to the woman he supposed he had married—a former opera singer, a journalist, a woman of fashion. She did miss her old comfortable life a little, but underneath all her appointments and teas there had been despair. Keeping busy was the opiate of a woman who hadn't found herself.

Now she preached to her dear Mouchy. She answered him, in Buddhist terms, that by acquiring knowledge (and not incidentally books) she was building a refuge for their old age together. In fact, she was looking years younger and feeling vivacious. The woman was sensitive to the glamour of her surroundings, aware that she was a privileged person during the largely beneficent years of the mature British Empire. The maharajas had lost their teeth and were quaint curios to play among, while war in Europe threatened evanescent as lightning on the far horizon.

At a small town on the Sikkim–Tibet–Bhutan border, on the June day before the Dalai Lama crossed into his own country—the time had been fixed by court astrologers—His Holiness was receiving only royalty. Nonetheless, folk streamed out of the hills to catch a last glimpse of this god on earth, and to the local nationalities of Lepchas, Bhutias, and Indians were added Chinese soldiers expelled from Tibet, evidently bearing no grudge. A bargain had been struck: the Han could go in peace if they left their modern rifles behind. These would be useful to a new-model Tibetan army trained by the British. The deal had Charles Bell's stamp on it.

While attendants kept back the curious crowd with knotted whips, Alexandra sipped tea with the Maharaja of Sikkim and Prince Sidkeong in a bungalow nearby. A tiny owl, a present from the two, looked on from its perch. Ceremony was followed, and the old maharaja's cup and saucer were of gold with turquoise inlay and a superb pearl, the prince's of silver with a button of coral. Alexandra was disappointed when tea was served her in a plain porcelain cup. She was developing a taste for position.

She accompanied Sidkeong, who would act as interpreter, to see the Thirteenth. They found the lamas uttering disjointed orders, the servants rushing about confused. The Dalai Lama was cordial yet hurried. Alexandra sensed that his mind was already in Lhasa, organizing his government. Her apparently casual remark can be taken in a literal sense: that the use of the thought form—a second, purely mental self that is detached at will—was practiced by adepts in Tibet. While Alexandra questioned the Thirteenth's good will, she didn't doubt his powers.

To Alexandra's surprise, the Dalai Lama handed her written answers to her abstruse questions. She could write to him for further explanations, their correspondence to be forwarded through Charles Bell. She realized that the Compassionate One had made a remarkable exception for her, a woman. Of his own wife, Bell wrote, "She was careful not to speak to His Holiness, for that would have offended Tibetan custom." Bell, who knew the Thirteenth better than any other Westerner, claimed he was "frank and open not only in conversation, but in his dealings generally." Neither did he neglect the spiritual side, being "strict in his devotions." Bell observed that "he was fond of gardening and would plant seeds and seedlings with his own hands. And he would visit his [pet] animals, the Bengal tiger and the other animals."

However, Bell did admit that with the passing years the Great Thirteenth became increasingly an autocrat who could punish swiftly and arbitrarily. He was to gather into his hands more secular authority than even the Great Fifth. During perilous times, he necessarily acted as the head of state. We are reminded of a Tibetan proverb: "In a powerful country religion goes down." The contrast with the Fourteenth Dalai Lama couldn't be more evident; his only power is moral, yet his influence is felt world-wide.

Whenever possible, Alexandra verified her accomplishments with photos, and she persuaded the Thirteenth to sit as she snapped away. But when she developed the film, the Dalai Lama appeared to be a vague form, like a ghost. She assured Philip that the film had been properly exposed. She had no explanation, but she was reminded of a story she'd heard about the Younghusband expedition. Its photographers had taken many shots of the interiors of temples, of bejewelled Buddhas, and elaborate altars, brushing aside the objections of the lamas. But when they tried to develop the pictures, nothing appeared. Alexandra felt she had been a victim of the same occult phenomenon.

Alexandra was favorably inclined toward one command given by His Holiness: "Learn Tibetan!" Her desire to master this difficult language had been awakened by an earlier, parallel incident. Shortly after their first interview, while she watched the Thirteenth bestow his blessing on the mob of pilgrims, she noticed a man seated on the ground wearing dirty, torn monastic garments, his hair wound around his head like a turban. He was sneering at the goings-on. Alexandra, through Dawasandup, learned that the man was a wandering *naljorpa* from Bhutan—a sort of ascetic who lives just anywhere and possesses magical powers. Soon afterward, the seeker forced the reluctant schoolmaster to accompany her on a visit to the naljorpa in his cell at a nearby monastery.

The strange man was stuffing his mouth with rice and answered their greeting with a burp. Alexandra tried to speak to him, at which he chortled and muttered a few words. Dawasandup refused to translate but indicated the man had called Alexandra an idiot. After a while, the hermit proved more communicative, damning the Dalai Lama's blessings as a sham. He pointed out that if the Thirteenth possessed real power he wouldn't need an army or allies to fight the Chinese but could turn them back by surrounding Tibet with an impenetrable psychic barrier. Alexandra was intrigued by this filthy fellow with his necklace of human bones and his wild air. But from the point of view of the individual traveler, there was an invisible barrier that prevented all who tried from reaching Lhasa, the forbidden capital.

Alexandra demanded to know who the naljorpa thought he was. He laughed noisily, comparing himself to a pig rolling in the mud. But he also claimed to be a disciple of Guru Rinpoche, as the Tibetans refer to Padmasambhava. Indeed, he spoke in a sort of code well-known to followers of the mystic Short Path, the daring but dangerous attempt to attain salvation by magical means. He repeated the alchemical formula that one must fashion gold out of dog shit!

Alexandra remained skeptical, and on their way out she gave Dawasandup a few rupees for the mendicant. The man disdainfully refused the present. When Dawasandup pressed the money on the naljorpa, he suddenly staggered and fell back against the wall, clutching his stomach. The magician hadn't moved an eyebrow, but now, with a grin, he got up and left the room. On a small scale, he had set up an invisible, psychic barrier.

Not long afterward, Alexandra met a more learned but equally irreverent naljorpa, known as the *gomchen*—great hermit—of Sakyong, a place in eastern Tibet. He also followed the Short Path, reminding Alexandra, in a ritualistic formula, that Enlightenment consists in "the absence of all views and imagination, the cessation of the thinking that creates illusion." This is difficult for Westerners to accept, since they prize their opinions and imaginings. Alexandra found it even less credible when the Sakyong gomchen predicted that she would travel to Tibet via China and be initiated into the Secret

Teachings. She was certain she would choose her own path, and that it led back down to India and the study of Sanskrit in Benares. Eventually, she hoped to compile some tome on comparative religion—the sort that would set heads nodding in the refined salons of Paris.

First, however, David-Neel responded to an inivitation from the Maharaja of Nepal, facilitated by Charles Bell, to visit the birthplace of Gautama Buddha at Lumbini and then make a sortie into the Tilora jungle on the Indo-Nepalese border. In December in Katmandu the maharaja received her in style and they soon became intimate on matters mystical. This ruler of a large, strategically located land was handsome, suave, and given to display. He assigned Alexandra a light carriage escorted by two footmen; the "boys" were under the orders of the British Resident to stick close by. Finally she was transported over the mountains into the jungle in a sedan chair, a dozen porters and four elephants trailing behind.

Alexandra came alive in the tropical nights, inebriated by the perfume of the foliage. Unfortunately, the Tilora was populated by man-eating tigers, and none of her retinue of coolies and servants cared to venture into its depths, not even taking one of the elephants. One afternoon, with a single boy, the Parisian pushed on until she reached a pleasant, cleared spot. She sat down cross-legged, admiring a bright blue bird chirping on a bough. Her boy wandered off somewhere.

Alexandra turned pensive. The eighth anniversary of her father's death, recently passed, had opened old wounds. She recalled her mother's mean triumph in watching Louis David die. But her father, too, had disapproved of her bohemian ways and studies. He couldn't bear the resemblance to what he might have become. Suddenly, she heard rustling, as though of a big cat, among dry leaves to her left. Gingerly peering into the brush, she spotted about twenty yards off a long reddish body stripped with black. The creature was half-hidden by foliage, and so she thought it might be a zebra. Then she realized that in this country there were no zebras—it was a tiger!

To run would be stupid; in two bounds the huge cat would be at her throat. Quieting her thumping heart, the former devotee of Paris cafes shut her eyes and forced herself into deep meditation. She knew that yogis could calm wild beasts by their detachment from fear.

She recalled the story of how the Buddha of a previous time gave his body to a mother tiger as a meal for her hungry cubs. But Alexandra's solution was to visualize the beast as reddish leaves mixed with black leaves. When, after some time, she looked up, the creature was gone.

Not content with this victory, Alexandra attempted to recreate the big cat's image. To a philosophical Buddhist, the idea of a tiger is as real as its physical presence. But in the spot where the cat had stood, she saw only a corner of blue sky. Interrupted by the arrival of her boy with an elephant, Alexandra returned to camp.

Philosophy aside, in how much actual danger was she? The naturalist George Schaller has pointed out that the notion of the tiger as inherently ferocious is a fiction perpetuated by trophy hunters, and that "tigers are even-tempered, gentle beasts which assiduously avoid any confrontation with a person on foot, an exception, of course, being the rare man-eater." Clearly, the European traveler wasn't expert on the gustatory preferences of tigers. When Madame Blavatsky was attacked by a man-eater—so she claimed—she had to call on a Master to overpower it, Tarzan style. Alexandra reacted with courage, will power, and discipline. Like the rest of us, she had to struggle to be brave.

That night the distant but startling roar of a tiger made the boys around the campfire jump. The big cat was getting a good meal, but was it the same one? Alexandra regretted that she hadn't taken her camera and photographed the beast. Then she could have sent the snapshot home for Philip to admire.

Chapter 10

In the Realm of Shiva

David-Neel had been a Buddhist for twenty years when, in Benares, surrounded by death and the dying, she came to a profound realization: the ego did not exist. She understood that what she had called "life" was a nightmare from which she hoped to awaken into the peace of the Buddha. On December 7, 1913, fleeing the heat and plagues of India, she returned to the tiny capital of Sikkim to an amazing welcome orchestrated by Prince Sidkeong. Some miles from town schoolchildren lined the road, teachers at their head. The principal offered her the traditional white scarf as a mark of honor. Farther on a deputation of lamas greeted her, followed by an assemblage of nobles and landowners, loading her down with scarves. Finally Sidkeong appeared, and he and Alexandra entered Gangtok in the midst of the procession—as though they were the royal couple. If this was a dream, it was a sweet one!

However, staying at the British Residence to avoid gossip, Alexandra became disillusioned. Here, on a hill overlooking both the town and a lower hill with the royal palace and Sidkeong's villa on it, she had to take English tea constantly and dress for dinner. The Europeans were kind, doubly so at Christmas when they gave an amateur concert followed by a sumptuous dinner. It made the adventurer feel like an old crank among a lot of frolicking children.

Events of major importance were occuring elsewhere, and Alexandra, had she admitted it, felt left out. She was hanging about waiting for an end to the lagging tripartite conference at Simla. Historian C. J. Christie writes: "In the course of 1912 and 1913 Britain put intense pressure on the Chinese Republic to redefine the status of

Tibet and to reach with Britain a new settlement that would maintain China's suzerain right while at the same time establishing Tibet's autonomy." China eventually agreed to talk and the conference convened in October 1913. While Sir Henry McMahon led the British delegation, Charles Bell, who was on excellent terms with the Tibetans, made the crucial decisions. Sidkeong was hurried off to Simla to no purpose except to pose for an occasional photo in unflattering tails and top hat. Alexandra was displeased by his dance to the Resident's tune.

She hoped to visit Bhutan—seldom allowed—because Bell had promised to intervene with its maharaja. Now the latter claimed to be involved in the treaty-making. But it is unlikely that Bell, concerned over India's northeastern border, would have permitted a European woman to travel about in Bhutan. To compensate, Alexandra began to study Tibetan, which she found much easier than Sanskrit. She didn't expect to become fluent, only to learn to read, and she hoped to travel there a little if permitted. Hearing Tibetan music again, the deep, pensive strains produced a pleasant distress, as if the beings wandering in the *Bardo* (purgatory) were calling out. The concert took place at the local burning ground for corpses, which underscored the effect.

For the New Year of 1914, the Sikkimese monks presented David-Neel with the robe of what she called a lamina. The garment had been duly consecrated. But more important, it identified her with the long tradition of coreligionists who had studied and copied manuscripts, pilgrimaged, deprived themselves, and even died for their beliefs.

The robe of dark red felt had a blue silk kimono-style collar and a yellow fringed waistband. High Lhasa boots of leather and felt embroidered in auspicious patterns accompanied the outfit, topped off by a bonnet of golden Chinese silk. The monks, besides bestowing a rare compliment on this foreign woman, had provided a warm garment to insulate her in the Himalayan heights.

Given time on her hands, Alexandra began to fret about her health. Whenever she didn't move, she lapsed into depression, fatigue, and complaints of feeling old. Wisely, she went on a round of the monasteries, explaining Buddhist *sutras* (discourses) to the young monks. At Rumtek monastery she set up a new tent that astounded everyone. It could be lived in even in the winter. She assured Philip she would send it home to him in one more year, when they could play explorer together. But she ignored his request that she send him a final figure for the cost until her return. She acknowledged his sacrifices, but she was more concerned about demonic forces that were secretly determined to keep her out of Tibet. Probably, she was sensing Charles Bell's influence.

Tramping about in the heights, Alexandra thrived by breathing the mountain air. The former gourmet wasn't bothered that she had to settle for coarse food and at times nettles and ferns. Still, she would dream of the peas and asparagus from the gardens around Paris. Another echo of her youth returned agreeably: she was able to march for hours across the Alps, never tiring. But at age forty-five she hadn't supposed it was still possible.

It happened that one evening after a long trek, as darkness threatened to close in before she could reach a far-off village, she suddenly felt sure-footed, her body light as a feather, and that she could walk on swiftly forever. The Tibetans made this occasional, subjective experience known to hikers into an esoteric science they called *lung-gom*, of which Alexandra had heard but wished to learn more. Inadvertently, because of the time of day and her previous fatigue, and due to her fixing her gaze on the distant goal, the trekker in the Himalayas had duplicated just the right conditions to become a trance walker. Night fell but did not impede her from reaching her goal.

Alexandra wished to master the technique, widely misunderstood as "flying," but further investigation would have to wait. Her movements at this period—which she appears to have suppressed—have been a mystery to her biographers until now. Growing impatient, Alexandra tried the first of her end runs around British (and native) bureaucracy. In the secret files of the India Office we found a communique dated 22 January 1914, Assam (northeast India—to the south of Bhutan, where she was not looked for), from B. J. Gould, a political officer:

> A French lady named Madame David-Neel, who is a Buddhist and is deeply interested in Buddhist philosophy . . . showed me a letter from the Viceroy which indicated that the Viceroy was interested in her projected journey, and [she] produced a letter of introduction from Mr. Bell to see the Maharajah of Bhutan. . . . Mme. Neel has proposed that she should visit the Chumbi valley and Bhutan by herself.

So the highest British officials remained supportive of Alexandra's scholarly researches, although within bounds that would not offend native rulers or break treaty commitments. But they were also playing cat and mouse with her. The same official continues:

> Privately the Maharajah has informed me that he is afraid that complications may ensue if a lady without a European escort wanders about Bhutan, and especially if she displays a desire to visit monasteries. He is also apprehensive that if he grants a lady permission to enter Bhutan on account of her interest in Buddhism, he may find difficulties in keeping missionaries out. . . . As to the Chumbi valley, there can, I imagine, be no question of her being permitted to go there.

Alexandra, turned back at the Bhutan border, switched her attention to southern Tibet. In India she had requested that the French ambassador pressure the Government of India to allow her to visit Tibet to study its religion and philosophy at Shigatse. In so doing she made a mistake. On February 2, 1914, an unnamed British officer responded unofficially to the ambassador's application, though not to the ambassador:

> [T]here was some reason to suspect that her [David-Neel's] objects were not quite so innocent as she would have them appear. . . . As regards Tibet we are pledged not to permit private travellers to enter the country without consultation with the Russian government. There seems no reason why we should allow a French traveller admittance which we refuse to our own officers.

Indeed, for years Charles Bell was not allowed to accept the Dalai Lama's repeated invitations to visit Lhasa, an issue over which he threatened to resign in 1918.

Alexandra was plotting her course carefully. Frustrated in one direction, she approached her goal via another. She knew how to apply political influence, even though this might backfire. Trying to enter Bhutan, she presented her letters of introduction to a lesser functionary in Assam, while nearly everyone's attention was focused on Simla far across India. Although it failed, it was a clever ploy. But when she was definitively blocked from Tibet, David-Neel dropped the niceties and went ahead anyway. She understood the likely consequences, did not act out of a foggy notion of destiny, and she could not have been surprised by the British reaction, as she later claimed.

In the meantime, the death of the old maharaja on February 10 caused Alexandra to hasten to Gangtok. Despite his agonies, the maharaja had persisted in trying to substitute his younger son as heir. Alexandra strongly backed Sidkeong's ascension to the throne. She found the funeral ceremonies impressive: processions, rites in the open air, lamas chanting gravely in the temples. From early morning until late at night the long horns blew and bass drums rolled, giving her delicious chills. This was one grand opera in which the former singer, as she preached a sermon before a large, rapt audience of monks, did not mind playing a supporting role.

Alexandra was happy to be reunited with her gamin prince, who now donned the robes of state as Maharaja of Sikkim. She was quick to scent danger in the air of the intriguing little court. One afternoon as the pair customarily took tea, she pleaded with Sidkeong to move with caution. This came rather late, since she had earlier encouraged the prince to defy the British and the clique of ultraconservative lamas.

A life-size statue of Padmasambhava stood imperiously in the corner. Since all the monasteries in Sikkim were unreformed Red Hat, he was venerated as their patron saint. Although his brand of magical Tantrism was beyond the ability of most monks, it was greatly admired. Meanwhile the new ruler had determined to become the Tsong Khapa—the Yellow Hat reformer of the fifteenth century—of Sikkimese Buddhism. Sidkeong would abolish drunkenness, sorcery, and living off the peasants.

To make her point, Alexandra, indicating the statue, teased that the local clergy had been worshiping an evil spirit for centuries. Her companion began to reply, but it was the statue, harsh features silhouetted by the flickering light of an altar lamp, who took the slur personally. A ghostly voice seemed to cut in, warning them both that he was master of this country, more powerful than any human ruler.

Alexandra told herself that she hadn't heard anything and must be imagining this reprimand from the long-dead Padmasambhava. Then why did the maharaja blanch and vigorously defend himself? He insisted that he would succeed. Had there been a message addressed to him, or was he able to pluck the thought from

Alexandra's mind? The incident may be taken metaphorically in that a religious statue usually will have enclosed within it sacred texts to give it power. Padmasambhava is supposed to have hidden potent secret writings in many places. No doubt, the ancient magician still speaks to Tibetans.

The young maharaja, disregarding the warning, swore to purge the monasteries and to employ the rod where necessary. The use of liquor and tobacco must go, the monks should pray regularly, banish superstition, and educate themselves as true Buddhists. Meanwhile Sidkeong had a more pressing problem. Once the mourning period was done, he was scheduled to marry Ma Lat, the Burmese princess whom he scarcely knew. Charles Bell was counting on it. The princess was allegedly hot-headed and modern in taste and dress. She even played the piano! Besides, the maharaja had a Sikkimese mistress, a commoner by whom he'd fathered a son. He turned to Alexandra for advice. She insisted that he do his duty and marry the Burmese. Once the newlyweds had children, because Sidkeong was so young at heart, all would go well between them.

When we consider Alexandra's adamant refusal to bear children, her advice seems two-faced at best. But her tender feelings toward the maharaja would be less disturbed by a dutiful rather than a love match. Not incidentally, she wished eventually to visit both Burma and Siam in company with Sidkeong. She went so far as to open a correspondence with the Burmese princess to encourage her. Imperial politics was to her a game she enjoyed playing.

In contrast, the maharaja grew so distressed by his marital dilemma that, on a jaunt with Alexandra to an outlying bungalow, he consulted with a high lama of exceptional powers. The lama's guru had been a seer, and he too could read the future. Without knowing the subject at hand, the seer fell into a trance, twitching painfully. He opened his eyes and seemed an entirely new man. In an odd, soto voice he uttered the strange prophecy that Sidkeong needn't concern himself about the matter. The oracle staggered off, leaving his royal patron bewildered.

Alexandra's troubles with her own spouse were coming to a head. Philip was threatening to look elsewhere for a tender, compassionate mate. In a more practical vein, he complained bitterly of having to rattle around in a big house by himself, and he warned her that if she didn't come back soon, she would no longer fit into his life. Alexandra intended to keep her husband at a distance, but nonetheless to keep him. Philip was her lifeline to Europe and America and their publishing houses, as well as an emotional anchor. Most important, he sent money. Had she been a poverty-stricken yogi, how warm a reception would the Frenchwoman have received at the courts and diplomatic residencies of Asia? So the errant wife assured her husband that she loved him better than ever.

It is remarkable how this woman kept up a live relationship through the uncertain mails of those days, during nearly a decade and a half of meandering in outrageous places. Sometimes she coyly complimented Mouchy, telling him how much she enjoyed his letters. At other moments, when Philip moaned about his lot, she subjected him to purgative doses of Buddhist philosophy. Alexandra could also resort to emotional blackmail. In May 1914 Philip sold the house in Tunis and moved to the headquarters of the railway in Bône, Algeria. The detachment of his wife turned to rage. How dare he take such a step without consulting her? Philip was the fickle one. She reminded him of past humiliations, of how he'd once taken advantage of her poverty and lack of prospects.

Alexandra knew how to pierce through Philip's armor to his vulnerable conscience. She sang well the ballad of the elder roué seducing the tender young thing. In secret she could watch a tantric sex rite with aplomb, but the Frenchwoman's announced morals were strictly Victorian. When she could no longer stall Philip, Alexandra threatened to become a hermit. She would go live in a cave and he would lose his last hold over her.

During the early fall, Alexandra came upon the four nuns of Chorten Nyima, actual recluses who lived amid wild scenery on the Tibetan side of the border with Sikkim. She was tramping in the mountains with her servants and the temperature had fallen below freezing. Sick with the grippe and an abscess in her ear, she felt taken by a determination to plunge into the land of mystery. Once having crossed the imaginary line, she found the weather crisp but dry and the sunshine radiant.

The little monastery was set high among eagles' nests and air so clear that the rocks glittered like semiprecious stones. Cliffs carved by erosion, sprinkled with pastel-colored pebbles, lent an air of serenity that calmed Alexandra's jittery nerves. Around the *gompa* an impassible, jumbled scenery emanated a serenity beyond expression. Chorten Nyima means "sun shrine," and an ancient legend held that a *chorten* (burial monument) containing precious relics had been transported on the sun's rays from India to here. Secret writings of Padmasambhava were said to be hidden on the grounds. According to popular belief, 108 springs—the Tibetan magical number—watered the area. While only a few were visible to the vulgar, the pure of heart surveyed a well-watered scene indeed.

Once thriving but neglected over the years, the gompa had deteriorated into a crumbly heap occupied by a handful of nuns. Alexandra was moved by the quiet courage of these women whose daily lives were fraught with danger. Snowed in for half the year, the nuns often came to near starvation or falling prey to wild beasts. More terrifying to them, they had to combat evil spirits who took on strange forms. A certain plant was most demonic, for it grew on the edge of dizzying precipices in order to lure victims down into the abyss.

David-Neel would discover that Tibetan women have a strong and determined character. They did not flinch from living or traveling alone over their untamed, bandit-ridden country. They willingly braved a hostile climate and terrain to make pilgrimages and practice their religion. In *Born in Tibet*, Chogyam Trungpa Rinpoche, the founder of meditation centers throughout the West, paid tribute to the fearless nuns who sheltered him on his flight into exile from pursuing Communist Chinese troops. The Tibetan woman's reputation for independence greatly helped Alexandra on her own pilgrimage to Lhasa.

The nuns at Chorten Nyima, despite dirty faces and tattered robes, proved as generous as they were brave. They begged Alexandra to share what they had, including their crude enclosure. After inspecting the ruined city, she chose to pitch her tent outdoors in sight of snowy, inviolate peaks jutting into an azure sky. Once the brilliant sun sank behind the mountains, and the gloom of night spread, everything froze. The warmth of her lama's robe and boots kept the outlander alive. She didn't dare budge out of the covers to save her dried foods from turning to ice. The brutal weather confirmed an old Tibetan proverb, "The coldness of this land will stop tea from pouring."

Woolen gloves didn't prevent the wind from cracking her fingers, nor did constant oil applications keep her face from blistering. Still, she found herself meditating in air that showed her breath as condensed vapor, and the hermit's way impressed her as a natural path toward self-realization. Did solitude create visions, she wondered, or merely permit one to discover that one has been blind till now?

Alexandra knew that she was no saint, but in the spring of 1914—while in Europe the major powers became deeply entangled in hostile moves and countermoves, hostages to fate—she hoped she was less of an imbecile than Western political leaders. She assured Philip that she was not following a whim but an ancient, trodden path that had opened before her. In fact she was marooned through the summer at the palace guest house in Gangtok, waiting for funds to arrive. Philip, after hinting that he'd found a mistress, hadn't written in months.

Alexandra's tedium was relieved when the young maharaja brought tidings from Simla: The British, Chinese, and Tibetan delegates had signed a convention that provided for Tibetan autonomy. While Bell hoped for the creation of an informal British satellite, the Chinese were appeased by dividing Tibet into Inner (Kham and Amdo—closer to China) and Outer (central and western) zones, with China claiming a vague suzerainty over the whole. "Autonomy" for Tibet and "suzerainty" for China, it should be noted, is the formula for a settlement currently favored by H. H. the Dalai Lama, and thus the official position of the Tibetan government in exile.

However, after six months of talks at Simla, British diplomacy had failed to satisfy anyone but Charles Bell and Sir Henry McMahon. The Tibetans had given up their claim to a large tract of mountainous tribal territory wedged between Bhutan and Assam in order that McMahon could draw his famous line between China and India over the crest of the Himalayas. In return Tibet was left still more dependent on British military advice and recognition. Worse, Peking would almost immediately disown its delegates and the convention. Chinese troops moved on eastern Tibet. The ensuing Sino-Tibetan border conflict would run parallel, in minor key, to the overwhelming theme of violence known at the time as The World War.

Alexandra heard the news from Philip in August, and she curiously responded that war with Germany was inevitable and, since France had reliable allies, a good thing. In a demonstration of

"Realpolitik" that would have been the envy of Bismarck, the Iron Chancellor, Alexandra asserted that Russia would suffer but hold up for a considerable period, Britain would be immensely valuable for its navy and its colonies, and Germany was bound to starve to death. That she turned out to be so bellicose (not to mention correct) is less surprising when we recall that her political godmother was the Paris Commune of 1871. The French left had wanted to fight to the last against the Prussians.

During the next few months, David-Neel wandered about in the mountains accompanied by a fellow orientalist, the Scotsman McKechnie, a specialist in Pali, and their retinue of servants. Her state of mind was unsettled, and as soon as she returned to where she could receive or send mail, she demanded news of the war in Europe. When Philip reproached her that someday she would regret being so far from home during these tragic hours, she responded that if she were a man she would return at once to enlist in the army. But to serve as a nurse—the role assigned her as a woman—she regarded as too insignificant.

The war proved convenient for Alexandra. She understood nothing of combat waged with machine guns, tanks, airplanes, and poison gas, and she was convinced it could be won fairly easily. The monster of Prussian militarism had to be crushed forever so the world could live in peace. Alexandra would learn the hard way the lessons that warfare teaches, but not before she had become, in a limited way, a resourceful captain of men.

In the meantime, the common cause reunited her in spirit with dear Mouchy, whom she longed to hug and kiss. Since the seas were too dangerous for her to sail home, talk of returning was put off indefinitely. Philip sent funds, and when the money was temporarily held up, others came to her aid; these included the Maharaja of Nepal, who found her a most interesting phenomenon. It was no peaceful disposition, still less a mushy mysticism, that drew this warrior to Buddhism. Rather, she most admired the yogis who lived in caves, alone with their daring thoughts. These extreme individuals she classed with intellectual freethinkers she had known, such as Reclus or Stirner. However, the yogis, Tibetan or Indian, went far beyond any European, for they possessed the Secret Teachings of tantric lore. This door to the mysteries had remained closed to her.

But now, she assured Philip, she had won acceptance as a disciple by a renowned *gomchen* (great hermit), and she was certain to make rapid progress. But first, as though to erase any lingering doubts, Alexandra was going to suffer a terrible blow.

On December 14 at Lachen, a tiny monastery in the mountains just before the high passes of Tibet, Alexandra heard that after a sudden, brief unexplained illness, the Maharaja of Sikkim had died at the age of thirty-seven. It took six days for the news to arrive. At first, because he had remained so youthful, she was simply shocked. Then she recalled their last outing together when Sidkeong, dressed in an Alpine suit, had climbed so quickly ahead of her that she thought his heart and lungs were made of brass. At the summit, savoring the stillness, they meditated on a rock like a pair of wild birds. Then he had to descend toward the cares of the court, while she was going higher into the Land of Snows.

Sidkeong, a mountain sprite, had leaped from boulder to boulder, waving his Swiss hat, calling back to remind Alexandra to return soon. Now she would never see him again. She was moved to confess, even to Philip, that she had loved Sidkeong, an orphan whose stepmother was his worst enemy. The two of them shared an identity of views, of wounds, that Philip Neel the man of affairs could barely understand. On occasion, the woman would hint at her despair at not finding that special someone who makes all the anguish worthwhile. By her unassuageable sorrow at the maharaja's death, we may conclude she *had* found him in the person of an Asian monarch, just before he was lost to her with grim finality.

However, Sidkeong was a *tulku*, a "phantom body" who, according to Tibetan belief, should only die when he wished, perhaps to be reborn at a more auspicious time. Thus the lamas were talking about mystical reasons for their ruler's passing. When Charles Bell pumped an informant, he got the following:

> Ku-sho says that he heard that the cause of the illness of the Maharaja Sidkeong tulku which was followed by [his] death was from his negligence of services to his ancestral Cho-kyong [demon defenders of the faith] and by his introduction of offering [them] candles instead of butter lamps. Secondly that he proposed to marry a princess of Burma, which angered the Cho-kyong, as she had been of an alien nationality, and that she does not follow the Cho-kyong. Moreover during his illness the late Maharaja failed to observe ser-

vices properly toward his ancestral deities or gods on the usual lines. But Ku-sho does not know the cause of his death.

If Bell learned any more than this, he did not commit it even to his private notebooks.

Sidkeong had pushed his reforms with undue haste, thereby making not only demonic but material enemies. He had invited to his country both Europeans and learned monks of the southern school. He appointed them as teachers over his own lamas and invited them to preach at the monasteries. David-Neel admitted she had initiated the practice of regular sermons before the assembled monks. In 1937 when the German Buddhist who became known as Lama Govinda visited Sikkim, he reported that the lamas still resented Sidkeong's introduction of "foreign thought."

Indian historian George Kotturan writes that Sidkeong "had voiced his opposition to the continuance of the privileges of the feudal aristocracy and the religious hierarchy of the state. . . . When he was taken ill, it is believed, they conspired with a British physician who was attending on him and engineered his death." Lal Basnet adds another sinister element: "Sidkeong Tulku, by his reformist zeal, had displeased not only the feudal landlords but also . . . Charles Bell. His death was as much a relief to the Political Officer as it was to the kazis and monks."

Bell admitted that Sidkeong was "in many respects an outspoken critic of British methods," but he insisted the maharaja was on the whole pleased by the effects of British rule in opening Sikkim to the outside world. Although Bell was not likely to be involved in Sidkeong's death, his successor certainly proved more pliable. And murder as a political weapon was and remains common in south Asia. Half a century later an American, Hope Cooke, married the crown prince of Sikkim, nephew of Sidkeong. His father the maharaja, a guilt-ridden old man haunted by the imperious ghost of his mother, was the younger son put on the throne by the intrigues of Queen Drolma. He soon died, and the American became Queen Hopela and pregnant. Browsing about the rather gloomy royal palace—the same that Alexandra knew—she came upon an unused room with a glorious view of the mountains:

> It's the room, I hear, in which my husband's uncle and previous incarnate, Sidkeong, was killed—either by gross ineptitude or delib-

erately—by a Bengali physician employed by the British because Sidkeong had proved too wise and strong an obstacle to British paramountcy in Sikkim. Although the details of Sidkeong's death are grisly . . . this room seems neutral, free of spirits, and is sun-filled, even though a sparrow-nested eave hangs over the window. . . I want this room for the baby.

In time Queen Hopela had to flee Gangtok to prevent the murder of her own son, the crown prince—by poison.

Throughout the Himalayas there grows a sinister flower, the blue monkshood. In former days an essence distilled from this plant was used to tip arrowheads; a mere scratch killed. The skill in concocting this subtle poison has not been lost, and Queen Drolma, practitioner of subtle arts, likely possessed it. In our version of events, after she had administered a dose to her stepson, she called in a physician to attend him in his last agony. Finding nothing specific, the doctor administered brandy and heaped Sidkeong with blankets. He listed the cause of death as heart failure.

Whatever effect Sidkeong's demise had on the pace of British colonial history, it shattered Alexandra's dreams. Throughout the winter of 1914, living in her tent at the remote monastery, she felt a great ache in the place of her heart. Wisely, she declined to attend the lengthy and elaborate funeral rites for the maharaja, culminating in cremation. She did go to a nearby ground to watch the burning of a peasant woman's body. She recalled mournfully how not long ago Sidkeong had spoken of their traveling together and how he would introduce her to his friend the King of Siam. It grew so cold she had to warm her feet by the crackling pyre. Suddenly, she couldn't help imagining Sidkeong aflame, his dark hair a torch, his crisp little hands sizzling, the abrupt explosion of the brain inside his skull. In Sikkim it is believed that if a person dies violently his ghost may linger for some time, apearing to those dear to him.

The transience of friendship, of love, were brought home to a sorrowful David-Neel. How stupid to cling to other people, who were bound one day to crumble to dust. Life on earth was the realm of Shiva the destroyer. The seeker, though learned in Buddhism, hadn't worked sufficiently on herself. She was now to turn from the perishable to the imperishable, spirit soaring like an eagle over the craggy heights.

BOOK TWO

The Pilgrim

Far hence in Asia
On the smooth convent roofs
On the gold terraces
Of holy Lhasa
Bright shines the sun.

—MATTHEW ARNOLD

Chapter 11
Cavern in the Sky

1914: the year the world went to pieces and Alexandra David-Neel took up the meditative life of a hermit. The death of the young Maharaja of Sikkim put an end to her notions of parading from one oriental court to another. The Great War prevented her return to France, and instead, in the heart of the mountains, she entered into an intimate relationship with another man, where he was the master and she the disciple. Often David-Neel had complained about the closed nature of Tibetan Buddhism. Its art and symbols, not to mention many of the lamas, didn't easily reveal their secrets to an outsider. But a miracle occurred when a great hermit, a reputed sorcerer, accepted her as his pupil.

Alexandra first met the Gomchen of Lachen—abbot of the monastery there—in 1912 at Gangtok where he had descended reluctantly to conduct a ceremony at court. When Prince Sidkeong introduced the Frenchwoman, he couldn't have imagined she would become the disciple of this revered mystic. Or could he? At any rate, it was his legacy to his dear friend. She found the lama, about fifty at the time, beguilingly ugly. Garbed for his part in the tantric ritual, he wore a five-sided crown, a rosary necklace of 108 pieces of skulls, an apron of carved human bones and a *phurba* (magic dagger—used in rituals to quell demons). The Gomchen's hair was plaited in a long thick braid that touched his heels, and from his ears dangled gold rings studded with turquoise. Alexandra had never seen such eyes—like hot coals. No wonder common folk supposed he could fly through the air, kill people at a distance, or command demons.

Lord Ronaldshay, the governor of Bengal, wrote that the

Gomchen was one lama who "commanded the deepest and most widespread veneration." Conversing with him, Ronaldshay felt that "he had reached the stage of Arhatship and was, therefore, beyond good and evil." Marco Pallis, mountain climber and seeker who was influenced by David-Neel, dedicated his excellent *Peaks and Lamas*, to "the great contemplator, abbot of Lachen." The awestruck Pallis described the Gomchen some twenty years after Alexandra knew him:

> His face was broad, with twinkling, humorous eyes, his hair long and wispy; from his ears hung a pair of large gold rings. . . . The whole effect might have been comic but for the aura of power that seemed to radiate from his person, making one feel at once that here was no ordinary mortal. Actually, I have never looked on a more impressive face, despite its grotesqueness.

During the following two years, Alexandra took part in occasional conversations with the Gomchen in his apartment at the monastery. This collection of a few humble structures, home to a handful of monks, was perched on a mountain slope overlooking the little Himalayan village of Lachen at eight thousand feet, inhabited by sturdy, superstitious hillfolk. Lachen means "the big pass," and the main occupation of the region in the northeast of Sikkim, aside from subsistence farming, was the raising of yaks employed to carry goods across the nearby high passes to Tibet. These good-humored, sure-footed, shaggy, horned beasts also provided the natives with meat, dung for fuel, and hair to weave into tents, and the female (a *dri*) gave milk to churn into the omnipresent butter.

The initial talks with the lama were difficult. David-Neel, a beginner at Tibetan, needed to use the Reverend Owen, from a nearby mission, as interpreter. The minister did his best, but seated stiffly in an armchair between the two Buddhists who assumed a lotus posture on the rug, he felt out of place. The Gomchen was dressed in a more everyday vein: a white skirt down to his feet, a garnet-colored waistcoat, and through the wide armholes, the voluminous sleeves of a yellow shirt. These long sleeves, which in the old photographs hang nearly to the ground, were a mark of the mandarin class, indicating that the wearer had enough servants not to need to use his hands.

Questions and answers flew between master and would-be disciple. The two ranged over the history and doctrines of Buddhism; they discussed everything from abstruse points to the need for ritual. Owen tried to keep up, but his translations grew perfunctory. The Buddhists took this as a signal to settle quietly into deep meditation, continuing their dialogue by other means. The minister, not daring to leave, fretted over being late for his Bible class at the mission.

Despite the barrier of language, Alexandra and the Gomchen were instantly delighted with one another. She felt that here was a clear-thinking skeptic who had penetrated the trappings of religion to its inner core. But even she was astounded by his reply to her question about the efficacy of a huge prayer wheel that was housed in a separate temple nearby—the largest wheel in Sikkim, reputed to make one and a half billion prayers per revolution. "These vain repetitions of wheels, the worship of images on an altar, even the beautiful mandalas, they mean nothing at all. Their only use is to attract and occupy the attention of average men, who fail to understand that nirvana is within their grasp. You have already seen this."

Alexandra felt certain she had much more to learn and that the Gomchen could guide her to it. So in the early autumn of the first year of the Great War's carnage, inspired by the nuns of Chorten Nyima, she determined to climb the dizzying heights to the hermit's hideaway, the Cave of Clear Light at De-chen, twelve thousand feet in the sky.

David-Neel rode beyond Lachen through Alpine scenery where dull green lichen "clung to the fir trees and streamed like great handfuls of frayed wool in the wind." Indifferent to a chilling mist, she stayed at the uppermost *dak* bungalow at tiny Thangu, a half-day's outing from the hermitage at De-chen. However, she had no horse on which to ride higher. The Sikkimese in charge, afraid his European guest might walk, offered his own horse, a small tame reddish beast. Alexandra mounted and the horse threw her into the air and down on a patch of grass. Knocked cold, she awoke in pain but not badly hurt.

The bungalow keeper was mortified and assured her he would make the pony behave. But as soon as the man grasped its bridle, the puny animal kicked him onto some rocks where he landed on his head. He was carried off ranting that the pony was perfectly tame. The natives attributed this episode to the power of the Gomchen, who they claimed had set up a psychic barrier to guard his hideaway. Alexandra's servants looked glum and warned her not to go. A lad of fifteen, Aphur Yongden, recently entered into her service, cowered in a corner crying. From her sickbed the seeker ridiculed their talk of harmful demons, and when two days later the lama sent a mare for her, she rode up the steep, barren trail until she spotted the waving prayer flags of a hermitage.

The Gomchen came out to greet her, and they shared a pot of buttered tea in a cave finished with a rough wall and gaping holes for windows. After tea the Gomchen retired to his own cavern about a mile farther up the mountain. Darkness fell before Alexandra could accustom herself to the surroundings. Her servants spread blankets on the bare rock floor and disappeared. No moon, she peeped out to spy a glacial mass of mountains above the gloomy valley. The roar of a distant waterfall punctuated the otherwise still night. Fearful of tumbling into the void below, she crept back inside.

The moment she lay down, the kerosene lamp went out. She had no matches and could not move an inch for fear of breaking a limb. A cold wind blew, while a single star was visible through the window. She thought it must be her lucky star because she had never before been so happy. She was at last free of the snares of luxury and ownership that others thought so wonderful. The hermit's life was the thing!

Next day Alexandra scrambled up to the Gomchen's Cave of Clear Light. In 1895, without fanfare, the lama had established himself in this cell. For five years he saw no one, subsisting on scraps of food left before his door by herdsmen. When these superstitious folk solicited him for a blessing, or more likely a curse on an enemy, he ignored them. The hermit's conduct so impressed the monks of nearby Lachen that he gained an authority over them, and they improved both his diet and surroundings. By the time of Alexandra's arrival, she found the master living in relative comfort.

The Gomchen's cave was larger and better furnished than the one below. A wooden step led to the entrance, which was hidden by a curtain; one entered into the kitchen, then back through a natural opening to a small grotto, the living room. Here wooden chests formed a sort of couch, large cushions were placed on the ground, and slabs of brightly painted wood were set up on feet as low tables. Farther back were the usual altar offerings: copper bowls filled with water, grain, and butter lamps. Religious scrolls covered the walls, and beneath one of these stood an inconspicuous cabinet said to house the demons subservient to the potent lama. On its solitary perch, this was truly a cavern in the sky.

Terms of a discipleship were agreed on whereby Alexandra promised obedience to the guru for an indefinite period. She must not take any journeys without his permission, a proviso her husband might have envied. In return the anchorite dropped his cherished plan to go into a traditional three-year, three-month retreat. Instead, Alexandra would teach him English while he improved her Tibetan. If she proved worthy, the Gomchen would reveal to her the secret oral teachings of tantric Buddhism, which were hardly known in the West.

After joining her tent to the lower cave, David-Neel moved in, filled with the spirit of adventure. Yongden and the other servants were housed in a hut a few yards away. The Frenchwoman had no intention of performing herself the menial tasks necessary to keep alive in the rarified atmosphere, and Yongden, just out of school, wasn't much help either. Alexandra found that life reduced to the essentials pleased her, and the Gomchen treated her like his younger sister. He supplied her with yak butter, milk, and fruits from his own limited store. Unfortunately, he fancied himself a cook and invited his pupil to dinner. His mutton soup was foul, and Alexandra, after she downed it with a smile, was forced to rush outside and disgorge it. She was sick all night.

In mid-November their idyll was broken up. The Gomchen, obliged to return to his monastery on business, didn't dare leave the foreigner alone to face the snows of a Himalayan winter. The hermitage was inaccessible for four whole months when drifts blocked the trail. So Alexandra accompanied her teacher and set up the tent at Lachen. She boasted that with a kerosene heater she could keep the temperature around 45 degrees Fahrenheit. Her lama's robe helped keep her warm, until one night in early January, weighted by snow, the tent fell in on top of her. It was like a bad dream, made worse because she had to move into a cell in the monastery.

The folk of Lachen and their primitive communal notions proved a real nightmare. There were some eighty families in the neighborhood, growing barley and potatoes, pasturing yaks in the summer, and all year practicing a caricature of a socialist government. Strict regulations prevented one family from gaining the slightest advantage over the others. According to Marco Pallis, Alexandra was "nearly forced to accept a whole pack of hounds because a family that sold her one dog was considered, by so doing, to have tried to steal a march on its neighbors." All fines went into a communal fund from which a feast would be given once a year. The elders and the monks got the good things to eat, the poor got scraps, and the women nothing. In response Alexandra threw a feast for the women and became persona non grata to the officious elders.

Other distractions at Lachen included the nearby Protestant mission, also not to Alexandra's liking. The British ladies had converted a few Tibetans by giving them clothes and presents, as well as Bible lessons. These acts of charity confused them, since poor as they might be they were accustomed to make offerings to their holy men. It smacked of bribery to the French Buddhist, although outwardly she remained on chatty terms with the missionaries. The women who came to her cell for tea and biscuit—which she baked herself—couldn't help staring at the Gomchen. Probably they considered him "a dirty old man," for the lama was fairly robust and his manners were those of a peasant. No matter, it was politic for Alexandra to keep on the ladies' good side.

She tried to put Sidkeong's death behind her, but her temper was frayed by unexpressed grief. When both the village and monastery celebrated the Tibetan New Year by a feast worthy of a Brueghel painting—eating and drinking in the open air—she could scarcely hide her disgust. She watched in glum silence as the normally hardworking peasants and frugal monks let loose. Shanks of meat sizzled and cooking pots bubbled, while the cooks stirred strange brews with their fingers. The valley teemed with racing and wrestling figures, and above a handful of monks danced clumsily in a sort of chorus line. Everybody was getting tipsy on *chang*, the local barley beer.

Alexandra sought out the Gomchen to complain that the dissolute clergy were showing disrespect to their late sovereign, as well as violating Buddha's precepts. She demanded that he put a stop to the carousing within the monastery grounds. Mocking her as *"Mem Sahib,"* the lama suggested she go commiserate with the prudes at the mission, who wished to force their notions of right and wrong on others. Pallis praises the Gomchen's "urbanity, tempered with a dash of satire," which enabled him to put Sidkeong's death in perspective. For he, too, had counted on the late maharaja to reform feudal Sikkim.

Now as the revels grew more feverish, men and women staggering about, Alexandra felt absurd. *She* was the outsider here. She headed for the mountains where the winter sun shone brilliantly on the snowy crests. A recent fall added to the silvery carpet. Alone, Alexandra planted herself on a rock and strapped herself upright in the Tibetan fashion. Master of miles of scenery, she let go of care, slipping into a deep meditation beyond joy or sorrow.

Through the winter, David-Neel made amazing progress in Tibetan. She found herself conversing fluently with the Gomchen, who spoke with a proper Lhasa accent, and she began to believe he was really a wizard. Her feelings toward him swung between repulsion at his peasant manners to awe at the clarity of his thought. When he spoke on Buddhist metaphysics, eyes glowing with fervor, the bond of *chela* (disciple) to guru was being forged; indeed, she was being tied in to the long line of masters who had preceded him.

In Tibetan Buddhism the telepathic method is regarded as superior to both written and oral teachings. However, there were few masters left able to employ telepathy, and fewer disciples psychically attuned to learning in this way. The Gomchen and Alexandra would sit together in silence in a darkened room, focused on the same object, the aspects of a diety for example. After a time the Gomchen would ask what she had seen and if it were the same as his projection. The goal was an entirely unified mental state. Later, camping in the wilds, Alexandra would record instances of the use of telepathy at great distances, of receiving messages the Tibetans termed "written on the wind."

In the summer of 1915, the Gomchen returned to his mountain hideaway and commenced preparations against the lengthy winter, and there Alexandra joined him. In sight of the five peaks of Kanchinjunga—called the storehouse of the treasure of the gods because its snows were first to reflect dawn's gold and last to don the sable of night—the seeker prepared for her personal exploration into the mysteries of being. But she could undertake this search only after performing the more mundane tasks that would ensure her survival.

Her cave, the lower one, was improved considerably by adding on a wooden two-story structure. On the ground floor the outer room was divided in two by a curtain: one half served as combination kitchen and study (the best place to keep warm), the other half as a bedroom that communicated with the cavern. Upstairs was a guest room, and any currently unused space was taken up with stored goods. Alexandra had the convenience of an indoor toilet (though not plumbing) and a tiny outdoor balcony. Unfortunately, the whole job had been done by local peasants who were terrible carpenters.

From halfway around the world, Philip sent practical advice about the building of what he called his wife's "Huron hut," since she had compared herself to a heroine in a James Fenimore Cooper novel. After months of mistakes the dwelling was completed, carpets laid on the floor, and the walls painted. An exultant Alexandra heaped praise on Mouchy for helping to accomplish her wildest childhood fantasy. Assistance came, too, from Sikkim's new maharaja, Tashi Namgyal, Sidkeong's younger half-brother, who sent a quantity of expensive brick tea. This and the twelve kilograms of yak butter furnished by the Gomchen, plus a little salt, were the ingredients of that beverage the Tibetans drank so constantly. Alexandra thrived on this rich brew, reinforcing her notion that in a past life she had been one of Genghis Khan's Mongols.

September brought the "little winter"—a prelude—and snow as high as a man, although Alexandra continued to bathe daily in her zinc tub. She plunged into Tibetan studies. The Gomchen spoke freely about the inner meaning of Buddhist doctrine, and he grew rhapsodical on the lives of famous mystics; but he turned reticent when she brought up hidden tantric rites. No doubt, he felt the force of the Frenchwoman's skepticism, and that someone as strong willed as she would have to make her own discoveries. Suddenly her old enemy neurasthenia struck. The crisis of spirit deepened until Alexandra could scarcely bear to be alone. At night she had pains in her heart and terrible dreams about the war. Desperate for information, she sent her boy Yongden into the snows to seek out the latest news on the fighting, so far away. Unknowingly, she was on the edge of a breakthrough in her practice.

To divert his pupil, the Gomchen took her climbing. If in thought he was wildly venturesome, in mountaineering he proved steady and taciturn. Alexandra, much slimmer from a sparse diet, felt chipper. She pushed out of mind earlier climbs with the handsome maharaja. The behavior of this rustic philosopher bewildered her, since one moment he was genial, the next sardonic. He could cry or laugh with the ease of a child. His Achilles heel was his love for a pet cat.

The pampered kitty lived in the hermit's cave and was accustomed to eating from the Gomchen's hand. One day, annoyed at the comings and goings of porters, the pet ran away. That same night, telling no one, the lama left in search of her. Without warm clothes or provisions he walked all night, feeling his way with a stick. The path led across dangerous waterfalls, around steep cliffs, and over fallen boulders. Finally, the Gomchen reached a spot where he expected the truant to arrive, but in fact the cat had circled home. The sage spent four nights in a dank cave, and when worried villagers searched him out, they received a scolding for their trouble. The exhausted lama trudged home, sneezing and coughing, to find his kitty yawning and stretched in her usual place by the fire.

By early autumn the Gomchen had retired into his cave and gone into a trance. This might last for days or weeks, during which time no one was allowed to approach him. Marco Pallis witnessed the Gomchen on the verge of entering such a state—"hovering on the brink, about to take flight to undreamed-of realms"—the timing of which was not entirely under his control. When Pallis explained that he climbed mountain peaks in order to find perfect solitude, the Gomchen scoffed: "The solitude to seek is the concentration of your own heart; if you have once found it, it will not matter where you are."

Alexandra couldn't afford to be so philosophical. All about her reigned confusion. In Tibet the warfare continued against the Chinese invaders, and in Sikkim the peasants were resisting conscription for the great war overseas. Nevertheless, many thousands of Gurkhas and other Himalayan dwellers volunteered to fight in Europe or the Middle East, willing to soldier for pay. The price of supplies shot sky high, and Alexandra was anxiously awaiting the last caravan of the year before snowfalls closed the passes. It finally arrived with loads of butter, rice, barley flour, potatoes, turnips, lentils, and beans: the whole of the former gourmet's diet for the next few months.

Christmas Eve 1915 found David-Neel in despair. She missed Philip and wanted to go home. Her rheumatism, troubling all along, had led to fever, nausea, and pain so severe she sometimes couldn't stand up. This night, asleep in the back of the cave where it was warmer, she was awakened by a servant. The roof of the upper level had caught fire. Out she trudged into the snow in her nightdress. Shivering, she watched the boys put out the blaze. At five in the morning, the mountains loomed like vast shadows, and an odd calm spread over her soul.

Once the heavy snows fell and she was trapped, Alexandra began to make great strides. All winter the Gomchen permitted his disciple to invade his solitude. Every other day, dressed in a heavy outer cloak and high felt boots, she set forth on the slippery path to the lama's cabin. There his wife—he was Red Hat and permitted one—removed Alexandra's wet things and hung them before the fire to dry. She served hot buttered tea to professor and pupil, who fell to work over the subtleties of Tibetan grammar, history, philosophy. The session done, Alexandra donned her cloak and boots and flung herself into the glittering light of late afternoon. Making her way down, she might sing an old chant:

> Alone on a mountain
> possessing nothing
> sleeping on the rocks of a cavern
> One feels free
> stripped of all beliefs
> greater than a raja
> greater than God.

Day in and day out the landscape, under the dominion of majestic snowcapped peaks, was extraordinarily quiet, all the streams and rivulets frozen. Alexandra was left to her reading and practice. Her sole diversion was a bear who came by in hope of being fed. She had no fear of so-called wild animals and got as close as the bear would allow. But with nowhere to go, Alexandra had to come to grips with her own phantoms. Desires, hopes, and fears dissolved in the acid of self-knowledge. In meditation her life was played back: childhood in Paris, youth in Brussels. As though she was watching a film, she pictured her parents quarreling, herself on stage singing opera, scenes of failure and humiliation. She viscerally felt the boredom and tension of her married years and the few triumphs of her career as a writer.

To herself she cried, laughed, and groaned, but she kept on sitting until what others thought of as her self—the perception they still carried in their minds—was like one deceased. No clear-cut stages marked the path toward Alexandra's enlightenment, and no transport of joy (samadhi) enlivened it. She experienced only steadily growing, quiet courage. She wondered if there was any more to it.

Alexandra's strength increased sufficiently to attempt an experiment with tumo breathing, one of the Tibetan practices that seems miraculous. She had stumbled on its good effects inadvertently, much as with lung-gom walking. One evening, huddled by the fire, she began to breathe rhythmically and felt her feet warm up. But she soon grew tired. From her reading she knew what was happening. Tumo was the most vital practice of the anchorites, enabling them to survive brutal weather without fuel, of which there is little in the mountains, naked or clad only in a light shift. The transcendental yogi Milarepa, its foremost exponent, praised tumo as the best clothing. About Milarepa's disciples, the Oxford scholar Evans-Wentz wrote: "They were proof against extremes of cold . . . and so needed to wear no other garment [than cotton] even in the arctic winter of the high Himalayan altitudes of Tibet."

Alexandra, although she had plenty of clothes, found the heavier ones burdensome. Remembering the warm breezes off the Tunisian desert, she could only sigh. In March as the weather moderated, she moved into her yak-hair tent and threw off bulky clothes—and caught cold. The Gomchen grew sufficiently alarmed to instruct his overeager pupil in tumo. The principle methods are auto-suggestion and retention of breath: tumo is a meditation on the fire within.

Like all Tibetan exercises, tumo is spiritual. The aspirant must have permission from his guru and a proven ability to concentrate. He must be isolated and avoid foul air and noise. Before sunrise he sits scantily clad in the lotus posture doing various drills to clear the

nostrils. Then with the out-breath he expels pride, anger, covetous-
ness, and sloth, and with the in-breath he draws into himself the
Buddha spirit. Slow, deep inspirations act as a bellows to fan a smoldering fire at the pit of the stomach. If the practitioner is successful,
warmth will rise to encompass his whole being.

Traditionally, graduates of this course were tested on a frosty
night with a hard wind blowing. They sat cross-legged on the bank of
an ice-encrusted river or lake while sheets were dipped in the water
and one was draped over each man's torso; using tumo, he was
expected to dry it. Then the sheets were soaked again and the exercise repeated. By daybreak the successful practitioner might have
dried as many as forty sheets.

Alexandra's final exam was less exacting. On a moonlit night in
spring she proceeded to a lonely mountain stream and bathed.
Afterward she sat naked and meditated until dawn. Although at first
she felt no ill effects, she soon came down with a flu. Still, she had
conquered a lifelong aversion to harsh weather, and now she could
step out on her balcony before dawn, clad in thin muslin, to catch the
first hint of gold on Kanchinjunga's five crowns.

By summer 1916, David-Neel's isolation was drawing to a close.
She could not relish the role of disciple for long, and despite her
threats to Philip, she had no intention of becoming a hermit. The
Gomchen guessed as much, and he habitually told his pupil about
his travels in Tibet as a younger man. He casually acquainted
her with the geography, inhabitants, and customs of the land. The
Gomchen hinted that she must continue her education on the
road—as a pilgrim—and convey what she had learned to the world
at large.

Certainly, Alexandra sometimes looked sadly, almost with terror,
at the path that wound down the mountain into the valley of Lachen,
which one day would lead her back to the mundane world of sor-
rows. That was the way to France, North Africa, home, and husband.
But there existed another direction, and with the arrival of warmer
weather the traveler turned her attention to the forbidden passes to
the north. In her writing she would indignantly point out that in the
past, before the Anglo-Tibetan entente, the Land of the Religion had
been far simpler to enter. Now she found roadblocks set up along the
Himalayan routes some fifty kilometers from the Tibetan border. Her

cave, although well within those posts, lay only a half-day's hike from this forbidden world of knowledge.

Alexandra's two difficult winters spent in cell and cave bore fruit many years later in a slim, deceptively titled volume, *The Secret Oral Teachings in Tibetan Buddhist Sects.* The book, written by David-Neel at eighty and first published in 1951 is not arcane but a reflection of the long rational conversations she had with the Gomchen while the buttered tea simmered and the wind howled outside. Alan Watts called it "the most direct, no-nonsense, and down-to-earth explanation of Mahayana Buddhism which has thus far been written."

Alexandra's thought is as cool and clear as a Tibetan lake. The spirit of Gautama Buddha pervades it, the pressing need to transcend the pain of isolation and to achieve the peace of knowing that all is Nothing. By the latter term Buddhists mean the Void from which all matter springs and into which we—our many perishable egos—are constantly dissolving. Alexandra tried to explain to Philip that she'd had to leave him; he no more could have held her than clenched the fine desert sand in his fist.

Shortly before parting from the teacher to whom she owed so much, Alexandra suggested the outline of a book about the knowledge he had imparted to her. The master scoffed that it was a waste of time: "The great majority of readers and hearers are the same all over the world. . . . If you speak to them of profound Truths they yawn, and, if they dare, they leave you, but if you tell them absurd fables they are all eyes and ears." He was playing the devil's advocate, since he, too, was a reformer at heart. Finally, he gave the project his blessing with one word: "Try!"

Some twenty years later, in the 1930s, another Western seeker, the young man of German descent who would become known as Lama Govinda, visited the Gomchen at De-chen. The land of his forebears had gone mad, and the world was drifting toward a second great calamity. Inspired by the example of David-Neel, the saddened scholar turned East for enlightenment. Tashi Namgyal the Maharaja of Sikkim, by then middle-aged, extended help by equipping a little caravan to take Govinda to the venerated hermit. The eager pilgrim had to halt for the night at the bungalow at Thangu, not far below the hermitage.

Strangely, before falling asleep, the young man felt as though another had taken over his mind and willpower and he was losing his identity. At once he "realized that it could be none other than the hermit, who . . . had entered my body and taken possession of it, probably quite unintentionally, due to the power of his concentration." Govinda fought the growing magnetism, jolted into action by the terror of annihilation. Tensely, he drew a self-portrait to prove that he still existed. Then he was able to sleep. In the morning he climbed up to the Cave of Clear Light. The hermit greeted him with a smile and served tea. They spoke of Alexandra David-Neel and looked over newspaper clippings about her that had reached the Gomchen. Govinda told him "how deeply I was impressed by his *chela's* works." The old lama in turn praised her "endurance and strength of character." Was he aware of what had gone on the night before?

The Gomchen warned against what he termed the disease afflicting the world—morality without wisdom—and he offered the seeker a subject for meditation: the Eighteen Kinds of Voidness. Before he left, the future Lama Govinda became convinced that the innocent-seeming yogi had purposely sent the force that invaded his inner self. He was equally certain the Gomchen had chosen Alexandra as the ideal person to broadcast the ancient, secret knowledge of which humanity stood in desperate need. Her works, translated into the major languages, were being read by millions. If they failed to alter the traumatic course of history, that was beyond the power of any sage or author.

Chapter 12
Asia Marvelous and Diverse

Charles Bell occupied a unique place in the diplomacy of the early twentieth century. He was charged with defending an empire that, at least to its subject peoples, appeared unshakable yet harbored within itself the seeds of dissolution. Neither a powerful Lord Curzon or a dashing Lawrence of Arabia, liable to grab headlines and attract biographers, Bell managed to accomplish more in the realm of understanding and trust than the theorist or the hero. Undramatic about his attachment to Tibet, he warmly supported its interests and set policies in motion that helped keep the country independent until the 1950s. In 1919 he would resign as Resident Political Officer in Sikkim, but in the next year he returned as special ambassador to Tibet. London had decided to grant him a stay in Lhasa.

Before the World War, Britain had agreements with both Russia and China that constituted a sort of Closed-Door policy to the Sacred Realm. By 1920 those other two empires had fallen into disarray, and the Foreign Office felt free to pursue its own policies, including strengthening the Tibetan army. Bell was sent to Lhasa, remained nearly a year, and gathered much material of interest. In 1921 he again resigned and retired to an estate in Berkshire. Amid a fine collection of oriental artworks, he wrote books on the people and religion of Tibet, as well as his *Portrait of the Dalai Lama,* about both the institution and his good friend the Thirteenth.

Bell was careful, astute, and sympathetic to Buddhism and its practitioners; his final loyalties were fixedly British. He seems to have fought the temptation of becoming, in Lawrence's words, "the man who could see things through the veils at once of two customs, two educations, two environments." Such a man, insisted the author of *Seven Pillars of Wisdom*, was bound to go mad. Bell was too much the diplomat for that, but occasionally he could act with a demonic fury and swiftness.

In July 1916, when Alexandra David-Neel set out for Shigatse in southcentral Tibet, she was crossing a line pencilled atop a mountain range on a map—a barrier invisible to the naked eye. She traveled at the express invitation of the Panchen Lama, and yet she knew she risked the wrath of the Resident in Sikkim. She was aware that the British policed the frontier, allowing only their own representatives and a few merchants to pass. She took care to skirt the Chumbi Valley where she would likely have been spotted. David-Neel understood from discussions with Bell himself that "Tibet would be delighted to be under a British protectorate," and that British soldiers, telegraphers, and trade agents in southern Tibet were the vanguard of this arrangement.

At this time, David-Neel failed to realize how closing the country to foreigners was also a Tibetan policy insisted on by the abbots of the powerful monasteries around Lhasa. The latter were afraid that foreign influence would weaken their own hold on affairs, and they vigorously opposed any modern ideas or visitors. As Hugh Richardson, a successor to Bell and dean of Tibetanists, has written us, "The Tibetans were far from simple and naive when their own affairs were concerned. They used the British as a cat's-paw to keep people out." One authority with a more open mind was the Panchen Lama, the abbot of Tashilhunpo monastery, who despite his exalted spiritual rank exercised only a local temporal power.

Alexandra, accompanied by Yongden, crossed the border on horseback, trailing a pack mule carrying two small tents and provisions. With a magic suddenness, masses of angry clouds dissolved and the sky turned into a deep blue setting for a sun whose light struck sparks against distant snow-shaded peaks. The houses were built of stone with flat roofs, and the cast of people's faces was Mongolian. At Tranglung, Alexandra visited a sorcerer who reputedly could make ritual cakes (*torma*) fly through the air to punish his enemies. He turned out to be mild mannered and polite, unwilling to harm a fly. The pair wandered on, sleeping in the huts of peasants when they could. The European didn't try to disguise herself, finding the people friendly and police as rare as crime.

Melting snows made the rivers tricky to ford. While the travelers were hoping to attain Kuma, a village of thermal springs, a freak storm stranded them short of their destination. Hail struck, then snow began to fall so quickly it soon reached to their knees. A nearby brook overflowed into their camp, and the discouraged pair had to spend the night huddled under one soggy tent. Alexandra felt that these trials were too fatiguing even for the Amazon that she had become. Yet she tried to soak in the indefinable atmosphere of Tibet, fearing she might never be so fortunate again.

Alexandra brightened when she reached Tashilhunpo, beyond the busy market town of Shigatse, and the large monastic city of red and white houses appeared even more splendid than she had imagined. Although she knew it was unheard of for a foreign woman to dwell among the celibate Yellow Hats, Alexandra sent Yongden to request lodgings within the enclosure. She was delighted when comfortable rooms were placed at her disposal. Inquisitive functionaries were soon quizzing the visitor on her origin and business. At first they confused Paris with Phari—pronounced alike— a village to the south. Then a debate ensued over whether the Frenchwoman was or was not a foreigner. She maintained that since *philing* ("stranger") literally meant someone from overseas, and you could reach her country by walking (in the eighteenth century Csoma de Koros, a Hungarian, had done this), she wasn't a foreigner. In the midst of the confusion, there appeared an unassuming gentleman in a simple habit.

Alexandra was won by the Panchen Lama's refinement. He knew where Paris was and pronounced it correctly. His conversation was that of an educated man and a sincere Buddhist. Alexandra had supposed that the country beyond the Himalayas would grow wilder, but she realized that, on the contrary, she was coming in touch with an old, truly civilized people. In 1906 the intrepid, not to say brash, Swedish explorer Sven Hedin had visited the Tashi Lama, another name for the same incarnation. He was struck by the abbot's unfeigned charm, his warm smile and kind expression. Even Charles Bell, concerned that the Panchen was a potential rival to the Dalai Lama, stated, "On account of his great sanctity his influence is very great." However, he sensed that the still young man didn't lack worldly ambition.

Bell points out that the Panchen Lama is considered to be an incarnation of Amitabha, the Buddha of Infinite Light, who is regarded as the spiritual guide of Avalokitesvara, the Lord of Mercy, whose emanation is the Dalai Lama; therefore, "it is held by many Tibetans that the Panchen Lama is spiritually higher than the Dalai." This bit of metaphysics mattered not to Alexandra, but she was delighted that the Panchen took seriously the Tibetan name bestowed on her by the Gomchen: Lamp of Wisdom. The prelate and his mother conducted their guest through the temples, halls, and palaces of the large monastic establishment. Alexandra was stunned by the splendor: gold, silver, and turquoise decorated doors, altars, and tombs. Household objects used by important lamas blazed with jewels. While there was no denying all this magnificence, the display finally struck the seeker as pointless. She couldn't help yearning for the solitudes where bears and leopards prowled, and for the Gomchen, whose manner of life suddenly seemed refined.

The orientalist did thrive on dialogues with the monks, some three thousand eight hundred strong, half of whom were scholars. Confronted with this vast storehouse of ancient information, a dynamo of psychic uplift, Alexandra realized how little progress on the path she had made. Yet the Panchen, impressed by the European's sincerity and knowledge of scripture, invited her to remain in Tibet under his patronage. She was tempted, but her keen nose for political winds warned her that the number two lama lacked the authority to make his word stick. A quarrel between the courts at Shigatse and Lhasa was brewing, principally over whether the Panchen would contribute to the building of a new model army, urged on by the British. In 1923 the Panchen decided to flee to Peking, where he became the focus of China's effort to reestablish influence in Tibet.

David-Neel's patron would die in Peking in 1933, and his successor, the Tenth Panchen Lama, held more or less a prisoner in China through much of his life, would die suddenly in 1989 after criticizing the harshness of military rule in Tibet. His successor, the boy Gedhun Choekyi Nyima, chosen in the traditional manner under the supervision (from India) of the Dalai Lama, has been spirited out of Tibet and is kept under house arrest somewhere in the Chinese country-side. Chinese authorities have chosen a candidate of their own, who—after he has been educated to their liking—will be instrumental in selecting the next Dalai Lama. Even before that time the true Panchen may meet the same abrupt fate administered to his prede-cessors. It is the old game of power politics mixed with religion, one that Alexandra had experienced to her sorrow.

Besides, she wasn't ready to live out her days as a yogi. Her luggage, books, notes, and photo negatives were stored at Calcutta. Paris and London were asking her to give conferences on Hinduism and Buddhism; why, even the Americans were interested! First she was headed to northern Asia, ready to brave the seas for a plenitude of untranslated texts. Once the war ended, she would sail home to her Mouchy.

She left Shigatse in early August with additional possessions. The Panchen bestowed on her the robe of a graduate lama and an hon-orary doctorate from the Tashilhunpo university. She took with her, too, the warm regards of both the Incarnated Buddha and his mother, the latter of whom continued to write to her. In return, she frequently nagged Philip to send the elderly dame postcards with views of the desert, as well as dried figs and dates.

Alexandra and Yongden wended their way back to Sikkim, stop-ping off at Narthang, Tibet's largest printing establishment. She admired the casual style of the printers, who did painstaking but beautiful work with primitive wood blocks. They chatted and drank tea as though their deadlines were in the next life. How different it was from the feverish agitation of a Western editorial office. Finally, exhausted, the pair arrived home at De-chen. They found their hermitage sacked, turned inside out, and the Gomchen in retreat, seeing no one.

The mystery was soon cleared up when Alexandra received notice she had two weeks to leave the country. Her trip across the forbidden border had become known to Charles Bell, who traveled to the area and fined the inhabitants of Lachen—the nearest actual village—a heavy collective sum. Furious, he reminded them it was their task to prevent foreigners from crossing the border. In turn these devastated peasants pillaged Alexandra's abode in hopes of finding valuable belongings. Bell fined her, as well. She claimed that he was dying of envy at her trip to Tibet, but because she was French, he could not lay a hand on her. However, he scolded and fined the Gomchen, who couldn't afford to antagonize the ruling power. Alexandra felt that behind it all was the jealousy of the missionaries.

These good souls chafed at being barred from the mission field of Tibet, rife with infidels. They resented Alexandra's free access and her espousal of the native religion. Through their converts they learned of her journey, then ran to the Resident. As for Bell, he had considerations of state; the British were suspicious of any unauthorized traveler in Central Asia. They remained concerned that, like the Mongol Dorjieff who'd claimed to be a devout Buddhist but was a Russian spy, Alexandra might be the agent of some European power. Bell's reprisals were harsh, and he may have felt personally betrayed. He couldn't help but resent the Frenchwoman's opportunity to gather material for books, since he himself wasn't allowed past Gyantse. That she was the sort who disobeyed the rules and consorted with magicians didn't weigh in her favor.

British suspicions were not entirely unfounded. In the secret files we found the following dispatch from the Gyantse Trade Agency (1917):

> Mme David-Neel, the Belgian [sic] who . . . was expelled from Sikkim for having paid an unauthorized visit to Shigatse, maintains a correspondence with the mother of the Tashi Lama and *also with the Lama Chensal Kushab, the confidential adviser of the Tashi Lama.*

Bell once described the Panchen Lama as "England's oldest friend in Tibet." He wouldn't tolerate David-Neel's meddling in Tibetan affairs, and since the correspondence referred to has been destroyed or lost, we can only guess whether she was in fact butting in as she had done in Sikkim. Willfully or no, "the Belgian" had become an influence on Central Asian politics.

Alexandra instantly understood the seriousness of losing the goodwill of British colonial officials. She was now persona non grata anywhere under the jurisdiction of the Government of India. She lapsed into depression and adopted a "good riddance" attitude in her letters to Philip. She disparaged the freezing Himalayan nights, of trying to make fires with yak dung, of eating an unvarying diet of lentils. She assured him that, once he sent her the money, she would return to France promptly via Japan, which she praised as modern, intelligent, and peaceful.

At Lachen, Aphur Yongden accomplished the packing of his employer's twenty-eight cases. From this moment he moves to the forefront of Alexandra's life, indispensable in many ways. A lad of sixteen from a modest background—his father was a petty official—he had served a Sikkimese nobleman in return for a little education. In spite of being a novice monk, the youth had ambitions to become a man of the world. He was sure this was possible in the Philippines, of which he had heard. Alexandra, promising him travel, adventure, and six rupees per month, took him into her service. The lad got plenty of what he was promised except for the pay. Yongden was short, attractive in a plain way—he wore rimless glasses—and quite capable of learning. One day he would become a lama in his own right and a considerable help to Alexandra in writing her books. What was more, he carried an invaluable British passport.

Frightened by the Resident's wrath, Alexandra's other boys snuck off, while Yongden stuck. He refused to heed his family's threats, and even when they offered him a wife and house if he left the foreign shedevil, he turned a deaf ear. No mere adventurer, he came to reverence Alexandra and was willing to do every sort of menial task for her, while she soon came to prize him. Eventually she legally adopted him.

However, now the pair had to descend the mountain into the bustling world denounced by the Buddhist and of which the lad of seventeen knew nothing. The threadlike path wound lower and lower, until Alexandra glanced back one last time at her shanty. The villagers hovered around the wooden structure, ready to set it ablaze. Her life in the hazy blue heights was already a dream. The might of the British Empire had triumphed, but silently the lone woman swore revenge—a witty revenge appropriate to her beliefs and to the spirit of her birthplace, Paris.

Voila, a miracle! Despite the deteriorating postal communications, a bank draft from Philip made its way out of war-torn Europe and found its way to Alexandra in August 1917. She and Yongden, having left Japan, were living in a monastery on Diamond Mountain,

Korea, surrounded by vertiginous peaks, breathing crystal-clear air. She slept in a bare cell, awakened at three in the morning to meditate, and spent the rest of the day tramping on the mountain paths to visit hallowed shrines. Unfortunately, it rained for three weeks straight, which caused her rheumatism to kick up. Otherwise she felt, at forty-nine, younger and stronger than ever.

All along the explorer had been consulting cartographic maps of Central Asia, searching for a name in tiny characters hardly visible among the shading that indicated mountains. This was Kum Bum, fabled birthplace of Tsong Khapa and the real-life model for James Hilton's Shangri-La. The monastic city was located in eastern Tibet's Amdo province—not France or North Africa. By early October Alexandra had reached Peking (now Beijing), China's former imperial city. She found it large, flat, and well kept, and as usual she took quarters in the precincts of a monastery. Allegedly—the mails were censored—she intended to leave for Mongolia in order to continue her studies where the lamas spoke and read Tibetan.

Alexandra had great respect for Chinese culture, and Peking proved agreeable to her. Because she didn't have a grasp of the language, she was lumped with the foreign diplomats, soldiers, and missionaries whom the people hated. Alexandra denied any association with this class, and she especially dreaded the obligatory teas given by the well-meaning missionary wives. Her plan to travel to Mongolia, if it was real in the first place, never materialized. There was an automobile that left from the railroad station, but no one had ever been able to afford it.

Alexandra, after complimenting Philip on improving with age, like a fine wine, sketched her actual route for him. She intended to cross western China to Tibet, then travel across the steppes of that large country to the northern reaches of the Himalayas. Finally, she would once again descend through the high passes to India. This was going to be her very last journey before returning home, and it must be kept secret. Of course she would need more money.

Alexandra assured Philip she hadn't gone mad and was really going to return this time. It was simply a question of putting one foot after the other. But he must never mention Tibet in their correspondence or in casual talk in Algeria. That would put her in great danger. She was making the trip against the will of the Dalai Lama at

Alexandrine David, mother of
Alexandra David-Neel

Louis David, father of
Alexandra David-Neel

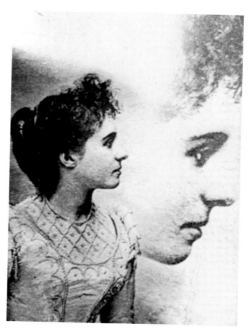

Alexandra, "première chanteuse" of the
Opéra Comique

Alexandra at 20, a youthful feminist

Alexandra, the married woman, 1910

Philip Neel, her husband, 1910

Sidkeong Tulku, Maharaja of Sikkim

Representatives of Tibet, Great Britain, and China at the Simla Convention, 1914.
Sidkeong Tulku is in the front row, second from left, Sir Henry McMahon is in
front row center, and Charles Bell is in the second row behind McMahon to his left.

The Thirteenth Dalai Lama seated with David Macdonald.

Tibetan nuns

Wayside Tibetans extend a typical greeting.

Alexandra's hermitage, at 13,000 feet in the Himalayas. The author is seated at right.

Tibetan rope bridge of the type Alexandra crossed on the way to Lhasa

Men and yaks clearing the road to the Chumbi valley
under deep snow.

Men in coracles on the Tsangpo river

Alexandra and Yongden in front of the Potala, 1924

The marketplace at Lhasa

Alexandra between two nuns of the Red Hat order

Kampa Dzong, a fortress

Dorje Phagmo (Thunderbolt Sow),
Tibet's only female incarnation, and
her sister.

Tibetan Ngagspa (wizard)

Lama Yongden, Alexandra's adopted son

Yongden

At Samten Dzong: Alexandra's cameras, gold jewelry, necklace of bone, "rings of the initiate"

At Samten Dzong: Alexandra's travel kit—watch, compass, pistol, jewelry pouch, cooking pot, bonnet

Alexandra at Samten Dzong at 87

Lhasa and the Resident at Gangtok, Charles Bell. She had learned that British intelligence had long ears.

Through the French Ambassador at Peking, Alexandra met a rich Tibetan lama from the Koko Nor district in northeastern Tibet, administered by China. He acted as a Chinese official and was in the capital to collect a large sum due him from the treasury. Tall, strong, imposing but homlier than the Gomchen, the lama was well read, the author of a grammar. Attired in a luxurious yellow silk robe over purple velour, attended by servants, he reminded the Frenchwoman of a Roman cardinal. When he played the tambourine and sang a sweet Tibetan air, he quite charmed her.

The lama quickly invited Alexandra to join his caravan on its return trip to Kum Bum, central to the Koko Nor region. He even offered to supply her with wood and water, both scarce, while she studied at the monastery. In return he expected Alexandra to help him with his major ambition: to write a book on astronomy. Knowing little about planets or stars, she still jumped at the chance. It constituted the first leg on her route, and with civil strife and an outbreak of black plague ravaging western China, the protection of an armed caravan seemed esential.

China, after the collapse of the Manchu dynasty, was in the midst of a chaotic interregnum that lasted until the final victory of the Maoists in 1949. Until his death in 1925, the Republican leader Sun Yat-sen usually held sway in Canton and much of the south, while local generals ruled over various provinces. These warlords printed worthless money, extorted provisions and labor from the people, and sold concessions to any foreigner rapacious enough to buy. Measuring their wealth in soldiers, the warlords were never secure, and when not battling one another they would combine to march on Peking to topple the kaleidoscopic, almost imaginary, central government. China's plight made David-Neel want to cry, but she didn't hesitate to plunge right in.

The lama never recovered his money. By the end of January 1915 he had decided to leave anyway. A draft from Philip arrived in the nick of time, along with news that Alexandra's senile, paralytic mother had died a full year earlier. Her daughter claimed to be deeply moved by memories. Now a woman of property, which was out of reach until after the war, she quickly sent Philip her will. She left him the bulk of her modest estate after debts were paid and her library was donated to the Buddhist Society of London. Alexandra instructed her husband to provide for Yongden, who by defying his family had amply demonstrated his loyalty.

Then she was off to the railroad station for a big send-off. An elaborate hospital car stuffed with medicines was appended to the train because of the pestilence raging in the countryside. Alexandra disdained those who displayed their fear by wearing face masks, and she was pleased when the hospital car became detached by mistake. At the railhead the party switched to mules and wagons. Alexandra found the armed guards atop the lama's baggage to be worthy descendants of the Golden Horde of Genghis Khan. For herself and Yongden she fashioned a large French flag from three appropriately colored strips of cloth. This she intended to fly during a battle, a talisman of neutrality. But at first the caravan was hung up for days in a squalid village on the border between Honan and Shensi provinces.

Here Alexandra became ominously ill. Philip had begged her not to expose herself, that she was all he cared about in the world. The plague was of the fatal pulmonary variety that had ravaged Europe in the Middle Ages. Initially the symptoms were no worse than the grippe—fever and dizziness—but if on the fourth day the victim coughed up blood, she was doomed to an excruciating death. Most likely there would be no one to help in the last agonizing hours. Yongden stayed close by, but Alexandra was determined not to infect him or others. She resolved that, on the sight of blood in her sputum, she would take the revolver she slept with and blow out her brains. On the fourth day she felt much better.

In spite of the archaic politeness of the armed men to the foreign woman in their midst, whom they addressed as "Your Reverence," tension filled the air like a thunderstorm about to burst. One morning Alexandra awoke to find a few severed heads impaled on a wall in front of her door. Bandits, she was told, but their contorted faces looked no more guilty than those of the government soldiers. She heard that in the warfare between Tibetans and Chinese troops that continued sporadically along the frontier, the winners of a battle made a stew of the losers' hearts—they ate them with rice.

Alexandra did not pretend to judge. Rather, she did her best to ward off violence. Slow progress through filthy villages made the lama official irritable and brought out his shady side. One evening at an inn, Alexandra was surprised to see young women clad in green pants and a pink jackets enter his room. After noisy haggling the harlots emerged, leaving the youngest to stay the night. This failed to appease the lama, and he fell into a quarrel with a Chinese officer. Soon heavily armed soldiers burst into the inn. The lama called his men to come running, guns in hand. It looked like a miniature war was about to erupt.

The foreign woman, aided by an interpreter, saved the day. Alexandra convinced the Han captain it was beneath his dignity to take notice of the ravings of a barbarian from the Koko Nor wilds. Then she remonstrated with the lama in Tibetan. How could he condescend to tussle with swinish soldiers? The quarrel evaporated and the caravan resumed its laborious trek toward Tibet's Amdo province.

The company Alexandra was keeping had turned into a liability. She and Yongden detoured via Tungchow where a small colony of Swedish missionaries offered her shelter. Immediately the walled town was assaulted. Bullets sang through the air, and the pastor and his family retreated to their chapel to pray with fervor. Alexandra jumped into a hot tub. She supposed the rebels would storm the city and take her prisoner, and she wished to get in a bath first. Fortunately, the attack was beaten off for the time being. The Swedes, convinced God had heard them, loudly gave thanks for their deliverance. Alexandra muttered that God should have prevented the attack in the first place.

The fighting continued with the invaders using ladders to scale the high walls, while the defenders, short on ammunition, hurled stones down on them. Alexandra couldn't help being roused by this classic panorama, a painting by Delacroix sprung to life. Sabers were unsheathed and blood flowed in the ditches, but compared to the mechanized warfare and poison gas in Europe, it looked quaint. The city's defenses held, and in April lilacs bloomed in the gardens.

The missionaries gave Alexandra accounts of earlier Western explorers to read, and these incensed her. The interlopers, who spoke neither Chinese nor Tibetan, had embarked with dozens of camels and horses, dozens of servants, all of which needed to be equipped. Naturally things went wrong, and about such misadventures the bunglers wrote their books. Worse, they had turned the natives against all foreigners by tricks such as slaughtering the pet animals of monasteries, stealing horses from nomads, and carving their initials into sacred trees. Alexandra traveled as a pilgrim, not a conqueror. Once the civil war cooled, she was ready to resume her jaunt.

Sian, capital of Shensi, was appointed as the meeting place with the lama official. It was essential that Alexandra enter Tibet in his caravan. Ignoring the military governor of Tungchow, who pleaded with her that leaving meant certain death at the hands of bandits, she snuck out through the gates in a train of three creaky carts, each drawn by two mules. The terrified drivers whipped their beasts through a scorched countryside, barren of peasants or travelers.

A rainstorm broke, and in the darkness the party approached a river beyond which they supposed themselves safe. They hallooed for the ferryman and were answered by a hail of shots. Somehow, they crossed the river on a raft, then bedded down with the fleas in a hovel; next day they continued on. Finally, looking up, Alexandra saw a wagon loaded with baggage and piled still higher with Mongols—Sian, the lama, they had come through!

Nearing Koko Nor, the impatient pilgrim began to walk. She had followed a tough regimen—sleeping on the ground, gulping coarse food, burned up by the sun—one she could not have tolerated in her youth. What nonsense were stories about fragile women or decrepit older folks. Robust and hearty, one day she surmounted a ridge to gaze down on the great Kum Bum monastery. The golden-roofed temples and flat, whitewashed houses of this Shangri-La gleamed in the mountain-rimmed valley.

In July 1918, sixteen hundred miles from Peking and gloriously distant from Europe, Alexandra and Yongden settled into a comfortable house to begin the more mundane task of translating Buddhist manuscripts. How marvellous and diverse was Asia, thought the scholar. Yet its thought remained locked behind a door closed to the Western mind. She must do her part to pry open that door.

Chapter 13
A Paradise

Before the onset of dawn in Central Asia, the conchs sound their eerie wail. Under a vast dome of sky in which the stars, soon to gutter out like spent candles, burn the brighter, shadows gather on the flat roof of the assembly hall. Novices, wrapped in togas against the bitter cold, are assigned to waken the slumbering monks of Kum Bum. Each begins to blow into his shell, and while one rests to breathe, the others continue to bellow forth rising and falling waves that crash against the far corners of this monastic city of hundreds of dwellings. Although the age-old call is not sufficient to raise the dead, it does rouse the living.

Lights flicker in the windows of the princely mansions of grand lamas, and domestic noises indicate stirring in the humbler quarters as the summons slowly ebbs. The sky pales to gray, rosy day breaks. Doors are flung open, and from every side some three thousand and eight hundred *trapas* (monks of basic degree) stream toward the imposing hall with its ornate tiers in Chinese style. With shaven heads and in uniform robes, the monks are reminiscent of trained performers scurrying to their accustomed spots. In a few moments the morning prayers will begin to ascend toward peaks so mighty even the sun has difficulty in scaling them. The Religion—the cumulative forces of light—once again will banish the demons of prehistoric darkness. As the wail of the conch drifts into space, albeit fainter and fainter, so the Doctrine when proclaimed echoes throughout the universe.

This was the unvarying routine of monastic life as seen and lived by Alexandra David-Neel. For centuries each one of the myriad monasteries scattered the length and breadth of the Lamaist domain—the immense territories of which Tibet is only part—had greeted the typically chilly dawn in the manner described. Such is the case no longer. Although the conch still sounds sporadically over the Central Asian steppes, it is in lament. The dozens of major *gompas* of the heartland, each a town in itself, have been sacked and demolished; their tens of thousands of monks are scattered, murdered, silenced. The Fourteenth Dalai Lama, defender of the faith, lives in exile in India and speaks openly of perhaps being the last in his line. David-Neel sensed that, even in her time, she had found a world both venerable and pristine, too precious to endure in the age of tanks, planes, artillery—or even highways. She is the witness to Shangri-La before its demise.

On the second-floor terrace of her house in the Pegyai Lama's palace sat the doughty woman during the frosty mornings of autumn 1918. Neglecting the rigors of tumo, Alexandra dressed snugly in a warm robe and high yak-hide boots in order to watch the daily pageant of life unfold. At ninety-five hundred feet, she inhaled air that tasted of snowy peaks. She could glance from the temple roofs burnished by sunlight to knots of yaks foraging for grass to a camel caravan of Mongols starting for Lhasa. Or she might draw within to savor her distance—here at what Tibetans call "the second birthplace of Buddha"—from the clamor of so-called civilization.

Alexandra wasn't permitted to attend the usual matins service, one of the few acts common to the entire brotherhood of a monastery, nor to share communal meals. The only exception was at important holidays, when the woman lama joined in with the trapas, whose shabby robes offered a marked contrast to the gold brocade vests worn by the dignitaries and the jewelled cloak of the ten-year-old *tulku* who was abbot of the gompa. Again she encountered the juxtaposition of the tawdry with the magnificent. Scrolls of paintings of Buddhas and dieties hung from the high ceiling, while a host of faded gods and demons peered at her from the walls of the dim hall. Rows of butter lamps illumined the large silver and gold reliquaries that housed the ashes of former disinguished lamas. A mystic atmophere enveloped all things.

The monks began, deep toned, punctuated by bells, drums, and roaring trumpets. The little novices seated on the benches in the back rows hardly dared to breathe for fear of the "hundred-eyed *chostimpa*"—the official disciplinarian—and the whip that ostentatiously hung from his elevated seat. This fellow was always a dark, strapping *Khampa* (native of Kham to the south) who overlooked the assembly with majestic disdain. Once Alexandra saw three men toward the rear, well hidden from view, make slight signs to one another. Up rose the chostimpa, and with his whip in hand, he strode across the hall like an avenging angel.

Stalking past the foreigner, he tucked his toga above his elbows, brandishing the knotted cat-o'-nine-tails in his large calloused fist. The malefactors shook but sheepishly awaited their punishment. With the panache of a hangman, the chostimpa lifted each man by the scruff of his neck, depositing him in the aisle where the poor fellow prostrated himself forehead to the floor. Whack! went the whip on each one's back, then the fearful personage resumed his dignity and his high place, looking for new offenders. Sometimes it was convenient to be a woman and not subject to the rules.

For the most part, Alexandra stayed aloof, if observant, from the daily routine at Kum Bum. She would arise at dawn, and after a bracing hour on the terrace during which she walked or meditated, a boy arrived to light the stove and boil water for tea. This she took in Tibetan style, with salt and plenty of butter. She did her toilette and read until taking an English breakfast at nine. Alexandra claimed to be fortunate in that she had good bread from a Moslem baker in a nearby village. Until noon she translated into French and English rare manuscripts the lamas loaned her from the monastery's extensive library. She needed help with the ancient literary Tibetan, but since these texts of Nagarjuna's (an early Buddhist philosopher, the Father of Mahayana) had been lost in the original Sanskrit, the scholar was elated at the find.

Midday meant a break for a hot tub, followed by more work. At four she dined on a thick soup of locally grown vegetables. Dessert might be a compote of stewed fruit. Again Alexandra bent to deciphering the texts until she retired to bed at nine. She had given the larger, lower room to Yongden, because the bright frescoes on the walls disturbed her rest. No hint of neurasthenia kept her from sleeping wonderfully well, and it seemed but a moment until the conchs woke her, proclaiming another dawn.

Alexandra felt that she could go on living in this manner for a thousand years. Of course there were occasional diversions. Lamaism is a form of Buddhism that can be actively practiced only by monks. The laity supports the religion, in practice the gompas, which is best done by bestowing gifts. At Kum Bum, greatly revered as the birthplace of Tsong Khapa, the founder of the Yellow Hat reforms, wealthy pilgrims frequently made an offering of a special feast for the brethren. It was a welcome change from the routine tsampa and tea, and although Alexandra couldn't attend the banquet, she was always brought a portion of the meal. She particularly relished "a certain Mongolian dish made of mutton, rice, Chinese dates, butter, cheese curds, sugar-candy, and various other ingredients and spices, all boiled together." Savory *momos*—meat enclosed in a ball of baked paté and steamed—were another favorite. These gave the lie to an old Tibetan proverb, "To eat lama's food requires jaws of iron."

At the end of November 1918, Alexandra wrote to Philip with tears in her eyes. It wasn't because a letter from him had finally reached her four months after mailing, nor even due to worry over Yongden, dangerously ill with influenza. She was tenderly nursing him, although she had a high fever herself. No, the rush of sentiment came at learning of the Armistice from some English missionaries who had heard the news before she did.

Once the flu ran its course—the pair caught their share of that deadly worldwide epidemic—Alexandra and Yongden sewed a huge French tricolor and trooped it to the top of a nearby mountain. The valley below showed green but patchy, the slopes splashed with touches of golden poplars. The sun shone brightly in a clear blue sky. Ceremoniously, they unfurled the banner, which had embroidered on it a common Tibetan prayer of thanks: *"Lha gyalo! De tamche pam!* Victory to the Gods, the Demons are Vanquished!" The pair watched with satisfaction as the flag flapped in the breeze.

Kum Bum was surrounded by many lesser monastic establishments, which occupyied mountain nooks and crannies. The monks, nuns, and hermits understood the efficacy of sending a message to the universe. But David-Neel had the more practical intention of informing others that the mighty Allies had defeated the dread Huns. If the great struggle in Europe was done, the little war for Tibetan independence was being waged more fiercely. The monks, who didn't shrink at fighting, were arming to defend Kum Bum and its treasures. Recently a nearby gompa had been pillaged and burned by Chinese irregulars. The brethren fled and took revenge by killing a Chinese interpreter, dicing his body in pieces and serving up his heart as a tasty morsel. No wonder that Alexandra slept with a loaded pistol under her pillow and kept two fast horses always saddled in the stable.

Neither fear nor temptations provoked by watching trains of yaks driven into the hills and beyond by hard-bitten men would lure Alexandra from her cell until she was ready. Subsisting largely on tea and a strange vegetable that tigers were supposed to eat, she went into retreat for the next six weeks to delve deeper into her studies. She was out and about by mid-February when, a hint of spring in the air, the New Year celebration took place. Kum Bum, located to the north of the villages and grazing lands of Kham, was also accessible to the populous Tibetan speaking portions of Kansu and Szechuan (China) to the east, and it could be reached by the Mongol horse breeders to its north and west. For this festive holiday, pilgrims and nomads poured into the monastic precincts to view its miraculous tree and to have a good time.

Legend held that after Tsong Khapa's birth, attended with portents, the umbilical cord was buried and from it grew a tree that became an object of worship. Pious visitors arrived to make offerings of ornaments and jewelry, a monk built a hut, and so the famed gompa began. In the 1840s the clever and learned French priest Evarist Huc sojourned at Kum Bum, writing of the tree, grown large and venerable, "We were filled with an absolute consternation of astonishment at finding that . . . there were upon each of the leaves well-formed Tibetan characters, all of a green colour, some darker, some lighter than the leaf itself."

The priest and his companion were eager to convert the natives to their brand of the miraculous, and so they minutely examined the leaves for fraud and tore off some bark. But the young bark also exhibited the "outlines of characters in a germinating state, and what is very singular, these new characters are not infrequently different from those which they replace." Indeed, Kum Bum means "ten thousand images."

As usual, David-Neel was indifferent to miracles, and she scarcely mentions the tree. But she observed with interest the pilgrims who arrived at the site hoping to see some wonder. The surroundings, especially at night, added a touch of magic. Snow covered the mountains and the monastic city, and soaring many-tiered temples and humble homes alike sparkled in the glow from innumerable lamps and candles. Red-garbed trapas carried resin torches, which glinted steadily in the frosty air. The populace surged through the streets, and all, both rich and poor, were dressed in their best. The women proudly showed off headdresses of 108 braided plaits, gleaming with butter and bedecked by red and green ribbons. The Golog women—nomads from the mountains—added a kind of mantle of large cups of silver, turquoise, and coral, as well as a bowler hat resembling those worn by Bolivian Indians. They clanked as they moved with the deliberation of treasure galleons. Most amazing were the many statues made of butter upon which the folk gaped and made endless comments.

These tableaux, composed of flour pasted over wooden frames and then drenched in butter of various colors that quickly froze to give a glassy sheen, could be images of famous kings or sages or fanciful dragons or other mythical beasts, even a scale model of Lhasa complete with a tiny Dalai Lama about to enter his palace. Executed with great care by the temple artists, the figures were to be admired for only the night of the fifteenth of the first month, which culminated the New Year celebration. They were destroyed by daylight and the butter sold as healing salve.

Whatever its potency, it couldn't compare with a blessing received from the incarnate *dakini* (mother goddess), who was ushered about the exhibits with all the pomp of a visiting archbishop. Resplendent in the flowered robe given her by the Panchen Lama, Alexandra moved in state, the crowds furiously attempting to prostrate themselves or kiss her hem. She could only nod in appreciation to her worshipers, since a cordon of guards continually beat them off. The folk seemed grateful for the blows. As for the skeptical Frenchwoman, she was reminded of an incident in the career of Madame Du Barry, Louis XV's favorite mistress, when she was first presented at Versailles. Of her descent from her carriage, gorgeously attired, she later remarked, "I would have liked to have been at a window to see myself pass."

What caught up Alexandra and took her outside herself was not adoration, which she regarded as proof of the aspiration of the common folk to higher things, but the trill of a Mongol flute accompanied by the irregular clang of copper cymbals. In the midst of a fawning mob this music, like the breeze over a camp of nomads on the vast steppe, thrilled the former diva to the bottom of her heart. The far distances called to her, and she was bound to succumb sooner or later to her lust to roam. Being alone in the wilds, no one in sight, camped under a tent . . . that turned her on.

In the spring of 1919, the civil war heated up. The central government at Peking, which had ruled over Amdo and Kham (referred to on older maps as Inner Tibet), although weakly and thus benignly, was losing its grip altogether. The Tibetan tribesmen, good fighters, were in continual revolt. Breakaway armies fought one another and brigandage flourished, especially among the fierce mountain *Gologs* (literally "heads on backwards"), who delighted in stealing mules from the Chinese generals. The Dalai Lama seized this opportunity to demand the total independence of all Tibet. But realistically, he had few troops to send to the frontier, a month's forced march from Lhasa over the world's worst roads. So along the Sino-Tibetan marches anarchy reigned, and to paraphrase Hobbes, life was short, brutish, and chancy.

Alexandra was inspired to go on some delightful jaunts. At a day's walk lived forty nuns in their "Fortress in the Sky," a poverty-stricken gompa atop a mountain surrounded by other needlelike peaks of somber red hues. Alexandra and the cheerful nuns got along well. These women thought nothing of tramping over the entire country on a pilgrimage. Their absolute faith and quiet courage helped to fortify their resolve. Although she refused an offer to take up residence, they went together on hikes, climbing slopes so steep that the middle-aged adventurer had to be hoisted along like a package. She found it exhilarating to attain ruined temples and shrines where hermits had meditated centuries ago. On the way down, Yongden, proud as a ram leading his flock, entertained the party with songs. He even flirted with the prettier nuns.

Summer found David-Neel at the head of a small expedition— including Yongden and several armed servants—headed for the barren but entrancing region of Lake Koko Nor to the northwest of Kum Bum. This was a year of pilgrimage—every twelfth—and caravans might arrive at the lake from farthest Mongolia, circumambulating its considerable breadth. Going around sacred mountains or lakes is essential to what the French scholar R. A. Stein has called "the nameless religion" of Tibet, by which he means the matrix of age-old popular magical beliefs and practices covered over by a Buddhist patina. The clear, high lakes were particularly employed for divination, peering into the future, and within their depths they concealed a variety of spirit beings, so that Tibetbans were fearful of eating one in the guise of a fish. This journey to the lake lasted ten days and for a time the party was lost. But with the aid of a rudimentary map and pocket compass, Alexandra led the way to Koko Nor, a mini-ocean for these parts.

The area was a rugged plain lacking even a single village. The great salt lake, together with mountain ranges on the horizon near and far, broke the monotony of the steppe, which was scarcely fit for grazing. Alexandra adored the solitude, the loom of a snowcapped peak reflected in the wavery blue water. Here was a landscape she knew deep down in her soul. Yet camping on the banks of this icy sheet had its drawbacks. It was impossible to buy or beg food, and although one shivered with cold at night, the mosquitoes were ravenous. There was also the threat of bandits.

In 1864 the explorer Dutreuil de Rhins had been murdered in this vicinity. Some years after Alexandra's visit, two Frenchmen, Louis Marteau and Louis Dupont, disappeared without a trace. So the little party, as it circled around the flat expanse, kept a sharp watch, alert for danger. The American missionary Robert Ekvall, who lived in Amdo in the 1930s, wrote in *Tibetan Sky Lines*, "A hairlike rift in the blue may mean a lance, and the fork of a gun rest. . . enemies and a raid. The bold outline of a distant mounted figure is sure to bring a sense of uncertainty, even menace."

According to Alexandra, there was an invariable etiquette followed when one party approached another. For example, she was jogging along placidly when one of her retainers warned of an armed band approaching. Quickly, she reached into her saddlebag for a revolver, while Yongden and another man rode forward in a show of force. Alexandra's horse took off, and when she tried to dismount, she found herself stuck in the saddle. Luckily, the intruders decided they were weaker, or less certain, and they beat a hasty retreat. Strength was measured by a party's number of weapons and their quality—many guns were old blunderbusses—and its determination to fight. A common greeting in this region was, "No closer, friend, or I'll shoot!" The weaker party must advance slowly and explain itself; to run would mean a hail of bullets in the back, no questions asked.

At the sacred lake on the border of Tibet, Mongolia, and China, Alexandra met more pilgrims than bandits, when she met anybody at all. The water, deepening in shade from azure to turquoise to lapis as the sun waned, compelled her gaze for hours on end. One evening three odd-looking characters planted their tent next to the traveler's. Dressed in shabby oranges and reds topped off by faded sheepskins, they were Bon priests, necromancers of the ancient faith who knew charms to kill a fetus in the womb or conversely to animate dry bones. Life in the open, and the practice of their occult rites, had given the men the knowing, crinkled faces of sages.

Alexandra was intensely interested in this sect, and some of her best writing would make use of dubious tales about its followers. On a different occasion, in Kansu on the edge of a primeval forest, a Bon disciple joined her company for protection against robbers. The man wore his long hair, wrapped in red material, as a turban. She fed him well and learned that he was going to join his master just then performing a ceremony on a hill some distance away. The rite was designed to quell a demon who had been angered by one of the clans that inhabited the region.

Alexandra was dying to observe the *ngagspa* (sorcerer) at his trade, but his disciple assured her it was impossible. The Bon priest couldn't be disturbed during the lunar month it took to perform the rite. The always curious orientalist was not about to be put off, for the ways of the ancient religion were little known and much feared. She made the Bonpo into a sort of prisoner, having her servants watch him carefully. He went on feasting, grinning, showing no interest in running away. Alexandra soon understood that the disciple had been trained in telepathy, and he was able to send his master "a message on the wind."

Sure enough, once their party crossed the Kunka Pass and came out on the Tibetan plain, a troop rode up at full speed, dismounted, and offered Alexandra presents of ceremonial scarves and butter. The ngagspa had sent his emissaries to beg the foreign lama not to visit him. None but his initiated disciple would be permitted to approach the spot where he had built a secret shrine. Alexandra wasn't boorish enough to persist, especially since the ngagspa had so vividly demonstated his powers of telepathy.

Magical occurrences were frequent in Tibet. Alexandra recorded them as they happened, often providing a rational explanation for the phenomena. She speculated that the country was hospitable to these psychic sports because of its consistently high altitude, the great silence in which it was bathed—permitting one to hear another's thoughts—and, above all, due to the absence of cities, crowds, and electric devices. These caused whirlpools of distracting energy. Then, too, the Tibetans were placid and open; to them the spirit world seemed as commonplace as their mountains, steppes, and lakes. Mystical training was, in the first place, the clearing away of the distractions of the mind.

The journey to Koko Nor had been a fine test of endurance, a warmup for the final journey that David-Neel was contemplating. By September 1919, she was pleased to be back in her comfortable house at the monastery. For her Kum Bum, with its pitched roof, Chinese style buildings that flew bright-colored banners and housed hundreds of chanting monks and silent meditators—but above all a treasure in manuscripts—was a true paradise.

It is ironic that Kum Bum served James Hilton as the model for Shangri-La in *Lost Horizon*. He located his hidden lamasary far to the west in the Kun Lun range, where in fact there is nothing. The nineteenth century Abbé Evarist Huc, on whose writings Hilton admitted he drew, resembled the fictional Father Perrault, the ancient abbot of Shangri-La. Huc came to dispute with and convert the lamas, but he succumbed to the lure of study. Unlike Perrault, he never lost his Christian vocation, and rather than don a Buddhist robe he left. Of all the early missionary travelers to Tibet, Huc was the most inquisitive, and he blandly reported strange goings-on.

Abbé Huc gave no hint of any elixir of immortality or fountain of youth associated with Shangri-La. It is disappointing that Hilton, who knew little about Tibet, attributed Perrault's living for a couple of centuries to "drug taking and deep-breathing exercises." Kum

Bum did have a notable school of medicine, specializing in the collection and preparation of curative herbs. Huc noted that "the pilgrims who visit Kum Bum buy these remedies at exorbitant prices." He accurately described the Tibetan physicians' method of urinalysis: "They examine [the patient's urine] with the most minute attention, and take the greatest heed to all the changes undergone by its colour; they whip it from time to time, with a wooden spatula, and they put it up to the ear to ascertain how much noise it makes."

David-Neel remained surprisingly silent on any aspect of Tibetan medicine. She was afflicted with arthritis and sciatica, but her remedy was to ignore the pain. When it became unbearable she dosed herself with patent medicines containing some narcotic. However, she was intrigued by the disputations engaged in by the novice lamas before receiving their higher degrees. While the entire faculty looked on, a master would question his pupil on the intricacies of Buddhist doctrine, standing over the seated, anxious young man, teasing him by alternately proffering or withholding the huge woolly ceremonial cap of a graduate. Or two candidates would debate philosophy, clapping hands or jumping up and down to emphasize a point. All questions and answers consisted of memorized portions of scripture. Still, the emotions of the participants were real, for the loser, in disgrace, had to carry the winner of the debate on his shoulders throughout the grounds.

Alexandra, a woman, no matter how learned could not engage in debates with the male lamas. Since winter was not the season for gadding about, she took to her reading. She informed Philip that she needed one more year at the monastery to complete her translations, and would he please send more money? Otherwise his wife might have to wander about like a nomad or a beggar.

When translating manuscripts had lost its charm, she turned to a deep form of meditation, shutting herself in *tsams*. Specifically, the term refers to certain small boxlike structures that used to be maintained on the outskirts of every monastery. Here monks who were already trained to isolation shut themselves up for months or years at a time—or forever. David Macdonald described the cells as tiny, filthy, devoid of any light whatever. Once a trapa took the vow of lifelong retirement, it was unbreakable. The door through which he entered his cell was bricked up and a little food placed outside a trap once a

day. lf this lay untouched for several days, the cell was broken up, to
disclose a withered corpse. According to Macdonald, ''Many of the
hermits become mentally afflicted, while others become fanatics.''
Their view was that the virtual denial of life assured them of attaining
nirvana, eternal bliss.

The French orientalist had nothing so ambitious in mind. The
tsams she entered in the winter of 1919–1920 was not so strict as cus-
tomary and took place in her own quarters. David-Neel's purpose
was experimental: she meant to create a *tulpa,* a phantom being
voluntarily produced by powerful concentration of thought and
the repetition of prescribed rites. She describes the incident but
unfortunately not the process in *Magic and Mystery.* She claims to have
succeeded, although in a way that frightened her thoroughly.

A tulpa, unlike a *tulku*, which is the successive incarnation of a
particular personality (such as the Dalai Lama), is a temporary phenomenon that is willfully created. It may take any form whatever but
is most often in human shape. These tulpas coexist with their creator
and can be seen simultaneously with him. The tulku, on the contrary,
does not coexist with his ancestor. Usually, the tulpa is sent to perform a definite mission. However, once the thought form is given
sufficient life to pass as a real being, it may free itself from its origi-
nator's control. Folklore in Tibet and elsewhere tells tales of the
created being turning on its magician-father and killing him, and we
are reminded of the fictional Dr. Frankenstein and his monster.

In his commentary to the *Tibetan Book of the Dead*, Evans-Wentz
wrote that "mediums in the Occident can, while entranced, automatically and unconsciously create materializations which are much
less palpable than the consciously produced tulpas by exuding
'ectoplasm' from their own bodies. Similarly, as is suggested by
instances of phantasms of the living reported by psychic research, a
thought-form may be made to emanate from one human mind and
be hallucinatorily perceived by another, although possessed of little
or no palpableness."

In traditional Eastern thought, there is no hard line between
the real and unreal. A dream or a vision is as actual or illusory as a
mountain, the perception of which depends on the viewer.
"Inasmuch as the mind creates the world of appearances, it can
create any particular object desired," continues Evans-Wentz. "The

process consists of giving palpable being to a visualization, in very much the same manner as an architect gives concrete expression in three dimensions to his abstract concepts after first having given them expression in the two-dimensions of his blue-print." In Alexandra's case she intended to manufacture an entity that hadn't existed previously but of a certain type—a fat, innocent, and jolly monk.

Through a focused meditation that lasted for months—somewhat like a prayer that asks for the intervention of one's *yidam*, or guardian deity—the phantom monk was formed. His appearance became fixed and lifelike. By then, with the coming of mild weather, it was time for Alexandra to take a complement of retainers, equipment to match, and to roam in the Koko Nor region. The monk tagged along, walking by her when she rode and stopping as they made camp. Sometimes the illusion rubbed against her, palpably touching her. Worse, the jolly fellow grew lean and mean, troublesome looking and acting. The tulpa had escaped his master's control.

What Alexandra had scoffed at came to pass. To make matters more complicated, others began to see the fellow and to speak to him. Although he didn't answer, his presence had to be explained. Years later, Alexandra wrote calmly of the experience, claiming to have found it amusing, but at the time she was beside herself. She felt that the incident called into question her motives in studying tantric Buddhism. She wondered if she was destined to take the left-hand path of the sorcerer? Typically, when something of real importance happened, Alexandra kept it from Philip Neel.

With her usual determination, Alexandra decided to dissolve the phantom before making for Lhasa. The tulpa clung tenaciously to life, and he only disappeared after six months of hard struggle and after she had again asked for the intervention of her guardian diety and steadfastly performed the appropriate rites. How to explain the affair? The orientalist admitted that she herself did not know for certain but was unwilling to dwell on it.

In western China the year's crops had failed, and by fall, 1920 there were outbreaks of famine and pestilence. At Chengtu in nearby Szechuan one hundred people a day were dying of cholera. The peasants were starving, and even honest folk had turned to murder and robbery. Talks between China and Tibet had failed, local governors were turning into warlords, fighting and pillaging one another. Alexandra, nearly penniless and growing ragged, hung on at Kum Bum waiting for funds. To Philip's demands that she return to Algeria she turned a deaf ear.

Alexandra David-Neel had sworn to go where no white woman had been before. She would reach the heart of Tibet, capital of Buddhist Central Asia, traveling on foot and without a tent if need be, begging her way. Akin to the simple herdsman of the high grassy steppes, the peasant on a small plot in Kham, or the fierce Golog in his mountain fastness, a splendid vision of the holy city rose before her eyes: Shangri-La. It was the dream she had as a child, the carry-over from her past life as a nomad or a bandit queen.

Chapter 14
The French Nun

Through the early winter of 1921, Alexandra and Yongden bent to their studies. The young man of twenty-three, who had been made a novice at fourteen, wished to become a *gelong*, or proper monk. Because he hadn't undergone the usual training, he was obliged to pass a special examination. Meanwhile, with the aid of a pair of magnifying spectacles, Alexandra worked through the nights translating texts by Nagarjuna. The Tibetan books from which she copied were actually collections of block-printed single sheets. Nagarjuna's most famous work, *The Diamond Sutra,* is contained in one hundred such volumes of a thousand pages each.

If the task seemed daunting, David-Neel was glad to be counted as practically the sole female member of—in Evans-Wentz's phrase—"that noble band of translators and transmitters who in our time have added fresh effulgence to the Light born of the East." Flourishing in the second century A.D., Nagarjuna was the first teacher publicly to teach the supreme doctrine of the Voidness, which though it dated to Gautama himself, had been previously elucidated only to highly advanced disciples. Nagarjuna formed the bridge from Sanskrit to the northern languages, from the select few to the aspiring many.

Marpa, the guru of Milarepa, the poet-sage, acted as a human bridge in a more literal sense, tramping over the Himalayan passes in all weathers, loaded down with sacred books, carrying on his back the wisdom of India to Tibet. David-Neel, too, would span not only grand distances on the map of Asia, but more importantly the cultures of East and West. She was able to leap the daunting chasm between meditation and action. The peasants and nomads of Amdo could not fathom the foreign lama's researches, but when she stepped forth from her cell, they worshiped her person.

These folk were labeled "people of the extremes" by the more sophisticated inhabitants of Lhasa. To Alexandra they looked romantic at a distance, skin shining like bronze. The men draped themselves in capacious cloaks that brushed the earth; the women sported vivid cottons of red, blue, and green, scarves dangling from their waists. Both sexes wore round or pointed bonnets trimmed with fox or lamb skins. Up close, they were grimy and unwashed, but she found them pleasant smelling.

It was common for bystanders to prostrate themselves as Alexandra passed. They were convinced she had solved the mysteries and could foretell the future in a bowl of water. Particularly when she donned her yellow vest embroidered with gold and silver flowers, a gift from the Panchen Lama, the effect was electric. Hordes clamored for her healing touch, and the local Moslems came in droves, certain she must be a prophet. Thubten Norbu, brother to the Dalai Lama and former abbot of Kum Bum, writes of being put into a similarly embarrassing position:

> Sometimes, because I am recognized as the reincarnation of [a venerated] Rinpoche, people came to me and asked for my blessing. I used to tell them that I had no power to give them a blessing . . . and that perhaps I was more in need of blessing than they were. . . . But they would reply that what I thought of myself did not matter, that they believed I must be a great person to have deserved such a high rebirth. Then I used to say a prayer with them . . . .

Thus David-Neel, in the minds of the common folk, was elevated to the lineage of beneficent incarnations. More willingly, she herself stepped into the ranks of a more questionable but colorful lot—the varied explorers of Tibet. Because they generally came to the Sacred Realm against the wishes of its rulers, Peter Hopkirk has aptly termed them "trespassers" and "gatecrashers." Always they attempted to reach the near-legendary capital of the Dalai Lama.

The first European to visit Lhasa, Hopkirk claimed, was a Friar Odoric in 1324. He set out from the Franciscan mission to the court of the Great Khan at Carnbaluc (Peking) to return to Italy via uncharted Central Asia, a route home not so different from

Alexandra's. However, on the way he hoped to find the lost Christian kingdom of Prester John. There were Nestorians among the Mongols, although the followers of this fifth-century Syrian heresy had adopted abominable practices, unheard of in Europe, such as "washing their lower parts like Saracens." They probably influenced the ritual of Tibetan Buddhism, which Abbé Huc declared to be similar to the Catholic.

Odoric wrote an account of his journey in which he stated:

> I came to a certain great kingdom called Tibet, which is on the confines of India proper, and is subject to the Great Khan. . . .The chief and royal city, Lhasa, is built with walls of black and white, and all its streets are well-paved. In this city no one shall dare to shed the blood of any, whether man or beast, for the reverence they bear a certain idol which is there worshipped. In that city dwelleth the Pope [Dalai Lama] who is the head of all idolaters.

The friar reached his home in 1330, and his tales of Tibet were embroidered and retold by the plagiarist who called himself Sir John Mandeville. All Europe thrilled to this imposter's account of *his* journey to fabled Cathay. This is the first instance of the recurring fascination with Tibet shown by Western missionaries, dreamers, and scholars. It is also a fine example of an armchair author filching travelers' tales for his own use.

Interest died down until the seventeenth century when Portugal planted a colony at Goa, India. Jesuit priests struggled over the Himalayan passes, still searching for lost Christians. The Tibetans welcomed them, and a mission was established at Shigatse. In the eighteenth century, the Capuchins founded a mission in the Buddhist capital. The young Italian priest Ippolito Desideri, a Jesuit, lived and studied at Sera monastery, learning about the religion he hoped to show as false. Eventually, the lamas grew to resent the influence of both the Jesuits and Capuchin fathers at the Dalai Lama's court, and by mid-century their missions had disappeared with scarcely a trace.

The British, after securing their rule in the Indian subcontinent, sent a different sort of envoy north over the mountains. Warren Hastings of the East India Company dispatched a young Scot, George Bogle, to open up trans-Himalayan trade and to gain intelligence of Russian and Chinese influence in Tibet. The Panchen tried to turn Bogle away, claiming he was subject to the Chinese Emperor "whose will it was that no Moghul, Hindustani, Patan, or Fringy be admitted to his realm." *Fringy* was the Scotsman's corruption of *philing*, or foreigner. Bogle won the Panchen's friendship for Britain, but both he and the Lama died soon after of smallpox.

The eccentric English scholar Thomas Manning, a friend of Charles Lamb, accompanied a Chinese general to Lhasa in 1811 and had an interview with the Dalai Lama. Although Manning dressed as an Oriental, he was contemptuous of Buddhist custom, infuriated the lamas, and had to flee Tibet. In contrast, Abbé Huc succeeded in 1846 in becoming the first missionary to Lhasa in over a century. He lived there unmolested until, jealous of his influence on the Regent, the Chinese Amban ordered him out. When Huc published two volumes of his firsthand experiences, set down in a lively, open style, the pedants of his day denounced him as a credulous fool.

Toward the end of the century, feeling threatened by both the Russians and British India, the decrepit Manchu emperors connived with fearful lamas and greedy nobles to keep the people of Tibet, and the Dalai Lama, in total ignorance of events in the outside world. The Land of Religion was closed to disturbing foreign influences. The policy invited evasion, and the British took to dispatching Indian secret agents across the border. These pundits, disguised as traders, carried concealed compasses and chronometers, and by counting their paces they managed to survey much of the frontier country.

Alexandra, too, on her journey to Lhasa, lacked proper scientific equipment for map making; nor was she as methodical as the most famous of the pundits, Sarat Chandra Das, a Bengali who found his way into Kipling's *Kim*. The high Tibetan official who unwittingly helped him to attain the capital was flogged and then drowned in the river. His family's properties were confiscated, his soul condemned to hell, and even his reincarnation—a small boy—was persecuted. The frontier officials were severely punished. This made their fellows desperate to catch any philing rash enough to clamber up to the roof of the world.

The prohibition only made Tibet seem more mysterious and alluring to outsiders. The formidable geographic barriers that surround the country are not insurmountable. The Russian Colonel

Nikolai Prejevalsky made two attempts to reach the capital from Siberia. On the first he lost fifty-five camels to the harsh winter before turning back. On the second try, in 1879, he had the support of the czar. "Nor was he going to take any truck from bandits," writes Peter Hopkirk, "being accompanied by an escort of seven carefully chosen Cossacks, all expert rifle shots, who had sworn to go through 'fire and water' with him." As a secret weapon, he brought pictures of Russian actresses to seduce officials.

A week's march from the holy city, Prejevalsky's expedition was stopped by two officials backed by hundreds of warrior monks ready to die to defeat the Russian invasion. When the colonel demanded to know why he could not proceed, an official replied, "All the laymen and monks of this Tibet of ours have frequently had sad experiences when we extended kindness to foreigners. Together we have sworn a sealed covenant not to allow foreigners to enter Tibet."

But if masculine bluster failed to clear a way, what of womanly determination combined with evangelical zeal? The missionary Annie Taylor, who resembled Alexandra in spunk and diminutive size, got on well with the cheerful Tibetan travelers whom she hoped to convert, but she had set herself the goal of bringing the Christian gospel to the Dalai Lama in person. She endured a four-month journey from western China over a tortuous road of ice and snow; she crossed high freezing passes and nearly starved to death, only to be intercepted a few days short of her destination, betrayed by a former servant. Taylor demanded provisions from a military chief, then trudged back the way she had come. When she arrived at Tachienlu, Szechuan, in April 1893, she had covered 1,300 miles in seven months and survived the rigors of a Tibetan winter. Although the plucky missionary spent many years in Sikkim serving God and awaiting another opportunity, she never attained Lhasa.

The surest means of gaining Lhasa was to shoot one's way in, as did the British expedition under Colonel Francis Younghusband. He was not in command of its well-equipped army, and witnessing the slaughter of monks who threw themselves in front of machine guns caused the young officer to turn from diplomacy to the mystical. Accompanying correspondents were sickened, and through their reports to their papers turned Parliament against the Anglo-Tibetan Convention. But Younghusband remained a hero to the public, who understood that the empire had scaled the Himalayas, and southern Tibet was open to the British and firmly closed to others.

Younghusband had wished to attain Lhasa by the most intriguing method of all: deception. The Indian pundits had donned disguises, and so had the Japanese Buddhist Ekai Kawaguchi, who sojourned at a Tibetan monastery in 1901. These were Asians, and it was a more difficult task for the Swedish Sven Hedin to impersonate a Buriat Mongol. That same year, starting from Chinese Turkestan (Sinkiang), he came within a five-days' march of Lhasa before being detected. In 1906 he arrived in India with the intention of crossing into Tibet. Lord Curzon, from London, privately backed the already famous explorer's mapping expedition. But a new government at Whitehall turned thumbs down, ordering the Swede arrested. The house of Rothschild had alerted them to Hedin's being a czarist agent in search of gold fields.

Still, the Swede slipped in through Ladakh. He spent two years in southern Tibet mapping rivers and mountains, discovered the source of the Indus, and eventually published twelve volumes of mundane prose and exquisite maps. The British knighted him, to which he responded by supporting Germany in both world wars. Traditionally explorers have been male, domineering, and neither imaginative or pleasant. Heinrich Harrer, of *Seven Years In Tibet* fame, fits the bill.

The most successful incognito previous to Alexandra's was that of Dr. William Montgomery McGovern, a canny British professor of oriental studies who passed himself off as a native caravan porter. Climbing up from India, he slept in cowsheds with the other men, lived on jerky, and struggled through heavy snows to reach Lhasa a full year before Alexandra, also at the lunar New Year. There he became terrified of a hostile mob. He gave himself up and, due to the pro-British bent of the Dalai Lama's chief minister, was kept under protective guard for a month while he recuperated. McGovern was sent down to India with an escort. He had seen enough to write a book—in Alexandra's wry phrase—about his misadventures.

Alexandra had read or heard of most of her predecessors in what we may term "the little game" of sneaking to Lhasa. From their failures she learned what not to do. Although she envied "Sweed Hadin" his modern equipment, especially a stove, she refused to

grow overly dependent on porters and she avoided showing anything of value. When she requested Philip in Algeria to construct a
camp bed for her, she ordered it be made severely plain. She was
used to traveling along unknown tracks, avoiding even peasants,
some of whom were descending to banditry. She had the flexibility to
change her itinerary instantly in order to outwit the British secret
service, which tried to keep tabs on her, or local Tibetan officers.
Although Alexandra was embarrassed over others seeing her in tattered garments, ultimately rags would prove her best protection.
Gradually, the Frenchwoman took the mental steps necessary to shed
her old self and assume the identity that would win her through.

In February 1921, in the thin light of a Tibetan dawn, a small caravan exited through the gates of a venerable monastery in Amdo
province. A few mules carried baggage, but the four native "boys"
went on foot. Wrapped in crude sheepskins and wearing fur hats,
yak-hide boots encasing their feet, their breaths steamed in the
painfully dry air of midwinter. Across their chests were slung ban-
doliers of ammunition, and they carried single-shot rifles with pride
if not military precision. Ahead of the pack strode a short, square
lama in a red cloak lined with fur, face nearly buried in a huge fur
bonnet. The temperature had sunk to below zero Fahrenheit. After
marching a while into the hills, the lama turned to stare at the white
buildings and red palaces of Kum Bum, its roofs molten with the fire
of sunrise. She understood she might never again see this sight. Yes,
she . . . for the bulky figure was Alexandra David-Neel, embarked on
her greatest adventure.

No sooner had Alexandra's party taken to the low road that ran
between steep earthen walls than they ran into a long caravan of
camels and drivers coming the opposite way. The road was so narrow, either she or the camels would have to back up for at least a
mile. The Mongol drivers felt, and Alexandra agreed, that it would
be far easier for her. But her boys took this as a loss of face and
refused. She was obliged to back them, or they would lose all confidence in her.

While Alexandra hesitated, the situation quickly deteriorated as
the camels fell to biting one another. A Mongol lifted his gun, and
now to back off meant being shot down. Alexandra scrambled to the
top of the bank for an overview, then signaled to her boys to unsling

their rifles. The Mongols, impressed with their opponents' rank, or their fairly modern weapons, backed down. They had a job to turn the camels around, tied as they were nose to tail in strings of ten. Once the cumbersome maneuver was done and the passage left free, Alexandra climbed into a small cart and traveled with assumed dignity along the road. She had won the loyalty of her men. On the sly, she slipped the Mongols two Chinese dollars for their trouble.

By noon the temperature had soared fifty or sixty degrees and the sun shone brilliantly in a sky of delft blue arched over clay yellow earth. The party slowed to shed some clothing, but since they were determined to cover forty kilometers during daylight, they wouldn't rest until dark. Their leader set the pace, and when they came to a treacherous ford across a stream she didn't hesitate to plunge in first. As the barely visible western mountains turned somber gray, sunset dying out behind their peaks, the travelers searched for a safe spot to camp. Perhaps in the lee of a hill they would be sheltered from the bitter night winds, and bandits, growing ever bolder, couldn't easily surprise them.

This evening they were lucky to fall in with a friendly clan of nomadic shepherds. Alexandra scoured the plain for yak chips— good fuel—while the boys gathered a little wood, lit a fire, and put up the tents. Yongden, the most trustworthy, tended to the animals, which had to be guarded. Then the former opera singer, clutching her bowl, made the rounds of the camp, shamelessly begging for milk—she was a vegetarian nun, she claimed—and blessing the nomads' sheep and yaks. She would sleep peacefully tonight, delicious curds in her belly, head cradled on folded clothes beneath which nestled her revolver.

Thus passed a typical day on the road to Lhasa, a journey that, with detours but not really tangents, was to take three full years and end in spectacular success. By February 1921, David-Neel felt herself growing older and more troubled by arthritis. Although she assured Philip that she yearned to return home, first she would accomplish what had become an obsession. She had numerous reasons to attempt Lhasa: prestige, fame, the pleasure of revenge on those who forbade it. Besides, what a story it would make!

However, something deeper called to her from this everlasting goal of travelers and pilgrims. In one sense she was content to wander over the steppes like any nomad. But Lhasa drew her in the same unreasoning way it still draws pilgrims from distant Mongolia: in greasy rags, they advance the whole way by prostrating themselves full-length on every third step, until each forehead is one big bruise while their eyes sparkle from the light within. Never mind the danger or discomfort or humiliation, Alexandra had determined to make the journey.

Then why did she take so long to reach her goal? The traveler moved concentrically, Kum Bum as approximate center, along a wheel within a wheel over the face of so-called Inner Tibet, western China, Mongolia, and down to southwestern China before she made a last dash across the treacherous Po country to Tibet's capital. She didn't plan this but responded to events, specifically setbacks in trying to reach Lhasa. Her mental gyroscope stayed on course, and the long, roundabout journey would prove its own reward as well as eventually successful.

But it all began badly. At Sining, the first sizable town en route, Alexandra was told by the chief of the Christian mission, the Reverend Ripley, that a money order sent to her by Philip had been lost. She supposed the Chinese postal authorities had pocketed the sum, ten thousand francs, more than enough to keep her going for a year. Even if Philip was willing to replace the sum, it wouldn't reach her for some time.

Alexandra fell back on any hospitality she could find, including that of brigands. The traveler wasn't above sharing a campfire and a bowl of hot buttered tea with these gentlemen, who must be distinguished from common thieves. Their calling was considered honorable and they followed a code of ethics. Punctilious brigands announced their attack beforehand, allowing victims room to defend themselves. Although they tried not to kill anyone, they appreciated a spirited fight, after which they left the losers a mule and enough food to reach safety. Times were so hard in parts of Amdo and Kham that all the men of a village went out to rob, while the women defended their homes. Euphemisms arose to describe the trade: pillage was termed "making commerce" or "gathering roots." A gentleman brigand, before stealing a mount, might intone the formula: "My horse is tired. Would you mind lending me yours?"

"It is natural that there should be brigands in Tibet," wrote

Charles Bell. He cited the wildness of the country with its vast empty spaces and that "by tradition and instinct the people are nomadic . . . hardy, living the simple life in clear, cold air, courageous, mobile, and fond of adventure." But their means of subsistence were precarious and the men at times found themselves robbing merchant caravans to feed their families. At other times these same brigands, even the fierce Goloks, would come to Lhasa as peaceable traders. They would not be arrested nor would they harm anyone.

In the shadow of Amne Machin in eastern Tibet, Alexandra once attended a festival of bandits at their mountaintop shrine; this was nominally Buddhist and contained such offerings as spears, broken guns, and flapping prayer flags. Each highwayman added a colored banner auspicious to his birthdate. The group, which surely included some murderers, showed no signs of bad conscience but enjoyed themselves by intoning chants exalting the deeds of mythic knights who roamed primeval forests slaying demons and rescuing maidens. Time was kept by striking an iron rod on a large caldron of bubbling soup. A photo taken by Alexandra shows a strapping Khampa, jeweled dagger hilt in evidence, staring unabashedly into the camera. He is not a fellow to fool with. However, in old age brigands often atoned for their deeds by going on pilgrimages or becoming monks. One rich and respected man who entertained the traveler had given up robbing only when his son was discovered to be the incarnation of a Grand Lama.

Alexandra had to keep her wits about her. Once, camping with a questionable bunch, she strung a rope across the bottom of her tent and during the night tripped up a robber. Another time she took a whip to a sturdy Khampa intent on having her knife. Because not all brigands were honorable and the conditions of survival went from bad to worse, outright ambush was a real danger. In 1922, the saintly Dr. Albert Shelton of the American mission hospital in Batang was senselessly gunned down on the road, although he was traveling with the prince of the region and an armed escort.

In uncertain country, Alexandra kept well ahead of her party, dressed in a dirty old robe like a Chinese peasant woman. Hobbling along, she looked too poor to rob, and she could scout for her men who followed. These were outfitted like soldiers and made a great show of their arms. Although the warning signal was a pious chant, Alexandra knew she was waging partisan warfare.

Her penchant for disguise—in particular as a harmless old crone—combined with an occasional judicious show of force reminds us of the tactics employed by Lawrence of Arabia in his campaigns. Granted the huge disparity in the size of the forces they led, both these warriors preferred using wiles to guns, and they were willing to expose themselves to harm before jeopardizing their men. They both appeared where least expected, thought always ahead of the enemy's moves, and never lost sight of their distant but realizable goals. These are classic guerilla tactics which necessitate a feel for the country and its natives that Lawrence manifested in the deserts of Arabia and David-Neel on the steppes of Central Asia.

Of course, the comparison ought not to be stretched. Alexandra, a Buddhist and a woman, better understood the consequences of violence. She claimed that she carried arms while traveling only to satisfy the desire of her boys to play soldier. She herself could hardly imagine an enemy she could not outwit. But this, too, is a posture. In fact Alexandra knew the thrill of entering a dense forest, weapons loaded, attentive to any rustle among the trees that might indicate an ambush by bandits. She enjoyed herself, much as did Lawrence setting out to dynamite a Turkish railway train.

As Alexandra's party traveled south along the border of Amdo and Kansu, famine prevailed and cholera raged; tigers and leopards were coming out of the woods to eat corpses. Yongden played tunes on a tin whistle to keep away the beasts, and more practically, he spread word through the villages that his mistress was an ancient sorceress. Donning her necklace of 108 pieces of human skull, she adopted the air of a dakini. Peasants appeared with their horded morsels, anxious to reverse the plagues afflicting them. Alexandra had to work for her and the boys' supper by blessing the new barley crop, the sheep and goats and pigs, exorcising the house where they were put up, and divining for its owner where a recently deceased relative would be reincarnated. It was useless to declare such business to be rubbish. Had she done so, the locals would suspect her of being a Christian missionary.

In areas that were predominately Chinese, Alexandra dropped her Tibetan disguise and attempted to look European. Amusingly, she was so accustomed to life on the steppes that she had come to look like a Tibetan nun of high rank. And to think like a Buddhist.

Once a Chinese coolie, who with others had done some work for her, attempted to grab away the bag of copper pennies out of which Yongden was paying the men. Everyone wanted to beat him, but when the others weren't looking Alexandra tossed the thief a silver dollar. He seized it and ran off. Alexandra knew she had been unjust but she had sensed the poor fellow's desperation. Compassion was more important than justice.

Still, Alexandra could take revenge on those who offended her personally. She usually received all the hospitality a visiting dignitary might expect. Abbots of both Buddhist and Bon monasteries welcomed her, while the peasants plied her with fresh eggs or barley flour. But on one occasion, when her party arrived at a village soaked after a day's trek in the rain, the folk were rude and grudgingly assigned her a campsite. It turned out to be the common toilet. Alexandra, furious, spat three times and solemnly cursed the villagers, not only in this lifetime but in the next. She strode off, declaring that she was going to sleep in a field and, to do so comfortably, would stop the rain. Within an hour the sky was filled with stars.

Next morning the headmen arrived to offer an excuse, but Yongden, often mischievous, seized a flashlight. He snapped on the light, terrifying the simple peasants. Then he invoked the flame within the lamp to do the bidding of the angry dakini. The village was cursed and not even their lama's prayers could save them. Leaving the folk in consternation, the party marched off. Alexandra felt they had gone too far, but Yongden, like a son to her, refused to countenance any slight. Her servants were sad, certain their mistress's curse would take effect.

By summer 1921, the wanderers were tramping through the forests of western Szechuan, braving downpours and mudslides—Alexandra praised her rubber-soled American boots—and crossing swollen rivers on rickety bridges of braided bamboo rope. One such span looked so unsteady, they spread planks atop it. They began to inch across, rocks falling from a cliff almost on their heads. Yongden called to hurry up, and no sooner had the boys and mules got over then the entire bridge crumbled into the rushing water. Up went the party into the perpetually white mountains, trudging along the steep, narrow paths hemmed in by walls of snow.

In her published works such as *Tibetan Journey*, David-Neel liked to present herself as hale and hearty, a French *voyageur* in a James Fenimore Cooper novel. She appears to be always good humored, ready for any adventure. But in letters to her husband she was more candid, admitting that she suffered greatly from arthritis and even depression. She wondered if she would ever succeed in her goal of reaching Lhasa. She was not, as she sometimes has been presented, an Amazon, but rather a normal although extraordinarily plucky woman. Will, and the power of an idea, drove her onward.

Officials caused more problems than did bandits, often being one in the same. The Chinese tried to fleece the travelers, but the Frenchwoman could threaten the wrath of her consulate at Chengtu—known as "Capital of the West"—or in a pinch invoke Yongden's British passport. When a Chinese petty bureaucrat refused to let them leave his village without an official stamp, that is to say a bribe, Alexandra refused, threatening to report him to Peking as an abuser of lamas. He backed down. The Tibetans could be thornier to deal with.

In early September, the party was well entertained by the rich abbot of Dzogchen gompa in Kham near the Yangtse. Alexandra, who earlier had been reduced to eating a dried sheep's head that gave her boils, delighted in feasting Chinese style with the cultivated abbot. Dessert came first, followed by dumplings, stews, fish, and meat and finally soup. Perhaps she dined too well, since soon after they left she came down with digestive difficulties that she termed enteritis.

She decided to proceed to Bhatang, further south on the Yangtse, to be nursed at the mission hospital presided over by the highly regarded missionary, Dr. Shelton. However, on a grassy plain Alexandra spotted two mounted men who were playing a fanfare and carrying a flag displaying a heraldic lion. Behind them rode a fat, ostentatious official (*gyapon*) from whom she sensed trouble.

Lhasa had newly asserted its authority over this area, and the gyapon was sent from the capital to investigate thievery. In a moment, his force of twenty-five soldiers appeared, headed by a sergeant. The official informed Alexandra that foreigners could proceed no farther into Tibet without a special passport. She must return to the monastery to await one. Very likely he supposed the philing was bound for Lhasa, and to let her pass would cost him dearly. Alexandra demanded that the detachment let her proceed. She described her dysentery in graphic detail. The gyapon acted sympathetic, but Alexandra soon discovered that he dreaded a powerful official at Tachienlu—the British consul in Szechuan—whose orders he was obeying.

Although this region was anarchic, the British remained influential. If Alexandra had known how interested in her whereabouts the Government of India remained, she would have become angrier and more concerned. The Foreign and Political Department of the viceroy's office issued the following communiqué on October 21, 1921: "Perhaps the minister at Peking may be able through the Chinese government or his French colleague to secure return of the French nun who is reported to be trying to enter Eastern Tibet."

Alexandra's disguise as a dakini, while impressing the locals, does not seem to have fooled the Tibetan or British officials. However, it was not until December 6 that the viceroy's office learned this was the same woman on whom they had kept a careful dossier: "We did not realize that the French nun was the well known Mme. Neel who crossed the frontier of India some years ago despite orders to the contrary. We hope she still can be turned back."

On the spot in Kham a standoff ensued. Alexandra was determined to press forward and the official and his soldiers were equally determined to stop her. Fear of being banned from the country altogether made her act cautiously. She agreed to leave the district, but by her own route. She now intended to go northwest to Jyekundo. This alarmed the gyapon, because not only did that town lie on the direct caravan route to Lhasa, it was also headquarters for a dangerous enemy, a Moslem Chinese general who was waging unrelenting war on the native tribes. The official, ordering the sergeant to draw up his men, insisted that Alexandra return to the monastery.

But secure in her right, she turned her back on the soldiers. The Tibetans became frightened at the thought of killing a European. They shouted the traditional benediction—"Long life!"— while the gyapon burst into tears. Still they kept her surrounded. Grasping her sturdy walking stick, the dumpy Frenchwoman attacked with the dispatch of a grenadier—whack! whack!—she cleared a path. She called to Yongden to bring her revolver and then threatened to shoot herself. The men were afraid of both the practical and karmic consequences of such a deed.

Poor Yongden was equally taken in by her performance as Alexandra strode toward her tent. He quickly hid the weapon and the drama fell a little flat. Still, the gyapon was sufficiently cowed to permit her to travel where she pleased. He gratefully acquiesced to her terms: yaks, supplies, an escort. Alexandra felt satisfied with her victory, temporary though it might be. She now realized the British would keep up their surveillance.

One day from a distance high on a snowy perch, the adventurers looked down to a valley with over two thousand yaks in line, divided in groups, hastening to the shrill cries of the cowboys who drove them. Large fierce dogs circling the yaks emphasized their masters' commands. It was a caravan bringing tea to Lhasa. When it had passed, Alexandra and her boys descended to the road. Yongden bowed to the ground three times.

Chapter 15

An Officer and a Gentleman

Jyekundo, under the control of a Chinese Moslem warlord, was as much a military garrison as a town. Its nondescript baked mud houses straggled up a bare hill toward an overlooking gompa of no distinction. The place failed to boast a single indoor toilet. At twelve thousand feet, set among frosty mountains on the edge of the Chang Tang, "Desert of Grass," it had a moderate summer climate. But winter promised to be bitter, and Alexandra, low on funds, was living in a leaky shack on top of a roof. She fought off the temptation to make a dash for Lhasa, some six weeks away. She was leery of another clash with Tibetan officials, who had been alerted by the Government of India and were on guard. So she and Yongden vegetated while water leaked from the roof onto her books and the wind whistled through crevices to torment her joints.

In late October Alexandra wrote to Philip that, although her heart bothered her, it would be preferable to get outdoors and search for another harbor for the winter. The fastidious traveler was offended by the dirt and lack of sanitation in the town. She was headed northwest to the Mongol camps in Sinkiang, where she hoped to rent a warm felt-lined yurt from the shepherds and to stay during the cold months. The summits she saw from her roof were already whitened, but perhaps the snows would not block the passes for another month.

The attempt lasted ten incredible days and failed. The pair couldn't struggle through drifts up to their waists, and their horses' hooves froze. Big gray wolves tracked the little party, one lean one coming particularly close. Yongden wanted to shoot him and use his skin to carpet their tent, but Alexandra preferred to try to tame him.

He was the leader, the most aggressive and the hungriest. She took a chunk of meat and moved cautiously toward the wolf, then tossed it to him. He seized it in his jaws and bounded away. The wolf returned but the game could not continue because Alexandra had not even scraps of food to spare. Back went the pair the way they had come.

Yongden found three rooms in a better house, but by midwinter Alexandra was seized by "cabin fever." Firing a little stove, she kept her room at a tolerable forty degrees Fahrenheit during the day, but at night it grew much colder. Outside the weather was dry and the sun shone in an azure sky. Alexandra, tired of aching joints, decided they would fight their way through to the warm valleys of the south where orchids bloomed the year long.

Again they set out. They walked for weeks, crossed mountain passes with snow up to their knees, slept in caves and nearly froze, and finally ran out of food. Fortunately, they were intercepted by Tibetan officials, who when they found a camera on Yongden, demanded that the pair turn back. This time Alexandra exacted horses, fuel, and money for the return trip. At Jyekundo she wanted to start immediately for the Gobi Desert, but the Moslem army commander—described by a British general as "a keen, energetic, honest, good man"—implored her to wait for warmer weather.

This general, Sir George Pereira, arrived at Jyekundo from Peking on June 23, 1922. He was a well-bred gentleman after Alexandra's own heart. She, in her fifties, had rheumatism and he, nearing sixty, limped from a childhood riding accident. His record in combat in the World War was heroic, and in spite of a troublesome digestion, he loved to roam the wild, far corners of the Orient. This splendid representative of the mature British Empire, a charming, unassuming scholar educated under Cardinal Newman had experienced a rough journey. He was weakened by hunger and thirst, his pack animals perished, and he had survived by the generosity of a passing caravan. Nonetheless, Sir George was as eager as Alexandra for further adventure.

The pair met daily to take tea, and the Frenchwoman, in her best robe, showed the Englishman the few sights of interest. The fellow explorers shared their most recent exploits. Sir George had hunted through the mountains of Szechuan in hope of bagging a giant panda, even at that time a rare animal that no European had shot.

He missed the prize, coming down with frostbitten toes instead. However the Buddhist Alexandra felt about such useless slaughter, she knew she needed Sir George's help. Stymied by petty bureaucrats, she was getting no closer toward her elusive goal.

Sir George was bound straight for Lhasa on a secret mission for the British Foreign Office, and he stayed in touch with the Government of India through Sikkim. He left at the end of the month, waited at Chamdo until early September for permission to continue—which was granted due to Charles Bell's influence at Lhasa—then he journeyed for six weeks over a difficult mountainous route to the capital. Sir George was well received and granted an interview with the Dalai Lama. In spite of deteriorating health, the general traveled during the next year along the wild Tibetan-Szechuan frontier, where he died at Kanze of a bleeding ulcer. He was a careful surveyor, and had he lived would have received the gold medal of the Royal Geographical Society.

Sir George was a genuinely brave man, and although he was warned about bands of brigands, he refused to travel in an armed caravan. Perhaps as a result, he became enchanted by Tibet. In a report to the Foreign Office, he wrote of ". . . the apparent happiness of the villagers. I have seen the children running about, playing games, and heard the laughter of the elders, and there seemed to be a freedom of care about the Tibetan peasantry, very different from village life in China." This foreigner could truthfully state, "Wherever I have been in Tibet I have received nothing but kindness and hospitality."

Sir George surely felt that his end was near, because he did a thing uncharacteristic of explorers: he shared his maps with a perfect stranger. Alexandra, who often navigated by instinct, now possessed more definite guidance. In return, she plied the general with information about the area where he was to lose his life. Both travelers were intrigued by the poorly known country of southeast Tibet, lying between Yunnan, China, and Lhasa.

One afternoon after tea a map was lying open on the table, and with the tip of his finger Sir George traced the supposed course of the Po River. "My information is that there are several accessible passes above the springs, where the river rises," he said. "If you went that way to Lhasa, you would be the first."

Alexandra was stunned. She had not said directly that she was

going to Lhasa, but Sir George had shown her the route. He acknowledged that it would be a journey fraught with danger. The inhabitants
of the Po country were deemed savages, maybe cannibals, and anyone
foolish enough to enter their domain supposedly never came out.

After giving Alexandra his lefthand blessing and a rough sketch
map, Sir George departed. To Major (soon Colonel) F. M. Bailey, who
in 1913 had explored part of the Po region and lived to become the
successor to Charles Bell at Gangtok, he wrote on July 28th: "I met
Mme. Neel, the French Buddhist lady, at Jyekundo, she had gone
from Kansu via Kantze to Jyekundo and [she] left the day after on
her return to Sinning and Lanchow." The latter two destinations
were to the northeast past Kum Bum and the Koko Nor Lakes, and
in the *opposite* direction from Lhasa. True, Alexandra was headed that
way at first. But chivalrous Sir George, who was aware of the wish of
the Government of India to keep her from the Tibetan capital, covered for her. He deceived his own government about time and place,
although merely by relating a partial truth.

His reasons are made clear in his confidential report to the
Foreign Department of the Government of India:

> At Jyekundo I met Madame Neel, the French Buddhist lady of some
> 50 summers, the only European I met between Tangar and Gyantse.
> She had been some years in China and had spent a year at Kum
> Bum monastery learning Tibetan and studying Tibetan books, and
> then she had adopted as a son an ugly Tibetan lama, whom I at first
> mistook for a Hindu waiting maid, who speaks English fluently. . . .
> After a study of Buddhism in Mongolia she is going to return to her
> husband in Tunis. Though told that she was very anti-British, it
> struck me that on the contrary she was well disposed, as she spoke of
> all the kindness she had received in India and said that British rule
> was the only thing for India. The only thing that struck me was that
> she did not seem to like British influence in Tibet . . .

Despite Pereira's somewhat mistaken time frame, his report confirms Alexandra's own account of her studies and travels (recalling
that he may have considered eastern Tibet to be "China") and tells us
that she had already decided to adopt Yongden, who was actually
rather agreeable looking. She had even told Sir George the truth
about her age!

Alexandra was stuck in hated Jyekundo until funds arrived from Philip. She and Yongden might wander the streets in rags, but she continued to acquire Tibetan books, which she sent on to Peking. By now Yongden was in his early twenties, and although slight and scarcely taller than Alexandra, a man of many talents. Besides acting as her secretary and helping with translations, he baked bread, cooked, washed linen, gathered wood, stitched together the remnants of their clothing, and performed any other task called for at the moment. In return he received not a rupee in salary, thus raising him from the class of servant to that of gentleman.

Yongden, like his mentor, was celibate, and he had decided to devote his life to helping Alexandra in her quest—so she informed Philip. Her husband must officially adopt and provide for him, because according to French law she herself could not. Once Philip met Albert, he would be happy to have him. Who was "Albert"?— merely Yongden with an anglicized name to suit his position, if not his attire. In any case, Philip's acquiescence was a fond assumption on her part.

Alexandra spent nearly a year at Jyekundo scheming her departure. She and Yongden could watch caravans of yaks trundling by on the route from Tachienlu across the Desert of Grass to Lhasa. One day when the frustrated adventurers were wandering the muddy streets, a huge Khampa, brandishing an antique sword, dashed from a house and was quickly followed by a score of fellows trying to catch him. Alexandra inquired of some women and learned that the warrior took himself for an incarnation of Dickchen Shenpa, minister to King Gesar of Ling, the hero of the Tibetan national epic that bears his name. Because King Gesar's enemy the King of Hor had reincarnated in town in the form of a young lad, when Dickchen downed too much chang, he roared off in search of the evildoer. The other men always stopped him from harming the poor boy.

Alexandra was delighted to learn that Dickchen was a wandering minstrel who sang passages from the long poem, which she supposed to have originated over one thousand years before. Next day she slipped in among the women gathered to hear him; the men sat opposite, everyone on a bit of carpet on the dirt floor. The madman was now composed, chanting, gesturing, all the while staring at a sheet of blank paper. Alexandra admired his stature and figure, his handsome features and bright, flashing eyes that at times seemed to reflect an inner world of visions.

Singing in the Kham dialect, the bard played out the numerous roles of the colorful epic and even provided his own accompaniment by imitating trumpets and other instruments. The audience, who had listened to the story many times before, interrupted on occasion with cries of, *"Om mani padme hum!"* (Hail to the jewel in the lotus!) The blank paper was put in front of the performer because on it he envisioned what he was about to sing. The minstrels of the poem have committed it to their subconscious memories and are able to call up passages when they wish. While some scholars claim that King Gesar is a mythical personage, Tulku Thondup Rinpoche wrote (in 1996) in an introduction to a new translation: "Gesar was a real person and his victories were true events. . . . Gesar's influence on the spiritual and social life of his people is still felt in many parts of Tibet, Mongolia, Buryatsia, Kalmykia and Tuva [Russia]."

Alexandra invited the minstrel to perform the epic in private, to which he agreed after she assured him that King Gesar would not be denigrated. As the man chanted, she and Yongden both scribbled, and in six weeks they had produced the most complete written copy in existence. Alexandra realized the minstrel lived more in the time of Gesar (the Tibetan "hour of glory" in the seventh and eighth centuries) than in the present. He would often disappear to wander over the grasslands dreaming of his old life as companion to the great champion of justice. But in earnest, he insisted he *was* Dickchen and could transmigrate back and forth between past and present.

Once, in midwinter with temperatures down to below zero Fahrenheit, the Khampa brought the foreign lama a fresh blue flower—sent to her by Gesar himself. The ground was frozen, the nearby Yangtse covered with ice six feet thick, and this species of flower normally bloomed in July. Where on earth had he gotten it? Equally puzzling was the prediction by Dickchen, based on the epic, that the Panchen Lama would flee to China in exactly two years. Alexandra scoffed, but on her way to Lhasa in 1924 she was shocked to learn that her friend, fearing for his life, had indeed taken refuge in Chinese territory. Even the boy supposed to be the evil King of Hor, then a novice monk of ten, seemed to possess an appropriately vicious nature: he delighted in killing birds with stones and pummeling his fellow novices.

There were too many local versions of the epic for Alexandra to produce a definitive text. But since the historical King Gesar had been a Khampa, their version was the most comprehensive. The tale of heroism, of knight errantry, is nominally Buddhist but pervaded by an earlier spirit of magic and wonders. Gesar, an incarnate god, rides a golden, winged stallion into battle against the demons of the four directions. He is the great hero, the tiger-god of consuming fire, sometimes fitted out in gold armor and at other times all in turquoise, including helmet, shield, bow and arrows. He is fond of quick changes and appears indifferently as a humble blacksmith's apprentice or the god Namthig Karpo, clad in white and riding a goat, or in the more suitable guise of the handsome, irresistible king who uses his soulful black eyes and enchanting smile to seduce his worst enemy's wife.

There is a touch of Rabelais about this rambling tale, sung not in classical Tibetan but the dialect of whichever region the bard finds himself. Gesar, like Buddha, comes to banish ignorance, but he is not squeamish about using force. After he has slept with the queen, and she has fed him dainties and quickly hidden him when her husband the King of Hor comes home—not under the bed but beneath the kitchen floor—Gesar cleaves the cannibal-demon-king's head in two. Then he gives the villain's spirit, which is wandering in the *Bardo* (purgatory), precise instructions on how to avoid hell and reach the Western Paradise. Sinners are to be redeemed.

The epic, Homeric in its proportions, functions on several levels. The simple folk love to hear it over and over, for it both reflects their concerns and transports them to magical realms. But as made clear by Chogyam Trungpa Rinpoche, this is a serious treatise on courage: "Gesar represents the ideal warrior, the principle of all-victorious confidence. As the central force of sanity he conquers all his enemies . . . who turn people's minds away from the true teachings of Buddhism . . . that say it is possible to attain ultimate self-realization." Sakyong Mipham Rinpoche, Trungpa's son, adds in a foreword to a new translation, *The Warrior Song of King Gesar*, "He represents our dreams; our hopes of overcoming incredible odds; of being victorious and kind at once; of being vast and at the same time noticing small pebbles alongside the road."

This sounds like a description of David-Neel's midwinter journey to Lhasa. The enemy, to be found in one's own mind, is cowardice. Her attraction to Buddhism, allegedly a passive faith, can be better understood if seen in this light. Once she overcame her doubts and fears, she attained her birthright, her self. Then no official, no army, no empire could stop her from going where she pleased.

In early August 1922 Alexandra, after selling two mules to reduce her cavalry to five, headed a small party traveling northwest toward the Gobi in China's Sinkiang province. The Moslem general loaned her a couple of his soldiers as an escort and a two-wheeled baggage cart. To Philip, she hinted about following an old caravan route, rich in Buddhist lore, to Samarkand, Russia, from where a railroad ran to Paris! It isn't likely she was serious. The czarist empire had startled the world by becoming the Soviet Union, and its eastern provinces were the scene of civil strife and epidemics.

Alexandra admitted that she was zigzagging, which greatly multiplied the distance to her goal. Her letters might be intercepted and read at any time. Earlier she had warned Philip that he might not hear from her for a lengthy period because she was headed where there was no post office. No matter, he must not send out a search party, which would put her life in greater danger.

David-Neel proceeded at a leisurely pace. She spent November and December at Kanchow on the edge of the Little Gobi just below the Great Wall. In a drafty house where she and Yongden had to sleep without a fire while the thermometer plunged to below zero, they polished their version of the Gesar epic, consulting several texts. Curiously, she complained that many of its incidents were too risqué, and the edition that she finally published in English in 1934 is (alas!) properly Victorian. The scholar had high hopes for her progeny and mistakenly supposed that the *Superhuman Life of Gesar of Ling* would make a best-seller. Instead, it remains the least known of the great world myths.

In January 1923, with a light sprinkling of snow on the ground, the temperature barely rising to the twenties Fahrenheit in the glare of the noonday sun, the party saddled up their mules and set off across the desert. Occasional low dunes were followed by stretches of spiny grass. They saw almost no one, but somewhere in this region Alexandra had her finest opportunity to observe a *lung-gom* runner.

One day, peering through field glasses, she picked up a moving black spot far in the distance. As she watched, this turned into a man heading toward them with incredible rapidity. The orientalist was thrilled as she realized she would be the first Westerner to verify the remarkable feats of these adepts, who are sometimes said to fly. She reached for her camera.

A trusted retainer warned her to keep her distance; she mustn't stop the lama or speak to him because it would kill him. The skeptic in Alexandra doubted this, but she had to respect even the grossest superstition if the people believed it. Reluctantly, she studied the runner but took no pictures.

She saw that his face was perfectly calm and his gaze fixed on an imagined object far, far away. Rather than run, the *lung-gom-pa* lifted himself from the ground, proceeding by leaps. He looked like a rubber a ball that bounced each time it touched the ground. He wore ragged monastic garb. In his right hand he held a *phurba* (magic dagger) and appeared to use it as a staff though it was high off the ground.

Lung-gom-pas were expected to continue in their even, ground-devouring stride for days on end without stopping for food or water. In the vast, nearly empty countryside of northern Tibet, such a feat might be termed practical. Only certain lamas indulged in such traveling, and their training was as curious as the accomplishment. Not really athletes, they were mystics who had meditated for years in a dark hole. Breathing exercises, chants, and visualizations were repeated until the adepts were able, from a seated posture, to leap straight up out of the hole. Another portion of the training consisted of going about for long periods in heavy irons, so that when the chains were removed, the practitioner felt feathery light. As in *tumo* breathing, skill at lung-gom was acquired by clearing the mind of distractions, followed by perfect concentration on a diety. It was both a mystical practice and a necessity in the Tibetan wilds. Soon Alexandra would have to call on this art to survive.

After traversing barren country that reminded her of the Sahara, and reaching Anhsi in Sinkiang, Alexandra wheeled her party around for a grand flanking move. She wasn't deterred by the cold, for although the occasional inns were miserable, sleeping on their Mongol-style *kangs* was comfortable. This was a cement platform on which bedding was placed and under which horse dung was burned. It smelled bad but kept the sleeper warm. However, a turn around Mongolia was ruled out by the hostilities between pro- and anti-Bolsheviks. In early April the expedition arrived back in Lanchow, where Alexandra took decisive steps. She sent on her books, certain valuables, and good clothes to the French Bank of Indochina at Shanghai. She dismissed her loyal Tibetan retainers, gave up the camp bed Philip had sent her, and her snug tents as well; not even her beloved tub was spared. From here on the once-particular Parisian would travel lean, depending on her adopted son to do the tasks she couldn't manage.

In May Alexandra crossed the dry, dusty land of Kansu under a scorching sun that raised the temperature to ninety degrees Fahrenheit. When night came, it plummeted forty or fifty degrees to leave her and Yongden shivering in their sheepskins. Since she was taking quinine, she likely had a touch of malaria, but she worried more about her son's violent fever until it abated. On they traveled, Alexandra carried in a sedan chair by two porters while Yongden brought up the rear. Still in poor health, he prodded a couple of mules with baggage.

Through the narrow gorges of Shensi, the poor woman sweltered in her bouncing black box. The inns were filled with vermin, and often she preferred to spend the night dozing outside the front door in the chair. She informed Philip that she was sending him two articles for the *Mercure*: one on "Socialism Among Primitive Tribes," the other a humorous aside on how to travel cheaply in China.

Toward the end of June, held up by seemingly random fighting, Alexandra arrived at Chengtu, Szechuan. Typically, she lodged with missionaries, in this case French Catholic nuns who ran a hospital. Again she was sick with dysentery and saw a doctor at the Institut Pasteur. He insisted that she live there so he could begin a course of treatment. The weary traveler moved in, reveling in good food and a lush garden. But she declined a series of injections of a supposedly infallible remedy because she was afraid of the hypodermic shots. Living genteelly, she mended, helped along by the sizable French community showering praises on her head. The consul gave a reception in her honor, which she attended with a slight fever, and he demanded that she accept a loan of money.

Alexandra also dined with the Catholic bishop at his palace, where she and Yongden were offered such unaccustomed luxuries as wine and cigarettes, coffee and cake. The clergymen present never spoke of religion, but they nevertheless encouraged their country-woman to join forces with the church. The bishop considered her an apostate but a very impressive one.

Fearful of being thwarted, Alexandra concealed her destination from everyone. The allegedly Republican government at Peking—still referred to as "the Emperor's household"—held the allegiance of a wavering number of Chinese provinces. From Canton, Sun-Yat-sen influenced much of the south, while most larger coastal cities were dominated by the European powers. Japan was powerful in the north, and the situation in the west was bloody and anarchic. The governor of Kansu was making war on the rebel governor of Szechuan, who had called on Yunnan to send troops to his aid. Alexandra, headed south across these provinces, expected to encounter famine, brigands, corrupt officials, and lots of adventure.

In mid-July Alexandra took to her sedan chair, traversing muddy roads, torrential rivers, and a combat zone in southern Szechuan. She found herself in the midst of the retreating northern army. The soldiers tried to stop her, but she chatted with the general and got a pass. Next she came to the rear guard digging in to impede the enemy advance. She felt sorry for the men, boys really, some holding parasols or fans. It reminded her of a scene from *Madame Butterfly*. At a deserted village, her coolies rebelled and laid down the chair. *Madame* hopped out and threatened to beat them, if not worse, and so they carried her onward. She wanted to stop to watch the battle, but the shrieking coolies persuaded her to go around through a rice paddy. She found the mosquitoes a nuisance.

More serious were the native bandits formed into sufficiently large armies that they defeated the regulars. The Lolo tribe had the nasty habit of kidnapping foreigners for ransom. So with much evad-ing and maneuvering, trekking in paddy mud up to their knees, Alexandra and Yongden reached Likiang in late September. This last Chinese town in northwest Yunnan was dominated by another tribe, the Mossos. Burma was to the south, Tibet to the north, and already there were Tibetans nearby. Staying at a Pentecostal mission where she was cordially received, although the food was plain, Alexandra wrote to her husband that she was ready to begin on the hard part of her adventure.

She crossed the Mekong River by a preposterous rope and pulley, a means of traversing a river that would soon look positively modern. Then, after paying a call on an isolated French priest, she wrote her "dear Mouchy" that he would hear from her in the spring. She was going to try something that her academic colleagues with big reputations would not dare.

Poor Philip in Algeria had a dream about his errant wife shivering in the shadow of a mountain, her fire gone out, the snow drifting over her tent . . . only the icy stars knew her whereabouts. He awoke startled, certain that either he or she was mad. He must do something.

Philip acted in his own way and made a difference. He contacted the French Foreign Ministry and they alerted their ambassador in London. Le Comte de Saint-Aulaire explained, in a note dripping with *politesse*, the purpose of Alexandra's journey to the one man who could from such a distance offer her protection: the Marquess Curzon of Kedleston, the British Foreign Secretary. Lord Curzon was impressed by Alexandra's daring, though he may have thought her mad. He requested that Viscount Peel, then the viceroy, instruct the proper Indian officials to ensure Alexandra's safe conduct. Instructions made their way through the India Office to the government of India, where they were received by the Political Department and commented on by a series of bureaucrats whose signatures are illegible or mere initials. The first of these complained on August 22, 1922:

Madame Neel is a lady of somewhat doubtful antecedants who was last heard of in the autumn of 1921 on the Sino-Tibetan frontier. She was then said to be contemplating a journey to Lhasa.

The French govt. now state that she will shortly cross India on her return from a journey of exploration in the Pamirs, and ask 'that she be made welcome.'

'Pamirs' is probably not used by the French govt. In the strict geographical sense, but . . . In the vague sense of 'High Asia,' and Mme Neel may be simply coming down from Tibet via Gangtok or Leh, or even direct from Lhasa via Gyantse. Even so the puzzling question arises of how the French govt. knows of her whereabouts. . . .

It is not quite clear what the French govt. expect the Govt. of India to do. The latter cannot be expected to go to trouble to provide positive facilities for a lady with Mme Neel's record. Possibly all that is expected is that the G of I should refrain from arresting her as an undesirable!

The second official commented that the Foreign Office in London "know nothing whatever about Mme. Neel." A third had no comment and a fourth remarked: "It is difficult to form any opinion of this lady's activities . . . I should gather she is a French agent of some importance." Finally, on August 28, the Political Committee translated Lord Curzon's generosity into carte blanche for the Government of India to take "such action as may appear desirable," which in effect meant that "Mme Neel's movements [will be] discreetly watched." The French Nun, a spy, was to be spied upon, providing she could be found. Alexandra, however, along with Yongden had launched herself into the unknown.

Chapter 16
A Long Walk

From David-Neel's farthest penetration of the Gobi at Anhsi in March 1923 to the northwest corner of Yunnan province, adjacent to where she designed to slip into Tibet, is a distance of over a thousand miles north to south across western China. That is as the crow flies, but she and Yongden had proceeded more like turtles, maturing their plans as they went. By the time the pair arrived at the Abbé Ouvrard's parish on the right bank of the Mekong in late October, they had likely covered at least twice that mileage. They were on the march since leaving Jyekundo in August of the previous year. They had traversed desert, jungle, and rice paddy, endured scorching heat and freezing cold—often in the course of a single day. The travelers were worn out and undernourished, health shaky, and the kind abbé looked concerned when they departed his mission on short notice.

Rumor was Alexandra's most feared enemy. If Tibetan officials got wind of her intentions, they would guard the few roads to Lhasa with greater care. Although the abbé had proved warmly cordial to strangers, Alexandra fooled him with a story about going on a search for rare plants. Inspiration had come from a chance meeting with the American botanist Dr. Joseph Rock, who tendered her an offer, naturally refused, to plant hunt with him. His large expedition, with its comings and goings, nevertheless provided good initial cover for the two outlanders to stray across the border. Rock would be responsible for spreading the erroneous idea that Amne Machin, in the region of Koko Nor, was a peak higher than Everest. His 1930 article in *National Geographic* contributed to the mysterious, Shangri-La quality of Tibet, where even the supposedly highest mountain on earth could go unremarked for centuries.

One bright autumn morning, his guests bid the ingenuous Father Ouvrard adieu and headed toward the Kha Karpo range. The snow mountain, glittering as a diety, guarded the threshold of the mysterious land. The explorers wore typical Chinese dress, while two coolies carried a week's provisions and a light tent made by Yongden. It would have been unthinkable for a European woman to carry her own pack. Alexandra, after evading the curiosity of botanist and priest, now had to rid herself of the servants.

The party spent its first night in a vultures' cemetery where on occasion the locals slaughtered an old mule in order to lure scores of the winged scavengers that they would bludgeon to death for their feathers. The site was littered with bleached bones, but Alexandra had eyes only for the highest of the mountains, illumined by a full moon in a starless sky. It was the season for pilgrims, come from the four directions, to tramp the long way around the sacred Kha Karpo. Among these pious folk, who spoke a variety of dialects, Alexandra intended that she and Yongden should blend—Tibetan mother and lama son.

Complaining that her feet were bruised and needed rest, which was true, she discharged the coolies one after the other. Paid and fed, they were sent in opposite directions to meet eventually and share their confusion. In directing one of the boys to a mission bearing a package of clothes for the poor, Alexandra gave away most of her and Yongden's wardrobe. She did not leave them with a single blanket. But they still had too much to carry, and they had to sacrifice a waterproof groundsheet.

Their kitchen equipment consisted of one all-purpose aluminum pot, a lama's wooden bowl for Yongden, an aluminum bowl for Alexandra, a case containing a knife and chopsticks, and two cheap foreign spoons over which she was to nearly kill a man with her new automatic pistol. Alexandra reluctantly gave up her thermos. They took so little because they meant to pose as *arjopas*, the mendicant pilgrims who in large numbers roam from one sacred spot to another. Many of these, while keeping back a few coins for Lhasa, begged for their supper. It was considered meritorious for people to aid them.

The pair headed for the Dokar Pass, gateway to Tibet proper, and at first they walked only at night through the heavily forested district. The track itself was sufficiently rough, but in the dark they knocked into trees or fell against thorny bushes. Although tortured by thirst, the power of will dulled their pain and drove them on— aided by small doses of strychnine. When taken homeopathically, this deadly poison is a central nervous stimulant and energizer. However, a slight overdose can result in a condition in which one's senses become overly acute and one sees and hears what isn't there. This partially explains why at first, Alexandra peopled the forest with spies and felt like a hunted animal. Then came an odd series of incidents.

Strange, feverish mirages arose before the pilgrims. When the pair spotted crows perched on a tree branch, the black birds circled around them, making highpitched noises like laughs. Yongden declared these were really feathered demons who played tricks with fire and music at night to seduce travelers from the right path. The orthodox young lama admitted that his great-grandfather had been a renowned magician. Then, to disperse the mysterious birds, Yongden recited formulas and made the appropriate ritual gestures.

Alexandra's unease deepened, accentuated by tramping through the darkness to the accompaniment of panthers roaring in the bush. Her bones hurt from sleeping by day on the ground hidden under a pile of moldering leaves. Even a pleasant morning during which the interlopers approached the Dokar through a beautiful valley white with frost turned bitterly cold as they began to ascend. They reached the pass by evening, the threshold of the guarded region. Tibetans had planted around it the usual flags inscribed with prayers. But even these seemed martial and threatening to the weary, drugged mother and son.

The two were welcomed to the Land of Snows by a sudden blizzard of sleet. Missing the path down, they began to slip and each had to fix a sturdy staff in the ground for support. They squatted on their haunches until two in the morning while snow fell, but when a faint moon rose they were able to descend. These staffs were furnished with sharp iron tips and were *de rigueur* for treks through the Tibetan wilds. By now the travelers had donned heavier clothes more suited to the weather. Yongden dressed in lama's robes, while Alexandra put on suede boots from Kham, a coarse, heavy dress in layers with long sleeves, and an old red sash twisted about her head. But none of this clothing could compare with the fleecy sheepskins worn by natives to keep out chill blasts.

On the far side of the Dokar, bizarre happenings continued. In a glade by a river a leopard came by to sniff. Yongden was asleep. Alexandra, remembering her Bengal tiger, condescendingly shooed the cat on its way. That same day the travelers stumbled upon a village unmarked on any map. They saw an oriental fantasy of palaces and villas in miniature, surroundeed by deer parks. Thinking it real, they retreated to cover till evening and fell asleep. When they awoke the strange town was entirely gone. Yongden insisted that it could not have been a product of both their imaginations. A vision, yes, but real in its own way, which he had dispelled with magic words and signs. Perhaps it was the work of someone who wished to hinder them.

Alexandra took the affair with a grain of salt. When Yongden warned that soon they would confront material villagers, soldiers, and officials, who would be suspicious of strangers, she assured him she would cast a spell over them. Feeling more herself, Alexandra revelled in the unbridled freedom of a pilgrim who carries all she owns on her back and is liberated from worldly cares. That evening she even performed the *chöd* rite, a mystic dance that involves certain formulas and exhortations to the gods and demons to aid the performer in freeing the mind from attachment. Within a few years she had become a *naljorma*, a female mystic.

Alexandra perfected her outward disguise as the pair moved along. She made braids out of jet black yak's hair and to match that color rubbed a wet stick of Chinese ink on her own brown hair. She wore huge earrings in native style and powdered her face with cocoa and crushed charcoal to darken it; her hands she blackened with soot. The proficiency with make-up learned in her operatic days helped greatly. Equally important was the role she ought to play, and quick-thinking Yongden devised one. When a group of pilgrims wondered aloud if the silent old woman—transfixed by dazzling white peaks jutting into a cobalt blue sky—were a *pamo* (a medium), he assured them that she was. Elaborating, he said his father had been a *ngagspa* (sorcerer), and therefore his old mother was a *sang yum* (literally "secret mother"), the spouse of a tantric lama. This instilled caution in the simple folk they had encountered. The pilgrims dreaded to offend even the consort of a wizard, whether he was living or dead. After offering mother and son tsampa and dried meat, they hurriedly went their way. The food was welcome, since the travelers carried only a small supply.

Yongden's strutting as a lama skilled in the occult arts was bound to cause complications. For a while the pair continued to avoid villages, skulking through before dawn and concealing themselves at daybreak, watching the stream of pilgrims flow past. Yongden tried to cadge food, tea, and information from these sojourners from eastern and northern Tibet, and in return they often demanded he perform *Mo*. This fortune-telling by means such as counting beads or staring into a bowl of water had as its object anything from predicting the future to discovering a lost domestic animal. It would have been unthinkable for a Red Hat lama to refuse an honest entreaty and besides, he was sure to reap a reward. Between mother and son positions were now reversed: *he* was courted for his knowledge, while *she* dumbly scoured their pot or did some other chore.

Ten days out, they reached the majestic Salween River, where they accepted a kind lama's hospitality for the night. The countryside in autumn had an eternal springlike freshness. They wandered on the river bank under a warm sun and the pebbles under their feet seemed alive; mother and son were strangely suffused with joy. They were entering a mythical region called Pemako by the Tibetans. It was a sort of Promised Land, the subject of an old prophecy that predicted Buddhism would be persecuted in Tibet, but "here they would find a land good to live, their religion would revive and eventually spread throughout the world."

While the congruence of the prophecy with actual events today is impressive, the Tibetans who relocated there in the nineteenth century did not find the territory—the lower Tsangpo Valley, on the frontier of India where Assam meets Burma—terribly cordial. They often fought with the local tribes, and in 1910 they were caught in the path of an invading, marauding Chinese army. Colonel Eric Bailey, who entered the region in 1913 to survey and map for the Government of India, complained of leeches in the woods and indoors "every species of fly which bit or stung." Yet Alexandra and Yongden spent a delightful few days loitering along the beautiful river valley.

The travelers had left behind the pilgrim route around Kha Karpo and needed to invent a new excuse for their wandering. A minor loss briefly shook their confidence. Alexandra carried a small compass that she took pains to conceal. After a night spent in a cave, she was putting on her overdress, which served as a blanket, when she discovered the instrument was missing. If such a foreign object was found, it would give them away to officials who might hunt them down. Frantic, the pair backtracked and finally located the compass, although Alexandra admitted the mishap set her heart to pounding.

Even their small tent could give them away. After ascending the Tondo-la (*la* means pass) at 11,200 feet and once again descending, the weary walkers pitched their tent by a stream. They dared to use it only under cover of darkness. In the morning a large party of pilgrims overtook them and begged Yongden to tell their fortunes. One farmer wanted to know how his cattle were faring during his absence. More serious was the plight of a young girl with sore feet who feared being abandoned on the trail. Such was the fate of those who failed to keep up on the arduous tramps; they might fall victim to wolves or perish from starvation.

Lama Yongden was both compassionate and clever. He slowly counted the beads on his rosary, tossed pebbles in the air, and consulted the auguries. He concluded that a wicked demon had swelled the girl's legs and that it must be exorcised by stopping for three days at a *chorten* (a burial monument containing a relic), which they would soon encounter. Here the pilgrims were to observe a ceremony that the lama explained in detail: these simple folk had to recite a spell that ended in a bleat, "Bhaaah!" Yongden made them practice it many times over until they got it right.

At least the girl would enjoy a much-needed rest. The bumpkins, overawed by the lama, reluctantly allowed him to leave and began to spread stories about his magical powers. At a nearby village, Yongden enthralled the whole population and the monks from the gompa with tales of faraway places and his making of *Mo*. The peasants brought him gifts, which he graciously accepted, while Alexandra, squatting in the dust, grew uneasy. She uttered a pious expression that secretly meant, "Let's beat it!" Yongden had to surrender his newly won celebrity and a comfortable lodging to tramp off with his mother. The scolding she gave him made him sulky for days. However, it was next his turn to berate her for a potentially fatal misstep.

The pair had stopped in midmorning to boil tea beside a primitive aqueduct. A dozen villagers gathered to watch, wondering who they were. Yongden, chewing on tsampa, refused to utter a word. Alexandra grew flustered and hurriedly washed the teapot. She forgot that the water would reveal her white skin to the locals. Doubtless these folk had never seen a European in the flesh, but they felt sure they were tallish demons with white eyes and gray hair. Nothing could be more ugly or dangerous. The people of Tibet were naturally friendly and helpful to strangers, especially pilgrims, but they had been led to believe that all philings wished to destroy their religion. So it was no joking matter when three soldiers joined the crowd. They demanded to know where the travelers were bound.

Yongden calmly spoke up, saying that he and his mother had made a pilgrimage to Kha Karpo and were returning to their own country, Amdo. They loaded up and started off on the road to Lhasa, leaving the villagers to argue about whether they were or were not Mongols—half-wild savages but at least not philings. Alexandra breathed a sigh of relief.

Mother and son trudged on through a cultivated, hilly landscape that was still green although it was nearly winter. The valleys of southern Tibet are so favored climatically that they can grow a winter crop. Food was for sale at the monasteries, which often owned the land worked by the farmers. But ironically, monks were more worldly than the common folk, and they might recognize Alexandra as a philing. So the travelers would hurry by the walls of a gompa in the early morning darkness and camp in the woods; at dawn, Yongden would return for supplies and intelligence. In one instance, becoming hopelessly muddled in a pitch black night, they decided to lie down where they found themselves, without shelter or a fire. They slept painfully on rocks.

The first rays of light revealed they were camped directly beneath the walls of a monastery in which lodged an important official. While Alexandra scurried off to the nearest field, Yongden went in to barter. He returned loaded down like a mule, and they breakfasted luxuriously on broth thickened with wheat flour and then continued on to a pilgrims' camp. The good-humored folk came forward to be blessed, and Alexandra chatted with the women about her yak-hair tent in the Koko Nor region, her flock of sheep, and her favorite holidays. She was no longer a philing but a nomad of the steppes, free as all her breed.

Soon thereafter, Alexandra found an old fur-lined bonnet on the trail. It was the sort worn by the women of Kham and would both complete her disguise and warm her head on the cold heights rising between them and Lhasa. But Yongden warned her against touching it. Tibetans believe that to pick up a hat, although it falls off one's own head, ensures bad luck. The Frenchwoman laughed and stuck the greasy fur onto her pack.

Their luck did change, but for the better. A close encounter with a *pombo,* posted by Lhasa to guard the road and interrogate suspicious characters, turned out well. Officials, soldiers, and monks were all on the alert against foreigners. This pombo carefully scrutinized Yongden but ignored his mother squatting in the dust, then gave the pilgrims a rupee as alms. Alexandra was so nervous she felt that needles were piercing her brain. She needn't have worried, since her son's twice-told tale was becoming as polished as a jewel.

Congratulating themselves, the pair hurried upward toward the next pass, the To-la. At the gusty summit, prayer flags flapping, they shouted to the ice-blue sky the traditional salutation:*"Lha gyalo! De tamche pam! Victory to the Gods! The Demons are Vanquished!"*

Alexandra soon found herself a guest of ordinary Tibetans while posing as a beggar. Already she had adopted certain habits of the country, such as blowing her nose with her fingers, sitting calmly on a dirt floor spotted with grease and spit, or wiping her soiled hands on her dress. Now, however, she would face additional affronts to her ingrained sense of cleanliness, offered out of hospitality. She was to live as did the common folk and to converse with women in a way that had never been done by a European. At the home of a wealthy villager, she had to eat anything that came her way. It was unheard of for beggars to turn down food put into their bowls. Here, at least, the householder was too frugal to offer the Tibetan luxury she most dreaded: maggoty meat.

The travelers gained valuable information at this place. Later, David-Neel, when creating her own legend, claimed to despise politics and to carefully avoid any involvement in such matters. In fact she was, and had to be, a shrewd political observer. Her sympathies lay with the Panchen Lama, who had treated her kindly and whom she found more philosophical and open-minded than the Thirteenth Dalai Lama. Thus she seemed ready to believe the worst of the government at Lhasa.

Alexandra listened attentively as the farmers complained of arrogant officials sent from the capital and of taxes levied to pay for the new, modernized army. She would be quick to inform her readers that the men of the border regions were trusted only with old, outmoded rifles. Some of them secretly preferred the governance of the defunct Manchu Empire, which had been distant and light. The Khampas particularly were independent to the point of anarchy, and it was for good reason Alexandra was able to impersonate one.

Well briefed on where the pombos held sway, the pilgrims tramped on. Feeling confident, they sought out habitations where the lama could tell fortunes or the mother beg from door to door. One housewife called them in for a meal and poured into their bowls curds and tsampa. Alexandra began to mix the two, forgetting her fingers were dark from wet ink recently applied to her hair: Black streaked the milky tsampa.. As the good woman drew near, Alexandra hastily swallowed the entire bowl of nasty tasting stuff.

Still less appetizing was a meal served by a poor couple who extended the hospitality of their hovel on a bitter night. These folks were no better off than beggars, so Yongden offered them the rupee given him by the generous pombo, in order to buy something decent to eat. The man exited and triumphantly returned with a parcel. By the embers of the tiny fire, Alexandra made out a stomach. She knew that sewed up in the stomach were the kidneys, heart, liver, and entrails of the animal. These had been decaying in there for weeks to create what Tibetans considered a delicacy. The housewife made a stew from this gelatinous horror, the children fell upon the scraps, which they devoured raw, and then bowls of the foul soup were presented to the guests. Alexandra had crawled into a corner, groaning.

Yongden announced that his mother was ill, but beneath his breath he muttered that she always escaped the worst of it. He bravely gulped a full portion of the nauseating liquid. Not surprisingly, he too fell down sick. The family joyfully feasted on the rest, smacking their lips, while the numbed travelers drifted off to sleep.

The pair had become true Tibetan wayfarers. If the trail led down and then up several thousand feet, it was gladly climbed. Officials delegated by Lhasa, each feeling obliged to demonstrate his importance, combed the villages in order to tax the inhabitants. The two beggars dodged them or, half-smirking, pleaded for alms. They lingered along the Nu Valley, chatted with its farmers, then struck out into unknown, barely explored country. Autumn leaves turned gold and purple were set off by the evergreens. Sometimes a fine snow sprinkled the grass to lay down a magical carpet. But this fairyland aura could be shattered by the suspicious stare of a nosy lama, or the whispered rumor that philings had been seen in the neighborhood—usually taken to be Chinese. Alexandra and Yongden reverted to nighttime tramps, once again fearful of discovery.

The lack of privacy among humble Tibetans caused the retiring Frenchwoman problems. Once so fastidious, a hot bath struck her as a memory from a former life. Going to the toilet in front of others remained trying. Aside from embarrassment, she couldn't afford to divulge the articles hidden beneath her voluminous dress. She had to complete her arrangements in the early morning darkness before their hosts stirred. She darkened her face with soot from the bottom of the cooking pot, then poked Yongden awake. They would position their heavy money belts containing silver coins—accepted currency—and, in Alexandra's case, gold jewelry given to her by the late maharaja of Sikkim. This hoard was sufficient to get them murdered many times over. They tucked away compasses, watches, and maps, and finally they secured their pistols, always kept loaded.

Alexandra wanted to carry a camera in her pack, but it meant added weight and if found would have made her position very precarious. She had been turned back earlier on that score, and therefore her precautions had become meticulous. She recorded everything she did bring, never mentioning a camera. Most significant, there exist no photos of the four-month journey, an opportunity for documentation the traveler would have seized. Then what of the various photos of Lhasa erroneously credited to Alexandra David-Neel? More on this later, although when she did pack a camera, it was as likely to be up-to-date as her seven-shot automatic pistol.

At the house of a well-off farmer on the bank of the Salween, the usual difficulties were compounded by his incredible stinginess. The man, having lost a cow, demanded that Yongden predict where he should find her. After much hocus-pocus on the part of the lama—and to his astonishment—the cow turned up on schedule. The farmer was so impressed that he insisted the lama bless his household and every one of his cattle and pigs. Yongden had to read scripture and sprinkle holy water throughout the extensive stables. Finally, the travelers' reward was served up—a thin soup of dried nettles. Then they were shown to their sleeping places on the dirt floor far from the fire. Out of respect, the lama was given a bit of ragged carpet on which to curl himself.

Tibetans, except for the highest class, traditionally slept naked, curled up like a cat. Often the peasants crawled into the same verminous sheepskins worn during the day. Alexandra watched as the daughters of the household performed this act, first stripping to the waist to reveal upper arms and breasts encrusted with dirt. But the weary pilgrims comforted themselves with thoughts of a warm breakfast next morning. It was the custom to reward a lama lavishly for making a successful prediction.

At break of day the imposters had scarcely finished secreting their gear when the mistress appeared. She kindled the fire and poured into their unwashed bowls the remains of last night's greasy broth. To add insult to injury, the old miser demanded an additional blessing from Yongden, who was obliged to grant it. Once on their way, the cheated lama hurled a traditional curse at the farmstead: "May the wool never grow on your sheep's backs, your cattle prove barren, and your fruit trees be blighted!"

Mother and son burst out laughing, echoed by the babble of the Salween, which chimed in, "Foreigners, you have much to learn about the Land of Snows."

Chapter 17

A Long Walk, Continued

"If you look at the map of the country north of Burma," wrote the British officer Eric Bailey in his *No Passport to Tibet,* "you will see a strange physical formation. Following from north to south are three enormous rivers, close to each other, the Yangtse, the Mekong and the Salween. . . . Now look at Tibet [i.e. to the west] and you will see a large river, the Tsangpo, flowing due east through the southern and most populous parts of the country." So much a terra incognita was this land that geographers, knowing the Tsangpo originated in distant western Tibet around Mount Kailas, were puzzled as to where its waters eventually flowed. This and other geographical mysteries were finally solved by intrepid explorers such as Bailey, nearly all of whom were trespassers.

The Tsangpo becomes, in the tangled mountains of eastern Tibet, the Brahmaputra, which before it joins the Ganges to debouch into the Bay of Bengal, forms the heart and veins of present-day Bangladesh. Similarly, the Yangtse constitutes the main artery of China, while the Salween descends through Yunnan and Burma to the sea. The Mekong snakes down through Vietnam to widen into a marshy delta no American of our generation is likely to forget. While coursing through the Land of Snows the rivers are more rapid and not so broad. Because they are older even than the Himalayas and rise in what Sven Hedin dubbed the Trans-Himalayas, deeper into Tibet, the rivers have had to cut their ways through the massive mountains to the seas, creating steep, impressive gorges. Tibetans have devised a variety of hair-raising schemes to cross from one bank to the other.

Bailey, who presently would act as host to a triumphant David-Neel, told of crossing above a river in 1913 while tied to a sort of saddle that slid along two twisted bamboo strands. He did not care to repeat the strange sensation. To cross the Mekong, Captain Kingdon Ward, a noted botanist, had to tackle a contraption similar to one that Alexandra described: kicking off on the higher bank and vaulting down a single bamboo rope to the lower bank. Descent was mercifully rapid over the roaring torrent. On calmer streams yak-hide coracles were used to float up to six passengers across. Impossible to steer, the craft might get swept away in the current. In the mid-1930s, when the American missionary Robert Ekvall rowed a high lama across the angry Yellow River in his inflatable rubber boat, it caused a sensation. The rest of the amazed pilgrims headed for Lhasa were ferried by stages in a barge pulled by horses attached to ropes. This boxy contraption nearly tipped into the swift water. Typically, the pilgrims could not swim, trusting rather in prayer.

To David-Neel must go the prize for the most frightening reported transit of a Tibetan river. On the way to the town of Zogong, she and Yongden were overtaken by two lamas acting as couriers for the governor of the Mekong district. The lamas grew suspicious, and so the pilgrims, after getting away, altered their route to traverse the sparsely populated country of the Giamo Nu River, the upper course of the Salween. They reached the station on a glorious day, and because a lama and his followers also wished to cross, they found a ferryman at this out-of-the-way spot. Alexandra was not put off by the sight of the narrow band of water at the bottom of the gorge, but the crossing device looked worrisome: a single, slack cable fastened to poles fixed at an equivalent height on either bank.

Alexandra, still disguised as an elderly dame, and a young Tibetan girl were unceremoniously bound together to a wooden hook meant to glide along the leather cable. A push sent them swinging into the void, dancing like puppets on a string. Down they went to the middle of the sag, from where ferrymen on the far bank jerked on a long towrope to haul them in. It snapped, and the pair slid back to the dip. Their lives were not in danger—unless one of them succumbed to giddiness and, letting go of the strap fixed under the hook, fell backward. In that case both would tumble into the gorge.

Alexandra, who boasted of nerves of steel, didn't waver, but her young companion, turning pale, fixed her eyes above. She was sure the strap was coming loose. Alexandra could see nothing wrong with the knots, but the girl's terror began to communicate itself. She probably knew more about these contraptions than did a philing. It seemed a question of whether the men would repair the towrope before the knots unraveled. What a fine subject for a wager!

Alexandra refused to countenance failure. Steadying the lass by telling her she had called on secret powers for their protection, she watched a workman crawl out the cable, upside down, the way a fly walks on the ceiling. Finally, attached once again, the couple were hauled to safety, fearing the strap might come undone with each jerk. On the far side, the ferrymen cursed the hysterical girl, and Yongden, cool as ever, demanded alms for his old mother, who had been frightened to death. In truth, the pilgrims were about to experience an episode that would come close to killing them both.

To reach the Po country, David-Neel had to choose between two roads. She had a sketched map of the first that clung to valleys and passed by villages and monasteries. Tramping through inhabited places no longer troubled the pair, for as soon as they approached a settlement they began crying for alms. This helped to keep off the huge, fierce watchdogs and often led to a simple meal with humble folk and a berth in the corner. From monasteries the beggars sometimes purchased such extravagances as molasses cakes, dried apricots, tea, and butter. Still, back in Jyekundo, General Pereira had become excited about a large blank spot on the map of southern Tibet. His remark that nobody had ever been there meant, of course, no white person.

There were problems with this route through an uncharted wilderness. Any travelers met on the path were likely to be brigands setting out to rob in more settled country. They might murder witnesses to shut their mouths. Worse, a high pass led into the long valley, then another out. If heavy snow fell after they managed to get in, and the second pass was blocked, the travelers would be trapped to freeze or starve to death.

Alexandra was drawn by the lure of the unknown. But she also had a chance to make her mark as an explorer. She struck out into the wilderness across an icy stream in weather so cold that, when the ice splintered and she got her feet wet and dried them with her woolen skirt, the skirt stiffened and froze. They had been warned in the last village to take ample provisions, but due to the exactions of the local pombo in his fort, the folk had nothing to spare. So to warm themselves, she and Yongden cooked a soup out of a piece of dry, dirty bacon, a pinch of salt, and tsampa. Her father's dogs wouldn't have eaten such a dish, thought Alexandra, downing a second full bowl.

Up they climbed until sunset in the face of a sharp wind. They found shelter for the night in an abandoned herdsman's camp. It had a roof, a hearth, and plenty of dung to burn, and the weary pair thought of it as paradise. They faced more climbing the next day. On the lookout for a *latsa*—the jumble of prayer flags that marks the summit of a pass—they stumbled over a high ridge without finding one. Instead, a vast landscape, previously hidden from view, revealed itself to them. It was an immensity of snow limited at a far distance by a wall of shiny snow-clad peaks. The valley before them ascended gently until it reached the summits on the skyline. For once Alexandra was struck dumb by the overpowering spectacle. Behind this magnificent veil, she felt sure, was the Supreme Face before which one could only bend one's knee.

The trail was obscured by snow, and the pair didn't know which way to turn. It was three in the afternoon, and to miss the path meant being caught on the heights through the night. Alexandra, quite in character, decided to go straight ahead. Fortunately, her bag was light, but Yongden was weighted down by carrying the tent and pegs. She forged ahead quickly through knee-deep snow, goaded by worry, then wondered if the lad had fallen behind. She glanced back.

Yongden, far below, amidst the white immensity, appeared as a small black spot, like a tiny insect that seemed to be crawling up the slope. Alexandra felt the disproportion between the giant glacier range and the two puny travelers who had pitted themselves against it. She understood the meaning of "compassion" as it welled up in her heart for her companion of so many adventures. She had to win through to Lhasa—if only to save the lad whose loyalty to her never wavered.

Alexandra plowed upward and, where the snow appeared too deep to walk, used her long staff as a pogo stick. In waning light, she discovered a white mound with a few branches protruding, and from them hung icecovered scraps—the *latsa* at the top of the pass. She waved to Yongden who slowly joined her. As she glanced round, in a stupor caused by weariness, the moon rose. Its silvery light fell on the glaciers and high peaks and unknown valleys through which they had to proceed. The pilgrims blessed this land of icy giants and every little unseen creature in it. Then they descended from the nineteen thousand foot Deo-la, hoping to come upon shelter and fuel. By moonlight they trudged through an eerily beautiful valley bisected by a frozen river, winds whipping them. To stop meant death.

The pair had been tramping for nineteen hours straight with nothing to eat, when at two in the morning they halted. *Lung-gom* (trance walking) had automatically taken over where even the strongest determination faltered. But here they found cow dung at a camping place near the stream. Once stopped, it was vital to start a fire at once. Fuel wasn't enough; the flint and steel on which they depended were soaked through.

Yongden suggested that his mother perform *tumo*—the practice of inner fire—while he moved around to keep warm. Alexandra felt she was out of practice in this occult art. But now was the time to remember the teachings of the Gomchen of Lachen. She sent Yongden to collect cow droppings, and then, tucking flint and steel and a pinch of moss beneath her dress, she sat down to begin. She drifted into a trance during which her mind remained concentrated. Imagined flames rose around her, crackling, growing higher till they enveloped her, curling above her head.

The loud report of ice cracking in the river startled Alexandra awake. The vision of flames subsided and she felt the cold wind against her heated body. Her fingers were like live coals. Confident, she struck steel against stone. Sparks leaped onto dry grass, spread to a hearty blaze. When Yongden returned he was amazed, not least by his mother's fiery face and glowing eyes. Although they enjoyed their fire, she feared her health might be affected. But the touch of the morning sun on the little tent roused the pair from a refreshing sleep. Alexandra never felt better.

At times, the travelers had been suspected by the populace, but more usually were helped. Tibetans tried to improve their karma by giving aid to pilgrims bound for holy places. However, the few poverty stricken herdsmen that they encountered wintering in the valley between the two high passes were downright rude. They learned that the Aigni-la to the Po country *might* still be open if they hurried. Yongden, glib as Ulysses, had a religious talk with one of the *dokpas* and not only persuaded him to guide them to the summit of the pass but to bring a horse for his aged mother. They accompanied the cowboy to his camp where they were lodged in the chief's own dwelling: dark, smoky, the dirt floor spotted with spittle.

When Yongden stepped out to beg for alms, the hospitality included an attempt to rob his poor mother. These bumpkins thought of banditry as good clean fun. The shame fell on the victim for not defending his property. In this case, Alexandra was curled up before the hearth, pretending to sleep but keeping an eye open to guard their packs. The chief, who had become curious, was on the point of setting upon Alexandra's bundle; she rolled around, calling on her son in her supposed sleep. Up she popped, claiming the lama had warned her from afar to awaken. Yongden returned and immediately fell in with the game. The superstitious dokpas were frightened and behaved themselves.

They all dined on broth made from yak's innards, and Alexandra gulped three bowls of it. She was distressed by talk of philings at the Kha Karpo. Had these rustics heard about them, or was the story several years old? In Tibet there was no knowing. News might travel with surprising swiftness from village to village via "yak telegraph," or it might linger in some out-of-the-way camp, being savored like ripe cheese. Next morning the travelers were glad to get going, and the guide proved true to his word. At the latsa that marked the Aigni-la, Yongden offered the dokpa a few coins, but he wanted only a blessing. Money he would spend but merit he could save up toward his next lifetime.

The pilgrims stood at the summit of the first and only pass they attained without the usual hard climbing. But under a lowering sky, both were filled with foreboding. The herdsmen had been concerned about the grazing come spring. The ground held insufficient moisture to grow healthy grass. To gain their goodwill, Yongden promised them snow if they would perform a simple rite, but only after he and his mother passed over the Aigni-la. Now the pair wondered if the dokpas had begun to pray too soon.

The air was laden with humidity as the travelers descended across barren pastures to a marshy stream. Alexandra realized she had discovered one of the springs of the Po Tsangpo, a tributary of the river that flowed placidly to the south of Lhasa. Despite her distrust of maps, she assumed the role of explorer, hoping to trump the professionals at their game. Although low on food, Alexandra was determined to range farther in search of additional feeder springs. So she led the way forward into the upper valleys.

In the evening snow began to fall lightly, drifting among black trees. It grew heavier, blocking the peaks and valleys from view, and the neophyte explorers pitched their tent in the form of a shelter sloping against a rock, boiled tea, and went to sleep. Alexandra was awakened by a sense of painful oppression. She instantly realized they were being buried alive under an avalanche of snow. The pair stayed calm, turned on their stomachs, and, heaving upward, broke free. They had to tramp the rest of the night, since another shelter might be similarly smothered.

At noon the following day they discovered an earthen cave where they holed up, sleeping until the following dawn. Still the huge, wet flakes came down. Undaunted, the adventurer strode out on the whitened terrain. Yongden, trailing behind, mistook snow for solid ground and plunged into a ravine. His frightened companion found him lying on the snow stained by spots of blood. The blood only from bruises, but the lad had badly sprained his ankle. Alexandra, more upset than her son, insisted on carrying him. But she lacked the strength to port him over deep snow riddled with pitfalls. So the pair, Yongden leaning on her arm, crept for hours back to the cave.

In the morning, Alexandra woke to the sight of Yongden, using his staff as a crutch, attempting to walk. His foot was swollen out of shape and could bear no weight. What was to be done? Turning back was impossible, and so the mother wished to hurry to the nearest village for help. But this would be Po country, and the Popa inhabitants were famous as bandits, even cannibals. Leaving Yongden alone in the cave was dangerous. At night wolves, bears, or a leopard might attack him. Staying put meant starvation.

Alexandra, deciding to take action, plunged into the snow in search of a dokpas' camp. She walked the whole day under falling flakes without meeting a soul. She started back with cow chips from an abandoned hut, wrapping them in her upper dress. Her Chinese underdress became soaked, and the bitter wind turned it to ice. Night fell and she couldn't find the cave. She had an urge to cry out in the darkness but suppressed it for fear that, if she heard no answer, she would go mad. Finally, a glimmer of light higher up showed the way, and at last she was reunited with Yongden, who was half dead from fright.

A bowl of hot water and tea dust cheered them, and the lama hoped he would be able to walk tomorrow. If not, Alexandra must abandon him and save herself. What happened to him had been no accident but the result of his previous deeds. Pondering karma, the pair slept soundly as the snow continued to fall until it had done so for sixty-five hours straight.

Next day they struggled through knee-deep drifts. Alexandra had fixed her son a primitive crutch from a stout branch and an empty provision bag for padding. With the weather clearing and Yongden hobbling along, she was able to enjoy fine Alpine scenery and the prodigious stillness of the strange white land. But her right big toe was peeping forth from its boot, and as the tear grew, her foot began to freeze from the fresh snow. They saw no signs of people or cattle or shelter.

Darkness came and with it snow once again. They couldn't take another night in the open. But the pilgrims' luck—or karma—was not all bad. Ahead, Alexandra bumped into a fence. She grabbed it, afraid it was illusory. She had stumbled on a herdsman's summer camp, complete with a snug cabin and firewood and dry dung under the shed. By the time Yongden came up, Alexandra had a fire roaring in the hearth and was preparing dinner: boiled water sprinkled with *tsampa*. The mere warmth was more pleasing to her than had been dinner at the poshest restaurant in the old days in Paris.

The travelers stayed on for a lazy, hungry day in the cabin. Yongden patched his mother's boots, and they dined on tea dust. Next day they started before dawn under snowy skies through a holly and oak forest of the sort pictured on greeting cards. It was Christmas Eve, and Alexandra broke off a small branch of berries, meaning it for an unidentifed friend in Europe. In this manner she reassured herself that the weakening pair would live to present it one day. Ironically, by the time they returned to France the intended recipient had died.

About noon, when the travelers realized they had taken the wrong path, their chances looked grim. They retraced their steps to the camp, boiled snow, and drank the water. Yongden went to scout, while his mother reflected how her European acquaintances, in her place, would surely give themselves up for lost, blame each other, and curse fate. A snatch of Buddhist verse came to mind: "Happy indeed we live/among the anxious, unanxious." But when Yongden returned, she saw that he looked pale, fever glowing in his eyes.

That night was a trial. By the dim light of embers, Alexandra awoke to see the lama tottering toward the door. He mumbled that the snow was piling up and would bury them; they had to start right away. Burning with fever, Yongden lunged for the door, showing white drifts against the blackness. He begged her to come out into the falling snow. Alexandra shoved him inside and wrestled him down. While he fought, she recalled that the clearing outside ended abruptly in a precipice a few feet away. She tossed an armful of branches on the fire and the sudden flare of light startled the young man to his senses. He ceased to resist her efforts to make him lie down. Dozing with an eye open, Alexandra spent the night watching over her son.

Christmas morning the pilgrims arose with hunger gnawing at their bellies. Yongden looked sane, but when he said that he was a mountain god bearing a gift, his mother wondered. Promptly the lama produced a bit of bacon fat he'd employed to waterproof their yak-hide boots, and some leftover leather from the soling. Into a pot of boiling water went the goodies, and they drank a beggar's feast.

The day was auspicious, one on which they were to meet their first Popa. As they proceeded, the Popa emerged from a cabin and invited the travelers to warm themselves. Inside they found a dozen men seated around a fire—burly fellows with free-flowing hair and Mongol features. They questioned Yongden, who admitted that he and his mother had crossed the Aigni-la. The men thought the pair had come this moment across the snow-blocked pass. They must have flown over it! The Popas immediately demanded that Yongden fore-tell the answer to a burning question. They were in rebellion against the pombo representing Lhasa, who had sent to the capital for reinforcements. In turn, the rebels had dispatched a band to intercept the courier, and now they wanted to know how it would turn out. The lama stalled, knowing the ruffians would treat a false prophet summarily.

Alexandra muttered from a corner that all would end well. Yongden went through the story of his mother being the consort of a sorcerer. The Popas plied their guests with buttered tea, then slunk out, afraid of such powerful magicians. Alexandra and Yongden slept well and in the morning tramped on to Cholog. Soon the whole village gathered around the magical beggars who had flown over the Aigni-la. These were presented with a true miracle—a thick turnip soup. The two gulped down bowlfuls to break a week's fast.

At dusk, as Alexandra and Yongden reached the outskirts of a village, farmers fled from them, warning their neighbors that pilgrims were approaching. Every house was barred, and at a prosperous dwelling they were attacked by furious mastiffs. J. Hanbury Tracy, an Englishman who mapped the Po in the mid-1930s, described these hairy beasts, each weighing up to 150 pounds, as being "the size of a small pony" and having "a crusty disposition." Heinrich Harrer remarked that "their usual diet of milk and calves' flesh gives them enormous strength." He fought a struggle to the death with an unfortunate mastiff that attacked him. Alexandra defeated these yapping beasts by raining blows on their muzzles with her staff and jabbing them with its iron spike. But at this village the pilgrims received neither alms nor a spot by the hearth.

After crossing a dense forest, the pair arrived at Sung Dzong. Originally *dzong* meant "fortress," but by David-Neel's day a dzong included any dwelling on a height that housed an official. Although the town was at the junction of two rivers and important to the Po country, it hadn't appeared on her map. She regretted that her disguise, and the need to be vigilant, prevented her from doing any serious mapmaking. She claimed that the discovery of scientific instruments in her pack could have doomed her and Yongden.

However, the Indian pundits of a previous generation, who entered Tibet by stealth, had carried simple concealed implements for determining distances. Alexandra's thermometer, if boiled in water—the method is described by Bailey—could have indicated approximate altitudes from sea level. Rather, the itinerant preferred to remain wholly in the role she had chosen, to become—not merely act—the mendicant pilgrim. In that way the philing disappeared, most of all to herself. In the last instance, when menaced by desperate characters, Alexandra had to be willing to employ the ultimate Western tool, her revolver.

The Popas hated the Chinese for devastating their towns and countryside during the invasion of 1910–1911, when the invaders also murdered their king, whose two wives managed to flee with their offspring. This scorched-earth warfare had further impoverished an already primitive district. But still the region celebrated the New Year in mid-January, which was according to the Chinese calendar. On this day the pilgrims passed an isolated farmhouse, and from it emerged a number of drunken, raucous men, guns slung across their shoulders.

The men shouted but the pilgrims continued on their way, seeking out a cozy cave to bed down. In the morning, a Popa showed up and quickly grew fascinated by their two cheap foreign spoons. To be rid of him, Yongden asked if he had any local cheese to exchange for sewing needles—a kind of currency. He did and would bring a sample right back. Instead the man fetched one of his cohorts, a bold rascal who first fingered and admired their tent, then seized the spoons. The other grabbed the tent, while both cast impatient glances toward the farm, as if expecting the rest of their gang. If the Popas found out what these supposedly poor pilgrims carried, including gold and silver, they would murder them.

Alexandra warned the robbers to let go of her property. They laughed in her face, turning to pillage the packs. The old mother pulled out her automatic and coolly grazed one fellow's scalp. Flinging the stolen goods on the ground, the pair took off like scared rabbits. Probably a battle was about to be joined, but luckily a band of thirty pilgrims arrived. They were from the Nu Valley and had already been attacked by, and fought off, Popas. But their monks, who did the fighting, were armed only with swords and spears. They were delighted to meet companions with guns and demanded to see the marvels. Yongden showed them his old revolver, claiming that he had fired the shot. Alexandra was pleased to have the pilgrims hail her son as a hero, because an automatic pistol wielded by a woman spelled philing, if not demon.

These people were friendly and Alexandra enjoyed their company for a few days. Then she let them race ahead, while she preferred to revel in the mild winter climate and to loiter amid spectacular scenery and lush vegetation, including orchids. Kingdon Ward commented on the "many kinds of small ground orchids, some of them deliciously scented" that he found in southern Tibet. This was the land of purple iris, yellow primrose, and the blue poppy. The Frenchwoman felt the peculiar psychic atmosphere of the hidden valleys of the Po country where snow-clad peaks towered over waving fields of barley; the yogi in her divined a long-lost time, a paradise of youth and simplicity.

Edwin Bernbaum, writing of Shambala, on which James Hilton based his Shangri-La, and which is myth for some and reality to others, remarks:

> It will look like other valleys, with the same sort of trees, meadows, and streams, but a person with a heightened sensitivity will feel something in the atmosphere, a sense of greater space or freedom, which will affect him in a deep and powerful way. In addition to obtaining food and shelter there without effort, he will also find various spiritual treasures, such as sacred images and mystical texts.

A special eye or awareness is needed to see Shambala, which as Bernbaum points out ultimately lies within the heart and mind of the yogi. That Alexandra found contentment and renewal in a land peopled by robbers and cannibals tells us more about her than about the Po. This pilgrim, though on the path, was neither saint nor Buddha.

A brief stay in a hut with a simple couple touched Alexandra's heart. They had invited the pilgrims to share their meager hospitality. Aging, plain, the two were as tender toward each other as first lovers. The man had a goiter on his neck—common among Popas—and the woman was wrinkled with a wen on hers. Once considered a beauty, she had been the mistress of a rich merchant until she ran off with her Romeo. Now the penniless pair lived en famille with a cow, her suckling calf, and a litter of baby black pigs who manured the floor. The lovers had no regrets and, rare for Tibet, didn't desire children, so wrapped up were they in each other. They shared turnip soup with their guests and gave them tsampa for the road. During the night, Yongden put a few rupees in a pot on a shelf. The snoring lovers, when they found the money, would think the gods had left it there.

Alexandra started before dawn to tramp to Showa, the Popa capital. Here she reverted to form, begging loudly at the gate of the Po king's dwelling. In those days each of the border regions of Tibet was a semi-independent principality. This king was then in Lhasa but would eventually fall out with the central government. A chief of brigands, he would be defeated by the Dalai Lama's new army and die wandering in the mountains. His stewards heaped the lusty beggars with butter and eggs to get rid of them.

One last major hurdle stood between the interlopers and their goal: a toll bridge across a gorge at Tongyuk, where a dzong was placed to watch over travelers proceeding toward the capital. A bridge-keeper controlled a gate, and as the pilgrims knocked on it, he set it slightly ajar to regard them. They pounced with the eagerness of cats on a mouse.

They demanded to know the whereabouts of the large party of their friends from the Nu. The keeper said they'd passed through in the morning. What, had not the monks left a bag of dried meat for them? No! But that was not like them. Had not he, the keeper, stolen their meat? On they went in this vein until the keeper, forgetting they needed permission from the pompo in the fort to pass, waved them ahead. He was glad to be rid of such pests, while Alexandra silently gave thanks to her friends the pilgrims who had proved useful on several occasions.

Crossing forest country containing scattered villages, staying out of sight by day, the travelers supposed their journey would surely succeed. They emerged on a stretch of land partly cultivated and partly pasture, which made Alexandra homesick for the French Alps. One evening, while Alexandra toyed with the idea of exploring to the north, a simply dressed lama appeared at their camp. He wore a rosary made from human bone and carried a staff surmounted by a trident. He sat down and stared hard at Alexandra. The man, who carried no provisions, not even a bag of tsampa, made her nervous. He produced a skull fashioned into a bowl and took tea.

"*Jetsunma*," he demanded, "why have you removed your rosary and your rings of the initiate? Whom do you expect to fool?"

Yongden began to spin a tale, but the tantric wizard ordered him away. Alexandra understood that deception was useless. The lama knew her, she could not say from where. "You cannot guess, Jetsunma," he half-teased, reading her thoughts. "I am not who you think and I am anyone you wish."

As the pair settled down into a long conversation about Buddhist philosophy and Tibetan mysticism, the ideas of the lama, his phrases, and finally his features, began to remind her of Sidkeong, her murdered prince. Then in a moment the lama vanished into the woods, as mysteriously as he'd appeared. Alexandra reassured herself that the wizard—or was it a genie?—meant her well. He had come to give his blessing to her journey to Lhasa.

One day in February 1924, four months after starting from Yunnan, the sojourners crossed into Lhasa territory. Here, the year before, General Pereira had been greeted by officials bearing cakes and peaches. Even poor exhausted Montgomery McGovern, dressed as a porter, "ran into a swarm of beggars, who followed our party for more than a mile, gesticulating and clamoring for alms." But no one took notice of this pair of dusty, weary pilgrims, no different from scores of others come for the New Year festivities.

Alexandra, giddy with excitement, spotted the golden roofs of the Potala palace. The sun striking them caused the roofs to glow brilliantly against the deep blue sky. The Potala seemed to crown the whole of Tibet. With a suddenness peculiar to the roof of the world, a storm arose, lifting clouds of dust high into the sky. The palace was obscured, the trespassers hidden from any prying eyes.

Alexandra interpreted this omen to be good and helpful, since the plain usually teemed with life. She assured herself that none of the inhabitants of the city dreamed it was about to be invaded by a foreign woman! Equally miraculous, as the pair entered the precincts, unsure where to find lodging during the crowded holiday season, a young woman approached. She offered them a narrow cell in a beggar's hostel. Remote from the center of town, it would make a perfect hideout. It even provided a fine view of the Potala.

Once inside, Yongden dared to declaim—in whispered triumph—*Lha gyalo!* The gods win!" The pilgrims had arrived at holy Lhasa.

Chapter 18
"The Potala Is the Paradise of Buddhas."

In 1949 the American Lowell Thomas, Sr.—broadcast media's original anchorman, although he rarely stayed in one place for long—and his son Lowell Thomas, Jr., were invited by the youthful Fourteenth Dalai Lama, or really his Regent and the *Kashag* (Council of Ministers), to visit his capitol. The spur was fear of Mao's Red China, victorious over Chiang Kai-shek's Nationalists and massing an army of invasion on the vulnerable Sino-Tibetan border. Thomas was granted this unusual privilege because no other newscaster of the time had so wide an audience and was so personally familiar with important government figures. If help was to be extended to Tibet, whether diplomatic or military, it must come from the dominant Western power, the United States.

Fortunately, both father and son were hardy, adventurous types, used to life in the outdoors. The Sacred Realm remained nearly as closed as ever. "The peaks are our sentinels," runs an old Tibetan saying. Reaching Lhasa twenty-five years after Alexandra David-Neel made her heroic effort had become only slightly easier. The means of travel had not changed in hundreds of years: horse, mule, or foot, or camel from Mongolia. "Tibetans absolutely forbid travel by air, by car, or even by carriage or cart," wrote the younger Lowell in the engaging account of his journey to Lhasa, *Out of This World*. Since Radio Peking had begun to call for the "liberation" of Tibet, the two Americans had to start from Calcutta in July, in the midst of the difficult rainy season.

Once inside the Sikkimese frontier, the expedition was halted by a giant landslide: "an immense wall of rock, dirt and stripped tree trunks . . . The whole side of a mountain had collapsed under the monsoon rains." The Thomases overcame this difficulty and others ranging from obdurate mules to leeches that attacked their coolies' bare legs to the serious danger of sodden, crumbly mountain trails. Up the forested slopes of the Himalayas they climbed, hoping to make it from Gangtok to Lhasa in the usual three weeks. They crossed the Tibetan border—near where Alexandra had caught her first glimpse of the Forbidden Land—at 14,800 feet under a yak-hair rope fastened to two boulders and festooned with hundreds of flapping prayer flags. They frightened off three bushy-tailed wild yaks.

Despite the biting cold of the plateau, incessant rains worked through the Thomases' rubber suits. In a pine forest they met their first inhabitant: a huge white monkey with a long tail and black face. Tibetan myth holds that humans are descended from monkey ancestors. The natives will not harm these or other of the photogenic creatures inhabiting this land of strange, magnificent scenery. Here Alexandra learned to admire the many-faceted yak, the sure-footed blue sheep of the peaks, and the furry black-and-white panda of the eastern mountains. Here she befriended the bear, the wolf, and searched for the elusive snow leopard.

There is one end to all journeys in Tibet. Lowell, Jr. wrote, "Late that evening . . . we suddenly caught a glimpse of our goal—Lhasa, far off, under a range of dark mountains—sparkling in the sunset; and the Potala, standing out above the city, its golden roofs beckoning like a far-off beacon." Montgomery McGovern, the British professor disguised as a mule driver, wrote of "a great and sudden thrill" on sighting the Potala: "I knew that on the other side of the hill on which the palace was perched lay Lhasa, the abode of the gods." Heinrich Harrer and his companion, after a grueling journey through western Tibet, entirely unsure of the reception they would receive, wrote that when they sighted the Potala, "We felt inclined to go down on our knees like the pilgrims and touch the ground with our foreheads."

In one way or another, all three parties would receive a royal welcome—McGovern clandestinely, Harrer in time, and the Thomases with full pomp and ceremony. David-Neel, the only Buddhist among the lot, was the least welcome. Yet she was delighted to have arrived during *Monlam*, the great festival to celebrate the New Year, and she was determined to keep herself incognito and to enjoy herself to the full. The first of her sex to crash the gates of the forbidden city, she would see everything beautiful, unique, or holy.

What did this so-called "Rome of the Lamaist world" look like? Lhasa, attractive or repellent, was very much in the eye of the beholder. At times other than the New Year, when its population swelled, Lhasa was a small city of some twenty thousand people, located near the bank of the river Kyi (tributary to the Tsangpo) in a large valley with an impressive horizon of stark mountain ranges. A hill to either side marked the town's extent, and on the smaller, more pointed one was situated the medical college, while stemming from the other, surrounded by its own little village, rose the magnificent Potala. However, Lhasa, a collection of flat-roofed, whitewashed houses of sun-dried brick, revolved around the Jokhang temple, the St. Peter's of Tibetan Buddhism. The temple existed before the town, which, in a way, constituted its outbuildings. The market ran right around the Jokhang, along the avenue known as the Barkhor, and twice daily each pilgrim would circumambulate this Holy of Holies.

Alexandra decided to visit the Potala first. She admitted its imposing appearance but sincerely felt that its architects had expressed power and wealth rather than beauty. On the other hand, McGovern, when he finally came to face the Potala, "halted almost dumbfounded by its splendor. . . . [I]t possesses a simplicity and yet a stateliness of style that cannot but impress even the most sophisticated." Alexandra, who was disguised as a *dokpa*, a nomadic herder, wanted to enter the Potala in a group of similar folk. She sent Yongden to inform a couple of simple lads from the borderland that they were to have the honor of "meeting" (a Tibetanism) the Potala. They replied they had met it already and were headed for a chang house before setting out for home. Yongden, with an air of compassion, brushed aside their objections and offered to take them on a tour, explaining to them the names and meanings of the myriad deities. Surely that was preferable to getting drunk? Fortunately, the pair turned out to be as religious minded as most Tibetans.

Curiosity drew Alexandra to the Potala. She still did not approve of the worship of graven images, nor giving fees to priests for opening doors to chapels and sprinkling a few grains of tsampa on the altars. Yet she followed the three men inside, head lowered and eyes cast down, as she prepared to tour the huge complex, which is a cluster of buildings that then included tombs, temples, and chapels, reception and ceremonial rooms, schools, and offices. The door-keeper, a gnomish boy in an ill-fitting robe, insisted that she remove her bonnet from Kham. This was a calamity. At the rooming house every act was public, and since Alexandra couldn't ink her hair, it had resumed its natural brown shade. Worse, it looked incongrous next to the braids of black yak's hair grown thin as rats' tails. Just such a nonsensical accident—the barking of a pet dog—had caused the unmasking of McGovern the year before.

An infuriated Alexandra had to trudge through the Dalai Lama's palace feeling like a clown. Luckily the other pilgrims ignored her, and she became absorbed in the labyrinth of corridors and galleries and especially in the life-sized murals that depicted the legends of gods and the lives of saints. In the shrine rooms were enthroned statues of the many deities of Mahayana Buddhism, bedecked with gold ornaments and inlaid with coral, turquoise, and precious stones, before them smoldering solid gold butter lamps.

If these houses of the gods were bright with the glow of lamps and festooned with silken banners in white, green, red, blue, and yellow—the five mystic colors—Alexandra could also veer off to investigate darker recesses where she found altars to the gods and demons of pre-Buddhist times, figures from what R.A. Stein has aptly termed "the nameless religion,"folkloric and magical. As the pagan gods had fought the introduction of Christianity to Rome, so the earlier deities battled against the Buddhist missionaries from India bearing new teachings. Shamans cast spells against the converts, until they themselves were subdued and converted by the superior magic of the holy men. Then the old gods were adopted into the Tibetan Buddhist pantheon of benevolent forces.

Far worse beings, hideously malevolent but invisible, were supposedly kept chained by the power of magic charms in special buildings. They were fed symbolic sacrificial offerings and watched with great care lest they escape and devour humanity. When writing about her journey to Lhasa, Alexandra distanced herself from what she termed the superstitious beliefs of the people; and she was troubled by the awe demonstrated by the horde of pilgrims before the huge golden statues of departed Dalai Lamas. These were not the teachings of Gautama Buddha, she claimed. Bowing down to idols could not break the karmic chain of births and deaths. Later on she would mellow toward the magic and mystery of a folk that might possess knowledge other than the rational.

Once atop the palace—which, including its mount, reaches to two-thirds the height of New York's Empire State Building—Alexandra took in the domain before her. Wisps of smoke rose from huge outdoor incense burners. Colored paper dragons sent up from rooftops danced in the crisp air. The triumphant traveler exulted in the panorama of Lhasa, its temples and monasteries, which she imagined to be a carpet rolled out at her feet. Scattered among the surrounding mountains were what appeared to be toy monasteries, some clinging to rock cliffs like eagles' nests. The two peasant lads were anxious to depart, and so the old mother trailed after them, reminded that her stay would be limited.

Alexandra found this capital to be a lively place inhabited by jolly folk who loved to loiter and chat outdoors. She described the streets as large, the squares as broad and on the whole rather clean. This conflicts with the accounts of certain other Westerners. Millington Powell, who went with the Younghusband expedition, portrayed Lhasa as "filthy beyond description, undrained and unpaved." It must have been "the scene of unnatural piety and crime." To Spencer Chapman, who arrived with a British diplomatic mission in 1936, everything seemed "mean and gloomy . . . repellent and sinister." The Lowell Thomases were far more relaxed about their adventure, and so was Hugh Richardson, who also accompanied the 1936 mission. He has written to us: "There was one terrible street near the public latrine but the main square was broad and quite well kept. I never found Lhasa either gloomy or sinister and for most of the year the intensely dry air kept down smells." The appeal of Lhasa was also in the nose of the beholder!

Alexandra went often to the Jokhang, wandering from the cathedral to the shops that fairly ring it. The Lhasans were and are very fond of bazaars, and in their capital, as in the Jerusalem of Jesus' day, temple and marketplace were intertwined. Alexandra found most retail trade in the hands, or better the laps, of women. She loved the market for its colorful folk: cunning traders, sheepskin-clad Khampas, turquoise-bedecked nomad women, Moslem merchants from Kashmir, and, as Harrer put it, "pretty women showing off their newest frocks and flirting a little with the young bloods of the nobility." However, Alexandra was disappointed by the show of cheap aluminum ware and other shoddy goods from abroad. This she blamed on the restriction of trade with China in favor of inferior goods imported from India.

One incident put her in grave danger, perhaps more than she realized. A policeman at the market made the browser nervous by staring at her. Instead of a uniform, these gentlemen were distinguished by a slouch hat and a single dangling earring. They were not known for their honesty and, under cover of dark, sometimes turned robber. Alexandra, reacting quickly, selected an aluminum saucepan and began to bargain for it loudly.

She offered the tradesman an absurdly low price. At first he laughed, saying, "Ah, you are a peasant, there can be no doubt of that!" The other merchants and customers joined in to ridicule the stupid woman who knew nothing beyond her cattle and the grasslands. But as she continued her ceaseless twaddle, the tradesman was ready to crown her with the pan. After the chuckling policeman had passed on, the old mother bought the loathed thing and scuttled away.

Had Alexandra been slower of wit and were she caught, she would have been taken not to the civil authorities but to two abbots from Drepung monastery. For the three weeks of the festivities they had absolute rule over Lhasa and could reprimand even the Dalai Lama. The ancient custom of their rule was necessitated by the streaming into town of up to twenty thousand *trapas* from the three great monasteries, Drepung, Sera, and Ganden, many of them so-called brawling monks. No one else could control these worldly types, who were given to drinking and quarreling. But the Drepung abbots were known to be fiercely antiforeign, and they might have turned the interloper over to an outraged mob. Her sex would not have protected her. Montgomery McGovern watched from a roof in the marketplace as a naked woman was whipped to within an inch of her life for the illegal sale of fireworks.

The atmosphere at the Monlam holiday was a mixture of

solemnity and gaiety. As a religious festival it commemorated Lord Buddha's victory over the malicious spirits that tempted him during his meditations. McGovern reported heavy drinking, rowdyism, but also more innocent activities: "The whole morning [of the first day] the marketplace was full of revelers of both sexes and from every part of Tibet. These were singing, shouting and dancing." Alexandra was charmed by the women's colorful outfits and how they would spontaneously begin to sing, to stamp their feet rhythmically, and to jangle the bells they held in their hands. The men joined in, and slowly the frolicking groups circumambulated the sacred Jokhang.

What one saw depended on one's point of view in the literal sense. In 1921 Charles Bell, brought out of retirement at the request of the Dalai Lama, had been His Holiness' guest for the Monlam festivities. From a privileged seat he watched spirited pony and foot races, wrestling matches, cavalry processions, and the beggars known as "white devils" who amused the crowd with bawdy jokes. Outside the gates, Bell sat in the reviewing stand with the highest officials to take in the scene of sparkling blue and white tents that dotted the plain. Men dressed as traditional warriors competed in contests of archery and displays of horsemanship to win prizes of Chinese silk or bricks of tea. The Khampa nomads in their fox fur hats and heavy beads looked for all the world like a detachment of Genghis Khan's horde.

More available to the pair of pilgrims were the events that took place in the wide avenue of the Barkhor. Normally it was the scene of devout Buddhists gaining merit by circumambulating the cathedral, reciting prayers, and making obeisances. The shrine contained as its chief treasure a venerable image of Siddhartha Gautama as a youth, supposedly painted from life. On the evening of the full moon of the first month (March), Alexandra and Yongden watched a procession of floats made of butter—a festival with its roots in equally ancient times. One hundred and eight floats presented images of deities, humans, and animals, the butter dyed and molded into the proper shapes. It was a parade meant to entertain the gods.

The pair pushed into the midst of an enormous crowd. Waiting for the appearance of the Dalai Lama, the excitement grew. Sheepskin-clad giants, forming a chain, ran for sheer joy although they knocked others down. Proctors from Drepung wielded long sticks and whips to no avail. Everyone pressed toward the center to get the best view. Alexandra found herself crushed against the wall of a house, barely able to breathe as she watched Charles Bell's new-model army march by to an English music hall tune. Then the Thirteenth Dalai Lama was carried by in a sedan chair covered with yellow brocade. The awestruck crowd could not have caught more than a slight glimpse of the Compassionate One. After the formal procession passed, nobles in their silks paraded by proudly, surrounded by attendants holding Chinese lanterns; high lamas with monk followers marched along, and then came rich merchants with their women in elaborate headdresses displaying their finery. Finally the populace joined in, catching up the pair of interlopers in the unfettered good humor.

People shied away from the monastic proctors with their sharp eyes and long staffs. Since she was quite short, Alexandra usually hid among tall, strapping herdsmen and let them take any indiscriminate blows. One day she happened to trespass where the upper class only was admitted. Without warning, a policeman hit the old mother with his truncheon. The confidante of high lamas and maharajas was so tickled that she wished to give the lout a tip. Her disguise was so perfect that even the police took her for a common beggar.

Although David-Neel missed her meditations among the tranquil steppes of Amdo, she could not deny that Lhasa was the hub of Tibetan life. Here she had to view the doings of its lamas and officials as just one of the crowd. In compensation she was able to penetrate deeply into the intimate lives of common folk. The hostel where Alexandra and Yongden occupied a narrow cell turned out to be a caravansary of talented, eccentric ne'er-do-wells. Dirty and ragged but unashamed, they often slept in the open courtyard. All of them survived on what they could beg, borrow, or steal.

Preeminent was a tall, handsome, former officer ruined by drink and gambling. Contemptuous of work, the captain each day strode out of the hovel, his bearing erect, courier bag slung over his shoulder, to chat with his many acquaintances. His conversation was lively, and those better off gave him what he casually requested. He returned in the evening with a full bag to feed his wife and children. However, affairs in these lower depths did not always run so smoothly; stealing and quarrels, adultery and accusations flourished. The neighbors would butt in, debating the right and wrong of the matter until the wee hours when everyone went away drunk. In one instance, the captain's wife received a blow meant for another woman, and the captain threatened to bring suit and to call Alexandra as a witness. This hastened her departure from the capitol.

Alexandra's rascally friends loved to sing the songs of the rebel Sixth Dalai Lama, nicknamed Melodious Purity. She owned, along with a variety of other Tibetan songbooks, a book of the Sixth's lyrical verses, devoted to his affairs with his sweethearts. One verse begins, "They call me the Profligate/For my lovers are many." In her *Initiations and Initiates*, Alexandra related that a half-secret cult was paid to the Sixth by the lower classes of Lhasa. Supposedly, a mysterious red sign marked the houses where he would met his lovers. She saw Lhasans, as they passed by, touch their brow to these signs—a mark of deep respect. Of the Sixth, the Oxford scholar Michael Aris has written, "He spent his nights with the girls of his choice in the town of Lhasa and in the Shöl village at the foot of the Potala." At any rate, until the advent of the Fourteenth Dalai Lama, the Sixth was alone in linking the pinnacle of Tibetan society with its humbler elements.

Alexandra's sympathetic view of the Sixth is another example of her bonding, in imagination at least, with the outlaw. When she turned to writing fiction, the trangressor of the moral code could be found at the heart of the action. The Mongol chieftain, Lajang Khan, who overthrew the Sixth Dalai Lama and sent him into exile, reminisced that "he had a wonderful charm, quite unlike ordinary people. He was tremendously bold." Alexandra shared not only these traits of character with Melodious Purity but his central dilemma: how to pursue enlightenment in an unconventional, worldly manner.

To take the analogy a bit further, after the Sixth was spirited off to China and died in 1706, surrendering his present life, biographies appeared that claimed he had survived another forty years and led a secret life as a wandering pilgrim. The conventional "facts" of his biography could not explain his inner life (or lives), nor the calm and dignified manner in which he finally acted for the good of his people.

The reverence Tibetans accord to the Sixth Dalai Lama, and Alexandra's fascination with his verse, is related to another custom that united all classes of Lhasans: the scapegoat. This was a man who willingly assumed the misfortunes, the karma, of the populace. By being driven out of town on the appropriate day, he purged the citizens of their collective guilt. During the week preceding the ceremony, the scapegoat was expected to wander about carrying an enormous hairy yak tail. He could demand money or goods of anyone, and woe betide the one who refused. Alexandra spotted the fellow in the market; if the offering was too meager, he threateningly raised the yak tail, and the shopkeeper quickly gave more. A curse from the scapegoat was certain to ruin a merchant's trade.

The volunteer gained a small fortune during his allotted time. Then, after a ceremony performed by the Dalai Lama, the scapegoat was obliged to flee to a nearby wilderness. Crowds along the route out of town were denser than any Alexandra and Yongden had gotten mired in, and the police more preemptory in beating them back. The crowd clapped and whistled—to chase out evil—as the scapegoat in a coat of fur, face painted half white, half black, was hurried past by officials. Although his exile would be temporary, the bad luck accrued by taking on others' sins nearly always proved fatal to the greedy one. The previous scapegoats had died promptly and painfully of no apparent cause.

That evening Lhasa celebrated its deliverance for another year. Alexandra recalled that people congregated outdoors, talking, laughing, and drinking chang. Beggars, deaf or blind, eaten up by leprosy, rejoiced as merrily as the wealthiest and highest class citizens. She met acquaintances who insisted on treating the old mother and son to a variety of dishes in a restaurant. Alexandra, a great fan of Tibetan cooking, pronounced herself pleased.

The final ceremony of Serpang occurred the next day. Weeks in preparation, it took place around the Potala but especially in the vast courtyard at its base. Thousands of monks carried hundreds of large multicolored silk banners. Dignitaries proceeded in state under canopies, while drums beat and bands played, including fifteen-foot-long trumpets borne on the shoulders of several men. Their solemn music filled the whole valley with an unearthly sound. Elephants plodded along, escorted by paper dragons performing all manner of antics. Young boys danced ritual steps whose origins were lost in antiquity.

Perched on the rocky mountainside, Alexandra, one among many, took in this array of splendor under the bright blue sky and the relentless sun of the Asian plateau. The brilliant colors of the crowd's dress, the alabaster hills in the distance, almost hurt her eyes. Lhasa lay at the beggar's feet, and she felt amply repaid for all the fatigue and danger she had undergone. Here indeed was a scene worthy of Shangri-La, a moment that has disappeared from earth. Since the Chinese invasion in 1949, the festival of Serpang exists only in cans of film stored in archives and on the pages of Alexandra David-Neel's writing.

In *The People of Tibet*, Charles Bell translated the blessing that officially closed the New Year revelries: "Lhasa's prayer is ended. Love is now invited." In early fall 1921, after nearly a year, his sojourn at the capitol came to an end. It had proved no paradise for the canny diplomat, whose curly hair was turning white. He had encouraged the building of a small but modern army and in the process received threats on his life, possibly inspired by the Chinese. He returned to his estate in England to write his books on Tibet. Because their basis is more political and official, they nicely complement those of David-Neel, who was more concerned with Buddhism, the techniques of mysticism, and herself.

After two months of gadding about, Alexandra left the capital as quietly as she had entered. She supposed that she was the first Western woman to behold the Forbidden City and that no one suspected she had been there. When Montgomery McGovern departed Lhasa the year before, he went under armed escort to protect him. Alexandra merely took the prudent step of promoting herself to a middle-class woman who owned two mounts and was accompanied by her manservant (Yongden). In *My Journey to Lhasa* she claimed that because she had bought numbers of books and intended to hunt for more in the south, she needed the horses to carry the baggage. In fact, she and Yongden had both caught influenza among the holiday crowds and they were down to skin and bones. Their mounts carried *them*.

The sun shone brightly the last time the pair rode past gardens where the trees were dressed in April's pale new leaves. After she had crossed the Kyi River and ascended to a pass, nostalgia gripped Alexandra. She stole a final glimpse at the shabby, splendid capitol, above which floated the Potala like a castle in a fairy tale. The pilgrim, who in six months would be fifty-six years old, called down the traditional blessing on all sentient beings who lived there. Then she set her face away from the holy city.

The newsmen, the Lowell Thomases, would spend only a few weeks on the roof of the world, guests of the Fourteenth (and current) Dalai Lama. At the time he was fourteen, already very interested in the world about him. In September 1949, it was their turn to leave Lhasa, bearing an urgent message for the President of the United States. This failed to impress the spirits that guard the passes to the forbidden land. The party had scaled the 16,600-foot Karo-la and were traveling in caravan when Lowell, Sr. was thrown from his horse and badly shattered his right leg below the hip.

The injured man was wrapped in a sleeping bag and borne along on an army cot until the cold, windswept darkness fell, when fortunately the party reached shelter. Lowell, Jr. wrote: "That first night was one of the worst Dad has ever experienced. The shock and exposure brought on high fever and frequent fainting. It was a long gasping night of agony and worry in just about the most out-of-the-way spot you can find on this planet." The Thomas expedition struggled for days to get its wounded member, carried by bearers, to Gyantse, where they knew there was a doctor. They crossed the same monstrous, freezing terrain as had Alexandra twenty-five years earlier. She was nearly as ill and had no servants to rely on.

At Gyantse the Thomas party rested, befriended by the Indian garrison. They continued by mounting the patient in a sedan chair, the poles of which were set on the shoulders of ten strong men. It took sixteen grueling days to traverse the two hundred miles over the Himalayan passes to Gangtok, and Lowell, Sr. was cruelly bounced and jostled the whole time. From there the Thomases would fly to Calcutta and then to the United States.

The senior Lowell's leg, healing incorrectly, had to be broken again and properly set. His son personally delivered the Dalai Lama's diplomatic note to President Harry Truman. The dignified plea for assistance was written in Tibetan characters with a bamboo pen on paper made from shrub bark. The president, who was soon to order American troops into Korea, refused to help Tibet or to recognize its independence. Landlocked and isolated, the Sacred Realm could not count on American support.

Ironically, Truman, the level-headed politician, sighed wistfully as Lowell, Jr. pointed out the route of his journey on a map. He had long dreamed of visiting Lhasa, but he supposed it was too late.

BOOK THREE

The Savant

Full of charm is the forest solitary for
the yogi with a heart empty of desire.
—BUDDHIST SAYING

Chapter 19
The Dream of Repose

"Alexandra David-Neel has never gone to Tibet." So wrote Jeanne Denys in her scandalous *Alexandra David-Neel au Tibet* (1972). The enraged Denys had spent a decade trying to make the case that David-Neel was a charlatan. Unlike later biographers, who have uncritically repeated the David-Neel mythos, she thoroughly read the accounts in English of explorers who had covered similar terrain. Denys' mainstays were Colonel Frederick Bailey and Hanbury Tracy; the former had explored in Tibet ten years earlier than the Frenchwoman, the latter ten years after. However, in the main these two knowledgeable writers do support David-Neel's *Journey to Lhasa,* with differences in description accounted for by their traveling in summer in better equipped parties, while Alexandra and Yongden went in winter, disguised, fearful, and often desperate for a meal.

Denys criticized her *bête noire* for vagueness on dates and places and for not displaying maps of Central Asia on her walls. But this sojourner had learned to distrust the often false assurance given by maps and preferred to follow the information she could glean from natives. True, she told Lawrence Durrell in an interview for *Elle* that she granted him in 1964, "I am foggy about dates." It was a constitutional aversion, since she also loathed clocks and never cared about the exact time. Certainly, there were contradictions in the woman's character, which Denys played upon, calling her derisively "an actress."

Denys was assiduous in carrying out her vendetta. She corresponded with French diplomats in Asia and with Christian missionaries who had known the traveler in the Sino-Tibetan marches during the Second World War, both Catholic and Protestant. But their memories had faded, and besides, they could know nothing of her earlier journeys. One valid point made by Denys is that, while David-Neel often poked fun at the missionaries, she would turn to them in times of need, rarely to be refused.

Alexandra's travail in the Po country came under Denys's closest scrutiny. Admittedly, her geography tends toward the hazy, and her findings are at slight variance with those of Bailey, who did meticulous cartographic work in the Po. In fact, he had with him a British army surveyor. The Frenchwoman knew early on of Bailey's efforts, since she referred to a British officer who had been to Showa, the Popa capitol. After her adventure, she met the man and swapped stories with him. Technically speaking, Alexandra David-Neel was not an explorer, since she carried no measuring equipment and made no maps. As Peter Hopkirk has noted, "[H]er contribution to the scientific exploration of Tibet has been nil." But the gentlemen of the exploring profession, including superbly trained British officers, had no difficulty in accepting her as one of them.

A further mystery remains. The English version of *Journey* includes eight photographs allegedly taken by David-Neel in and around Lhasa; these have turned up in recent books and museum shows, credited to her. One, of petty traders from Lhasa, she may have snapped elsewhere. Alexandra developed a flair for capturing the wild yet genial looks of nomadic types. But she took no photos in Lhasa because she carried no camera. Braham Norwick, a Tibetanist of long standing, pointed out that in the French version of *Journey*, published several months after the English, the author admitted to not bringing a camera because it would have been too bulky and liable to be discovered.

Norwick suggests, "They [the photos] had been taken by Tibetan photographers in Lhasa, and this explains . . . how they were made without exciting suspicion." However, it is not likely that there were any Tibetan photographers at that time, especially with access to a darkroom. We do know of at least one resident Nepali photographer, about whom we are told by Montgomery McGovern: "He was somewhat acquainted with the mysteries of photography, and while I was cooped up as a prisoner he went around the city and took several pictures for me." The Nepali, a member of the good-sized artisan community at Lhasa, may have had ties to Johnston and Hoffmann of Calcutta, a commercial studio that also had agents in Nepal and southern Tibet.

Another related mystery is that of the curious photo of Alexandra, Yongden, and a little Lhasa girl posed against the back-drop of the Potala, which appears rather like a stage set. Denys, certain it was faked, made much of the shot, while other, more reliable writers have suggested it may be a composite. But if the photo is viewed in the original larger size in which it appeared in 1926 in *Asia* magazine, before it was shrunk to suit a book format, it regains its natural depth. Moreover, the traveler sent this single photo to her husband as his Christmas present for 1924. It is an additional item of proof, as intended, that Alexandra's journey took place in the real world.

Jeanne Denys was a would-be orientalist who preferred to carp rather than seek knowledge in the field. Much of her tirade consists of a long, fatuous digression on Eastern themes. More ominously, an apparent anti-Semite, she became convinced that Alexandra's father and mother were Jews who spoke Yiddish at home. Her attitude was typical of the French ultraright, but because Denys was accurate on other personal matters, we cannot dismiss the suggestion out of hand. The librarian of the Paris Alliance Israelite has stated that a search of their files turned up no mention of Louis or Alexandrine David. Still, Alexandra used to speak of her ancestor, King David, and as with Genghis Khan she seemed to be referring to blood lines. Toward the end of her life, she became intrigued with the theme of Jesus as the culmination of the Hebrew prophets. That, and a couple of other hints, are all we presently know of the matter.

Even in her extreme old age, Alexandra remained reticent about her personal life. Forgotten, in the image that she projected, were her earlier identities as a student radical, a bohemian, an opera singer. To one confidant—her doctor—she entrusted the secret of her excursion on the left-hand path of Tantra. For her readers she adopted the detached pose of a reporter. Nor do even her personal letters reveal the hidden woman. Jacques Brosse was correct to claim that she feared to say too much. But in private, Alexandra told a still more hair-raising tale of her journey than she would present to the public.

Alexandra wrote to Philip on her arrival at Lhasa on February 28, 1934, her first opportunity since she set out from Yunnan the previous October. She informed him of her success, admitted the trip had been an act of lunacy, and assured him she would not attempt it again for a million dollars. She and Yongden were not much more than skeletons, and they had got by on stimulants, that is the home-opathic strychnine. But she was really planning to come home—if only she could figure out how to collect her baggage—rare books, ancient manuscripts, and objets d'art—that was strewn across China in the keeping of French banks, officials, and especially missionaries. Philip must help.

Alexandra didn't mail this letter at once. The Tibetan postal system, only a year old, was mainly employed, in the words of Montgomery McGovern, "as the most efficient means of keeping the unofficial European intruder out." Both letters and telegrams were used to dispatch warnings from the capitol to border stations. Further, not only stamps but "a small present to the postman" made the mail go. As far as Gyantse, at any rate, where it would have to be transferred to the British post office in the fort overlooking that city. From there a letter could be sent to the outer world. Had Alexandra mailed her letter to Philip in Algeria from elsewhere in Tibet, he never would have received it, and she would have been quickly detected.

Alexandra continued to write to her husband against the time when she could post the letters. In March she wrote that both she and Yongden had the flu and were coughing up blood, although they were beginning to recover. She was anxious to leave Lhasa, about which she claimed to be not very curious. It had been a great joke to come here in defiance of both the British and Tibetan governments! This is a side of Alexandra, weary and cynical, totally absent from the heroic personality she would present to her readers. She also made demands of a practical sort on Philip. On his next trip to Algiers he must ask the governor to use his influence with the press on her behalf. He should stress that her father had been an influential publisher and a Deputy in 1848. She wished to become an Asian correspondent for a major newspaper.

In April, after a difficult excursion to view Ganden monastery, founded by Tsong Khapa and the fountainhead of the Yellow Hat reforms, Alexandra complained that she was feeling her age. She had purchased a pair of scrawny horses to cross the treacherous snowy passes of the Himalayas in spring—trekking would have killed her and Yongden both—and she claimed she needed money. Her necklace of graded, nearly solid gold coins given to her by the late Maharaja of Sikkim was meant to serve as the money of last resort. Alexandra kept the necklace a secret from Philip.

Charles Bell bitingly commented about Alexandra that "travelling as a beggar, her opportunities were limited." Because of the disguise in which she took such delight, the pilgrim had barred herself from the high life of the capital or its continuing educational and intellectual traditions. On her way out of town, she passed the Jewel Park, the Dalai Lama's summer palace. She wondered how he would react if he had learned of her presence. In fact, the Omnicient One was aware of her feat and he looked the other way. Alexandra's disguise as a mendicant had worn pretty thin. Hugh Richardson related to us an anecdote told him by Tsarong Shappe, the commander-in-chief of the Tibetan army, about a woman he thought was David-Neel. One of Tsarong's servants anxiously reported to him "a strange nun who actually had a towel!" He had detected her in the act of bathing. Unmistakably this was Alexandra, whose obsession with cleanliness had overcome her prudence, marking her as a philing.

The year before Tsarong had clandestinely interviewed McGovern and shepherded him out of Lhasa. A reformer and a self-made man, he was secretly working to open Tibet to the world. Because he was personally close to the Dalai Lama, he would have reported Alexandra's presence to the Thirteenth. But, especially during Monlam, they both dreaded the wrath of the monks of Drepung. Best to ignore the interloper lest they create a nasty incident.

One must not take Alexandra's pretense of a cool objectivity too seriously. Her route, with all its detours and circumambulations, had always been aimed at Lhasa—since her first glimpse of the Sacred Realm a decade before. By early April, however, she was as determined to leave as she had been to invade it. What she could not forget was her tramp through the Po, the warm, fecund valley where during January wild orchids grow. So special is this country that some Tibetan students of the ancient texts hold it to be the location of *Shambala*, or paradise, known to Westeners as Shangri-La. Ringed by massive snow mountains glistening with ice, spiritual powers are needed to find the way there. Travelers will find food and shelter, perpetual youth and health, and they will not wish to leave. Alexandra had felt something of this, and she tucked deep within her the secret of the lush, carefree valleys.

Now she set her gaze toward the snowy peaks standing between her and acclaim. Burning with a long-nurtured ambition, Alexandra put aside her dream of repose. An uneventful journey of three weeks over rugged terrain included a stopover at Sanding monastery to visit Dorjee Phagmo, the "Thunderbolt Sow," a personification of female power, who unfortunately was not at home. The ragged pair descended on David Macdonald, the British Trade Agent at Gyantse, in early May while he was calmly dozing in the fort on the hill overlooking town. To the weary adventurer, their meeting was a crucial moment. She later claimed that instinct caused her to reveal her identity to the British. Really, she had no choice but to throw herself on the mercy of her old antagonists. Neither she nor Yongden had got much better, and exhausted, they could not go on without help.

Macdonald, who had served under Charles Bell, knew his duty. He questioned Alexandra and then wrote hastily to the viceroy:

> Mme. informed me that she left Yunnan seven months ago and entered Tibet by an unknown route disguised as a Tibetan lady. . . . She appears to have avoided Chamdo and other places where Tibetan troops are stationed. She traveled through the Po country[,] Gyamda [and] thence to Lhasa, and remained there for two months in disguise . . .
>
> Questioned why she visited Tibet she simply states that her object was to collect religious books and see the country, but otherwise she is very reticent in her reply. She now intends travelling to India via the Chumbi valley . . . [S]he proposes visiting America.

There in the terse wording of a communiqué is the essence of *My Journey to Lhasa*. Had Jeanne Denys read those words, she might have spared herself a decade of furious effort.

In any event, the daring of Alexandra's exploit overcame bureaucratic scruples, and the British extended their hospitality. Macdonald sheltered the wayward traveler, fed her at his table, expedited her mail, and even loaned her the sum of four hundred rupees. The Trade Agent was not a wealthy man, and after retirement his family was obliged to run a boarding house at Kalimpong for the British stationed there. (This has become the Himalayan Hotel, well known to travelers from many nations.) More important than money or the gifts of clothing from his daughter Victoria so that Alexandra might arrive in India in style, was Macdonald's agreeing to verify his guest's stay at Lhasa. He knew the capitol and would have been impossible to fool. However, the half-Scottish official waited until August 21 to sign and date a letter to that effect. The reason is readily apparent: It was then that he was repaid his loan!

The travelers took most of May to mend. Alexandra was sick and dispirited for days. Although the handful of Britons at Gyantse—including Captain Perry, Macdonald's son-in-law—were clearly in awe of her, she felt foreign among these whites with their stiff manners. Once again she had turned her back on Tibet and was beginning to regret it. Over dinner at a table covered with linen, porcelain, and silverware, everyone seated demurely and chatting about nothing, the veteran of the steppes had to struggle to keep from tears. Still, by the end of the month she was ready to leave for India.

Crossing from the windswept plain of Gyantse to the flower-filled Chumbi Valley, home to the Macdonald clan, Alexandra and Yongden dawdled for nine days. They stayed in comfortable dak bungalows along the way. Macdonald's wife, informed of her coming over the telegraph line, pampered and fattened the adventurer. Although Alexandra would pose in pilgrim's garb for a photograph taken in Calcutta, her explorings were at an end. It was reassuring to learn from Victoria Williams that she had treated the young woman kindly and kept her sense of humor, because her letters to Philip were raspy and demanding as ever.

Alexandra, aside from wanting money, ordered her sometime husband to employ the Argus press agency to clip articles certain to be written about her. He should keep not only her letters but the envelopes postmarked Tibet. Let anyone who wished doubt her, she would have the proofs handy. So absorbed was Alexandra in self-promotion that when she heard her friend General Pereira had died in the mountains of western China, she muttered only that it was an appropriate death for an old soldier. But while resting at Chumbi, Alexandra was troubled by nightmares in which she relived scary moments of the journey. She would awake in a warm bed shivering, overcome by a surge of fear. Bewildered, she imagined she and Yongden were lost on the trail, climbing upward, tiny and frail amidst the immense snowy peaks.

Although Alexandra rejoiced in modest comfort, she couldn't regain the strength necessary to attempt crossing the Himalayas, even mounted. So Macdonald's older daughter, Annie (Captain Perry's wife), loaned her a dandy and porters to carry the conveyance. This hardy woman had to be toted out of Tibet like a package, in little better shape than the injured Lowell Thomas, Sr. It was nothing to be ashamed of. The Land of Snows, forbidden then and still a difficult country in which to travel, does not yield its secrets lightly.

Alexandra put behind her the stinging plateau, the blizzard haunted mountains, and like Conway, the hero of *Lost Horizon*, reentered the world of everyday. She came down to the fetid air of the tropics at rainy season to be the guest of the British Resident at Gangtok, Sikkim. This was now Colonel Frederick (Eric) Bailey, the explorer, who held court with his wife Lady Irma. Alexandra was well received, and she was correct to claim that everyone admired her. If she detected an air of reserve in the Resident's treatment of her, it merely expressed the ambiguity felt by agents of the Government of India. They felt obliged to laud her but wished she would somewhere else.

Bailey himself—a tall, handsome man of bearing who spoke in a soft voice—had been a daredevil as a young officer. He disobeyed orders by entering Tibet and charting the course of the Tsangpo River. Tramping a portion of the same ground as Alexandra, he was more methodical if less imaginative. Badly wounded in the Great War, Bailey managed to carry off a secret mission in Russian Turkestan; employed by Bolshevik intelligence, he was searching for the British spy, Captain Bailey! By 1924 the colonel had settled down to administering Sikkim and pursuing his passion, collecting rare butterflies. His important books on Tibet were written later.

Alexandra sensed that most of the British officers were jealous of her. They couldn't fathom how this diminutive, frail Frenchwoman and her ordinary-seeming Asian son had beat them at their own game of heroics. Their wives, such as Lady Irma, the only child to Lord Cozens-Hardy, were intelligent, charming, and decorative. But whatever his personal feelings, Colonel Bailey was the man best able to comprehend Alexandra's achievement. Reversing the expulsion order of his predecessor, Charles Bell, he invited her to stay as long as she liked at Gangtok.

The Resident could not help the weather in his Lilliputian capitol, which was hot and sticky. Prices had shot sky-high. Alexandra was amazed how native servants, previously submissive, had become almost scornful of their European employers. She wondered why the British tolerated such behavior. Due to her isolation, she had not realized how the war sounded the death knell of the old colonial society. As well, she was troubled by memories of friends she had known from a time that seemed long past.

The Panchen Lama had fled to China. The old maharaja and Dawasandup the interpreter were dead. All she had left of Prince Sidkeong were gold trinkets, valuable but of cold comfort. Gangtok no longer struck her as a romantic hideaway. Desperately, she hoped for a letter from her dear Mouchy, from whom she hadn't heard in a year. Her inquiries about his health were truly anxious.

Alexandra was overjoyed when, on June 9, 1924, she received word from her husband. In replying, she attacked a French novel by Pierre Benoit—a book she hadn't read—set in the Sahara. It was the rage in Paris, and she wished to hear of no triumph but her own. Impatiently waiting through the rainy season for funds with which to return home, she accepted the invitation of French Franciscan missionaries to occupy a bungalow at Padong in the Darjeeling district. Once again missionaries would provide her with shelter free of charge. Here the altitude was higher, and she could breathe more easily, as well as begin writing of her adventures. These she intended to serve up to the public while still warm.

Monsoon rains fell throughout the summer, turning the streets of the village to mud. The bungalow, a former post office, was small and leaky. Alexandra felt like a prisoner. She hounded Philip for money, to which he agreed, though it took time to arrange. What surprised him was his wife's declaration that she wished to rush home to his arms. She assured him her travels were finished but admitted that she needed a place to write the articles American editors were clamoring for.

Alexandra refused to face the reality that, after an absence of nearly fourteen years, she had abdicated her marriage. Soon letters arrived to cheer her exile: first one from the president of the Geographical Society of Paris, then one from the French ambassador to China, an old acquaintance. He was seeking a government subsidy to be made available to her at Peking. Professor Sylvain Levi, the renowned Sanskritist, sent his warm congratulations and an offer for her to lecture at the Sorbonne. More immediately, he referred her to his son Daniel, consul at Bombay. Only Philip remained aloof, no had funds arrived to pay her debts, about which she was scrupulous, and passage to France.

Toward the end of August, Alexandra received a sufficient sum along with a note from Philip, taking the mineral water cure at Vichy. Elated, she assured him she intended to spend the winter at their home in Bone, but she hoped he would help her to give conferences at Paris in the spring. But the next moment Alexandra admitted that her true destination was America. Having been raised in Belgium, she felt a stranger among the French. She was most used to those she lumped together as "Anglo-Saxons." She was certain to succeed in the New World.

Philip, even had he wished it at this late date, could never hold onto his comet of a wife. No wonder he felt melancholy and hypochondriac. Alexandra promised that once she and Yongden arrived home, they would cheer him up. With her star in the ascendant, she did not consider how Philip had blocked her out of his emotional life. Worse, she did not realize that bringing home another man—no matter how related—was more of an affront than her husband could swallow.

While Alexandra prepared to leave the Himalayan region for Calcutta, a strange regretfulness crept over her. The nightmares had turned to dreams of a beautiful, peaceful valley where one was forever young at heart.

Chapter 20
Success at Paris

In his autobiography Alan Watts wrote of "that incredible and mysterious Russian lady Helena Petrovna Blavatsky, who founded the Theosophical Society in—of all places—New York City in 1875." Fifty years later Alexandra David-Neel dreamed, perhaps, of emulating her predecessor's feat. At least she instructed Philip Neel, bearer of a Protestant name, to obtain from the French president, a Huguenot, a letter of recommendation to the consul at New York. Circumstances, including a lack of ready money, would alter this plan.

In October, Alexandra received instant acclaim in Calcutta, a welcome contrast to her husband's coolness. The newspapers were filled with stories about her. As she arranged for her valuable belongings to be shipped from Shanghai via Colombo to Algeria, she was beset by many small problems. Government of India officials went out of their way to help. The Governor of French Indochina presented her with a parcel of land on which she might build a house, so that she would have a pied-a-terre in the Orient. She was at Benares in January, where she began to outline the story of her journey to Lhasa, in the larger sense, in three hefty volumes.

At Bombay, which she reached in early February 1925, Alexandra had to concentrate her thoughts. The *Revue de Paris* urgently cabled for her Tibetan memoirs, and the American magazine *Asia* promised an advance of three hundred and seventy-five dollars for three articles. The cash settled the question of how Alexandra's adventures would first appear: serially, aimed at an audience interested in the East but by no means specialists or inclined to Buddhism.

An appropriate tone of detachment, yet openness to the wondrous, when once she had mastered it, infused the author's most successful and influential works. Her original account of her journey to Lhasa—written in English, not translated, and published in five monthly installments the next year—is travel writing at its most compelling. These *Asia* articles are fresher, more true, and quite different from Alexandra's later book-length accounts, whether in English or French.

When the adept of tantric mysteries met the famous Indian poet Rabindranath Tagore, he reinforced her decision to write for a wide if literate public. At a lunch to honor the Nobel laureate, Alexandra managed to become the center of attention. The director of the Musée Guimet, who was returning from Afghanistan, insisted that she install at the museum a genuine Tibetan Buddhist chapel. Since at the Guimet she first started down the road to Lhasa, the suggestion gave her particular pleasure. Tagore, too, proved encouraging, and at a private interview he offered to help place her articles in Latin America, from which he had recently returned. To this day, Alexandra has a dedicated following among Latins.

Ironically, Professor Sylvain Levi actually launched David-Neel's worldwide reputation, but by reminding her that success must begin at Paris. His son Daniel, whom she'd known as a boy, seconded his father's urging that she proceed directly to the French capitol. Levi was working hard to assure Alexandra's triumph in her natal city. He could scarcely wait to delve into her collection of four hundred rare Tibetan books and manuscripts, and he requested a catalog at once. Only Philip remained aloof, claiming he lived in too small a house to accommodate her souvenirs, especially a certain young man. Alexandra, reminding him what old friends they were, ignored the hint.

On May 4, accompanied by Yongden and mounds of baggage, Alexandra landed at Valencia, Spain, hoping still to rendezvous with her husband in the south of France. Spanish customs, after taking a look at her books, robes, masks of the supposed devil dancers, and other unusual mementos, indicated they would prefer she continue to Le Havre. This meant she was not to see Philip until months later, but it placed her at the door to Paris. She responded to the challenge by an attack of her old nemesis, facial neuralgia. However, on land-ing, her admirers were many, congratulations poured in, and then she—and surprisingly, Yongden—became the talk of the town.

From the moment of Alexandra's arrival at the railway station, she had to suffer the pop of flashbulbs and the intrusive questions of reporters. Although she clung to her stated aversion to the worldly life, the returned pilgrim handled interviews with aplomb. She permitted the men and women of the Paris press to see in her what they wished: French heroine in the mode of Joan of Arc, magician, studious orientalist. The most amusing, and telling, of these interviews—by one Simone Tery—was not published until March 31, 1926, in *le Quotidien:*

> Mme. David [still no husband!] has the air of a very tranquil woman. She wears well a high bonnet of black velvet, strange, pushed down on her head, which serves to bring out the pallor of her face—but, this detail aside, she resembles the average French housewife [literally, "all the mothers of families"]. She speaks in a soft voice, a little sharp, without ever raising her voice, as though she were telling her neighbor about the illnesses of her children or [trading] kitchen recipes. Mme. David has a horror of "chic," of lyricism and easy success.

For journalists of her day and biographers of ours, the handiest means of coping with this *formidable* character who had broken the implicit rules against a woman thinking and acting heroically was to domesticate her, to pretend she was like other women except rather bizarre or freaky. Along with this view goes the notion that Alexandra was the plaything of some imperious Destiny. Philip Neel understood that it would be impossible for his wife to resume the role of a bourgeois homemaker, but it was because she had freely chosen a life of study and discipline, of adventure and loneliness.

Tery's remarks on Yongden were nakedly racist:

> He is dressed in a monk's habit, small and squat, with an impassive face, a small flat nose and narrow and alert eyes. He speaks of things in Tibetan, moving very rapidly his ten sharp fingers. Then he intones some weird chants to make your skin crawl, interspersed with inhuman cries.

The article concluded by suggesting the duo ought to have ahead of them a stunning career in music halls. In this regard the reporter perceived a bit of the truth. For two years after her reentry, David-Neel became once again a performer, although in the guise of an itinerant lecturer. First, worrying over Mouchy's health and the misunderstanding between them, she pressed for a meeting with her husband. This was finally achieved shortly before Christmas 1925 in a side parlor of the Hotel Terminus, near the railway station at Marseilles—neutral ground.

A tense conversation ensued between Alexandra and Philip to which Yongden was a witness, along with whomever else happened to overhear. The engineer, in his mid-sixties, retained a dapper appearance. His hair had turned gray, although he blackened his mustache. However, monsieur's boiled collar and stickpin-in-the-cravat elegance was hopelessly out of date in the 1920s. Albert—the anglicized version of Yongden's first name—was dressed in a more *au courant* stripped suit and tie, which fit his stubby frame without grace. Only in the guise of a tantric lama, a *tulku*, did he appear handsome, slightly resembling the late Maharaja Sidkeong.

These days when traveling, Alexandra favored a prim suit, starched white blouse, and a beret set squarely on her broad forehead. Beneath the amply cut clothes her body remained slimmer than it had been. But the coquettishly plump figure that could be enhanced by the latest Parisian mode remained only a distant memory for Philip. This woman, strange to him, her face deeply lined from exposure to harsh weather, eyes keen but hard, resembled some errant uncle returned from a voyage to far shores and set to relate his lengthy, incredible tales.

After meaningless kisses on both cheeks and the obvious exchanges, Alexandra began to extol the virtues of the younger man: "We have been together for eleven years in the wilds. A number of times we have nearly frozen to death, been set on by savage dogs, beaten off bandits. As a matter of honor, you must help me adopt this boy, who I treat as my son."

"I won't stop you," Philip replied. "I don't think it is a good idea. But I don't uphold an old-fashioned law that demands you obtain my permission."

"I thought to have a son would give you pleasure," Alexandra reminded him. "Albert could accompany you on your walks—he is very amusing."

What the young man of twenty-five said, or what he felt, can only be imagined.

"I never opposed you in anything," Philip reminded his wife. "I gave you freedom to leave me, to roam around the world. I have helped you to satisfy your taste for things Asiatic."

The Frenchman's glance toward Yongden showed that he regarded him as a rival. Alexandra, aware her husband was concerned about old age, turned wily. "Albert has proved his loyalty," she argued. "Isn't he better able to care for you than some strange servant?"

Philip, as ever, surrendered: "Do what you wish, I will give you the necessary authorization." But the negotiations broke down over the question of money. Alexandra, putting aside thoughts of America, demanded a large sum to buy a house in the south of France. Philip took umbrage at her offer that he could come to stay in it whenever he wanted. The discussion flared into a quarrel, spilled into the lobby to the astonishment of the hotel guests, and ended out in the street with bitter words barked back and forth. Fortunately, Marseilles was not a town to care about a husband and wife fighting over a young man.

Did the street fight come to curses or blows? We can't know because Alexandra, embarrassed, had much of the correspondence from this period burned along with other material she considered compromising. At any rate, the storm had blown over by March of the following year when Philip agreed to wire her six thousand francs toward her living expenses. Her inheritance had been eaten up by the postwar inflation. Alexandra thanked Mouchy from the bottom of her heart and added that she needed peace of mind to compose a far more complicated work than *Journey*, which she considered a story of adventure.

In order to make ends meet, and for the publicity, David-Neel launched a series of conferences. The first was held at the Sorbonne in the autumn of 1925, under the sponsorship of Professor Levi; it proved as colorful and successful as those to follow. In the same lecture hall where she had sat as a student, an overflow audience listened breathlessly as "the first white woman to reach Lhasa"—a phrase she used in her advertising—told a tale of daring, disguise, and hardihood, and even let drop morsels of information on the secret, exotic tantric rites. Still, she was careful to strike a pose that if not scientific was at least dispassionate.

To Alexandra's surprise, Yongden upstaged his mother and brought crowds to their feet cheering his improvisations of Tibetan poetry. She claimed he had picked up his style from watching Tagore. Declaiming in his lama's outfit, his poetry—which she would translate—was studded with "coral red mountains" and "turquoise blue skies." Or the young lama would enthrall his listeners with an anecdote of *ngagspas*, grinding human bones into life-prolonging powders.

That winter the pair toured the south. They packed the large municipal casino at Nice, then went on to Marseilles and Toulon. Handsome in colorful flowing Tibetan robes, Alexandra received from her audiences all the acclaim bestowed on a renowned diva. But she did not bask in her triumph. She hated living in hotels and the rooms were expensive. At Paris she had solved the problem of accommodations by setting up her dark, yak-hair tent in the courtyard garden of the Guimet and moving right in! The best she could do in the provinces was to pull the mattress off the bed and sleep on the floor.

Returning to Paris in the following spring, David-Neel spoke before standing room crowds at the College de France, the Guimet, and the Theosophical Society. To vary the show, and likely put Yongden in the shade, she introduced slides made from her striking photos of nomadic men and women, merchants with wares, so-called devil dancers in masks, high-up monasteries like fortresses, and the snowcapped Himalayas. To document their travels, Alexandra had taken hundreds of photos and asked Yongden to snap many of her. Now viewing these made her miserable. Although she was off to Lausanne, Brussels, and London for additional conferences and more applause, deep down she felt bereft. Dr. A. d'Arsonval of the College de France, a leading psychologist and both the orientalist's academic sponsor and her doctor, diagnosed the malady as colitis brought on by nostalgia for the country and life she'd left. At heart Alexandra was a nomad who loved best her tent, horses, and the open country.

To keep off neurasthenia, David-Neel wrote up to sixteen hours a day in various nondescript hotel rooms. The initial article for *Asia* appeared in March 1926. The five-part series, collectively titled "A

Woman's Daring Journey into Tibet," is hard to come by but far more candid than the full-length work that would follow. David-Neel was working so diligently to complete the latter that in March 1927, at Toulon, she contracted an eye inflammation that blinded her for a week. Then, peering out of one eye, she resumed editing the proofs. *My Journey to Lhasa* was supposed to be issued simultaneously in the spring by Plon in Paris, Heinemann in London, and Harper in New York. Actually the English language editions appeared in early fall, the sharply abridged French one in November.

Luree Miller has observed about *Journey*: "Included were all the ingredients of a fantastic adventure: traveling in disguise; mistaken identities . . . a faithful companion . . . dangers to Alexandra's life . . . miraculous escapes accomplished by cleverness and an almost supernatural good luck." Contemporaneous reviews were mostly favorable. The *New York Times* declared that "as a traveler she [Alexandra] has performed a brilliant feat." In London the *Saturday Review* found the work "a thoroughly absorbing tale," while in more sober style *The Times Literary Supplement* felt certain the author had imparted "a considerable measure of useful and trustworthy information." Sir Francis Younghusband reviewed the book for the *Journal* of the Royal Geographical Society from a unique perspective. Just two years earlier he had compiled General George Pereira's diaries into a consistent narrative entitled *Peking to Lhasa*. Few Westerners knew Tibet better than Sir Francis.

The "short, stocky, and warmly gruff little man with a bristling moustache"—Alan Watts's description—who in 1936 was to convene the World Congress of Faiths, and who leaned toward mystical ideas, missed the essential nature of Alexandra's writing. After the obligatory praise of her daring and courage, he complained, "The geographical results are very meagre, for there is no map attached to the book and no means of knowing exactly what route she took." In contrast, Pereira traveled over six thousand miles continuously, mapped every step of the way, and died of exhaustion. It was no accident that his precise map of Tibet and western China was sent to the British War Office and reproduced by their permission. This exploring by military officers was no mere academic avocation, and it is ironic that the British should have supposed Alexandra to be a spy.

Journey to Lhasa, recently reissued in both Britain and the United

States, is a pilgrim's tale, and if we would travel to where David-Neel went, especially today, we must do so in the realm of the spirit. This is a book of exploration but only secondarily of terrain. The pair of pilgrims on their way to the holy city, forbidden to outlanders, plumbed the depths of their physical endurance, their wit and comprehension, their faith in anything at all. On a deeper level, *Journey* is of the genre of a spiritual autobiography, comparable to the tales told by and of the enlightened souls of other religions. The eighteenth-century Hassid Rabbi Nachman also overcame disaster after disaster—some of his own making—to pilgrimage to Jerusalem. He donned disguises, lied or cheated when necessary, but always he was careful to perform the proper rites to propitiate a God jealous of outlandish success.

David-Neel, her Asian son in tow, voyaged to the most austere regions on earth, but also within the self. She loved the lad with the fierce love of a mother tiger for her cub. On the edge of the hostile Po country, unknown even to explorers, the pair had to hole up in a cave while Yongdon nursed his badly dislocated ankle. They had not a morsel to eat, and wet and shivering, they wondered when the snow would stop falling and if they would end as a meal for the wolves. Yet Alexandra found a certain charm in her lonely situation. She forgot her pain and worry and entered into a deep meditation, seated, motionless, silent.

The snow continued to fall as the voyager sat, making no effort to peer beyond its curtain into the uncertain future. Mind stilled, for a timeless instant seer and seen became one. Finally, at this desperate juncture, Alexandra reached the *samadhi* sought by the yogi through meditation, the union devoutly prayed for by the mystic Christian. Seeing by the clear light of wisdom, she glimpsed the Void from which all stems and into which all dissolves.

There was, however, a limit to the spiritual intimacy that David-Neel allowed her readers. Rather than follow Emerson's dictum "My life is for itself and not for a spectacle," the former diva stage-managed what she was willing to show. In matters delicate or profound, she often employed the "twilight language" typical of the Tantra, symbols with a double meaning. All in all, *Journey* is a voyage through space and psyche that bears comparison with classics of the genre, such as Lanza Del Vasto's *Return to the Source* or Gurdjieff's

Conversations with Remarkable Men. These seekers, through exploring the world about them, illumined an inner terrain. They did not provide the usual geographical guidelines, but if maps of their wanderings were drawn they would resemble the mariner's charts of the early ages of exploration: colorful, lacking detail, and slightly fantastic. The intent, rather than to mislead, is to direct the reader to unexpected places.

Sales of David-Neel's seminal work were healthy from the start— nine French printings within two years—and translations were made into a number of languages, including German, Czech, Italian, and Spanish. The Americans, who compared this supposed Amazon with the conquerors of the North and South Poles, were especially partial to the book. David-Neel, whose idea of America was as fictional as American ideas of Tibet, thought of sailing to New York to reap more laurels and enormous royalties. The dollar was very strong in relation to the franc, in the ratio of one to fifty. But the web of events was drawing the author in a different direction.

The French were quick to applaud their own, awarding honors and subsidies to David-Neel. First came the silver medal of the Belgian Royal Geographic Society, then the Chevalier of the Legion of Honor and the gold medal of the Societé Geographique. To the latter was attached a much-appreciated six thousand francs. One award that David-Neel accepted tongue-in-cheek was the grand prize for feminine athleticism from the French Sports Academy. A great lover of the outdoors, she couldn't consider herself an athlete or trekking through Tibet a sport. Ironically, she received the medal in May 1927 when, hobnobbing with the literati in Paris, she felt she was suffocating and her heart troubled her. Her feet grew red and swollen from wearing high heels. She never had loved big cities, and her living in the wilds had confirmed her solitary streak.

As long ago as her "Huron hut" in the Himalayas, Alexandra dreamed of acquiring a home with enough land on which to grow vegetables. Turning from thoughts of America, she focused on the south of France, although not the coast, which she considered overbuilt. In the fall she went on a walking tour of the Basses Alpes above the Riviera—prescribed by Dr. d'Arsonval to regain her health—and there the keen-eyed traveler discovered a likely spot. The German edition of *Journey* had netted ten thousand francs, and in addition she was able to sell several articles, the most noteworthy being a contribution to *Man and His World*, a reference work edited by Paul Reclus. He was the nephew of Elisée, Alexandra's old mentor from student days. For a change she had money, but she was careful to keep Philip informed of her plans. According to French law she might buy a house on her own, but if she wished to sell she would need her husband's permission.

Not just any location would do. Occasionally Alexandra liked to damn civilization and its works, but she insisted that her new home be accessible by rail and served by electricity. She understood the necessity of publicity and that she needed to be accessible to the press and visiting dignitaries. In May 1928, outside the quiet spa town of Digne, ninety-five miles northwest of Nice, Alexandra purchased a small villa on a hill with a good view of the attractive surroundings. She named it Samten Dzong, Fortress of Meditation. The road to Nice, lined by trees, ran past her door; a river flowed just below that, and mountains loomed in the background. Alexandra invited Philip to visit her and Yongden whenever he pleased.

Samten Dzong did become a refuge for the sixty-year-old savant, although for work rather than contemplation. The series of books on Tibet she was planning to write nearly fell victim to too much admiration. French president Gaston Doumergue, a moderate elected in 1924, became a fan of his redoubtable countrywoman. The president made available to the author sixty thousand francs to undertake a mission through Siberia into Mongolia to study the tribes of Soviet Central Asia, in particular the effect of the revolution on women. The interaction between Buddhism and native shamanism fascinated her.

Turmoil in the areas Alexandra needed to visit caused Moscow to refuse her a visa. Stalled, she appealed to her friend, the writer Romain Rolland, who interceded with the Soviet delegation to the League of Nations at Geneva. Their Minister of Education Lounatcharski seemed kindly disposed, and so forgetting her other plans, the would-be traveler began to make arrangements. However, within a short time the minister fell from grace and was shot. In the end, the applicant received the famous Soviet *nyet*.

This apparent setback proved fortunate. While Alexandra had to swallow her disappointment, she kept open her contacts with the

French government; she would need its backing for future expeditions. No more eager to chain herself to a desk than other authors, she surrounded herself with her unique collection of Tibetan books, her superb demonic masks, and other souvenirs from fourteen years of wandering on the roof of the world—including Yongden. Alexandra commenced on the next decade of fruitful study and the writing of books.

Chapter 21
The Short Path

Digne, a small cathedral town of winding streets, is best known from a memorable episode in Victor Hugo's *Les Miserables*. It was there the tormented exconvict Jean Valjean stole silver candlesticks from the bishop who had befriended him. Out of pity, the good cleric lied to the police, claiming that he gave the candlesticks away. Perhaps Alexandra David-Neel, like Hugo's hero, was hoping to begin a new life. More likely, she was attracted by Digne's thermal baths, which date back to Roman times and are beneficial for chronic rheumatism. At eighteen hundred feet, the climate is nearly perfect.

During the summer of 1928, once she'd settled into Samten Dzong, Alexandra's misgivings cropped up. She let Philip know the surrounding mountains were too skimpy for her taste, nothing compared to the Himalayas. There were trees on the property, but she and Yongden would plant additional ones: cherry, pear, chestnut, and lime. If the neighborhood wasn't wildly picturesque, at least the sun shone year round and she could sleep on a rug on a roofed-over terrace.

The country around Digne could boast of magnificent wildflowers. With Yongden, Alexandra explored the mountain paths, admiring gentian, edelweiss, marguerites, and fields of lavender. She endorsed the air over that of the seaside, and she begged Philip to visit them before the winter. People were scarce; only a couple of houses stood anywhere near, and their inhabitants gave the woman and her Asian son a wide berth. Pen and paper were the company she craved.

Alexandra planted a vegetable plot at her new hermitage. Her first crop turned out to be a bumper one and she sold the excess. Growing her own food suited her pioneering nature and appeased an increasingly frugal streak she had inherited from her mother. In the East, she became used to pinching pennies, and although currently prosperous, she did not forget the lean years. Once her Eastern acquisitions were thoroughly installed, she intended to work with the speed of a *kyang* (wild donkey) bounding over the Tibetan plateau.

The new householder ordered Philip to ship various objects that he had saved for her, including her letters to him, the only *journal de voyage* she'd made. Surprisingly, she did keep a meticulous inventory of everything sent from Asia to her husband, down to numbering each of the hundreds of photos. Where was the quilt from her student days, she wanted to know, and books by her favorite authors— Flaubert, Anatole France, Jules Verne, and Tolstoy? Philip must immediately send on her bicycle. The roads were pretty, and she wanted the exercise of pedaling.

By the end of the year, Alexandra was as snug in her sun-dappled retreat as she had been at snowy Lachen. But she was growing more distant from her academic mentor, Sylvain Levi, who chided her for not devoting herself entirely to works of philosophy. He had suggested she do a philological study of Tibetan literature, not unconnected with his own labors on a dictionary of Buddhism. The orientalist realized that the authority of her statements rested on how well she stood with the professors, never mind they didn't dare venture to Tibet. But works for a select audience failed to pay expenses, and these were mounting alarmingly as she renovated Samten Dzong. Without a university salary, the author deemed it impractical to write esoteric treatises.

Levi was angry that his former pupil didn't turn over to him certain rare manuscripts. Dr. d'Arsonval, who had superseded him as David-Neel's patron, wrote to her amusingly that Levi, a devoted library rat, was disappointed that his favorite pupil wouldn't give him some old Tibetan papyrus to gnaw. The author, ignoring the rivalry between the two men, worked diligently. In 1929 Plon brought out the French version of the book that would be titled *Magic and Mystery in Tibet* when published in New York in 1932. This has proved to be David-Neel's most durable and popular work, having been translated into Portuguese (Brazil), Hungarian, and Annamite

(Vietnam), as well as the Scandinavian and other European languages. Here, despite an assumed air of detachment, the author discussed the rational mystics close to her heart, adepts of the Short Path to Deliverance who risked its dangers in the hope of winning enlightenment in one lifetime.

The Short or Direct Path is considered hazardous in a psychic and even a physical sense. Its methods are extreme and uncompromising, and failure can lead to a spritual breakdown, a fall from grace like that of Lucifer in the Christian tradition—from angel to devil. This doctrine of complete freedom can be subject to abuse, especially since its founder, or really its eighth century translator to Tibet, Padmasambhava, was a powerful tantric magician. John Snelling, author of *The Buddhist Handbook*, writes, "He alone possessed the occult know-how necessary to subdue the demoniac forces inimical to the transmission of Buddhism." However, as Snelling notes, the old shamanic spirits were not annihilated but continued to play a role in Tibetan Buddhism. Alexandra found that those who claimed to be on the Short Path ranged the spiritual and social spectrum from beggarly fortune tellers to high lamas. Fortunately for us, she was acquainted with every sort of Tibetan, from the Panchen and Dalai Lamas to cutthroat brigands.

To our knowledge, Alexandra was the first foreigner to actively participate in Tibetan tantric rites, including those of the Left Hand, and to report back on them. The *chöd* rite, for example, was known but spoken of in a whisper. David Snellgrove and the Italian scholar-explorer Giuseppe Tucci wrote about it only from hearsay. This is hardly surprising since chöd has always involved secret oral teachings handed down directly from master to disciple. Evans-Wentz learned of chöd from Kazi Dawasandup and assisted in the translation of ancient texts. Alexandra, meanwhile, performed a mild version of chöd, which she continued to practice after her return to France.

She began to experiment with the so-called mystic banquet under the supervision of the Gomchen of Lachen. The rite is intended to be a one person drama, chanted while dancing ritual steps to a drum made from two human skulls, the skin stretched over them and pellets attached; it is played like a rattle with one hand. A trumpet made of human thighbone is played, and magical implements manipulated: the *dorje*, (vajra) or thunderbolt symbol, the *tilpu*, (ghanta) a handbell, and a three-sided magic dagger used to stab demons. Coordination is essential, and the performance must be rehearsed to go according to formula, because a misstep could prove fatal.

Traditionally, ascetics from Kham, *naljorpas*, whose hair plaited into a single braid fell nearly to their feet, were masters of chöd. On her travels through the borderlands, Alexandra had watched them dance under an infinite starry sky to the throb of drums and wail of the trumpets. They looked like the demons they called upon as they strained every sinew into intricate contortions. Their faces shone as they ecstatically trampled down their own feverish egos, daring death itself in the effort to halt what Buddhists term the mad race toward mirages. The initiate understood that the demons envisioned were imagined, but in the trancelike state these symbols became realities to the practitioner. An old lama warned Alexandra to beware of the tigers of her mind, even if she had given them birth, or if another had unleashed them on her.

Once, camped among cowherds in northern Tibet, Alexandra happened on a funeral. She stayed to witness the ceremonies, but she was even more intrigued by a nearby ascetic, Rabjoms Gyatso, who had established himself in a cave and was attended by two disciples, one nearly a skeleton. She guessed that the emaciated lama was performing chöd as the essential part of his spiritual practice, and she knew it was best acted out in a cemetery or other wild spot where a fresh corpse had been disposed.

Along with a large gathering of Tibetans, the foreign lama ate and drank copiously before the corpse, which was placed in a seated position in a large caldron. Friends of the deceased arrived from all directions to bring presents to the bereaved family. Rabjoms Gyatso's disciples read religious books over the dead man, after which he was carried to a likely spot in the mountains. The body would be cut into pieces and left there, an offering to the huge vultures.

Alexandra, herself dressed in the costume of a naljorpa, waited until dark and walked to the cemetery to spend the night meditating under a full moon. She was musing on the contradiction between the happy nature of the Tibetans and certain of their grim practices when she heard hoarse cries rising above an insistent drumbeat. Hiding in the cleft of a hillock, she recognized the tantric master's wasted-looking disciple. Playing his role in the macabre drama on an apparently deserted stage, he jerked his frame into frenzied postures. He accompanied his dance with staccato yells, which summoned demons by name to feast on his carcass.

The chöd celebrant is acting in a sense. He imaginatively creates a feminine deity in exact detail, and she, sword in hand, will cut off the actor's head, while troops of ghouls hover around clamoring for their banquet. Then the merciless goddess severs his limbs, flays his torso, and rips open his belly. Bowels falling out, the aspirant must urge on the hideous demons to attack with invocations of surrender. Thubten Norbu, the Dalai Lama's elder brother and former abbot of Kum Bum, has pointed out that the ceremony derives from human sacrifice in early times.

"[F]or the adept performing the rite of Chöd," adds Norbu, "there is a very terrible reality to the demoniacal form that advances upon him to sever his head." The celebrant may easily lose hold of himself and the ritual, acutely feeling the terrors being recited. Alexandra watched as the emaciated monk adopted a defiant stance. She heard him invoke the ritual formula: *I the fearless naljorpa, I trample down the self, the gods, and the demons*. He whirled, genuflected to the four corners, and stamped wildly as he followed the formula to vanquish anger, lust, and stupidity. All the while he stared at pieces of the previous day's corpse strewn before him.

But the disciple soon became muddled. He entered the small tent he had erected, leaving the corpse to a natural wolf come down from the hills to feast on it. The apprentice wizard, hearing the animal growl, took it for a demon. "Feed on me!" he cried out. Furiously blowing his trumpet, he jumped up and collapsed the tent on top of himself. When he struggled free, face madly contorted, he was howling with the pain of being bitten. Even the wolf became frightened and backed off.

Alexandra felt that the young man had lost his mind and her pose as disinterested observer would not do. Giving way to sympathy rather than compassion, she rushed toward him. But the poor fellow took her for a hungry ghost from a Tibetan hell. He offered her his flesh to eat, his blood to drink—before he tripped on a tent peg and fell heavily to the ground.

Alexandra, herself frightened, ran off to inform Lama Rabjoms. Guided by a feeble light from an altar lamp high on a nearby hillside, she found the cave. She saw the master seated cross-legged in deep meditation but still let fly her news about his disciple. She insisted that he was on the verge of dying from the illusion of being eaten by demons.

The naljorpa smiled. "As he is the victim, so he is the devourer," he replied.

Before the lama's calm, Alexandra began to regret her impetuous action. He had known through telepathy what had happened to his disciple and that she was on her way. Rabjoms proceeded to lecture her good-naturedly, reminding her of how hard it was to free oneself from illusions and fanciful beliefs. He was sure that her path, although more refined than his disciple's, was equally difficult. Illness, madness, and death were the risks of seeking enlightenement on the Short Path. Chastened, Alexandra agreed, and she stayed on for several days to study with this tantric master.

The unwillingness of David-Neel to suspend her faculty of criticism, to in a sense lose her mind, whatever obstacle it may have presented among the Tibetans was hailed as admirable once she returned to Paris. In his introduction to *Magic and Mystery*, Dr. d'Arsonval praised David-Neel as a philosophical skeptic, a disciple of Descartes, a scientist who had impartially observed and recorded phenomena in Tibet. d'Arsonval was president of the Institut General Psychologiqué, and his imprimatur on David-Neel's work was intended to remove it from the realm of the mystical or occult. Considering the general condescension at the time toward things Eastern, she was content to hide behind this smokescreen.

Fortunately, *Magic and Mystery* is written in a sprightly style reminiscent of David-Neel's articles in *Asia*. It introduces us to a gallery of intriguing real-life characters: Dawasandup, the profound scholar who liked his bottle; the Gomchen of Lachen, who despite his frightening apron of human bones was a pushover for a pussy cat; and the Maharaja of Sikkim, handsome, dashing, and doomed. We meet a collection of ngagspas and naljorpas, wise, magical, sly, and human. Of these the learned lamina is not the least subtle. About her own deeper self Alexandra would drop hints throughout her writings, but they must be watched for with the keenness of a cat eyeing a suspicious mousehole.

During the years 1928 to 1936, except for an occasional conference held in London, Belgium, Switzerland, or Eastern Europe,

David-Neel remained at work at Samten Dzong. Other than Philip she didn't encourage visitors. Some came anyway, including a reporter from Milan dispatched at the behest of an old acquaintance, Benito Mussolini, to interview her. In April 1931 she begged off an invitation to visit the Italian dictator at the Villa Borghese, Rome. Professing no use for politics of any sort, she was able to maintain a distant friendship with a clear conscience. Even Adolf Hitler took an interest in the orientalist's work. She claimed that *der Führer* planned to attend one of her conferences, held in Berlin in 1936, but had to regretfully cancel at the last minute. The swastika, we may note, is an ancient symbol of lightning found in the ruins of Troy, among native American tribes, and especially in Tibet.

Hitler's fascination with the Land of Snows was of long standing, and as a corporal he was assigned to infiltrate a German cult concerned with Tibetan magical rites. According to Otto Rahn, his interest in David-Neel's investigations had a practical side: he wished to learn about *tumo,* the breath of inner heat. Was Hitler thinking this early of equipping his storm troopers with, in Milarepa's phrase, "the best clothing" in order to facilitate their invasion of the snowy plains of the Soviet Union? If so, the Nazi dictator had failed to grasp the essentially spiritual nature of the practice.

David-Neel's *Initiations and Initiates in Tibet* appeared in its French edition in 1930. Following so close on the heels of *Magic and Mystery,* it failed to achieve an equal popularity, and indeed Alexandra complained that foreign editions were being held up by the proximity of publishing dates. Yet *Initiations,* denser and less anecdotal than its predecessor, remains indispensible to the serious student of tantric lore or even the do-it-yourself occultist. It contains more precise observations and specific methods of Tibetan mysticism. Many of these arduous practices were elucidated for the first time in the West, and by one who was herself an initiate and had practiced several of them. Now, when initiations are regularly given en masse in European and American capitals, the work is even more relevant.

David-Neel took pains to dispel the misconception that an initiation necessarily meant the revelation of a secret doctrine. In her day, initiation was a one-to-one affair, often preceded by lengthy preliminaries and testing of the disciple by his guru, sometimes nearly to the point of death. Also, initiations were accompanied by particular esoteric teachings. But she insisted that initiation was, above all, "the transmission of a power, a force, by a kind of psychic process." It represents a step on the path to enlightenment. It conveys the ability to see more deeply than most, or in her words, "to find out who really is the person we think ourselves to be and what really is the world in which we move."

Alexandra's knowledge of esoteric tantric methods was hard won, and because so much of traditional Tibet lies in ruins, her experience could not be duplicated today. Yet Buddhist teachings may be obtained from the many Tibetan lamas in exile. The secrecy so insisted on in Alexandra's time has given way to apprehension that the *dharma* (the doctrine) may be lost forever. She prepared the way for Tibetan Buddhism to be accepted in the West, where it makes its home for the forseeable future. The question does arise as to whether the Gomchen of Lachen, Alexandra's tantric master, gave her permission to reveal to the world a cornucopia of formerly secret knowledge that had been passed on orally to a chosen few. Lama Govinda, who was in a position to judge, supposed that he had done so.

The great Padmasambhava wielded only the *dorje* (thunderbolt) to tame and convert the native demons to Buddhism. The dorje is masculine and symbolizes compassion or method. Alexandra wore this on a gold ring on her right hand; on her left, a tiny bell on a silver ring, feminine to symbolize knowledge. The union of the two energies is crucial to tantric Buddhism, and possession of the rings stamped her as an adept, perhaps aspiring to the status of *naljorpa*. Literally this means, "One who has attained perfect serenity." However, that was not in Alexandra's character or karma.

Initiations elucidated in a more technical manner the themes introduced in *Magic and Mystery*. The author's next book, *Grand Tibet* (Paris, 1933), harked back to her first success, as its English title— *Tibetan Journey*—makes clear. This is an account of the author's adventures upon leaving Kum Bum in 1921 to travel among the merchants, brigands, and desperados of the Sino-Tibetan borderlands. It is straightforward and enormously enjoyable and deserves a wider audience. Captivated by the rolling, untilled steppes, the quiet and aloneness, a simple life under canvas, David-Neel came into her own. In an experience more archetypally American than European, the highly cultured woman, who yet was able to relate to the wildest of beasts, came face-to-face with brute uncaring nature, indeed became one with the primeval forces.

David-Neel had always admired the frontier fiction of James Fenimore Cooper, and according to Jacques Brosse, a Cooperian haste had begun to show in the author's own writing. In order to meet contract dates she fell into a variety of sloppy errors. But David-Neel worked best when under the pressure of a deadline, and each of her early books was written from an inner compulsion and has a distinctive excellence.

Of her several shorter efforts, "Women in Tibet" (*Asia* 1934) was an unmitigated triumph. She boasted that the article was an international success and that female readers from countries as far apart as America and China were writing to her craving more information. The piece analyzed the means by which Tibetan women mastered a harsh environment and gained sway over their men. The women had achieved a de facto equality despite law and scripture unfavorable to them, this by virtue of innate independence and physical stamina. Tibetan women were clever and brave and therefore valued by their husbands. It helped also that a large portion of the retail trade was in women's hands. The tenor of the article showed that David-Neel remained a firm feminist—no less than during the period when she had crusaded for the legal rights of housewives and unwed mothers, still more for their economic independence.

In the article Alexandra casually mentioned that she passed one summer as a guest of the Gologs in northeast Tibet, in the shadow of Amne Machin (twenty-one thousand feet), settling down amidst their black tents and herds of yak and sheep. The Gologs, a tribal people, have never been conquered, and even the Red Army has agreed to let them be. They are not hospitable to strangers, and in Alexandra's day their avocation was highway robbery. They preyed on merchants' caravans carrying goods from China into Tibet. But she was accepted by order of the ruler of the federated Golog tribes— a woman chieftain.

Another intriguing aspect of the article was the author's assertion that polyandry was widespread, if unadvertised, and that the women involved did not necessarily suffer in body or status because of it. David Macdonald, in corroboration, mentioned certain cases among the peasantry where a woman married all the brothers in a family despite there being five or six! She would be expected to bear each a child, and the offspring would treat the eldest brother as father and the rest as uncles. Thubten Norbu contends that the custom exists to keep land in one family and is harmless. Clearly, it has helped to keep the population low, which proved disastrous for Tibet in confronting China.

David-Neel, with the help of Yongden, was at work on more abstruse topics. Their version of *The Superhuman Life of Gesar of Ling* appeared in 1931 in France and 1934 in London, published by Rider, the venerable purveyor of titles occult and Eastern. The author writing first in French found a new translator Violet Sydney, who remained her collaborator over the course of several books. David-Neel thought of her as a snob and sometimes criticized her translations. Whatever their merits in general, Sydney's translation of David-Neel's attempt at an epic added to its old-fashioned feel. This has helped to keep Gesar's story one of the least known of the great national epics.

Aside from repeating the tale of chivalric heroism that she heard in Jyekundo, Alexandra related a prophecy of deep importance to the Central Asian peoples. Gesar—so goes his legend—is bound to return in some guise and, at the point of his sword, first sweep the white man from Asia and then conquer his homeland. A well-educated Mongol monk, acting as secretary to a merchant at Peking, described to David-Neel toward the close of World War I how the Chinese nation (he included Mongols, Tibetans, and the Han) would awaken from their centuries of slumber to follow Gesar in throwing the occupying Europeans into the sea, then sweeping over their homeland with the ruthlessness of the Golden Horde. She was stunned by this vision of a new Genghis Khan. It has come about in part, and if the whole seems unlikely, we may ask ourselves what might happen if China, instead of confronting the rest of Asia, became its leader.

In a very different vein is David-Neel's *Buddhism: Its Doctrines and Its Methods*, which appeared in French in 1936 and in English in 1939, and which once again is in print in the United States. In his foreword to the English-language edition, Christmas Humphreys, the eminent British Buddhist, praised the work as outstanding but little known. In it the Western student could find "the principles of the oldest school of Buddhism, that of the Theravada as practiced in Sri Lanka, Burma and Thailand, viewed by a mind learned in one of the later traditions, that of Tibet." Humphreys added that, since she had authored several books on Tibet, he was surprised when David-Neel turned back to the first principles of her adopted faith.

Humphreys first met Alexandra in 1936 on the occasion of one of her conferences in Nice. They discussed her latest work at length, yet he apparently did not realize that it was mostly a rehash of her *Modern Buddhism* published previous to the Great War and her sojourn in Central Asia. The tract was ignored at the time, and as early as 1926 the triumphant orientalist thought of redoing it. Editors in several capitals were clamoring for any manuscript of hers. By the midthirties demand had waned as Europe was faced with the rise of fascism. That Alexandra was able to squeeze in this project during her busiest decade is in itself remarkable. However, she merely borrowed much of the text from the earlier work, interlarding Tibetan variants concerned with the central themes of Buddhism. The result is instructive almost in the how-to-become-a-working-Buddhist vein.

Here is David-Neel the rationalist. Although *Buddhism* is spiced by the faint flavor of youthful idealism, we can find no tales of anchorites performing wonders in caves high above the earth, no dashing brigands or celebrants in gorgeous robes performing ancient rituals, no naljorpas meddling with cadavers in wild places inhabited by vultures. Instead we are treated to her distillation of the Buddhist doctrine into a two-page chart. Her observations on how to observe the mind are excellent, her discussion of karma essential to the novice, emphasizing that the concept has nothing to do with the Western idea of destiny, but rather depends on free will. The Buddhist admonition that "by pure deeds man becomes pure, by evil deeds he becomes evil" was a message the 1930s world refused to hear. It is the essential wisdom that mighty China in its dealings with unarmed Tibet refuses to heed.

Two significant reconciliations occurred during Alexandra's middle years. The first was with her origins and unhappy youth. In the summer of 1934 she visited Brussels to pay her respects at the graves of her parents. If she was moved to weep, she didn't record it. She admitted that the rancor of an earlier time had gone: her father, despite his reserve, she always loved, and now she could see her mother as a victim of circumstances. Next, possessed by nostalgia, she visited her old boarding school, and then the seaside village where as a teenager she had been taken on vacation and from which she sneaked away to England. How fervently she had wished to explore the wide world! Yet she now recognized Belgium as her native land.

More urgently, Alexandra achieved a rapprochement with her husband Philip. Their correspondence had gone on unabated during her travels, at least whenever there was a post office. Their relations ran the gamut from affection and concern to raging hostility. Philip appears to have given as good as he got, but in the end, he always sent money and his moral support. Now their relationship waxed mellow. On occasion the aging but still debonair gentleman traveled from Algeria to visit his wife at Digne.

Alexandra urged her husband to make frequent and longer stays. She kept a well-heated bedroom ready for him and invited him to spend the entire winter at Samten Dzong. If he became bored with their walks and chats about old times, he could take the train down to the casino at Nice. For Alexandra could spare her dear Mouchy only so much time.

During the same year the orientalist, feeling she must accomplish a more scholarly work to enhance her reputation but begrudging the lack of recompense, set Yongden to roughing out a translation of a text by Tsong Khapa. The result she meant to dedicate to Professor Sylvain Levi, who had not long to live. Yongden bogged down in the archaic Tibetan and Alexandra decided they needed help. She was aware that Giuseppe Tucci, the Italian Tibetologist, was working on the same book, and she intended to beat him to the book stores.

Alexandra told one and all that she and her son had to leave for Peking. In the Tibetan temple there they knew of a well-versed lama who could assist them. Surely this was an excuse to return to Asia, which she had been plotting since 1926. She had even considered crossing the steppes with an expedition of mercy funded by Citroen, the Yellow Cross, which was to encompass thirty cars and trucks, two hundred pack camels, and dozens of French volunteers. She abandoned the scheme, admitting it struck her as more dangerous than going alone.

It took Alexandra nearly three additional years to complete her work at Digne and to raise funds through her royalties and a grant from the French Ministry of Education. On January 9, 1937, a glacially cold night, the pair of pilgrims boarded an express at the Gare du Nord in Paris bound for Berlin, Warsaw, Moscow, and the Far East. The train silently left the station, slipping into the pitch black pierced only by falling snowflakes. Alexadra's mood was as gloomy as the night.

Chapter 22
Storm Clouds

Beginning on her new and final great adventure brought the perpetual seeker no comfort. Rather, on the train Alexandra chafed at having to wear pajamas and to sleep under blankets that had covered countless others. She raged at the passport requirements that had replaced letters of introduction to local notables. "I can leave countless times," she told herself, "but I will never arrive. Not even the last resting place will hold me."

Alexandra and Yongden stopped briefly in wintery Warsaw, to see pictures of themselves in bookstore windows. This did not lessen her feeling of impending doom, of menacing influences. Considering the destruction that soon enough would overtake this city with its crammed Jewish ghetto, Alexandra may be forgiven for her morbidity. She was preoccupied with the *Bardo Thodol, The Tibetan Book of the Dead,* and certain of its occult theories. She understood that once the animating spirit had left the body, the person was in effect dead. But that body, a sort of robot, might go about its everyday tasks and appear alive—to the other robots doing the same. Europe was a corpse waiting to be buried under the rubble of the coming war, and Alexandra herself didn't feel quite alive.

Russia, the next destination, at this season wasn't likely to bring cheer to the pilgrim's heart. As a small child, its snowy immensity had fascinated her. As a young radical in Paris, tales of czarist cruelty had reached her through exiled intellectuals. Then, after the revolution, the Soviet Union became the mecca for those desiring drastic social change. Thus it was out of a long-held curiosity that Alexandra booked a day's tour of Moscow—at the depth of Stalin's purges.

She found the railway station heavily guarded and the porters wooden and mute. Her female Intourist guide, who spoke perfect English, brushed aside her suggested itinerary in favor of a rushed tour of factories, capped by Lenin's tomb, and accompanied by a recital of the party line. Afterward, the guide deposited the weary travelers at a fancy hotel where indifferent waitresses served up overpriced ham and eggs. Alexandra realized that the average Russian couldn't afford these prices and that the revolution by no means had abolished the antagonistic classes of servant and those who could afford to be served.

The entire population appeared devoid of spirit, dead. With only a couple hours left before their departure, the pair were kept busy filling out a multitude of forms. Alexandra hadn't expected to find a heaven on earth, but daily life in the Soviet Union impressed her as a poor comedy, with worse food and no manners. She was delighted to claim her seat on the next express bound for Vladivostok. She didn't mind the long ride across Siberia because at the end she would reach Asia. She thought of her darling maharaja, now gone, and took solace in the love she had felt for China. She should have known such affairs are difficult to renew.

On the next to last day of 1937, David-Neel was having a pleasant lunch on a terrace with a French doctor in Hankow, a southern port city on the Yangtse River. It had been nearly a year since she and her son had boarded the trans-Siberian express, bound east. Six months earlier the simmering tension between Japan and China had burst into the flames of war. Forces of the Rising Sun, already in control of Manchuria, advanced rapidly south of the Great Wall. Europeans caught deep in the country generally headed for the seacoast cities where their home countries maintained concessions with extraterritorial rights. Those remaining within the folds of the stricken giant, whose power seemed paralyzed, found themselves glancing toward the skies from which death might descend with lightning swiftness.

Both Alexandra and Yongden (because he carried a British passport) could have been evacuated on a special train reserved for Europeans. It would leave Hankow the next day, and no Chinese were allowed aboard. The train, bound for Hong Kong, would not even stop at Canton but would proceed directly to Kowloon within the Crown Colony. The consul had urged them not to miss this last opportunity. Each car would have the flag of its occupants painted on the roof, a talisman to ward off Japanese bombs.

Alexandra had written to Philip, retired in the south of France, to describe the horrors of warfare that, although making use of the latest technology, was actually a throwback to savagery. The Japanese were slaughtering young, male, Chinese civilians to make sure they would not become soldiers. They were bombing hospitals. Neither side would take prisoners. The Europeans behaved no better, running for their lives. The Chinese now despised their former masters. Servants, if you could obtain them, were opium smokers or drunkards.

Why didn't Alexandra and Yongden board the train and escape? She informed Philip that, were she to reach Hong Kong, she lacked sufficient funds to sail to Europe. But her husband's drafts could more easily reach her in British territory than in war-torn China. In reality, the traveler, nearing seventy, sensed adventure, and she had no interest in returning to tame France. Instead, she decided to journey from Hankow on a rickety steamer up the Yangtse to Chunking, then to travel farther west and perhaps reenter Tibet via her old route, as Yongden was urging. She gave her next address as in care of the French consul, Yunnan-fou.

While David-Neel chatted at lunch, she heard the scream of warplanes diving down on the airfield. Bombs exploded to rain debris and spread black smoke over the neighborhood. She wondered about the steamer anchored in the river with Yongden, their baggage, and many others aboard. It made a tempting target for the Japanese planes. The worried mother commandeered the doctor and his car and they sped to the dock, but they could see no boat. The woman's heart sank till she learned that the savvy captain had maneuvered his tub a few kilometers upstream. After the attack was over he dropped back down, and mother and son were happily reunited. Next day the steamer, packed with fearful humanity, mainly Asian, departed for the upper reaches of the Yangtse.

How had the usually prescient Alexandra managed to get herself booked on this floating sardine can as vulnerable to rocks in the riverbed as to stray aircraft? She and Yongden had arrived at Peking a year earlier in midwinter 1937, anxious to get on with their research. She was impressed by the assured behavior of the Chinese and still more by their capitol. She felt the charm of a rejuvenated Peking. Alexandra was a guest of Madame Rosa Hoa, a Polish friend from Paris, who with her Chinese engineer husband lived in a lovely villa surrounded by gardens. Here the Frenchwoman met young Chinese intellectuals who were playing a role in building a new China.

Yet each time Alexandra left the villa to be pulled through the city in a rickshaw, she felt like crying. She didn't mind the police spy who followed her everywhere, but the people themselves seemed menacing, more antiwhite than anti-Japanese. At the end of June that same year Alexandra gladly quit the capitol to head for Wutaishan, the sacred Mountain of Five Peaks, slightly to the southwest but just below the Great Wall. The trip by train and mule was arduous; however, sighting the summits brought an expansive, joyful feeling.

Wutaishan provided a rugged yet hospitable setting, eight thousand feet above the North China plain, for a stunning complex of hundreds of monasteries, temples, and shrines. Its history went back to first-century missionaries from India who had arrived bearing the treasure of Buddhist texts. It was the object of an annual pilgrimage for the devout from China, Mongolia, and Tibet, and Alexandra and Yongden joined in observances with thousands of their coreligionists. While staying at Pousa-ting, the largest monastery, she mused that it was probably the last time she would live in a gompa.

Wutaishan, decked with flowers and surrounded by additional green and purple mountains, nonetheless had an occult atmosphere, perhaps because of the many Tibetans come to pay homage to Manjusri, who is compassion in action and wields the sword of wisdom. While the pair searched the libraries for ancient texts, they also roamed the mountain trails, exploring for a secret passage, open only to the pure of heart, that would lead one to Lhasa in five days. They did not find it, although long talks with Tibetan lamas brought them there in spirit. From the lamas Alexandra obtained "precious pills." These supposedly contained, among many ingredients, flesh taken from the cadaver of a revered Tibetan hermit to make her immune to sickness and assure a long life. She would need them to survive the gathering storm.

In July, after a provocative skirmish at the Marco Polo Bridge, Japanese troops stormed into Peking. From the Nationalist capitol at Nanking, Chiang Kai-shek temporized, but an August attack on Shanghai forced him to defend the nation. Unannounced, World War II had begun in the Pacific. Shanghai fell to the Japanese in November and Nanking the next month. Chiang responded by shifting his government fifteen hundred miles inland to Chunking, Szechuan. Fortunately, instead of immediately pushing on to Hankow, the Japanese consolidated their position by taking control of the railroads. Military lines began to stabilize with the Rising Sun flying over the north and the coast, the Nationalists ruling the mountainous southwest, and between and behind the lines, circulating among the mainstream of the peasantry, Communist partisans spreading the message of Mao Tse-tung.

David-Neel hoped that Wutaishan, although within the Japanese sphere of influence, was sufficiently remote to be ignored by the soldiers. She was only sorry she had left her baggage, including a whole library of books, at Peking. This became a blessing in disguise. Forced to postpone scholarly work, the author turned to the novel, to elucidate a theme constant in her mature thought.

In September 1934, Alexandra had received from her French publisher comments on the manuscript of a novel she had sent to them. The editors found it charming and colorful and were certain it would make at least a *succès d'estime*. It had to be cut it down, and the next year Plon brought out *Mipam*, or *The Lama of Five Wisdoms*. But allegedly this was the work of Lama Yongden, who in a prefatory note complained about Europeans who wrote falsely about Tibet and its people. These attempts he supposedly found hilarious, and so he had put pen to paper to correct the myriad misconceptions of his native land.

This raises the question of Alexandra and Yongden's collaboration not only on *Mipam* but also on two more superb novels, all three of which have been translated into English but remain unjustly neglected. Until David-Neel's remaining papers and manuscripts are placed in scholarly hands, we shall never know precisely how the pair divided up their work. Certainly, Yongden supplied the story line (from folk sources) for *Mipam*, and he likely did a draft in Tibetan, or possibly even in English. The novel was at first ascribed solely to him—the author is listed as "Lama Yongden"—and it was referred to by Alexandra in private correspondence as Albert's book. But to judge by style, he wrote neither the French text nor the author's note. In fact, Yongden never learned much French.

Alexandra was irritated by the astonishing success of James Hilton's *Lost Horizon,* published in 1933. It instantly swept America, where President Roosevelt named his vacation retreat Shangri-La. She must have supposed that a novel authored by a genuine Tibetan lama was bound to trump a fabricated tale by a Briton who had never set foot in the Land of Snows. *Mipam* sold well enough despite the hard times of the Depression, and it was soon translated into a half-dozen languages. Although it has been described to us as the Tibetan *Dances with Wolves*, attempts to transform it into a film have not yet succeeded.

Mipam, an unrecognized incarnation, is a fascinating, carefully drawn character, but his conflicted psychology is unlikely for a Tibetan; rather, he is a David-Neel alter ego. His adventures are compelling, including communion with a snow leopard reminiscent of Alexandra's meetings with remarkable wild animals. Mipam's determination and fearlessness echo David-Neel's own nature, her unwillingness to accept defeat. Yongden lacked the psychological resources to create this dogged fighter who, despite his lowly origin, eventually ascends to a higher spiritual plane. Alexandra, like Mipam, had to do battle with her own egotism, but the result wasn't as clear-cut. Little by little she smothered her adopted son.

Encouraged by their initial success, the pair decided to cooperate on a second novel, *Magie d'amour et magie noir.* Its name rightly suggests a tale of black magic, lust, and murder. David-Neel, trapped in a psychic paradise threatened from all sides, turned to the genre now termed "horror-occult." *Mipam,* written with a wry sweetness, has an upbeat resolution: Dolma, the hero's love since childhood, by sacrificing herself helps to elevate him to the throne of the Lama of Five Wisdoms. They had known each other in previous lifetimes and would meet again in the next. In contrast *Magie noir* is a bitter, bleak story that presents a similar theme: romantic love between man and woman is an illusion and an obstacle to the enlightenment of both. While *Mipam* is suffused with the light of the steppes, *Magie noir* plumbs the depths of unreasoning desire.

The novel's hero Garab, a dashing brigand, falls in love with the beautiful, kind-hearted Detchema, a prize from his raid on a caravan of pilgrims bound for Lhasa. She reciprocates his passion, giving him her virginity and her heart. Garab, whose father was a demon, makes a pilgrimage to Mount Kailas in western Tibet to investigate his paternity. But a little piety undoes him, as Detchema is ravished by the very same demon. Garab's jealousy leads to murder, followed by his attempt to give up the world by becoming disciple to an anchorite. When Detchema seeks him out in his solitude, he murders once again to protect her. Each time the deed becomes harder to bear because he is now conscious of the karmic implications of his crime.

David-Neel makes clear in her foreword that Garab was an actual pastoral chieftain of some wealth, who related this autobiographical story to her over many bowls of chang. She didn't doubt his "tale of love and magic"—the English title of the book—especially because she was familiar with its main locale, the Tibetan province of Gyarong, in the southwest on the border of Szechuan. David-Neel held back from relating the story because it included certain occult practices attributed to black Bon magicians. However, at Wutaishan she heard from two Tibetan lamas of the region that they, too, believed that black Bons held persons captive and confined in order to drink the juices of their putrifying bodies—an elixir to produce extremely long life. Securing this confirmation of strange rites of the Left Hand, David-Neel, with Yongden's aid, wrote a gloomy yet brilliant novel noir, in which she even described techniques she herself employed to ward off falling victim to a more subtle vampirism—that of love.

Magie noir reflects both the author's personal tension concerning desire and the tense circumstances under which it was written. The monks of the Mountain of Five Peaks conjured demons to keep their enemies at bay. They engaged in the wildest rumor mongering, such as that an armed, Japanese-trained column of orangutans was bearing down on the sacred mountain. Alexandra, since she never knew when she might have to dash for safety, not only composed on the run, but also she and Yongden carried their sole copy of the manuscript on the day hikes they took to keep fit.

Conditions soon grew worse. Their Chinese paper money depreciated to nothing, and cut off from Peking, they had no way to cash a check or draft. The hardy travelers were reduced to eating boiled rice and roots they dug up, seasoned with a little vinegar. Alexandra typically fattened on the excitement of wartime. She slept well and woke up hungry and cheerful. Still, as the Japanese approached, she decided to head for Taiyuan to the south. She supposed Madame Rosa Hoa had fled there, and she hoped to borrow some hard money. Alexandra and her son finally obtained mules and servants and set out. Disclaiming any animosity toward the Japanese, she took the precaution to drape herself in a French flag.

Predictably, the route was infested by black-market operators, bandits, and assassins. The laws, usually ignored, were apt to be enforced with a sudden severity. The pair watched as a handsome young soldier was shot by a firing squad because he married without his captain's consent. The Chinese proved more of a hindrance than did the invaders. One petty official detained Yongden, accusing him of carrying a forged British passport; he must be an imposter because he didn't have fair hair and eyes. The pest summoned his cronies to substantiate his brilliant detective work. He made Yongden write his name and the word *London* in the Roman alphabet. Astonished by the lama's facility, the officials let them pass.

Alexandra's muleteers deserted. There were no trains, no trucks, but the pair obtained space in a cart that bumped along. Not far from their destination, she was violently hurled from the cart to the ground, limbs askew like a rag doll's. A box of books that struck her on the head knocked her into a semicoma. Alexandra had to be lifted back into the cart and endure its jolts. Yongden covered her with a piece of greasy oilcloth of the sort used over corpses being returned from the front. But her yogic training permitted her to project herself temporarily outside her body. As the vehicle trundled in and out of ruts, she recalled an ancient formula of the Stoics: "Pain, you are but a word."

After nine days on the road, hurt, exhausted, and filthy, Alexandra arrived at Taiyuan to find it under attack by the Japanese. Her European friend was gone, and her entire fortune consisted of four Chinese dollars. However, the French consul loaned her money, and in time Philip would cable her a considerable sum. As usual, the seventy-year-old spurned any thought of a hospital or medical treatment. She couldn't be so cavalier about the daily air raids, which had to be sat out in cellars. Even this she turned to advantage, toting the manuscript of *Magie noir* with her in a suitcase. It is precisely because the book was written under fire that it is relevant, in the way of a work of art, to today's bonecrushing occupation of Tibet by the Red Army.

At Taiyuan, for the first time Alexandra was able to observe detachments of blue-clad Communist troops. Their military discipline and willingness to fight the Japanese marked a sharp contrast with the Nationalists. With her typical political savvy, the Frenchwoman predicted a civil war once the Japanese were beaten, an outcome she didn't doubt. For the moment, Alexandra once again found herself obliged to missionaries, Baptists this time, who received and conveyed money to her. David-Neel and Yongden boarded a train at Taiyuan bound for the city of Hankow, still in Nationalist hands. The trip lasted three days and nights, and the two were crammed in among refugee families under squalid conditions. The train was bombed and some died. Alexandra observed the futility of flight, as villagers from the south fled north and vice versa, the main thing being to run.

By the time of the pair's arrival in Hankow in December, they had been accidentally spat on by peasants, urinated on by infants, and stepped on by soldiers in their boots. Due to the milling crowds and changes of train, they had lost additional Tibetan books, manuscripts and notes. In this strategic but threatened port city on the Yangtse, Alexandra's choices were clear: go east by the special train for Europeans to Hong Kong and then by ship to France, or west into the unknown. She felt disposed to laugh at her own predicament, until she feared that Yongden and her baggage had gone down on the ferry moored in the river. Then she realized that she too had become a fugitive.

In January 1938 the travelers' voyage up the Yangstse from Hankow to Chunking went smoothly enough at the pace of earlier times. At each port passed on the way thousands of people were jammed onto the dock, pushing and jostling one another but passive en masse. They stared mutely as the ferry steamed by without stopping. Although the winds blew bitterly, Alexandra was able to marvel at the majestic beauty of the Yangtse gorges. She found that formerly picturesque Chunking, the temporary Nationalist capitol, which was crammed with officials, troops, and refugees, had turned filthy and ill-tempered. An open dislike of Europeans was manifested by children screaming the ubiquitous "Foreign devil!" and pelting the pair with stones.

This war without a face, the seemingly random violence of air raids on the civilian population, began to fray Alexandra's nerves. The river was too low to proceed farther up by boat, an airplane to Chengtu was too expensive, and a chair and bearers couldn't be found at any price. Soldiers, deserting from the inept Nationalist army, were pillaging the countryside, no longer acting in the chivalrous fashion of the brigands of old. Nonetheless, the resourceful Frenchwoman was writing to her husband from Chengtu by early March. She and Yongden were comfortably installed in a small, detached pavilion near the French medical mission, where they had stayed a decade and a half earlier. They watched dubiously while the doctors and nurses painted huge tricolors on the roofs of the buildings. David-Neel had learned that flags made fine targets for the Japanese, who were determined to drive all Europeans from Asia.

Good tidings awaited the weary, impecunious travelers: dear Mouchy had sent them ten thousand francs. During most of the war, while armies marched and countermarched, the Chinese national post office continued to function—after a fashion. *Magie noir* arrived safely in Paris in eight months time. Meanwhile David-Neel had begun work on a more immediate account, *Sous des nuees d'orage,* or *Under the Storm Clouds.* She wrote about events in China at the time they were happening. In Paris her editors were convinced the book would sell. Ironically, had it appeared earlier, the French might have found in *Storm Clouds* a warning of their own impending doom. At any rate, the author needed a more peaceful place to write about the hostilities. Chengtu, crammed with refugees, attracted Japanese bombers.

Alexandra fled toward Tibet, hoping once more to take up residence in a monastery. In mid-June, once the snows had melted, the travelers rounded up porters and two chairs to carry them westward over a pass 13,500 feet high. Ten days later they arrived at the middle-sized, frontier town of Tachienlu. They were buffeted by spring storms but elated to be in the Tibetan-speaking (if Chinese-ruled) world. Alexandra didn't know the town, but she was familiar with the mixed, seminomadic population of the borderlands. At eight-thousand feet, the air crisp, Tachienlu occupied an attractive cuplike valley. Alexandra took comfort in realizing that just ten miles on the other side of the western hills Tibetans were grazing their sheep and goats where the forests allowed.

But Tachienlu was busy with refugees, and Alexandra couldn't find accommodations. The monasteries held more troops than monks. While families camped in the steets, at the mercy of the weather, English missionaries befriended the orientalist and offered her shelter. By midsummer she escaped to a hermitage on the plain of Pomo San, a few miles out of town. The pair liked to stroll about the neighborhood, David-Neel in baggy suit and cloak, a battered man's hat atop her head, stout stick in hand, Yongden trailing after. She would jot down notes and he would snap photos to send to Philip or her publishers. Not surprisingly, they aroused the suspicion of the Nationalist authorities. The Chinese officers forbade her from gazing at the nearby mountain passes through binoculars. They even ordered the foreign devil not to stare out her window at passing columns of troops.

Alexandra made the best of a deteriorating situation. She purchased fur robes in anticipation of the harsh winter, but by November she and Yongden were practically freezing in the unheated hermitage. Bothered by arthritis, she was too rusty to attempt tumo breathing. Like the other foreigners, she felt hemmed in by events, not knowing where to turn. Emblematic of the convulsions shaking Asia was an attack in the street on the French Catholic bishop by a screaming mob, which nearly killed him. Meanwhile Japanese bombers penetrated deeper into the west, hitting Chengtu three times a week and, to the south, Yunnan-fou, on David-Neel's possible escape route to Burma. She informed Philip that the Japanese were proud of their massacre at the elementary school for boys. Chamberlain, acting a toady to Hitler, would not save Europe. Alexandra's joints might creak but her brain worked better than ever.

In late November, after Alexandra had heard from Philip about the Allied capitulation to the Nazis at Munich, she returned to the mission in Tachienlu. Snow fell for fifty hours straight, and shortly thereafter the English missionaries ordered Madame David-Neel

and son, bag and baggage, into the street. Jeanne Denys, who corresponded with the missionaries, claimed that Alexandra had tried to
sublet her dwelling to a tenant, in order to live more cheaply elsewhere and pocket the difference. Space was desperately short, but
Alexandra was able to turn to an order of French Catholic nuns who
rented her an old granary. The wooden shed had several rooms and
its own courtyard. After a good cleaning and airing, she was able to
create a cozy apartment for her and Yongden.

David-Neel settled in to write about what she had recently seen
of China. By midsummer 1939, she had completed *Storm Clouds,* and
in September Violet Sydney arrived to translate the manuscript. This
she accomplished between air raid alerts, when much of the town
gathered in a nearby cemetery. Chinese and Tibetans, Buddhists and
Bons assembled in an atmosphere of camaraderie and indifference to
danger. In November, David-Neel was able to send off her French
manuscript by diplomatic pouch from Chengtu to Paris. David-Neel's
carping about the translation made Sidney anxious to escape, but she
was stuck, with no means of crossing the war-torn country. How the
woman in her midsixties made her way out of China in May 1940
is unclear. Certainly, no English version of *Storm Clouds* has ever
appeared.

The work is an example of personal journalism, of reporting
events as they occurred to the writer. Because of her own undoubted
importance she was able to endow the often trivial with significance.
Still, this account of David-Neel's travails as once again she crossed
China from east to west, although it may evoke admiration, lacks the
truly heroic. No longer able to order her environment, she was more
at the mercy than in command of her servants. The former *dakini*
had been reduced to a refugee. An everywoman, Alexandra like
countless others could flee only before frightening, impersonal
forces. Her saving grace was that she saw far more clearly than the
leaders of her day. The madness of men had created this evil, and
they were going to die by the millions for it.

By the time *Storm Clouds* appeared in the spring of 1940, France
was on the edge of a devastating defeat. Poland had fallen to Hitler's
blitzkrieg and Europe was in disarray. China seemed too distant to
worry over. By June the Germans had marched into Paris, and this
book written and dispatched with such a sense of urgency disap-

peared into history. Alexandra wrote to Philip, who had retired to Gard in the south, that she was occupying herself and Yongden with work on an erudite project, a grammar of spoken Tibetan. Desperately in need of official aid, she was hopeful that the grammar, which she regarded as drudgery, would bring her funds from the French Foreign Ministry.

Alexandra preferred to devote herself to a book more in her free-wheeling style, A *l'ouest barbare de la vaste Chine*. We like to translate the title as *In China's Wild West*. The work, which would meet with some popularity after the war, is a study of the borderlands and the native tribes that inhabited them. Alexandra lacked anthropological training, but she had a feel for writing about the anarchic nomads of the Sino-Tibetan marches and the status of women among them. She had hopeful things to say about the relations between the Chinese and Tibetans. In this region the two peoples had mingled and inter-married for centuries and were mutually tolerant if not entirely respectful. She failed to foresee, however, the fierce fighting between the Chinese occupying army and Tibetan Khampa partisans that would mark the 1950s.

During the early 1940s Alexandra hung on at Tachienlu, within reach of the French consul at Chengtu, the Catholic missionaries, and above all the post office, her link to Philip Neel. The war always threatened to bring destruction closer, but correspondence with France remained possible, if tardy. She fretted about Philip's safety under the German occupation and sent him advice about keeping up his health and spirits. The elderly engineer was failing, and he informed her of his will, adhering strictly to their marriage contract. He expressed his gratitude toward Yongden for being such a help to his wife. On February 14, 1941, Alexandra received a tattered, grimy envelope containing a telegram. Weeks before she sensed that Mouchy had died. Once she saw the telegram came from his niece Simone, who had nursed him, her fears were realized.

From youth, Alexandra had hardened herself against any show of emotion. She slept on a board, read the Stoics, then discovered the subtle philosophy of Gautama Buddha. She had consorted with magicians and brigands, not hesitating to make an experiment of love. Now she stared unbelieving at the slip of paper, reading it over as though it was in a foreign language. Tears welled up and spilled over. Yongden, nearby, was amazed to watch his mother weep unashamedly.

Alexandra was not aware that just the month before Professor d'Arsonval, her academic sponsor, had also died. She probably didn't know that her friend the Panchen Lama had passed into another incarnation. The Gomchen of Lachen, who would live on for a few more years, was out of reach. The men whom Alexandra cared for, the braces of her world, were gone.

Chapter 23
The Wife of the Chinese

From 1938 through mid-1944, during a prolonged but vicious stalemate in the war, Alexandra and Yongden were paying guests of the French Catholic hospital at Tachienlu. They suffered more from the general uncertainty than from serious privation. King rumor ruled, and David-Neel admitted she had no sure means of learning what was happening elsewhere in China, let alone Europe. She kept in touch with the consul at Chengtu, and she read, wrote, and collected information for her books. But she couldn't easily shake off the effect of Philip's death.

Her familiar enemy, neurasthenia, stalked her. She quit eating, vomited, lost weight. She felt violent pains in her lower back. A Chinese medical doctor diagnosed the maladay as nervous exhaustion. The skeptical one had her own remedy for the problem: she got up, first beat a servant, and then Yongden. Afterward she felt fine.

Such acting-out couldn't assuage the inner hurt. Expressing love or feeling grief were opposed to Alexandra's view of herself, and so she tried to suppress these unseemly emotions. The result was rancor against those closest to her. She found fault with Yongden, who to escape her ill humor spent much of his time in little tea shops, chatting with the owners and customers. Formerly an abstainer, he now turned to drink. Although everyone else found him agreeable, his mother threatened to disown her middle-aged son. The woman of seventy-five had a growing fear of old age and helplessness. She began a refrain that she would often repeat: I should have died in my tent in the Tibetan solitudes.

Instead, Alexandra soon would have to respond to new challenges. In 1944, once the snows had melted, Japan launched a final desperate drive to divide China and secure an overland route to southeast Asia. The Nationalist armies melted before the onslaught, profiteering increased, and the police turned more brutal. Inflation soared, ruining the horde of teachers and students who had migrated to the west carrying their universities on their backs. Many joined the Red Army, under the direction of Chairman Mao, nipping at the heels of the advancing Japanese. David-Neel, although she is alleged to have read the poems of this political genius based somewhat to the north, gave no clue of it in her published writings of this period.

Japan's kamikaze offensive was bound to fail, if only because of the increasing presence of American forces in the Chinese southwest. "Vinegar Joe" Stilwell commanded—along with his arch-rival Chennault and his famous Flying Tigers—while thirty-five thousand GIs built and ran the world's busiest airport near Kunming, Yunnan. From India over the hump of the Himalayas came more men, material, air support. In a decisive retreat that spring, Alexandra abandoned her converted granary at Tachienlu and returned to Chengtu.

In the capitol of Szechuan, David-Neel encountered John Blofeld, then a captain in the British army attached to the British Embassy at Chunking. At thirty-two, Blofeld was an admirer of the Frenchwoman's writing who hoped to follow in her footsteps. Due to our own admiration for his work, especially the autobiographical *The Wheel of Life*, we made every effort to contact him. Our query finally reached him in Bangkok, bedridden, in pain, but gracious. Blofeld has written us:

> During the early 1940s, I happened to run across [David-Neel] at a very comfortable hotel at Chengtu, west China. Jokingly, I asked why she chose this luxurious abode in preference to the exhilarating hardships of a lonely mountain cave. In reply she gave me a highly detailed description of a recent journey into Tibet, during which she had been robbed of her possessions and thus forced to return immediately to a city where she could obtain credit and hope to receive funds from France. Only later did I discover that the whole long story, doing much credit to her self-image, was pure fiction!

Why would Alexandra deceive a young man whom she knew to be a dedicated Buddhist? Unlike Blofeld, who forty years later was still shocked by "Madame's capacity for detailed deception," we don't suppose it was a matter of self-image. The key question is how did Alexandra afford an expensive hotel in the midst of World War II when she could not tap either her own or her late husband's funds? Her French biographers relate that through their consul at Chengtu the French Foreign Ministry paid Alexandra a stipend of thirty thousand francs per annum (about six hundred dollars). According to Jacques Brosse, the consul asked nothing of Alexandra and Yongden except to be of service to them. Jean Chalon, in another unlikely explanation, insists that the money was support for writing their Tibetan grammar, a text that after the war no publisher or government agency showed the slightest interest and that was finally privately printed after David-Neel's death.

Remember, this was the Vichy (or profascist) government that was allegedly making these funds available for a recondite project on the Sino-Tibetan border, while in France the occupying German troops and the Resistance slaughtered one another, and the Allies bombed military and industrial targets. To us this appears a taller tale than Alexandra's feigned journey into Tibet. We suggest her story may have been told to Blofeld, a well-connected British officer, as a deliberate cover-up by a woman embarrassed to have been in the pay of Vichy, and who with her usual political acumen realized it might soon prove a real liability. We can't blame her for accepting the money, without which she would have fallen on hard times. But the question remains—did Alexandra supply the French consul at Chengtu with information in return? Certainly, the Chinese Nationalist authorities supposed that she had. We are left on the edge of what may be a thrilling spy story, but until the Digne archives are fully opened to investigators, a biographer can only peer over the precipice.

Alexandra and Yongden spent a little over a year in what Blofeld has described as ". . . a walled gray-bricked city affectionately styled Little Peking. Its residential lanes bordered by low grey walls pierced with bronze-studded lacquered gates . . . and the charming court-yards lying behind produced a sometimes startling resemblance to the Empress of Cities." Here David-Neel completed her grammar and also *China's Wild West*, spending odd hours listening to Hitler's final insane broadcasts relayed via Radio Saigon in Japanese-controlled Indochina. Here she learned of the end of hostilities in May 1945. In late July, courtesy of the new Gaullist government of France, she and Yongden were flown to Kunming. After spending two months there, she flew over the Hump to Calcutta, again at government expense.

Alexandra spent the next nine months based at the Grand Hotel. Her approaching return to France loomed like a Himalayan peak on the horizon. Later she told intimates that she undertook it solely to settle Philip's estate, and that she had been unable to return to Asia because of her arthritis. In any event, she could no longer live the life about which she wrote. Without Neel as an intermediary, she needed to be closer to publishers, the newspapers, the adulation of admirers. The south of France was the right distance from Paris.

While waiting for conditions in France to improve, Alexandra calmly watched through her hotel window as, on the eve of Indian Independence, Moslem and Hindu mobs alternately burned, pillaged, and murdered one another. Troops with tanks and machine guns were sent in to end the carnage. She didn't suppose the Europeans were any more moral. She was incensed by their newly adopted freedom of manner and dress. She disdained women in uniform who showed their legs. The brief shorts worn by handsome young officers bothered her. These are the complaints of a woman born in the middle of the nineteenth century, the heyday of hypocrisy. It is the sad song of a woman who has lost her husband and her prince, the men who knew her youth and beauty and whose existence, never mind at what distance, made her feel attractive.

Alexandra probably didn't hear of the death of her former nemesis Sir Charles Bell in late 1945 in British Columbia. Knighted in 1922 on his return from a year in Lhasa as special envoy from Lord Curzon's Foreign Office, Bell had become disillusioned with British policy in Central Asia in the 1930s. He saw that in preparation for eventually withdrawing from India, Britain was trying to accommodate China. Bell, however, remained a staunch advocate of an independent Tibet. So much so that when he traveled through Tibet, China, and Mongolia in 1933–1935, he was forbidden by the Foreign Office from giving advice to the Panchen Lama, then in exile in China, or any other Tibetan or Mongolian officials. Bell's last act was to write a monograph—or epitaph, since it was published after his death— advocating that Tibet, Ladakh, Sikkim, and Bhutan be encouraged to form one independent Buddhist nation.

In India, Alexandra had not entirely lost her way with military men, especially those who were young and dashing. In April 1946 another British captain, Ian Davie (Intelligence, HQ Burma Command) approached her for help. He was part of an RAF expediton that hoped to make contact with two British wireless (radio) operators employed by the Tibetan government, one of whom had become gravely ill. The expedition members were staying at the Grand Hotel, and Davie, who knew Alexandra's work, was excited to find her name on the register, the sole woman at the requisitioned hotel. He immediately applied to her for advice on Tibet, and she invited him to tea. Davie has written us as follows:

> She said she had considered my request, and that the most effective help she could give would be to write a letter of introduction to any Tibetan officials or lamas we might meet on our way. This she had already written in Tibetan script, and it simply asked the recipient to extend to the bearer the full welcome of Tibetan hospitality. It proved, indeed, to be invaluable since it had instantaneous effect when we presented it to abbots and *gyapons* (local government representatives) on our journey.

The mission was successful, and the assistance that Alexandra provided to its members is typical of her free-and-easy relations with men of action and authority. Be it Captain Davie, Colonel Bailey, or General Pereira, or on a different level the Gomchen of Lachen or the Maharaja of Sikkim, Alexandra felt a comradeship with these gentlemen, and from them she was ready to learn and to them she freely gave. That the men with whom she was most intimate in her long life—her father, husband, and adopted son—were vacillating types disappointed Alexandra but permitted her own heroics to flourish. The bizarre suggestion made by biographer Jean Chalon, and parroted by Ruth Middleton, that Alexandra hated men simply reflects the offical hokum swallowed by these writers.

Alexandra showed at her finest in the mountains. On a trip to Darjeeling, she rose before dawn to stand in the brisk air, watching the sun burst into flower over five-crowned Kanchinjunga. She recalled how some thirty-five years ago this had been her first enticing view of the Sacred Realm, forbidden to her race, her sex. Yet she had dared to enter, to travel and learn. Now, though she must return to Europe, no one could take from her the soul of a Tibetan.

David-Neel's actual departure from the Orient occurred at the Calcutta airport on the rainy morning of June 30, 1946. She ruefully boarded an airplane. As it took off with a roar and glided into the clouds, she felt numb to the core. She wondered if she were already dead, a shadow wandering in the bardo. But no, she had merely said goodbye to India, where once she had been young. Were her adventures at an end?

The return of Alexandra and Yongden to Paris didn't go unnoticed in the press. However, the journalists still referred to her in terms of "the first white woman to enter Lhasa," or "the great traveler and explorer," episodes of her life that were past. Her brief stay in the capital, still suffering from wartime shortages, was dominated by nostalgia, as she looked up old friends, many of whom were no longer living. Yongden, who understood French better than he spoke it, liked strolling the boulevards and going to the cinema. He was not so pleased as his mother to return to Digne.

They found Samten Dzong in good repair except for the furniture, damaged by the police who had occupied the villa during the war. Alexandra, turning in her pilgrim's staff for a sturdy cane, could still hobble about the countryside. Nearing eighty, her stride had slowed but her mind was busy with projects. *China's Wild West*, appearing in 1947, looked both forward and backward. The author, noted Lowell Thomas Jr., "was a keen observer [who] learned a great deal about China's far west and the intrigues of the border country."

Although Alexandra was pleased to have explored Central Asia before its colorful, mysterious way of life was ground under the rails and wheels of progress, she warned the West to stop thinking of Asians as passive. The Chinese especially, even the peasants and laborers, were an energetic and able people. Asia was going to be ruled by Asians, she stated flatly, a good portion of it from Peking. She advised Europe and America to initiate diplomatic, cultural, and commercial relations with whatever regime emerged from the postwar turmoil. She had little doubt it would be led by Mao. This came at a time when the United States still backed Chiang Kai-shek with money and munitions, and the Soviet Union, taking advantage of the civil war, had seized the former Japanese railroad concessions in Manchuria.

The late 1940s and early 1950s proved a fine productive time for David-Neel. However, her next two books were not financially successful. *Nepal: The Heart of the Himalayas* appeared in 1949 and *India Yesterday, Today and Tomorrow* in 1951. The titles are translated into English but the books were not. They were useful in educating some Europeans to a deeper sense of the Indian reality during the time the Subcontinent was achieving independence and splitting into what would become three major nations. The author had significant ties to India; still, she failed to make it hers as she had with Tibet. Most intriguing about these works are the personal anecdotes, in particular David-Neel's detailed descriptions of *pancha tattva,* or tantric sex rites, which we have discussed earlier. Although the events described took place in the period 1912 to 1914, she never would have published her account of them during the lifetime of Philip Neel.

Both *Nepal* and *India* contain a variety of recollections from an amazing storehouse of experience. But the French in the lean postwar years were preoccupied with keeping body and soul together. Conditions were better in Digne, where in the 1950s other houses began to encroach on the neighborhood of Samten Dzong. David-Neel, her legs growing worse, purchased a car, a Citroën 4CV. The good burghers, watching Yongden chauffeur her around in this mechanized tin can, dubbed her "the wife of the Chinese." That he was her son and Sikkimese made no difference to them.

On the town's main square, nowadays named Place General de Gaulle, sits the Librairie Sicard, which sells books and stationery. The proprietor, Madame Sicard, well remembers the frequent occasions when Yongden and his mother would putter up in the Citroën. Yongden, squat and nearsighted, would come in with the order, and the clerks would hurry to fill it. If they were too slow for the imperious one waiting in the car, she would loudly honk the horn and everyone would scurry faster. Later, when she grew too arthritic to leave the house, David-Neel would order by telephone the writing materials dearer to her than food.

Across the square from Sicard stands Lorion Photo. Here Alexandra had developed, and in some cases rephotographed, her old glass plate negatives for illustrations for *Nepal, India,* and other works. The proprietor recalls the shot of her and Yongden against the backdrop of the Potala and is certain it is genuine. What bitter-sweet memories these photos must have evoked in this voyager becalmed! The traveler, stranded, reached out for companionship.

She sought out Judith Jordan, teacher of English, in order to speak the language that had stood her in such good stead in Asia. She heard of a woman, Maria Borrely, who for years had been studying Sanskrit texts on her own. Alexandra asked her to come visit, and Borrely's son Pierre drove his mother. "Alexandra," he told us, "wanted to get to know the other bird in the countryside." At Samten Dzong, while the women talked, he was left with Yongden. It was very awkward, "because he spoke only English."

A few years later, in 1954, Pierre was a student at the university of Marseilles. His professor of philosophy, Gaston Berger, suggested he ask David-Neel for an article to be printed in the college review. She recalled the handsome, curly-haired young man and agreed to see him. She received him in the garden at Samten Dzong dressed "in a light green two-piece Italian summer dress topped by a hat with a big bird feather." She greeted the nervous student with a remark that translates as, "Hello, good sir, I am about to end a miserable life."

When Alexandra demanded what he wanted, Pierre hesitatingly began, "I am a student of philosophy."

"Philosophy, what do you want with that, sir? Presumption! Vanity! Don't you know this Western culture is a vacuity? It is . . . *insipide! insipide!*"

Pausing for breath, Alexandra returned to the attack, "Bergson! This Bergson was a cretin, Immanuel Kant mentally ill, nuts. They have written books and books up to here [she gestured with her hand] to fill them with nothing. But, thousands of years ago the [Sanskrit] poet Valmiki said it all and much better."

The intrepid student pressed on, requesting an article for the *Revue d'etudes philosophiques de Marseilles.* The orientalist broke into a loud laugh. Poor Pierre reported to Professor Berger that Alexandra was too tired to write anything for the review. She was eighty-six and although her productive capacities had dimmed, they were far from extinguished. Monsieur Borrely, who kindly related the above anecdote complete with gesture and intonation, has retired from his post as professor of philosophy.

During the 1950s David-Neel edited and translated into French previously unknown (to the West) Sanskrit and Tibetan texts. These were published quietly and had a limited circulation. She was able to cull them from her magnificent personal library, which included over four hundred rare Tibetan books and manuscripts. Considering the holocaust that has taken place in Tibet and the wanton destruction of Buddhist artifacts, this collection of an adventurous lifetime has become all the more valuable. Certain of the books were priceless in a more material sense, including a Tibetan-Mongol dictionary written in gold dust.

In 1954 Alexandra and Yongden published another folk novel, the title of which in a recent American edition (1982) has been rendered as *The Power of Nothingness*. Originally the brief tale of suspense appeared under Yongden's name alone, and of the three fictional collaborations of mother and son, it is the most recognizably novelistic— a thriller. The translator, Janwillem van de Wetering, well known for his own "Zen" mysteries, generally credits Yongden with creating plot, characters, and outline. This story, however, was based on the actual murder of the aged guru of Kazi Dawasandup, who had related it to David-Neel in Sikkim. Certainly the main character, a loyal but not especially brave monk named Munpa, has feelings close to Yongden's own.

Munpa finds himself tracking the murderer of his guru, and the tale ranges over the Sino-Tibetan borderlands so familiar to its authors, even to the Gobi Desert. In the manner of Eastern storytelling, while the plot opens outward it simultaneously spirals down toward the core of reality, at once empty and dazzling. Munpa doesn't exactly fall into a landscape, against which David-Neel was warned in her youth, but in solitary meditation he is obliged to paint a colorful epic upon a blank wall with the brush of his thoughts. Unwilling to believe the imaginary mural has a reality equal to any other aspect of his life, the monk becomes frightened by his own mind and runs away. Later he accepts the proposition that the so-called real world is nothing more than a series of pictures painted on an imaginary wall. This cleverly constructed piece is amiably, yet deeply, Buddhist.

Alexandra's search for an intellectual companion in the south of France was finally answered when in 1953 she heard of Dr. Marcel Maille. When we met him in a village near Toulon, a two-hour drive from Digne, the doctor was in his seventies, retired; because of his poor eyesight, he navigated the streets from memory. But in 1953 this dapper gentleman was in his handsome prime. His upright slimness and the way he carried himself when he came to call on her about her health reminded Alexandra of Philip Neel. That she sent for him is not surprising since he was known as a Tibetanist, and there were precious few of these at hand.

"She was enormously fat with swollen, painful knees and legs," Dr. Maille told us. "She could hardly walk."

Alexandra soon dropped the subject of her health. She began to quiz the doctor on his knowledge of Buddhism, in particular the obscure tantric rites. He was not abashed because he was well read in the texts and more importantly, after the war, had lived with the monks in Indochina and Burma. Alexandra quickly realized that here was a man whose passion for Buddhist philosophy equaled her own.

The aging orientalist returned the visit, ostensibly to consult about her legs. Yongden stayed in the car, which was parked the wrong way on a one-way street. "Her legs were terrible," recalled Dr. Maille, "with varicose veins and bleeding ulcers, which she wrapped up in cloth. She would let me do nothing for her."

It was Tibet Alexandra wished to talk about. When she learned the doctor was planning a retreat in the mountains she insisted that they practice the ritual of *chöd*. The term means "to cut up," and the world-famous author understood she still needed to cut her ego down to size.

"Take me with you!" she demanded.

Thinking of the terrain, the doctor protested, "But I can't carry you on my back, Madame!"

Alexandra gave in and recommended the ideal place in the Alpes Maritimes for the retreat; it was rocky and isolated, a little dangerous to reach but with ancient Celtic ruins. As she spoke she recalled an earlier time, on her journey to Lhasa, when she had paused at a natural clearing among tall trees, overcome by the desire to perform the mystic dance of abnegation. Despite the danger of detection, Alexandra sent her son to fetch water, while she drummed and rattled and wove the arcane figures, calling on the demons to come to feast.

Over time the two Tibetanists grew closer. Dr. Maille visited as often as he could, and they even translated texts together. He was very impressed by Alexandra's library and by her excellent knowledge of Tibetan. "I would be searching for the meaning of an obscure term," he recalled, "but before I found it in the dictionary, she told me. She was always correct." She told him stories—"thrilling!"—not found in any of her books. At five o'clock a servant cleared everything away and they concluded with tea in the English style.

When Alexandra suggested that she wished to move to Dr. Maille's locale, that she would give up Samten Dzong if he could find her a house on one level, he was taken aback. "You will be my doctor," she insisted.

"What doctor? You refuse to take drugs. You don't give a damn for medicine."

In reply she looked taken aback. "At least we could talk more often about things Tibetan."

If the doctor was dubious, it was no doubt due to the orientalist's habits. She hardly slept because of pain, and she lived in a mess of newspapers, books, manuscripts. He would find her in her chair surrounded by mounds of papers, immersed in the latest projects. Then, too, she had, as she admitted, a difficult character.

"She was a woman of authority who would not brook contradiction," recalled Dr. Maille. "She would defend her ideas, even if false, tooth and nail."

"She was *very friendly* to me and I liked her a lot, but there were times when I wanted to say, 'Enough!' I could have slapped her. Because she was so irritating, preemptory in her judgments. She never listened to your arguments."

Alexandra's scheme to move fell through and instead she took on a Russian housekeeper. Dr. Maille was relieved, but their friendship, which continued into the 1960s, grew ever more intimate. "She didn't tell me in a formal way," Dr. Maille told us, "but she explained to me that she had practiced sexual rites . . . sexual rites of left-handed tantricism. She never wrote of it . . . She mentioned it to me because as her doctor I was not shocked. But I am persuaded she spoke of it with *actual knowledge*."

"I have translated a number of texts concerned with tantric sex," continued the doctor. "They must be read from two points of view: one actual, the other symbolic. There are certain medical observations in them. She [Alexandra] spoke of this as an adept who had actually done these practices."

Their conversation on the subject began when Dr. Maille remarked to her that, in his university days, he had been given a hoary Tibetan text to translate for its tantric vocabulary. "My professor was an old prude, his interests were strictly academic."

Alexandra explained that the texts were not reliable because the tantric tradition was essentially secret and oral. "I assure you," she said emphatically, "there is much to be gained by *doing* it."

Dr. Maille added that she was ninety at the time of this conversation and that her eyes glowed with delight at the memory of the midnight rites. We inquired where he supposed these might have taken place. He could not be sure, but he thought either in Sikkim or Nepal.

Chapter 24

The Sage
of Digne

In early October 1955, a Saturday, Yongden, known as Albert, his name as a European gentleman, drove the car to get groceries. After he returned, Alexandra and he ate veal cutlets for dinner. They listened to the radio and he went to bed. It had been a day like any other at Samten Dzong. But during the night Albert became very ill. Alexandra, awakened, tried to bring his high fever down. First thing in the morning she sent for Dr. Maille. By the time he arrived Albert—or Yongden—was dead. He was fifty-six, the cause of death, uremia.

"He ended up an alcoholic," according to Dr. Maille. "Completely depressed because he was thoroughly uprooted." Interviews with several *citoyens* of Digne who knew Yongden elicited a similar response. In the end, the cautious Philip Neel was correct about the unwisdom of transplanting the young Asian man from his native soil.

Part of the problem was that David-Neel took a "colonial" attitude toward her adopted son, treating him with the condescension the British and French had showed toward their subject peoples. Yongden complained that his mother sometimes treated him more like a servant than a son. She admitted she tended always to regard him as the teenager she took into her service in Sikkim. When Yongden was nearing forty, Alexandra told Philip that he was a child in most ways. She was mainly concerned that he do her bidding and be at her beck and call. Thus she kept him dependent, her "boy."

The boy had grown into a thickset man wearing thick glasses and traveling in somber European clothing that scarcely flattered him. At Digne he was popular, going about his errands in a beret and striped shirt and blue pants. When a café owner offered him a glass of beer, or a patron a cigarette, he didn't refuse. He learned to speak a little café French. Tongues wagged that he was interested in women but afraid of his demanding "wife." Certainly, Yongden wished to live in or visit Paris for the amusements it offered. Alexandra preferred her remembrances of times past.

Yongden made the best of things. He rose early and accompanied his mother on her increasingly painful walks. When these became impossible, he grew roses, worked on their books together, or meditated, performing a thousand helpful tasks. We learn from General George Pereira—not from David-Neel—who kept this quiet—that "she had adopted as her son a young lama of the Red Hat sect who was a minor 'living Buddha' from South Tibet." Yongden a *tulku*, like Sidkeong *tulku*, didn't live long enough to express his innate talents. It may be he is already doing so in his next incarnation.

Alexandra never recovered from the blow of losing her companion of the last forty years. Without him at eighty-six, she would not write another significant book on the East. Yongden had been her last living tie to Tibet. She had the lama's body cremated and placed the ashes in an urn at the foot of a Buddha in the shrine room. She felt that something of his tranquil spirit remained at Samten Dzong. Feelings aside, the orientalist had lost her legal and literary heir. Yongden was to have received her rights of authorship and to act as the guardian of treasures she collected so passionately. David-Neel in her last years, for work as well as companionship, would have to turn to strangers.

When Lawrence Durrell visited this "most astonishing woman" in 1964 perhaps his most intriguing observation was to compare Alexandra to Prospero in *The Tempest,* and to claim that, like the Shakespearean magician, she kept hidden a shy, pretty Miranda. That retiring young woman—Marie-Madeleine Peyronnet—is now in her sixties, yet her determined, pointed face framed by graying hair hasn't greatly changed. Slim, and her manner far more assured, she still prefers to dress casually in pants. Originally hired in the capacity of housekeeper, she has become the custodian of David-Neel's home, papers, and photographs and editor of her posthumous works, indeed the arbiter of her memory.

The two women were cast from radically different molds. Where Alexandra was born a Parisienne, to a family on the political left, Marie-Madeleine was raised in French Algeria in a family of soldiers. The budding orientalist began her travels as soon as she was old enough to run away, while Madeleine remained at home, dominated by a father who had been colonel of a battalion in the Sahara. Still, she dreamed of far-off places, particularly Canada. In her late twenties she became nanny to a wealthy family and traveled to Aix-en-Provence. Here, in 1959, she was recommended to the notice of the famous author who, due to her bad temper and bizarre habits, couldn't manage to keep either a servent or a secretary.

On the first night the reluctant Madeleine spent with Alexandra—the author had phoned her to come at once to her hotel, she was dying—she watched the suddenly revived octogenarian wolf down her dinner. When she went to prepare the supposed invalid's bed, she learned this was an armchair padded with cushions over which would be draped, once Alexandra was in it, an old Tibetan blanket. The scholar insisted that her books, pencils, and pads be kept handy. She only drowsed and a vital thought might strike at any moment. She scoffed at the difference between day and night.

Soon the pair left in the battered Citroën for Digne. Madeleine, in high spirits, drove. When at the end of the journey she tried to help her employer out of the car, Alexandra called her a fool. Needing assistance made her furious. Yet the basis of the relationship between the two strong-willed women would be one of dependence laced with affection, a struggle between age and youth, knowledge and conviction, that only Madeleine with time on her side could win.

Madeleine's first glimpse of Samten Dzong was of the *former* garden, presently abandoned to weeds higher than the car. The interior of this little Tibet looked still worse: low-ceilinged rooms hung with grimy red tapestries. The ragged furniture appeared ready for the junk heap, and the kitchen appliances might have come from there. Madeleine followed Alexandra as she clumped through on her canes, raising swirls of dust. When she shyly suggested sweeping, the orientalist growled.

If the novice found the house disconcerting, its shrine room terrified her. The smell of incense, the sight of tables covered by human skulls and phallic symbols, a tanka on the wall that depicted bodies wrapped in the poses of desire, the tiny case by the Buddha that contained the ashes of Yongden, all caused Madeleine to silently make the sign of the cross. She spent that night in her bedchamber in a nervous sweat. A large black spider hung from a beam, but it didn't bother her nearly as much as the strange bells, butter lamps, and thunderbolts she had seen strewn about, nor the emanations from a *phurba*, a bejeweled magic dagger. But not lacking in grit, Madeleine successfully fought off her fears and became indispensable to her employer. Later on she amused herself by scaring others with the phurba.

It was the very disarray of David Neel's life that drew Madeleine to her. The former's bedchamber and office were one: a large wooden desk and a writing table—heaped with books and papers—a chair, chests containing odds and ends, in one corner a turn-of-the-century suitcase packed with camping gear ready to go. A Tibetan altar with the usual offerings dominated one wall, and tankas decorated other spots. Each night Madeleine had to tuck her mistress into an armchair, prop her feet on a cushion covered with cloth from her old camp tent, and then massage her legs covered by sores. Alexandra's pain must have been constant. Ever vain, the older woman ordered the younger to wrap up her legs so they couldn't be seen.

Alexandra would drift off but often awaken to jot down an idea. Then she would ring for Madeleine to bring her tea, never mind the hour. Aside from housekeeping, she had to assist the author in such tasks as providing quotes, whether she knew the language or not. Her employer would not hear of a holiday. She did help Madeleine to bring her mother and sister out of Algeria to live nearby. During the next decade the younger woman's only time off, three half-days, was to attend funerals. Throughout this period the orientalist worked on her memoirs, on rewrites of earlier books, and on *Four Thousand Years of Chinese Expansion*, which accurately predicted the rise of China to a world power.

Wrapped in her claret robe, thick white hair plaited in a pigtail, Alexandra always kept near her a simmering tea pot, a magnifying glass to decipher small print, and her daily schedule and notes for current books. In the later 1960s, she saw less of Dr. Maille, so Dr. Julien Romieu, the mayor of Digne, became her physician. When he advised her to get reading glasses, she replied that she did not yet need them. When Christmas Humphreys visited his fellow Buddhist, he was "impressed to find her, at the age of ninety-five, correcting proofs without spectacles in a room made dark against the summer sun."

Yet this admirable, egotistical woman, in many ways larger than life, was heartbroken in her loneliness. She sometimes took a morose pleasure in supposing that, as she would be no more, *her* Tibet was vanishing beneath the tidal wave of Chinese expansion. Only at Samten Dzong could Alexandra rule with an iron, if arthritic, hand. Madeleine was ordered to attack the weeds in the garden in order to plant peas, beans, parsley, and chevril. These vegetables would be cooked into thick soups reminiscent of the good meals at Kum Bum. During her journeys in Asia, Alexandra had been more or less a vegetarian, and she always preferred this diet. However, she remained fond of pasta, coffee, and sweets, unhealthy for a woman in her nineties suffering from arthritis. During the last several years she could not walk at all, and Madeleine had to carry her from chair to chair. Fortunately, she was not as heavy as she had been.

One bone of contention between the two women, who developed a deep but tense relationship, was David-Neel's Buddhist reverence for all forms of life. The shrine room was a refuge for mice who were eating up the Tibetan rugs and manuscripts. Alexandra refused to put out traps and instead experimented with taming a few of the little creatures. Secretly, Madeleine poisoned the lot, just as she surreptitiously, then openly, waged war on the dirt and disorder of Samten Dzong. When it came to the realm of ideas, the elder woman was relentless and the younger one sentimental. Alexandra forced her companion to examine the framework of her conventional beliefs.

In turn, Madeleine probed for the chinks in the old stoic's armor. She deeply missed her husband, and the mere mention of Yongden's name brought a wounded look to her face. Madeleine was the first woman since her youth to break through Alexandra's hard shell. Three-quarters of a century before, her mother's lack of understanding left a deep scar. Since then, the orientalist had tended to measure her accomplishments against those of men, whether they were admirers, teachers, or rivals. This relationship of her last decade was more intimate, more feminine. The imperious one criticized her employee for being too slow to carry out her commands, then affectionately dubbed her *Tortue* (tortoise).

In the 1960s curiosity seekers bombarded Samten Dzong with letters and visits. Convinced of David-Neel's powers, these extravagants came from the four corners with outlandish petitions. One South American fell down and began to kiss Madeleine's feet as she opened the door. Numbers of women begged to live as celibates with one they supposed was a great medium, while others expected her to help them succeed in business, cure an illness, or commit a crime. A refined-looking woman was eager to learn if her dead husband was wandering in the bardo or already reincarnated. Perfumed letters had made her suspect his fidelity and she wanted to demand of him the truth. Another irate wife implored the wizard of Samten Dzong to kill, at long distance, her straying spouse. Alexandra chuckled, thinking of the number of widows this would create if it were made a general rule.

Caravans of hippies often stopped at Digne on their pilgrimages to the East. They idolized the sage who had lived among Tibetan hermits, but to her credit she disdained to promote a cult or proclaim herself a guru. Girls in miniskirts were declared unwanted at Samten Dzong, since David-Neel considered such revealing garb inappropriate for well-bred women. But she liked to chat with and was rejuvenated by her young admirers. If they had read a book or two of hers and a little Eastern philosophy, she would entertain them like old friends.

David-Neel warned that the serious business of vagabonding was not for the fainthearted or faddish. First one must master the language of a country. To depart without money was a disservice to native beggars. She proposed that ten years of residence was necessary to speak of a place with real authority. Otherwise, the Buddhist set down no dictums, nor would she assign her admirers mantras to chant or exercises to perform beyond what could be found in her writings. To end a tedious interview she closed her eyes and dozed off.

The ancient one sometimes grew morbid. She regularly quoted the Greek maxim: "Those who die young are loved by the gods." Instead, she claimed to be paying for her sins with a cruel old age and a ridiculous end, armchair-bound. She longed after the Central Asian plateau, cursing herself for leaving. She had visions of dying on the steppes near the Koko Nor lakes, the earth beneath her, above the infinite starry sky. The lamas would chant from the Book of the Dead to ensure rebirth in a more kindly realm. Then the huge vultures would descend to partake of her body—the "sky burial." She would sigh, struck by the grandeur of it.

Yet Alexandra realized that, due to her own choices, she had been brought full circle: hobbled, dependent on domestics. This was reminiscent of her mother's last days, a fate that in the flood of life she had despised, never dreaming it might resemble hers. Madeleine preferred to distract Alexandra by baking special desserts. Visitors were an unfailing tonic, but the younger ones annoyed the harassed cook/secretary. Looking on these youthful seekers as a lot of unkempt beggars, she once burst out that were she president of the republic she would ban David-Neel's books because of the mischief they encouraged. The explorer of outer limits, making no reply, stared into space. Was it then she thought of implicating the younger woman in the destruction of portions of her correspondence?

When Jacques Brosse inquired of Madeleine about considerable gaps in the manuscript letters, she "confided that under the order of Alexandra herself, she had very probably burned them [the missing letters], without knowing what they were about." These gaps in the record exist for several tumultuous years after her marriage to Philip, and they become evident to obscure other embarrassing instances, such as illnesses and demands for money. Equally important, David-Neel's letters as published posthumously in French, edited by Madeleine Peyronnet, contain only about one-third of those extant. Often, at precisely the most interesting moments, the reader is confronted by an ellipsis. The frequent series of dots mask the reality these authors have attempted to realize.

Both women perked up when distinguished guests visited Samten Dzong. The Bishop of Digne, Monseigneur Collin, was an erudite man with whom David-Neel liked to discuss everything from politics to the Bible. The iconoclast had always got on remarkably well with the higher clergy. Teilhard de Chardin was another Catholic intellectual with whom she kept in touch. Once when he chided her for not believing in miracles, she replied that she made them.

It took a different sort of man to bring out Alexandra's sprightly, coquettish air. When Lawrence Durrell interviewed her in 1964 for *Elle*, he was struck by her "magnificent eyes," her "small and beautiful ears" and "delicately designed nose and mouth." At first she was difficult, relating to Durrell that, after first crossing the border into Tibet, she became ill and was dying in the snows. Charles Bell, the Resident in Gangtok, received word of her plight, yet because she had disobeyed his order, he would do nothing to help her. "You English are not gentlemen!" she remonstrated.

Whether the story is true or not, the old fox liked to test people. Durrell had come prepared for the eventuality. Struck by one of the postage stamp-sized illustrations from the French version of *Journey*— *Voyage d'une Parisienne à Lhassa* taken by an outmoded plate camera, he had it blown up. As he informed us, "It showed a young woman of quite exceptional beauty and spirituality dressed as a Buddhist pilgrim with beads and begging bowl and a little pointed wicker hat that I remembered from my own childhood"—when he first became acquainted with Alexandra's writing.

To soften Alexandra's mood, Durrell produced the photograph. He recounts her reaction:

> "Yes," she said, "it was a farewell picture I had taken on the eve of my departure from Darjeeling." Then becoming grumpy once more she added most reproachfully, "I think you might have brought one for me." I replied, "Madam, I have brought four for you." At this her face relaxed into its pretty youthful lines and she took the pictures from me with delight and said, "Ah monsieur, you see that I was once beautiful." It was very touching, very feminine, and from then on we were firm friends.

So the two authors chatted amiably, and Alexandra, hair not entirely white, appeared to Durrell as a woman of perhaps sixty. Here was another triumph of will over pain by the adventurer who opened the hidden world of Tibetan Buddhism. Or was it method— did she practice any form of internal yoga? Durrell believed she did, and we are convinced that she kept up some silent practices concerned with concentrating the mind, meditating on aspects of the Void, and preparing to die. Tantric methodology was Alexandra's forté, and it is not likely that she had forgotten what she so arduously acquired, or that she would discuss it with any but an initiate.

Nearing a century on earth, the woman began to crumble physically. Now and again a tooth would crack and fall out. Her skin itched terribly, and she would scratch off pieces of flesh. However, she retained the spirit of adventure. At one hundred she renewed her passport, much to the puzzlement of the official in charge. This was no empty gesture but the prelude to a journey. David-Neel did not like to fly but in her mind an itinerary had crystalized. Casually, she put the grandiose scheme to Madeleine: they would drive the Citroën first to Berlin where she knew of a doctor who claimed to cure arthritis. Then it was on to Russia, driving the length of that vast country to Vladivostok. There she and Madeleine could embark for their final destination, New York. Did she envision a tickertape parade up Broadway?

Alexandra had thought it out in detail, down to sleeping in the car and cooking to trim expenses. Seeing new places would make her feel young and well again. Madeleine vetoed the proposal, and not to provoke an argument gave the excuse that her legs were too long to curl up in a tiny vehicle. This put an end to the centenarian's long-held wish to see America.

In 1969 David-Neel was promoted to the highest order of the French Legion of Honor. Scholars paid her homage. Rene Grousset, the orientalist, praised her erudition and added that his Tibetan acquaintances uniformly held her in high esteem and accorded her the title *Jetsunma*. Similarly, the Fourteenth Dalai Lama from his Indian exile spoke favorably of the explorer in an interview with Arnaud Desjardins. The spiritual leader wanted to meet the woman who had known his predecessor, and added, "We have read her books and we recognize there our own Tibet."

But when the French government decided to cast a bronze medal in David-Neel's honor, she refused to pose. She claimed to be too old and ugly. The medal had to be cast from a photo without the subject's cooperation. She did choose the motto to be engraved on the reverse: Walk Straight on Following Your Heart's Desire. It is from Ecclesiastes and had caught the attention of the youthful rebel three-quarters of a century earlier.

Reluctantly, Alexandra engaged in a television program about Tibet that devoted twenty minutes to her exploits. She acted strange, replying to the interviewer in French, English, or Tibetan as she fancied. She couldn't help but oblige the mayor Dr. Romieu, and the councilors of Digne, when they wished to celebrate her hundredth birthday with a party. She descended into a dark mood for weeks before the gala. While Madeleine, impressed by the magnitude of the occasion, tried to tidy the villa against the expected invasion of reporters and notables, her mentor took refuge in her Tibetan books, mumbling the syllables aloud.

The cameramen on the occasion shot a beatific Alexandra, chignon neatly arranged, in a robe of Chinese silk. On each hand she wore the appropriate ring of the initiate given to her long ago by the Maharaja of Sikkim. She chatted with reporters as zestily as she had on her return to France in 1925. The municipality had contributed champagne to commemorate its most famous citizen, and the author's office was transformed into a bar that rang with toasts to her courage and longevity. Gawking locals and sophisticated Parisians made Samten Dzong teem like a three-ring circus.

The one-time hermit's goodwill eroded under the onslaught. She snapped at the camermen and even let loose at a troop of girls from the grammar school who shyly waited to present a bouquet of roses. After the crowd left, Alexandra communed for a few hours with her Tibetan volumes. Honors were as useless to her as old hiking boots. Although sitting upright in her wicker desk chair made hot irons jab into her spine, work was her one reliable painkiller. She accepted her trials, once informing Madeleine that suffering refines the character of men and women.

David-Neel was touched when Digne named a projected secondary school after her. Along with Dr. Romieu, she pored over the plans, sad that Philip Neel had not lived for this moment. How wise of the councilors to memorialize her before, rather than after, death. Even more on the scholar's mind was her will, the disposal of her invaluable library and extensive collection of Tibetan artifacts, especially the stunning masks. Dr. Maille was consulted, and he agreed to contact his good friend Professor R. A. Stein, head of the French Asia Society. Thus France's two leading Tibetanists conferred at Samten Dzong.

David-Neel wished her library and artifacts kept intact and placed where they might be studied. She hoped that Stein, author of *Tibetan Civilization*, a distinguished scholar but decidedly of the old school, would oversee the installation of her collections in Paris. In return he would have her ashes strewn in the Ganges. To sweeten the deal, she offered him certain ritual bone items. Professor Stein refused, acidly commenting to Dr. Maille, "This woman is not very interesting."

Perhaps conflict was inevitable between these two proponents of rival versions of the epic of Gesar of Ling. David-Neel was stung by the rejection, but we are reminded of an old saying that she liked to repeat: "Who knows the flower best—the one who reads about it in a book, or the one who finds it wild on the mountainside?"

In a panic, David-Neel cast about for means to assure the continuity of her work. She felt that Madeleine was too inexperienced to take proper charge of her legacy. According to an informant, "Each week she wrote another will [and] the last one was used." Her entire library of French, English, and Tibetan books was donated to the Musée Guimet, where she had begun her studies as a young woman. Today only the Tibetan books—440 of them—are to be found there. Her personal library of French and English books—of great interest to a biographer—has been scattered.

David-Neel's valuable collection of artifacts was left in limbo, with the most unfortunate results. Shortly after she passed away a truck came to carry away the precious rugs, tankas, statues, ritual objects of bone, and rare masks that the orientalist had collected, with a superb eye, over her years of arduous travel in corners of Asia where it is difficult to venture even now. Madeleine saved what she could, but twelve large containers of these items were shipped to Paris. Under supervision of the executor, these were to be allocated to several museums. Try to find them if you can.

Only David-Neel's letters and unpublished manuscripts were to remain at Samten Dzong under the immediate care of Madeleine, supervised by her literary executor, Dr. Monod Herzen of Paris. The proceeds of past and future publications would go to the municipality of Digne, which became the author's legal heir. Unfortunately, Dr. Romieu, a quasi-Buddhist, died before matters could be put on a sound footing. In her will, David-Neel stipulated that Samten Dzong was to become a true Tibetan Center: a building would be constructed in the garden to house those on the Path—Buddhists, scholars, and students—at very low cost. The purpose was to combine study and meditation, to re-create the Tibetan institution of *tsams* (deep, secluded meditation), but for Westerners, as Alexandra herself had practiced it at Kum Bum. The scheme never came to fruition, and Samten Dzong today is a brief stop on the tourist path in the south of France.

One of Madeleine's first experiences had been a summons to witness Alexandra's final breath. Throughout the next decade her employer rang her bell persistently, usually in the middle of the night, to signal the supposed last act. Naturally, Madeleine learned to disregard these false alarms. Against reason, she came to regard Alexandra as immortal, a notion abetted by her strong will, which showed no signs of withering. But in July 1969 Madeleine understood that the old explorer was beyond searching for sympathy. At breakfast her pinched face had a blissful glow, the aftermath of an illumination given to her the night before.

"God, the Father, spoke to me," whispered Alexandra. "He has made a great light in my soul and I have seen the nothingness of all that was myself."

These words, at once Christian and Buddhist in tone, are a quote from Anatole France's *Thaïs,* made into an opera by Massenet. Alexandra in the role of the heroine—a courtesan converted to religion, who nonetheless seduces a monk—had once sung them.

From this point on the world-weary one showed little emotion, only a certain sweetness, an affability, that Madeleine had not seen in her before. Her major regret concerned giving up current investigations: the lives of Jesus and Mao. She wished to approach the Christian savior as a typically Hebrew prophet, a patriot, and to treat the Communist Party Chairman as an incarnation of the mythical Gesar, righter of wrongs suffered by the Asian peoples. Whatever else may be said of David-Neel, she wished to share the rare knowledge she had acquired. She was a staunch warrior in the common human struggle to be free of ignorance.

David-Neel, like Conway in *Lost Horizon,* returned from her Himalayan paradise to the mundane world out of a sense of duty. The sadness about her life, inextricably mixed with her triumph, was caused by the knowledge that she could not find her way back to Shangri-La. On September 8, 1969, at three in the morning, with Madeleine by her side, Alexandra ceased fighting for breath. The traveler departed on her final journey.

On September 11 at Marseilles the remains of Alexandra David-Neel were cremated. Madeleine and Dr. Romieu were present, along with several old explorer friends and a niece and nephew of Philip Neel. As the departed had wished, there was a minimum of ceremony, and her ashes were placed in an urn to be kept with Yongden's at Samten Dzong until Madeleine could transport them to the River Ganges. Newspapers, radio, and television in many countries announced the explorer's death—to a world caught up in the Vietnam War and the popular struggle to put an end to it.

Yet Alexandra David-Neel has been far from forgotten. Along with her obituary, the *International Herald Tribune* showed a photo of Alexandra riding a yak; it was captioned, "Woman on top of the world."

Coda: The Legacy

Including posthumous works, thirty distinct titles bear Alexandra David-Neel's name. While each is concerned with the East, at least in part, they vary from early utopian to the highly erudite, from the formality of grammar to the intimacy of private letters. Her books range over philosophy, anthropology, orientalism, philology, geographical discovery, historical and political nuance, and the tangle of tantric practices. Always they are crammed with adventure.

Alexandra's most *astonishing* bequest—to use Lawrence Durrell's word—may be her life itself. This is riddled with as many contradictions as her character. Born in the eye of a revolutionary hurricane, the radical student ultimately disdained politics but remained a keen observer. Once an opera singer, she later chose to perform on the vast Central Asian plateau. A staunch feminist, she learned mainly from men, loved her father, husband, and son, and was welcomed as a compere by the most rugged of the lot. Colonel Eric Bailey, then the Political Officer in Sikkim, in his confidential letter to the Government of India informing the viceroy of David-Neel's forbidden jaunt to Lhasa, could not help raving about her "wonderful journey."

George Schaller, the savior of the Himalayan snow leopard, remarked of David-Neel, "She accomplished so much more and in such [a] seemingly offhand manner than most explorers in that part of the world." Although she ranged over great unmapped distances and conquered terrain from ice-clad peaks to leech-ridden jungles, she delved still more significantly into the crevices of the human psyche. Ultimately, this willful woman who was not above beating a recalcitrant servant, this beneficiary of turn-of-the-century imperialism who defied an empire, stands for individual liberty, for the full expression of the "I" that her Buddhist philosophy denied.

David-Neel took refuge in the Buddha in her midforties. Her true career began at an age when others begin to think of retirement. She studied and meditated amid the snows of a Himalayan winter ensconced in a cave; most difficult, she subordinated her will to another. The Gomchen of Lachen taught her much. She then employed the knowledge she had gained to explore, to record, and to explain to others. She never cut herself off from the world for long but fought for a hearing as determinedly as she had battled the brigands of Koko Nor.

There has been some complaint against David-Neel that she was unorthodox. Jacques Brosse believed that because she left her guru before spending the traditional three years, three months with him, she failed to attain enlightenment and finally lacked compassion in the Buddhist sense. But he did not know the woman and depended on Madeleine Peyronnet for a description of her final, illness-ridden years. In contrast, Ian Davie has written us, "She was serene, and the person she most resembled, in appearance and graciousness, was Mother Teresa."

John Blofeld claimed that "David-Neel was so deeply concerned with her public image that her most widely read books are limited to Tibetan Buddhism's popular aspects. Little is said about its spiritually or philosophically profound aspects." This judgement is superficial and perhaps prompted by envy. The public has determined which of David-Neel's books remain popular; it is not her doing or a valid criticism. That her more profound works such as *The Secret Oral Teachings*, but especially her novels, are not better known is largely the fault of her estate, which does not know them either. Still, David-Neel's writings have reached the right persons in the right places far enough to make a difference in their and our lives.

Lama Govinda, a German who became perhaps more Tibetanized than David-Neel, consciously followed the path she blazed. At Sikkim's royal monastery of Podang, he was pleased to occupy "the same room in which she had lived and where a strange voice had warned the young Maharaja . . . of his impending end and the failure of his intended religious reforms." Lama Govinda, like David-Neel, learned from the Gomchen that, "Mere goodness and morality without wisdom is as useless as knowledge without goodness." Blofeld's observation that David-Neel "remained basically a fundamentalist Buddhist to the last" is correct, if by this we mean a follower of the teachings of Gautama Buddha. She took literally Buddha's injunction to accept nothing on the basis of authority but to test every supposed truth by the clear light of reason and experience.

In 1972 George Schaller and Peter Matthiessen were studying the habits of wildlife near the Nepalese-Tibetan border, terrain that was both difficult and politically dangerous. Areas along the route were inhabited by Khampa bands, hard-bitten from years of guerrilla warfare against the Chinese army. Hampered by late monsoon rains, the pair settled into a small hotel in an isolated Tibetan village to the west of Annapurna. Rain continued to fall, the travelers needed porters, and the locals refused to be of service. So they remained in their sleeping bags for days and read, entranced by Alexandra's books, especially *Magic and Mystery*. Eventually the weather cleared, porters materialized, and the pair trekked on. Their journey resulted in two splendid—and popular—travel accounts, Schaller's *Stones of Silence* and Matthiessen's *The Snow Leopard*.

Ten years after the death of David-Neel, the first all-women's rafting trip down the Colorado River through the Grand Canyon began; it was 115 degrees in the shade, if you could find any. The rafters poured buckets of water over each other to keep cool. Some rowed, others paddled, a few talked. China Galland, who has described this and other adventures in *Women in the Wilderness*, wrote, "Our group is extremely diverse . . . Still I know there must be a common thread that has drawn us all together."

In the chapter titled "How We Got There," the author recalls making a most important discovery: the life of Alexandra David-Neel. At a time of crisis in her own life, Galland identified with David-Neel's despair at successive early frustrations. Galland continued, "I ponder the change in my spirits that has come over me since beginning to read about Alexandra . . . the triumph of implacable spirit, the danger and the merit of following one's own path, and the realities of living out a dream." Alexandra inspired China Galland to take chances and to communicate her victories.

At the opposite end of the world, 18,500 feet high on Annapurna in Nepal, Dr. Arlene Blum, leader of the first all-women's expedition up the giant mountain, spoke into her tape recorder: "I keep wondering when the next avalanche will come. I'm spooked . . . Risking our lives; God, it's crazy. Why? Well, in another six days someone can be on top."

Dr. Blum was profoundly affected by finding a copy of *My Journey to Lhasa* in a secondhand bookstore in Katmandu. She carried the message of the book with her up that towering mass of ice and snow, and the dogged determination of the Frenchwoman stiffened the women's will to succeed. The party conquered the world's third highest peak, although on the descent two climbers, roped together, plunged to their deaths. Dr. Blum's *Annapurna: A Woman's Place* surely counts as a fruit of the tree of many images David-Neel conjured up.

In August 1985, sixteen years after the "sky-walker" (*dakini*) crumbled to ashes, a young American woman, Letha Hadady, found herself at the ornate entrance to the Jokhang, Lhasa's "cathedral," festooned with flags to celebrate the twentieth anniversary of the People's Government of the Tibet Autonomous Region, and the arrival of the Tenth Panchen Lama to bestow his benediction on the occasion. Many rural folk, following age-old custom, had flocked into Lhasa for the event—complete with Mardi Gras-like floats proclaiming the new Tibet and "Twenty Years of Progress." Townsfolk, peasants, and nomads smiled broadly, only partly because they had been warned to for weeks in advance over the loudspeaker system that permeates every nook of the City of the Sun. Taking their lead from the Dalai Lama, the common folk never doubted that the Panchen Lama, who had been held in close custody by the Chinese government for most of his life, had the interests of his country at heart.

Tall, lanky, blond, the woman's typically Tibetan outfit of dark felt failed to disguise her nationality, and when she spoke it was with the slight twang of the western plains. Glancing around as though looking for someone, she began to circumambulate the baroque, swoop-roofed building. She held her rosary of one hundred and eight wooden beads, chanting "Om Mani Padme Hum!" along with other pilgrims treading the clockwise path taken for centuries. Some hobbled, some prostrated themselves full-length, others were absorbed in prayer. The American's journey to Lhasa, half a century after the original, was triggered by reading and translating several of Alexandra's books.

At Katmandu she had been informed by the Chinese consulate that she couldn't cross from Nepal into Tibet. But in New York they had assured her the border was open, that China welcomed tourists. Well, yes, replied the official, but there had been problems and she would have to obtain a visa in Hong Kong. It was useless to point out she would have to fly there and back for a prohibitive sum. Despairing, she solaced herself by having a lunch of savory *momos* at a little dumpling shop. Fighting back tears, she felt like David-Neel after her first glimpse of the forbidden land.

Three young Tibetan men approached and informed the American they knew of her difficulties. One produced an air ticket from Calcutta to Hong Kong. It was hers if she agreed to deliver a package to Lhasa. But what about the return ticket? They had none, suggesting instead she cross to Guangzhou (Canton) and travel through China by rail to Kunming, Yunnan; from there a truck took two weeks through the Po country to Lhasa. That was the safest way because there would be a less thorough search at the Tibetan border. She wondered if these genial lads in their twenties were anti-Chinese guerrillas, the source of the "problems" alluded to. Partisans operated out of Nepal, and even the Dalai Lama could not always control them. Besides, what was in the package?

She was forbidden to open it, that was the stipulation. But to whom should she deliver it? She needn't worry, a person would claim the parcel; they could say no more. She asked herself, what would David-Neel have done? Certainly not turn back after coming this distance. She accepted the medium-sized package of ten or twelve pounds—heavy enough for a bomb—and within two days found herself in ultramodern Hong Kong. At Guangzhou she boarded the train and spent the next three and a half days crossing China in fourth class: rock-hard benches, compartments jammed with poor families, the women wrinkled, the children asleep under the seats, the toil-worn men chain-smoking cigarettes. The toilets were unusable, and the aisles were full of sick people.

At Kunming the American learned the Tibetan border was

closed, visa or no. Hotels in Lhasa were full due to the celebrations. She might try flying from Chengtu, Szechuan. But there, too, the answer was no, although she was told to try again. Suddenly one day both the skies and Lhasa opened miraculously, and from the plane flying over southeast Tibet she looked down on a range of snow-capped mountains plunging toward the horizon like a school of humpbacked whales at sea. Finally, the mountainous wave broke, and as they glided down onto the plain, the Potala glinted white and gold, changing shades like a faceted diamond ring. She had made the journey that took David-Neel four months of intense struggle in a couple of hours.

The Barkhor around the Jokhang runs through the heart of Lhasa, past the din of the marketplace, and a pilgrim must concentrate on her mantra not to be seduced by colorful nomads hawking their wares. Where this street widens and the peddlers thin out about halfway around, the American spotted propped against a wall by a huge incense-burner an elderly Tibetan woman of no distinction, a beggar, if such were allowed. She gestured to her and the pilgrim obeyed the summons. The crone deftly slipped her a rolled-up sheet of rice paper, and then, with a gap-toothed grin, motioned like a wheel. She understood she must complete the circumambulation.

At the trekker's hostel that evening when her roommates had gone out—they were randomly assigned without regard to nationality or gender, and the toilet was a unisex hole in the ground—the American unrolled the flimsy paper. Poorly printed in Tibetan, Chinese, and English, it was the authentic cry of a people ground under the boot of history, declared abolished, yet still placing faith in the conscience of the world. "Long live His Holiness the Dalai Lama!" it began, then in a breathtaking unraveling of language:

> We want to Free Tibet. We against by forc 20 celebration of [indecipherable]. Go out Red China. We against Chiness Goverment. We want to Howmen Right—U.N.O. We want to Justics. Justics. Justics. Long live Free Tibet! Free Tibet!

This sheet so thin as to be transparent, this mangled English, was sufficient if intercepted by the police—and their spies were everywhere—to lead to prison, torture, and finally the dawn gift of a pistol bullet in the back of the head for any number of Tibetan patriots.

The American quickly tucked it away as her British, French, and German roommates returned.

Next day the beggar woman was absent from her spot; she was not sighted until it was nearly time for the American to fly back to Chengtu. Each day, carrying the mysterious parcel tucked under her Tibetan robes, she went around the Jokhang, meandering a bit obviously through the market, but in vain. The last morning she had stopped at a stall to buy a trinket from a peddler woman of Amdo, colorfully dressed and loaded with turquoise, when she felt a hand grasp her arm. Turning, she saw those withered lips curled into a splotchy smile.

She followed the crone down a narrow side alley. Without knocking she entered a door; the dimness within was further obscured by smoldering incense, but the American was able to make out several lamas praying before an altar. This was a clandestine Buddhist temple. The religion is strictly curtailed and controlled in its old home. But rites are held in secret, and lads are designated and educated as monks while appearing just like their comrades. *Tulkus*, such as Sidkeong or Yongden, are still discovered. Over the altar hung a framed, faded portrait photo of the Fourteenth Dalai Lama beaming with youth.

One of the lamas, in hesitant English, asked the visitor if she would like to make an offering. She understood, revealing the package. Opened, it contained nothing more sinister than hundreds of pocketsized photos of His Holiness, who at fifty had retained the aspect of youth but looked sadder and more benevolent. Under the photo was printed a blessing in Tibetan. The American grew so excited on discovering what she had been lugging about that she cried tears of joy. The blessing was given to her by the lama, a sturdy Khampa. His ruptured English reminded her of the "Free Tibet!" flyer. The Dalai Lama, the incarnation of Chenresi, Bodhisattva of Compassion, blesses impartially Tibetans, Chinese, and philings.

The American left for New York. She had visited the monasteries of Drepung and Sera, slowly being restored, which hold a few score of friendly monks. She had "met" the Potala several times—necessary because on each occasion she was rushed through by the obviously fearful guide. Rather bizarre were the Dalai Lama's private quarters, which have been kept untouched since he fled to India in 1959. One dawn she watched as lamas prepared a corpse for the "sky burial"

and chanted to guide the deceased's soul through the bardo as they
waited for the eager vultures to swoop down. She walked many miles
to the site of Ganden, but found no crowds of pilgrims around the
tomb of Tsong Khapa, made of pure gold and silver and encrusted
with jewels. The tomb had been broken into pieces and melted down.
Ganden, which once housed thousands of monks and Tibet's leading
university, is a shadow of its old self.

The American realized that the true stream of Tibetan life flows
underground, disguised, in the style of David-Neel, as a poor old
beggar woman. Buddhism, returned to its roots as an outlaw
faith, finds expression in artists who continue to paint tankas with
unchanging devotion; in the market folk at Lhasa, who as they deal
continually chant under their breath the holy names; in pilgrims
from far places who refuse to stop short of their goal. After all,
Shangri-La was not made of bricks and mortar.

Shortly after the American's departure, the desperation of the
Tibetans erupted in the first of several uprisings in Lhasa, followed
by ever harsher retaliation by the occupying Chinese forces. At the
time of writing—August, 1997—the repression of traditional Tibetan
life in their ancient capital has become nearly total. A May article
in *The Far Eastern Economic Review* titled "Lhasa Is Turned into a
Chinatown" reports that "as Chinese flock to the Tibetan capital"—
lured by wages five times as high as in China proper—
"skyscrapers and traffic jams are redefining the city." Lhasa has
become another Chinese boomtown on the order of Guangzhou or
Shanghai. The old city has been largely demolished, corruption
of all sorts rules, and the Tibetans themselves are marginalized.
A Tibetan businessman puts it succinctly: "Lhasa is a lost cause."
Except in two recent American movies, filmed in Argentina and
Morocco respectively, where an ersatz Lhasa has been constructed
out of cardboard.

The fantasy of Shangri-La remains compelling. We need to
believe that somewhere there is a land of Enlightened Masters who
can teach a secret knowledge that will free us from care and worry.
Strangely enough, Alexandra David-Neel found that place—just
where Madam Blavatsky had said it would be—in the Himalayas.
She studied with the Masters—call them lamas, naljorpas, or the
Gomchen of Lachen—and she returned to the West with the express

purpose of relating that which she had learned. This she accomplished in a witty, prolific, and entertaining fashion. This is the path of the *bodhisattva*, one who postpones enlightenment so that he or she may help to enlighten others.

For many centuries the Tibetans had amassed the knowledge of the ancient world. In the form of books or manuscripts they carried it on their beasts of burden from China, or on their backs over the Himalayas from India—sometimes they carried the precious secrets in their minds. David-Neel reversed that process, a transfer of the Dharma that today has been vastly accelerated by the outflow of refugees from Tibet. Buddhism has come to us in a manner parallel to the transfer of Greek learning to the rest of Europe after the fall of Byzantium, a cataclysm that resulted in the Renaissance. Are we once again on the threshold of such a powerful fusion of Eastern and Western thought and art? If so, Alexandra David-Neel's place is in the vanguard of humanity's progress.

To us personally there exists a snapshot from the travelogue of Alexandra's life that captures her way. In 1936 Europe trembled before the extortionate demands of Hitler. Czechoslovakia would soon be swallowed by the Nazis, but that did not prevent the orientalist, at the height of her renown, from going to Prague to give a conference. While there she visited the home of the sixteenth-century kabbalist Rabbi Loew, adjacent to a very old synagogue. In order to defend his people, this learned mystic had made a golem, or so legend held. He created this being by fashioning the statue of a man from clay, then animating it through magical sayings. The creature possessed extraordinary powers for good or evil.

Alexandra didn't believe in golems. She felt the conception was too physical. This sort of work was best done as a mental creation. Yet, when the guard left her alone in the rabbi's chambers, she scarcely hesitated before pulling aside the silken cord that barred access to Rabbi Loew's chair of office. Sitting there, she felt the electric charge of her lineage.

Throughout her life, Alexandra David-Neel sought substance behind the screen of shadows. She, too, fashioned a protector for her people: her works will help keep alive the true Tibetan spirit. After a century of endeavor, she departed for that dim shore to which we all journey one day. What she discovered there is hers.

Sources and Acknowledgments

Concerning biographers, Leon Edel has observed, "They think too little about art and talk too much about objective fact, as if facts were as hard as bricks or stones." We can name no one worse served by this state of mind than Alexandra David-Neel. For many years the facts of her long life were obscure, partly because she preferred to conceal her intimacies, human frailties, and even illnesses, which she considered signs of weakness. Unfortunately, David-Neel's posthumous plans for Samten Dzong, her collection of Tibetan artifacts, and her personal papers have been largely circumvented. There is an urgent need for these documents and photographs to be placed under professional supervision and subjected to scholarly study and free access. David-Neel's reputation deserves no less.

The significant gaps in portions of David-Neel's papers, coming at crucial moments in the story of her life, have caused us to take some liberties with her spoken dialogue. The words (and thoughts) attributed to her are not necessarily on record. Our method rather parallels John Blofeld's in his autobiographical *City of Lingering Splendour*: "I have employed the methods of fiction to reconstruct conversations or to refurbish settings fading from memory. So all I have written records truthfully either what was or what easily may have been." In our case, this applies to Alexandra herself and occasionally Philip Neel or Yongden. Third-party sources, spoken or written, and of course archival sources, are reproduced as accurately as humanly possible.

We have spent much of the last two decades unearthing the hidden facts of David-Neel's life, as well as living our own in a manner she might find sympathetic. There is no use in interpreting the evidence either in the spirit of attack or hagiography. We have aimed for a more objective, if equally enthusiastic, work. We have been concerned to show the moral and spiritual significance of David-Neel's life and writings, and what she continues to mean to others.

We began with Dorothy Middleton's *Victorian Lady Travellers,* which stirred our interest in these phenomenal, neglected women. Becoming acquainted with Mrs. Middleton, honorary vice president of the Royal Geographical Society, has been one of the great pleasures of this endeavor. Luree Miller, in *On Top of the World,* wrote one chapter that shone light (in English) on corners of Alexandra's life. A third woman, Letha Hadady, author of *Asian Health Secrets* (foreword by H.H. the Dalai Lama) is the godmother of this book. We cannot thank her sufficiently for her translations of idiosyncratic French, probing insights into Alexandra's character, and arduous travel on our behalf, when she wielded camera and brush to good effect.

We cite our equal gratitude to three gentlemen—in the full sense of the word—each British. Peter Hopkirk, author and foreign correspondent, was generous with his time in reading the manuscript and making suggestions for its improvement. His casual remark about the India Office Secret Files led us to a mine of information. This material, never before drawn on, provides the first third-party verification that David-Neel went where she said she did. It shows why she took detours and evasions. Here is the key to the mystery of her roundabout route.

To Hugh Richardson, dean of Tibetanists, we are more than thankful both for his meticulous guidance and amusing but informative anecdotes. Our correspondence with Mr. Richardson, Britain's last Political Officer for Sikkim and Tibet, grew to monumental proportions. Through his eyes we obtained a view of the actual world in which David-Neel moved. Without this precious knowledge, evaluating her actions would have been mere guesswork. Lawrence Durrell provided another view of our subject, personal and incisive. We are grateful for his time, attention, and encouragement.

We are sorry to have to thank Christmas Humphreys posthumously for recounting his meetings with our subject. We have relied on Mr. Humphreys's *Popular Dictionary of Buddhism* for both meanings and spellings of Buddhist terms. In general we have fallen back on the most commonly accepted forms, not necessarily those used by David-Neel, but contemporaneous with her. Consistent with that policy we have spelled Chinese and Tibetan geographical names in the fashion known to her and her time. The choice is essentially an aesthetic one. However, the adoption of current Chinese spelling of Tibetan names might imply a recognition of the legitimacy of their regime in Tibet—a political act we are not prepared to commit. Similarly our maps—drawn by Letha Hadady—conform to the boundaries agreed upon by the Simla Convention of 1914, the Asia that David-Neel knew.

Until now, no one had thought to interview a variety of people close to David-Neel. Doing so proved both enlightening and entertaining. Our thanks to Professor Pierre Borrely for his candor (and imitations), and to Frank Treguier for his helpfulness. We are truly indebted to Dr. Marcel Maille for his deep learning and interest in Tibetan Buddhism, and his willingness to share his unique insights with us. Additional thanks to his charming wife, Michele, for her contribution to our knowledge of the enigmatic one. And to Dr. Yves Requena, prolific author, physician of the soul as well as the body, for introducing us to Dr. Maille. The intelligence conveyed by these wonderful people, and by a number of tradespeople at Digne, came to us precisely when we could make the best use of it.

Among institutions whose collections we have consulted, we are particularly indebted to the India Office Library of the British Library, London; and to the anonymous librarian at the British Museum who directed us to the unpublished notebooks of Sir Charles Bell. These contain material Bell considered too personal to include in his several fine books on Tibet. The library of the Royal Geographical Society, London, is beyond compare in the field of travel; one may simply reach out and take what one needs, it is all on hand. Our thanks also to the Musée Guimet and the Bibliothèque de l'Opera, as well as the Bibliothèque National, Paris. It was our pleasure to use the specialized, but excellent, collections of the Sri Aurobindo ashram, Pondicherry, and the Theosophical Society, Adyar, India. Closer to home, the librarians of Dartmouth College, the New York Public Library, and Columbia University proved consistently helpful beyond the demands of their profession. Our profound thanks must be given to the following librarians of Hunter College, CUNY: the late Magda Gottesman, Norman Clarius, and Harry Johnson, who obtained for us books we never dared hope were available, and from the most remarkable places!

It was a pleasure to correspond, and later meet, with Professor Robert Thurman of Columbia, a scholar who knows Tibetan Buddhism firsthand, and with that intrepid traveler in his own right, Lowell Thomas, Jr. of Alaska. We profited from the advice of Marion Meade, biographer of Madame Blavatsky, an author who understands what it means to deal with a giant of a woman.

Once again in Paris, our thanks to Dr. Gabriel Monod-Herzen for sharing with us memories of the woman he knew so well. In New York, Braham Norwick, Tibetanist and long-time admirer of David-Neel, was the source of expert information. The enthusiasm of Dr. Arlene Blum (mountain climber par excellence) and the commitment of Valerie La

Breche helped to keep us on track. We are obliged to Sir John Thompson, former British ambassador to the United Nations and to India, for his wise and witty comments on Charles Bell and the diplomat's life in the Orient.

A few words on the previous biographies in French, on which we have drawn in differing degrees. Jeanne Denys' *Alexandra David-Neel au Tibet* (1972) is scandalous and motivated by hatred, yet it cannot be ignored. One's worst enemy often knows a good deal about one. Handle with care. Jacques Brosse's *Alexandra David-Neel: L'aventure et la spiritualité* (1978) is out of date and print but interesting and fairly balanced. His judgments show a real knowledge of Buddhism. The book has been unduly neglected.

Jean Chalon's *Le lumineaux destin d'Alexandra David-Neel* (1985) is a lengthy authorized biography. Chalon shows only a superficial acquaintance with Eastern thought. The author lacked the advantage of certain vital sources in English. Moreover, he has hatched some theories that, out of *politesse*, we may term misguided. The value of the book lies in its feel for narrative, lively style, and extensive treatment of Alexandra's younger, bohemian days and marriage. In English, a pallid attempt at biography is Ruth Middleton's *Alexandra David-Neel: Portrait of an Adventurer*. This is impressionistic, unresearched—a pastel miniature of a great woman.

We wish to take this opportunity to thank our guides to the profound world of Buddhist thought and practice: John Blofeld, Alan Watts, and Allen Ginsberg. To our astonishment, we received from Mr. Blofeld a lengthy, helpful critique of our manuscript written from his sickbed shortly before he died. We humbly thank our spiritual guides Chögyam Trungpa Rinpoche, and the Dharma Master, monks, and nuns of the Chinese–American Buddhist Association, Chinatown, New York. It ought to be abundantly clear we have no quarrel with the Chinese people, but only dissent for the policies of the People's Republic in Tibet.

We realize that we have made errors, and these we claim for ourselves alone. The good in our work we dedicate to the Tibetan people, wherever they may live.

Barbara Foster
Michael Foster
New York, N.Y.
1997

$\mathcal{S}$elected $\mathcal{B}$ibliography

ARCHIVAL AND UNPUBLISHED SOURCES

Bell, Charles. Unpublished Notebooks on Tibet, Bhutan, Sikkim and Chumbi Valley. 4 vols., manuscript notes 1936; Diary vol. 3-21, manuscript notes 1907-1938. The British Library, London.
The Political and Secret Annual Files (1912-1930), L/P&S 11, India Office Records. The British Library, London.

WORKS BY ALEXANDRA DAVID-NEEL

ENGLISH

David-Neel, Alexandra. "Behind the Veil of Tibet." *Asia* 26 (April 1926): 320-328, 346-353.
Buddhism: Its Doctrines and Its Methods. New York: Avon, 1979.
"Edge of Tibet." *Asia* 44 (January 1944): 26-29.
"A Frenchwoman Secretly Headed for Lhasa." *Asia* 26 (March 1926): 195-201, 266-271.
"High Politics in Tibet." *Asia* 43 (March 1943): 157-159.
Initiations and Initiates in Tibet. Berkeley: Shambhala, 1970.
"Lhasa at Last." *Asia* 26 (July 1926): 624-633.
"Lost in the Tibetan Snows." *Asia* 26 (May 1926): 429-435, 452-454.
Magic and Mystery in Tibet. New York: Dover, 1971.
"Mohammedans of the Chinese Far West." *Asia* 43 (December 1943): 677-679.
My Journey to Lhasa. New York: Harper & Brothers, 1927. Reprint, Boston: Beacon Press, 1986.
"New Western Provinces of China I: Ching-hai." *Asia* 42 (May 1942): 286-289.
"New Western Provinces of China II: Sikang." *Asia* 42 (June 1942): 367-370.

The Power of Nothingness. Boston: Houghton Mifflin, 1982.

"The Robber Land of the Po." *Asia* 26 June 1926): 312-316, 563-566.

The Secret Oral Teachings in Tibetan Buddhist Sects. San Francisco: City Lights, 1967.

The Superhuman Life of Gesar of Ling. Boulder, CO: Prajna, 1981.

"Theatre in China Now." *Asia* 44 (December 1944): 559-560.

"Tibet Looks at the News." *Asia* 42 (March 1942): 189-190.

"Tibetan Border Intrigue." *Asia* 41 (May 1941): 219-222.

Tibetan Tale of Love and Magic, Jersey, UK: Neville Spearman, 1983.

"A Woman's Daring Journey into Tibet." *Asia* 26 (March 1926): 195-201, 266-271.

"Women of Tibet." *Asia* 34 (March 1934): 176-181.

FRENCH

David, Alexandra. "Aupres du Dalai Lama." *Mercure de France* 99 (October 1912): 466-476.

"Le bouc emissaire des thibetains." *Mercure de France* 176 (December 1924): 649-660

"Les colonies sionistes en Palestine." *Mercure de France* 80 (July 1909): 266-275.

Grammaire de la langue tibetaine parlee. Paris: n.p. n.d.

"L'lliade thibetaine et ses bardes." *Mercure de France* 166 (September 1923): 714-725.

L'Instruction des indigenes en Tunisie." *Mercure de France* 74 (July 8): 61-72.

"La liberation de la femme des charges de la maternite." *Le Monde* (1908): 115-119.

"Le pacifisme dans l'antiquite chinoise." *Mercure de France* 67 (June 1907): 465-471.

"La question du Thibet." *Mercure de France* 140 (May-June 1920): 366-375.

Socialisme Chinois; Le philosophe Meh-Ti et L' idee de solidarite. Londres: Girard et Briere, 1907.

Les theories individualistes dans la philosophie chinoise. Paris: Girard et Briere, 1909. Reprint, Paris: Plon, 1970.

"Un Stirner chinois." *Mercure de France* 76 (November 1908): 445-452.

David-Neel, Alexandra. *A l'Ouest barbare de la vaste Chine.* Paris: Plon, 1947.

Ashtavakra Gita; Discours sur le Vedanta Advaita. Paris: Adyar, 1951.

Au coeur des Himalayas; Le Nepal. Paris: Dessart, 1949.

Avadhuta Gita. Paris: Adyar, 1958.

En Chine: L'amour universe! et l'individualisme integral: les maitres Mo Tse et Yang Tchou. Paris: Plon, 1976.

La connaissance transcendante. Paris: Adyar, 1958.

Grand Tibet; Au pays des brigands-gentilshommes. Paris: Plon, 1933. English edition, London: Bodley Head, 1936.

Immortalite et reincarnation: Doctrines et pratiques en Chine, au Tibet, dans l'Inde. Paris: Plon, 1961.

L'Inde ou j'ai vecu; Avant et apres l'ndependence. Paris: Plon, 1969.

L'Inde hier, anjourd'hui, demain. Paris: Plon, 1951.

Journal de voyage; Lettres a son Mari, 11 aout 1904-27 decembre 1917. Vol. 1. Ed. Marie-Madeleine Peyronnet. Paris: Plon, 1975.

Journal de voyage; Lettres a son Mari, 14 janvier 1918-31 decembre 1940. Vol. 2. Ed. Marie-Madeleine Peyronnet. Paris: Plon, 1976.

Le lama au cinq sagesses. Paris: Plon, 1935. Reprint, Paris: Plon, 1970.

La lampe de sagesse. Paris: Le Rocher, 1986.

Magie d'amour et magic noire; Scenes du Tibet inconnu. Paris: Plon, 1938. English edition, Jersey: Neville Spearman, 1983.

Le modernisme bouddhiste et le bouddhisme du Bouddha. Paris: Alcan, 1936. Reprint, Paris: Plon, 1977.

"Le phenomes psychiques au Thibet." *Revue de Paris* (December 1929): 566-594.

Le puissance de neant. Paris: Plon, 1954.

Le sortilege du mystere; Faits etranges et gens bizarre recontres au long de mes routes d'orient et d'occident. Paris: Plon, 1972.

Sous des nuees d'orage; Recit de voyage. Paris: Plon, 1940.

Quarante siecles d'expansion chinoise. Paris: Plon, 1964.

Textes tibetains inedits. Paris, 1952. Reprint, Paris: Pygmalion, 1972.

"Le Thibet mystique." *Revue de Paris* I (February 1928): 855-898.

Le Tibet d'Alexandra David-Neel. Paris: Plon, 1979.

Le vieux Tibet face a la Chine nouvelle. Paris: Plon, 1953.

Vivre au Tibet; Cuisine, traditions et images. n.p. Morel, 1975.

Myrial, Alexandra [pseud]. "Les congregations en Chine." *Mercure de France,* 47 (August 1903): 289-312.

"Moukden." *Mercure de France* 56 (July 1905): 69-79.

Pour la vie. Bruxelles: n.p., 1898.

WORKS CONCERNED WITH ALEXANDRA DAVID-NEEL

ENGLISH

"Alexandra David-Neel is Dead: Writer, Adventuress, Traveller, *New York Times,* I (September 9, 1969), 47.

Anderson, Walt. *Open Secrets*. New York: Penguin Books, 1979.

Dedman, Jane. "Walker in the Sky." *Quest* 78 (May-June 1978): 21-26, 90-92.

Galland, China. *Women in the Wilderness*. New York: Harper & Row, 1981.

Hopkirk, Peter. *Trespassers on the Roof of the World*. London: J. Murray, 1982.

Middleton, Ruth. *Alexandra David-Neel*. Boston: Shambala, 1989

Miller, Luree. *On Top of the World*. New York: Paddington, 1976.

Thomas, Lowell, Jr. *Out of This World*. New York: Greystone, 1950.

Tiltman, Marjorie. *Women in Modern Adventure*. London: G. G. Harrap, 1935.

FRENCH

Brosse, J. *Alexandra David-Neel: L'aventure et la spiritualite*. Paris: Retz, 1978.

Chalon, Jean. *Le lumineux destin d'Alexandra David-Neel*. Paris: Perrin, 1985.

Champy, Huguette. "Quelques Exploratrices." *Revue Economique* 68, no.2 (May 1955): 32-35.

Denys, Jeanne. *Alexandra David-Neel au Tibet*. Paris: Pensee Universelle, 1972.

Peyronnet, Marie-Madeleine. *Dix ans avec Alexandra David-Neel*. Paris: Plon, 1973.

OTHER SOURCES

Agulhon, Maurice. *The Republican Experiment, 1848-1852*. Cambridge: Cambridge University Press, 1983.

Akar, Tinley N. "Tibetan Uprising Observed in New York." *Tibetan Review* (April 1976): 7-8.

Avedon, John. *In Exile from the Land of Snows*. New York: Knopf, 1984.

Bailey, Frederick. *China, Tibet, Assam: A Journey*. London: J. Cape, 1945.

——. *No Passport for Tibet*. London: Rupert Hart-Davis, 1957.

Basu, Chandra. *Esoteric Science and Philosophy of the Tantras*. Allahabad: n.p., 1914.

Battaglia, Lee. "Wedding of Two Worlds," *National Geographic Magazine* (November 1963): 708-727.

Beauvoir, Simone de. *The Second Sex*. New York: Knopf, 1973.

Bell, Charles. *The People of Tibet*. Cambridge: Clarendon Press, 1928.

——. *Portrait of the Dalai Lama*. London: Collins, 1946.

——. *Tibet Past and Present*. Cambridge: Oxford University Press, 1924.

Bernard, Theos. *Penthouse of the Gods*. New York: Scribners, 1939.

Bernbaum, Edwin. *The Way to Shambala*. New York: Doubleday, 1983.

Beyer, Stephen. *The Cult of Tara*. Berkeley: University of California Press, 1978.

Bharati, Agehananda. *The Tantric Tradition*. New York: Weiser, 1975.

Bishop, Barry. "Wintering on the Roof of the World." *National Geographic Magazine* 123 (October 1962): 503-552.

Bishop, Isabella Bird. *Among the Tibetans*. New York: Revell, 1894.

Blofeld, John. *The Tantric Mysticism of Tibet*. New York: Causeway Books, 1974.

———. *The Wheel of Life*. Boulder, CO: Shambhala, 1978.

Blum, Arlene. *Annapurna: A Woman's Place*. San Francisco: Sierra Club Books, 1980.

"Triumph and Tragedy in Annapurna." *National Geographic Magazine* 155, no. 3 (March 1979): 295.

Burchell, S. C. *Upstart Empire*. London: Macdonald, 1971.

Burton, Richard. *Personal Narrative of a Pilgrimage to Al Madinah and Mecca*. 2 vols. London: Tylston & Edwards, 1893.

Candler, Edmund. *The Unveiling of Lhasa*. London: Edward Arnold, 1905.

Carey, William. *Adventures in Tibet*. New York: Baker & Taylor, 1905.

Carroll, John. *Breakout from the Crystal Palace*. London: Routledge & K. Paul, 1974.

Chapman, Spencer. *Lhasa; The Holy City*. London: Harper & Bros., 1938.

China's Three Thousand Years. New York: Times Newspapers, 1974.

Cobban, Aldred. *A History of Modern France*. London: Penguin, 1961.

Conze, E. *Buddhism; Its Essence and Development*. Cambridge: Oxford University Press, 1953.

Cooke, Hope. *Time Change*. New York: Simon & Shuster, 1980.

Cutting, Suydam. *The Fire Ox and Other Years*. New York: Scribners, 1947.

Dalai Lama. *My Land and My People*. New York: Potala Corp., 1983.

Das, Sarat Chandra. *Journey to Lhasa and Central Tibet*. London: J. Murray, 1904.

———. *Narrative of a Journey to Lhasa*. Calcutta: n.p., 1885.

De Bary, Theodore. *The Buddhist Tradition*. New York: Modern Library, 1969.

De Riencourt, Amaury. *Roof of the World; Tibet Key to Asia*. New York: Rhinehart & Co., 1950.

Desideri, I. An *Account of Tibet*. London: Routledge & Sons, 1937.

Dhondup, K. *Songs of the Sixth Dalai Lama*. Delhi: Library of Tibetan Works, 1981.

———. *The Diamond Sutra*. Tr. by A. F. Price. Boulder, CO: Shambhala, 1969

Doig, Desmond. "Sikkim: Tiny Himalayan Kingdom in the Clouds," *National Geographic Magazine* 123 (March 1963): 398-429.

Donaldson, Florence. *Lepcha Land*. London: S. Low, Marston, 1900.

Duncan, Jane. A *Summer Ride through Western Tibet*. London: Smith & Elder, 1906.

Edwards, Samuel. *Victor Hugo; A Tumultuous Life*. New York: David McKay Company, 1971.

Edwards, Stewart. *The Paris Commune, 1871*. New York: Quadrangle Books, 1977.

Ekvall, Robert. *Tibetan Sky Lines*. New York: Farrar, Straus & Young, 1952.

Eliot, Charles. *Hinduism and Buddhism*. 3 vols. London: E. Arnold, 1921.

Ellis, Havelock. *From Rousseau to Proust*. Freeport, NY: Books for Libraries, 1935.

Evans-Wentz, W. Y. *The Tibetan Book of the Dead*. London: Oxford University Press, 1957.

——. *Tibetan Yoga and Secret Doctrines*. London: Oxford University Press, 1958.

——. *Tibet's Great Yogi Milarepa*. London: Oxford University Press, 1971.

Fleming, Peter. *Bayonets to Lhasa*. New York: Harper & Bros., 1961.

Forman, Harrison. *Through Forbidden Tibet*. New York: Longmans, Creen, 1935.

Franke, Wolfgang. *China and the West*. Columbia, SC: University of South Carolina Press, 1967.

Garrison, Omar. *Tantra: The Yoga of Sex*. New York: Causeway Books, 1964.

Ghosh, Suchita. *Tibet in Sino-Indian Relations*. New Delhi: Sterling, 1977.

Ginsberg, Allen. *Indian Journals, March 1962-May 1963*. San Francisco: Dave Haselwood, 1970.

Govinda, Lama Anagarika. *Fundamentals of Tibetan Mysticism*. New York: Dutton, 1959

——. *The Way of the White Clouds*. Berkeley: Shambhala, 1970.

Grousset, Rene. *In the Footsteps of the Buddha*. London: Routledge & Sons, 1932.

Guenther, Herbert. *Treasures on the Tibetan Middle Way*. Berkeley: Shambhala, 1976.

Hanbury-Tracy, John. *Black River of Tibet*. London: F. Muller, 1938.

Harding, James. *Massenet*. London: Dent, 1970.

Harrer, Heinrich. *Seven Years in Tibet*. London: Dutton, 1904.

Hedin, Sven. *Adventures in Tibet*. London: Hurst & Blackett, 1904.

Hilton, James. *Lost Horizon*. New York: Pocket Books, 1960.

Holdich, Thomas. *Tibet the Mysterious*. New York: F.A. Stokes, 1906.

Hughes, E. R. *The Invasion of China by the Western World*. London: A.C. Black,1937

Humphreys, Christmas. *The Buddhist Way of Life*. London: Curzon Press, 1976.

——. *A Popular Dictionary of Buddhism*. New York: Citadel Press, 1965.

Karan, P. K. *The Changing Face of Tibet*. Lexington, KY: The University Press of Kentucky, 1976.

Knight, Captain. *Diary of a Pedestrian in Cashmere and Tibet*. London: Edward, 1863.

Krimmerman, Leonard. *Patterns of Anarchy*. New York: Anchor Books, 1966.

Landor, Arnold. *In the Forbidden Land*. *2 vols*. New York: Harper & Bros., 1899.

——. *Tibet and Nepal*. London: A. C. Black, 1905.

Lantier, Jacques. *La theosophie*. Paris: Culture, Art, Loisirs, 1970.

Lattimore, Owen. *Silks, Spices, and Empire*. London: Tandem, 1968.

Lawrence, T. E. *Seven Pillars of Wisdom*. New York: Dell, 1969.

Ling, T. O., *A Dictionary of Buddhism*. New York: St. Martins, 1972.

Macdonald, David. *The Land of the Lama*. London: Seeley, Service, 1929.

——. *Twenty Years in Tibet*. London: Seeley, Service, 1932.

McAleavy, Henry. *The Modern History of China*. New York: Praeger, 1967.

McGovern, William Montgomery. *An Introduction to Mahayana Buddhism*. London: K. Paul, Trench, Trubner, 1922.

——. *To Lhasa in Disguise*. London: Century Co., 1924.

MacCregor, John. *Tibet; A Chronicle of Exploration*. New York: Praeger, 1970.

Maitron, Jean. *Histoire du mouvement anarchiste en France, 1880-1914*. Paris: F. Maspero, 1951.

Maraini, Fosco. *Secret Tibet*. New York: Viking, 1952.

Massenet, Jules. *My Recollections*. Westport, CT: Greenwood Press, 1970.

Meade, Marion. *Madame Blavatsky*. New York: Putnam, 1980.

Middleton, Dorothy. *Victorian Lady Travellers*. London, Routledge K. Paul, 1965.

Millington, Powell. *To Lhasa at Last*. London: Smith & Elder, 1905.

Morgan, Kenneth W., ed. *The Religion of the Hindus*. New York: Ronald Press 1953

Norbu, Thubten. *Tibet Is My Country*. London: Dutton, 1960.

Norwick, Braham. "Alexandra David-Neel's Adventures in Tibet." *The Tibet Journal,* I (Fall 1976): 70-74.

Pallis, Marco. *Peaks and Lamas*. London: Cassell, 1940.

Patterson, George. *Tibet in Revolt.* London: Faber & Faber, 1960.

Rato, Khyongla Nawang Losang. *My Life and Lives.* New York: Dutton, 1977.

Rhys Davids, T. W. *Buddhism; Its History and Literature.* London: Putnams, 1926.

Richardson, Hugh. *A Short History of Tibet.* New York: Dutton, 1962.

Rijnhart, Susie. *With the Tibetans in Tent and Temple.* Chicago: Revell, 1909.

Rockhill, William Woodville. *Diary of a Journey through Mongolia and Tibet in 1891 and 1892.* Washington, D.C.: Smithsonian Institution, 1894.

——. *Land of the Lamas.* London: Longmans, Green, 1891.

Rodzinski, Witold. *A History of China.* 2 vols. Oxford: Pergamon Press, 1983.

Roerich, Nikolai. *Shambala.* New York: Stokes, 1930.

Ronaldshay, Lawrence. *Lands of the Thunderbolt.* London: Constable, 1923.

Rowell, Calen. "Nomads of China's West." *National Geographic Magazine,* 16 (February 1982): 244-263.

Rudortf, Raymond. *Belle Epoque.* London: Hamish Hamilton, 1972

Runkle, Gerald. *Anarchism Old and New.* New York: Delacorte, 1972.

Sandberg, Graham. *The Exploration of Tibet.* Calcutta: Spink & Co., 1904.

Saraswati, Janakananda. *Yoga, Tantra and Meditation.* New York: Ballantine Books, 1975.

Sanborn, Alvan. *Paris and the Social Revolution.* Boston: Small, Maynard, 1905.

Schaller, George. *Stones of Silence.* New York: Viking, 1980.

Schecter, Jerrold. "Official Atheism Has Killed Religion in Remote Tibet." *Smithsonian* 7 (January 1977): 78-85.

Scoffield, John. "Gangtok: Cloud Wreathed Himalayan Capital." *National Geographic Magazine* 138 (November 1970): 698-713.

Shakabpa, Tsepon. *Tibet; A Political History.* New Haven, CT: Yale University Press, 1967.

Shelton, Albert. *Pioneering in Tibet.* New York: Revell, 1921.

Shelton, Flora Beal. *Shelton of Tibet.* New York: G. H. Doran, 1921.

Snellgrove, David, and H. Richardson. *A Cultural History of Tibet.* New York: Praeger, 1968.

Stablein, William. "Tantric Medicine and Ritual Blessings." *The Tibet Journal I,* nos. 3-4 (1976): 55-69.

Stein, R. A. *Tibetan Civilization.* Stanford, CA: Stanford University Press, 1972.

Suyin, Han. *The Morning Deluge.* 2 vols. London: Panther Books, 1979.

Teichman, Eric. *Travels of a Consular Officer in Eastern Tibet.* Cambridge: Cambridge University Press, 1922.

Thomas, Edith. *Louise Michel*. Montreal: Black Rose, 1980.

Thomas, Lowell. *With Lawrenee in Arabia*. New York: Century, 1924.

Thornton, Richard C. *China: A Political History*. Boulder, CO: Westview, 1982.

Tibet the Sacred Realm: Photographs 1880-1950. New York: Aperture, 1983.

Tolstoy, llia. "Across Tibet from China to India." *National Geographic Magazine* 90 (August 1946): 169-222.

Topping, Audrey. *The Splendors of Tibet*. New York: Sino, 1980.

Trungpa, Chogyam. *Born in Tibet*. New York: Harcourt Brace World, 1968.

Tucci, Giuseppe. *Shrines of a Thousand Buddhas*. New York: R. M. McBride, 1936.

——. *Theory and Practice of Mandala*. London Rider, 1961.

——. *Tibet Land of Snows*. New York: Stein & Day, 1967.

——. *To Lhasa and Beyond*. Rome: Instituto Poligrafico Dello Stato, 1956.

Vasto, Lanza del. *Return to the Source*. New York: Simon & Shuster, 1971.

Waddell, Laurence. *The Buddhism of Tibet*. Cambridge: Wilteffer, 1967.

——. *Lhasa and Its Mysteries*. London: J. Murray, 1905.

Ward, F. Kingdon. *The Land of the Blue Poppy*. Cambridge: Cambridge University Press, 1913.

——. *Life in Eastern Tibet*. London: Windsor, 1921

——. *The Mystery Rivers of Tibet*. Philadelphia: Lippincott, 1923.

——. *On the Road to Tibet*. Shanghai: The Shanghai Mercury, 1910.

——. *A Plant Hunter in Tibet*. London: J. Cape, 1934.

Watts, Alan. *In My Own Way*. New York: Vintage Books, 1972.

——. *Way of Zen*. New York: Random House, 1974.

Welby, Montagu. *Through Unknown Tibet*. Philadelphia: Lippincott, 1898.

Woodcock, George. *Into Tibet*. New York: Barnes & Noble, 1971.

Yogananda, Paramhansa. *Autobiography of a Yogi*. New York: Philosophical Library, 1946.

Younghusband, Francis. *India and Tibet*. London: Oriental Publishers, 1910.

——. *Peking to Lhasa*. London: Constable, 1925.

Index

ALEXANDRA DAVID-NEEL'S JOURNEY TO LHASA

February, 1921	Alexandra leaves Kum Bum, via Sining.
Spring, Summer, 1921	Through Kansu Province, western Szechuan, via Lanchow, Labrang.
September, 1921	Arrives at Dzogehen Gompa (monastery), leaves for Batang — intercepted early and heads for Jyekundo.
October, 1921	Arrives in Jyekundo — intercepted trips north toward Gobi and south toward Po territory.
June, 1922	General Pereira arrives in Jyekundo, he leaves in July for Lhasa.
August, 1922	Alexandra leaves Jyekundo, north via Sining, arrives Kanchow in November.
January, 1923	Leaves Kanchow for Anhsi, Gobi Desert.
March, 1923	Farthest penetration Gobi, returns via Kanchow, Lanchow.
April, 1923	Leaves Laxchow, south via Shensi Province, Szechuan Province.
July, 1923	Arrives Chengtu, leaves for Yunnan Province, arrives Likiang in September.
October, 1923	Leaves Christian mission, right bank of Mekong River, via Dokar Pass, Kha Karpo Range (Snow Mountains).
November, 1923	Travels Salween River Valley. Finds springs of Po-Tsangpo River.
January, 1924	Through Po Yul (Po territory), to Showa.
February, 1924	Arrives Lhasa. Lha gyalo! (Victory to the gods!)

Approximate miles: 3,900 as the crow flies. Likely miles covered by Alexandra on horse, sedan chair, and foot: ca. 8,000.

CHINESE TURKESTAN

Yarkand River

KASHMIR

LADAKH

Indus

Sutlej River

Simla

B

NEPAL

Katmandu

Ganges River

INDIA

Tsangpo River

Shigatse

Gyantse

Mt. Everest

Sikkim

Phari

Gangtok

Kalimpong

B

Statute Miles

0   135

1 inch = 135 miles